Sociology and Scotland: An Introduction

Edited by

Tony Sweeney
John Lewis
Neil Etherington

UNITY PUBLICATIONS Ltd

Unity Publications Limited
Registered Office: Sherwood House, 7 Glasgow Road, Paisley, PA1 3QS.

First published 2003.

British Library Cataloguing in Publication Data
A catalogue record for this book can be obtained from the British Library.

ISBN 0-9545987-0-9

Text designed by Tony Sweeney, John Lewis and Neil Etherington.
Cover designed by Printcare.
Typeset by Printcare
Printed and bound by Bell & Bain Ltd., Glasgow

promoted within this Book, that students would reap the benefits of their own educational *Odyssey*. Like Homer's hero, Odysseus, HNC/HND and university degree students will be expected to travel a significant 'distance' and undertake many difficult challenges in order to reach their own 'destination', yet it is, or should be, these very challenges that make the final 'arrival' all the more worthwhile.

How to Use this Book

Throughout this Book there is a general theme – that of Scotland – with each chapter following a broadly similar pattern of development. The topic is introduced; the reader is led along a pathway through the different sociological approaches, and then arrives at a part of the chapter that addresses issues and studies pertinent to that topic. It is generally among these issues and studies and beyond that sociology and its application *to* and/or focus *on* Scotland is brought to bear by the authors. Each of the chapters, where appropriate, seeks to address issues of sociological interest in and to Scotland, by drawing on comparative examples and making appropriate references to relevant areas of public policy. Since, at the time of writing, we are now barely into our second legislative session after an almost 300-year absence of the Scottish Parliament, a book that attempts to address the impact of decision making emanating from that institution perhaps adopts a greater poignancy – time will, no doubt, tell! In this sense, as the Parliament develops, and along with that its administration of public policy, this Book particularly requires to be viewed as 'tool' with which to work at developing a sociological understanding of social life in Scotland.

Each chapter is equipped with what have been functionally referred to as 'Triggers', which are intended to either 'trigger' further discussion into the topic being studied, and/or, where such discussion is already underway, to help 'trigger' the student's 'sociological imagination' (Mills, 1959) so that (s)he might bring into focus his or her broader sociological knowledge. With this in mind, and to help encourage students to develop their 'sociological imagination(s)', each chapter contains within it regular invitations to 'see' what is in another chapter that is of relevance to the issue or topic in question. As C. Wright Mills (1959) advocated, encouraging individuals to try to link their own experiences – as many of the 'Triggers' seek to do – to their understanding of the wider world, but to try to do so from an 'informed' perspective (by using this Book as a 'toolkit' of resources), should hopefully help students develop a heightened awareness of the impact of wider and deeper social structures – such as the institution of the family in Scotland, institutionalised healthcare provision, e.g. the Scottish NHS, and Scottish cultural practices – on our own lifestyles and experiences.

In addition to the 'Triggers', each chapter contains within it 'Boxes', and/or 'Tables' and 'Figures' with which to help illustrate various topics and issues. At the end of each chapter a 'Chapter Summary' highlights some of the key points to consider

Chapter 1   Introduction

John Lewis, Tony Sweeney and Neil Etherington

Introduction

> [L]ooking at Scotland is not some kind of parochial endeavour, but has much wider implications for how we do social science in the modern world. [....] [O]bjections to constructing a sociology of Scotland is that in essence sociology is concerned with generic processes, not what happens in and to particular places. You can't have then a sociology of Scotland any more than you can have a sociology of Aberdeen, Auchtermuchty, or even to be utterly parochial, 22-26 George Street.
>
> (David McCrone, 2001a)

What we should perhaps state at the outset, then, is that this Book is not, nor ever intended to be, a sociology *of* Scotland. Almost two years or so ago, when this editorial team decided to undertake what now seems like a sociological version of Homer's *Odyssey* (1996) (in terms of endeavour, if not classical literature), we thought it right and proper – not to mention useful – to produce an introductory textbook that could be used as a supplement to our teaching, but that uses Scottish case studies, examples and evidence, where appropriate. The very large number of introductory sociology textbooks that adorn the shelves of academic bookshops and were crammed into our workspaces, are fine and varied, but they, with few exceptions, shared one common feature: they generally did not provide for an adequate *range* of Scotland/Scottish-featured discussion, let alone studies. Hence, the fruits of our (and the other contributors') efforts you presently have in your possession.

This Book has been produced as an alternative to the proliferation of introductory sociology textbooks available. It is aimed at students undertaking courses in sociology and related courses (social policy, social work, social care and health, for example) at SQA levels 7 and 8; that is, Advanced Higher Sociology, first year undergraduate level, Higher National Certificate Social Care, Higher National Certificate (HNC)/Higher National Diploma (HND) Social Sciences (both under the old SQA framework and the new).

The contents of this Book have been written with the 'new' sociology student in mind, who is positively encouraged to delve into the topic(s), through the use of activities intended to act as a stimulus for personal and classroom-based teaching and learning. In this sense, then, the interactive aspects of each chapter in this Book will be a useful accompaniment to classroom activity-centred learning. It is through such promotion and encouragement of independent and classroom-focused study skills reflects a team effort, but also to recognise that through collective endeavours such as this, we can begin to overcome some of the more individualising tendencies that are all too apparent in the education sector today.

The Open University in Scotland and the Faculty of Social Sciences at The Open University in Milton Keynes are delighted to be associated with this project. On behalf of my colleagues at the 'OU', I would like to congratulate both the editors and all the contributors for the efforts they have made here. It has not been easy undertaking a task of these proportions when there are all too many other commitments to be met. From all of the contributors involved in ***Sociology and Scotland: An Introduction*** to all our colleagues in further and higher education across Scotland, and to the students taking sociology and related courses, who are using this book, we hope that you will find this an engaging, informative and, dare I say it, enjoyable book. The editors are keen to have some feedback on this book so please do feel free to contact them at the Unity Publications address provided.

Good luck with all your sociological endeavours and I am sure that ***Sociology and Scotland: An Introduction*** will enhance your 'sociological imagination'.

Gerry Mooney,
The Open University in Scotland
Edinburgh, August 1 2003

Preface to Sociology and Scotland: An Introduction

Sociology and Scotland: An Introduction aims to provide sociology students and sociology teachers with a textbook that locates and explores sociological debates and arguments in a Scottish context. The choice of title is important: this is not, nor does it aim to be a Sociology *of* Scotland. It is an attempt to meet a long identified need on the part of both students and teachers for a sociology text that both considers and applies sociological ideas and concepts through the use of 'Scottish' examples and case studies. This is not to argue that Scottish examples are any better than those that are found in the vast array of introductory sociology texts that are available elsewhere. More that through the use of case studies and examples from recent and contemporary Scotland, Scottish-based students will be helped to see the relevance of sociology for understanding their own worlds. This is not, then, 'just another introduction to sociology'!

Sociology and Scotland: An Introduction represents the culmination of two years hard work on the part of a dedicated team of sociology and social sciences lecturers drawn from a range of further and higher education institutions from across Scotland. Led by three very experienced social sciences lecturers from the further education sector in Scotland, this book is very much a team effort. The contributors here teach on a diverse range of sociology and social sciences courses from Access to Social Sciences, NQ (Higher), Higher National Certificate (HNC), Higher National Diploma (HND) to Honours Degree level and above in the University sector. A number of Scottish colleges and universities are represented here: Glasgow College of Nautical Studies and Cardonald College in Glasgow, Bell College in Hamilton, Aberdeen College, Stevenson College in Edinburgh, the University of Abertay Dundee, Aberdeen University, Glasgow Caledonian University, The Open University in Scotland and Strathclyde University. Many of the contributors also teach with The Open University in Scotland on a variety of social sciences and sociology courses and The Open University's approach to teaching and learning is reflected in many of the chapters. This team have worked hard to take advice on the format of this book, on its content and 'level' from a large number of teachers from the secondary school sector, through further education to the universities. We pass on our thanks to them for their help and advice.

In order to make this venture possible **Unity Publications Ltd** has been created not only to produce and publish this book, but also to provide a forum whereby other publications can be supported, particularly from those teaching in the schools and further education sectors. The title *Unity* was chosen not only because this book

- **Defining Culture**   338
  - ○ Non-sociological definitions   338
  - ○ Sociological definitions   338
- **The Rise of Popular Culture**   341
- **What is Culture?**   345
  - ○ Elite culture, mass culture and culture as a way of life   347
    - ▪ 1) *Elite culture or 'the best that has been thought and said'*   347
    - ▪ 2) *Mass culture*   348
    - ▪ 3) *Culture as 'a whole way of life'*   350
- **Hegemony and Subcultures?**   351
  - ○ Cultures as dominant, residual or emergent   352
  - ○ Resistance through 'sub-cultural' rituals   353
  - ○ Case studies of youth subcultures   353
    - ▪ *Punk*   353
    - ▪ *Rude boys*   354
    - ▪ *Disco*   355
    - ▪ *Rave*   356
  - ○ Subcultures as 'symbolic resistance' or 'symbolic incorporation'?   357
- **Postmodernism, Identity and Consumption**   358
- **Cultural Discrimination?**   360
- **Conclusion: The Politics of Culture**   361
- **Chapter Summary**   362
  - ○ Further Reading?   364
  - ○ Useful Websites   364
  - ○ Bibliography   364

Index   366

- **Medicine as an Institution of Social Control** — 305
  - Medicine: knowledge, power and social control — 305
  - The functionalist approach — 306
  - Parsons' concept of the 'sick role' — 306
    - *'Sick role' – patient* — 306
    - *Professional role – doctor* — 307
  - The 'medicalisation thesis' — 308
    - *Clinical iatrogenesis* — 310
    - *Social iatrogenesis* — 310
    - *Cultural iatrogenesis* — 310
  - The Marxist approach — 311
  - The symbolic interactionist approach — 313
  - Medicine as 'surveillance' — 315
  - The feminist approach — 317
- **Health Inequalities** — 319
  - Health inequalities and social class — 319
    - *The 'Black Report' (1980)* — 320
  - Explaining health inequalities — 321
  - Recommendations of the 'Black Report' — 323
    - *The* Health Divide *(1986)* — 323
  - Regional variations in health — 324
  - Conclusions of the 'Black Report' and *The Health Divide* — 325
  - Health promotion – the focus on prevention — 325
- **Health, Illness and Inequality: the Scottish Context** — 327
  - The *Widening Gap* — 328
  - *Edinburgh and Glasgow* (1999) — 329
- **Scotland's Health: The International Context** — 330
  - What can be done? — 331
- **Conclusion** — 332
- **Chapter Summary** — 332
  - Further Reading — 333
  - Useful Websites — 333
  - Bibliography — 334

Chapter 13 Culture — 337
- **Introduction** — 337

		▪ *Psychological factors*	272
	o	Individual theories – the sociological critique	272
▪	**Sociological Theories on Crime and Deviance**		272
	o	Subcultural theories	274
	o	Labelling perspectives	276
	o	Conflict and Marxist perspectives	277
	o	Feminist perspectives	279
		▪ *Women as victims*	279
		▪ *Is crime related to masculinity?*	280
	o	Crime as 'rational choice'	280
	o	Control theories	281
	o	Left realism	281
▪	**Crime in Contemporary Society**		282
	o	Is Crime increasing?	285
▪	**How Do Countries Compare?**		286
▪	**Who is Convicted of Crime?**		286
▪	**Girls and Violence**		288
▪	**Crime in Cities and Towns**		289
▪	**Controlling Crime: Punishment and Crime Prevention**		289
	o	Why punish?	291
▪	**What Happens to Offenders? The Main Sentencing Options**		292
	o	Community sentences	292
	o	Probation orders	293
		▪ *What happens on probation?*	293
	o	Community service orders	293
	o	Custodial sentences	294
▪	**Do Prisons Work?**		294
▪	**Crime Prevention**		295
▪	**Conclusion**		296
▪	**Chapter Summary**		296
	o	Further Reading	298
	o	Useful Websites	298
	o	Bibliography	299

Chapter 12 Health — 302
▪	**Introduction**		302
▪	**Historical Development of the Sociology of Health, Illness and Medicine**		303
▪	**The Biomedical Model of Health and Illness**		303
	o	The biomedical model	303

o	Useful Websites	229
o	Bibliography	230

Chapter 10 Work and its Organisation   233

- **Introduction**   233
- **The Problem of Defining Work**   234
- **Classical Interpretations on Work: Anomie, Alienation and Rational Commitment**   237
  - o Durkheim and the promise of industrial society   237
  - o Marx and alienation in a capitalist society   240
  - o Comparing Marx and Durkheim on work   242
  - o Weber and the commitment to rational economic activity   243
    - *Work and the Protestant ethic*   243
    - *Rationalisation and bureaucracy*   244
  - o Comparing Marx and Weber on work   245
- **Labour Process Theory**   246
  - o Braverman and the 'degradation of work'   246
    - *Braverman versus 'Taylorism'*   247
    - *Strategies of control or consent?*   249
- **A Changing Context and New Methods of Work?**   250
  - o From Taylorism to 'Fordism'   250
  - o Alternatives to Fordism/Taylorism   251
- **Bureaucratic or Post-Bureaucratic Organisation of Work**   254
  - o 'McDonaldization'   254
- **Insecurity in a Changing Labour Market?**   257
  - o 'McJobs' for Britain and Scotland?   257
  - o The 30:30:40 society   257
- **Alienation and Control Revisited – Call Centres**   259
- **Conclusion**   264
- **Chapter Summary**   265
  - o Further Reading   266
  - o Useful Websites   266
  - o Bibliography   266

Chapter 11 Crime and Deviance   269

- **Introduction**   269
- **Defining Crime and Deviance**   269
- **Explaining Crime and Deviance**   271
  - o Individual theories – are criminals 'different'?   271
    - *Biological factors*   271

- **Conclusion** — 197
- **Chapter Summary** — 197
  - Further Reading — 198
  - Useful Websites — 198
  - Bibliography — 198

Chapter 9 Education — 200

- **Introduction: What is Education For?** — 200
- **Theoretical Perspectives on 'Differential Achievement'** — 200
  - The functionalist perspective — 200
    - *Evaluating the functionalist approach* — 202
  - The Marxist approach — 203
    - *Evaluating the Marxist approach* — 204
  - Interactionist approaches — 205
  - Resistance theory — 205
- **Reproducing the Class System** — 206
- **Postmodernism, Education and Differential Achievement** — 208
  - Evaluation of postmodernist views of education — 209
- **Differential Achievement and Social Class** — 210
  - Intelligence and Learning — 210
  - Material conditions — 212
  - Parental attitudes — 212
  - Working class culture — 215
- **Differential Achievement and Gender** — 216
  - Why do girls choose different subjects from boys? — 218
    - *The single sex school* — 219
- **Differential Achievement and Ethnicity** — 219
  - Statistics relating to attainment — 220
  - Factors in the school — 220
  - Factors in the home — 221
- **Educational Reforms** — 222
  - The New Right and the marketisation of education — 223
- **New Labour and Education** — 224
  - *The economic argument* — 225
  - *The raising of standards* — 225
  - *The egalitarian argument* — 226
- **Conclusion** — 227
- **Chapter Summary** — 228
  - Further Reading — 229

▪ **The Family in Scotland**	151
o Economic and material dependence of 'older' children	153
▪ **Lone Parent Households**	153
o Challenges for lone parent families	154
o Teenage pregnancy in Scotland	157
▪ **Functionalist Approaches to the Family**	160
▪ **Critical Approaches to the Family**	163
o Marxist perspectives	163
o Feminist perspectives	165
▪ **The 'Dark Side' of Family Life**	169
▪ **Conclusion: The Future of the Family?**	170
▪ **Chapter Summary**	172
o Further Reading	173
o Useful Websites	173
o Bibliography	173
Chapter 8 Poverty	177
▪ **Introduction**	177
▪ **Distinguishing Poverty and Inequality**	177
▪ **Defining Poverty**	178
o The 'absolute measure' of poverty	179
▪ *Booth and Rowntree*	179
o The 'poverty line'	181
o The 'relative measure' of poverty	181
▪ *Townsend's* Poverty in the United Kingdom *(1979)*	183
▪ **From Poverty to Social Exclusion**	185
o New Labour and social exclusion	186
▪ **Explaining Poverty**	188
o 'Cultures of poverty' and the 'cycle of deprivation'	189
▪ *Cultural explanations*	189
▪ *Citizenship-centred explanations*	190
o The 'underclass'	190
▪ *The underclass and social exclusion*	192
o Marxist explanations of poverty	192
▪ **Poverty and Social Exclusion in Modern Scotland**	193
o Scotland's poverty 'problems'	194

▪	**Conclusion**	115
▪	**Chapter Summary**	116
○	Further Reading	117
○	Useful Websites	117
○	Bibliography	117

Chapter 6 Race and Ethnicity — 119

▪	**Introduction**	119
▪	**Race as a Concept**	120
○	Non-sociological definitions	120
▪	**Sociological Explanations of Race**	121
○	Race and/or ethnicity?	121
○	What is 'ethnicity'?	123
▪	**Institutional Racism**	125
▪	**Theoretical Approaches to Understanding Ethnic Stratification in Britain**	127
○	Marxist theory – racism and capitalism	127
○	Weberian theory – a racial underclass	129
○	Functionalist/pluralist theory – 'host-immigrant'	130
○	New Right theories	131
▪	**A Brief History of Immigration to Scotland**	133
○	United Kingdom Immigration, 1950s-2002	136
▪	**Race, Ethnicity and Differentiation**	138
▪	**The Asylum Issue**	141
○	Racially motivated violence	142
▪	**Conclusion**	142
▪	**Chapter Summary**	144
○	Further Reading	144
○	Useful Websites	144
○	Bibliography	145

Chapter 7 The Family — 147

▪	**Introduction: Defining the 'Family'?**	147
▪	**Organisation and Structure of the Family**	147
○	Alternatives to marriage	149
○	Relationships and adoption	151

- **The Marriage Contract**   95
- **Feminism**   95
  - o   What is feminism?   95
- **The Historical Development of Feminism**   96
  - o   The 'first wave'   96
  - o   The 'second wave'   97
  - o   A 'third wave'?   98
- **Feminist Perspectives**   98
  - o   Liberal feminism   98
  - o   Marxist feminism   100
    - ▪   *Productive/reproductive labour*   101
    - ▪   *Services to capitalism*   101
  - o   Radical feminism   102
    - ▪   *'Patriarchal' ideology*   102
    - ▪   *Reproduction*   103
    - ▪   *Sexuality*   103
  - o   'Dual-systems' feminism   104
  - o   Black feminism   104
    - ▪   *The myth of 'sisterhood' in second wave feminism*   105
  - o   Postmodernist feminism   106
- **Challenges to Feminism**   107
  - o   Backlash and the media   107
    - ▪   *'Feminism is now obsolete'*   107
    - ▪   *'Feminism has made women unhappy'*   108
  - o   Post-feminism   108
  - o   Standing up to the challenge?   109
- **Gender and Employment**   109
  - o   Employment segregation   110
    - ▪   *1) 'Horizontal segregation'*   110
    - ▪   *2) Individual Choices*   111
  - o   Range of professions   111
  - o   Public sector work   111
  - o   Part-time work   111
- **The Sexualisation of Women's Work**   112
- **Women and Political Careers**   112
  - o   Supply and demand of candidates   113
  - o   The Scottish Parliament   114
    - ▪   *The '50:50 Campaign'*   114

o	Official social classification in the UK	62
▪	*The Registrar General's Socio-economic Groups (SEG) model*	63
▪	**Theoretical Approaches to Social Class**	65
o	The functionalist approach	65
o	The Marxist approach	65
▪	*Evaluating the Marxist approach*	67
o	The Weberian approach	69
▪	*Evaluating the Weberian model*	71
▪	**Debating Class Structure Today: Continuity and Change**	72
o	The upper class	72
o	The middle and working classes	73
▪	*Embourgeoisement*	73
o	The service class	75
o	Professionalisation	75
o	Proletarianisation	76
o	Contradictory class locations	77
o	A radical middle class	77
▪	**Social Exclusion and the Underclass**	78
▪	**Social Mobility**	80
o	Social mobility studies	80
▪	**Class Structure in Scotland: Classless or Class-ridden?**	82
o	Is there a ruling class in Scotland?	82
o	The middle and working classes in Scotland	83
▪	**Social Mobility in Scotland**	85
▪	**Conclusion: The Continuing Relevance of Social Class**	86
▪	**Chapter Summary**	87
o	Further Reading	88
o	Useful Websites	88
o	Bibliography	88
Chapter 5	**Gender**	91
▪	**Introduction**	91
▪	**The Distinction Between Sex and Gender**	92
o	Sex	92
o	Sociobiology and gender	92
o	Gender role socialisation	93
o	Masculinity and femininity	93
▪	**The Sexual Division of Labour**	94

Chapter 3   Sociological Methods   36
- **Introduction**   36
- **Theoretical Underpinnings to Sociological Research**   36
  - o   The positivist approach   36
  - o   The anti-positivist (naturalistic) approach   37
  - o   The realist approach   37
- **Sources of Data**   38
- **Types of Data**   38
- **Choosing a Research Method**   39
  - o   Official statistics   39
    - ▪   *Alternative secondary sources*   41
  - o   Interviews   41
    - ▪   *Structured interviews*   42
    - ▪   *Unstructured interviews*   42
  - o   Questionnaires   44
  - o   Sampling   46
  - o   Surveys   48
  - o   Observation   48
    - ▪   *Participant Observation*   48
    - ▪   *Non-participant observation*   50
  - o   Experiments   51
  - o   Case studies   53
  - o   Documentary and content analysis   55
- **Methodological Pluralism or 'Triangulation'**   55
- **The Research Process**   56
- **Conclusion**   57
- **Chapter Summary**   57
  - o   **Further Reading**   58
  - o   Useful Websites   58
  - o   Bibliography   58

Chapter 4   Social Class   59
- **Introduction**   59
- **The Uses and Abuses of 'Class'**   59
- **Defining Social Class**   60
  - o   Subjective definitions   60
  - o   Objective definitions   61
- **Objective Measurement of Social Class**   62

Chapter Contents

Preface to Sociology and Scotland: An Introduction   1

Chapter 1   Introduction   3
- **Introduction**   3
- **How to Use this Book**   4
- **Why 'Sociology *and* Scotland'?**   5
- **Sociological Development in/and Scotland**   6
  - Useful Websites   8
  - Bibliography   8

Chapter 2   Sociological Theory   9
- **Introduction: Why Theory?**   9
- **Beginnings: 'Classical' Sociological Theory**   11
- **Society as 'Consensus'**   12
  - Functionalist theory   12
- **Society as Conflict**   15
  - Karl Marx, Marxism and neo-Marxism   15
    - *Marxism 'today': neo-Marxists*   19
  - Feminist thinking   20
- **Individuals and Interactions: Micro-sociology**   21
  - Weber and 'action theory'   22
  - Phenomenology   22
  - Ethnomethodology   23
  - Symbolic interactionism   24
- **Giddens' Structuration Theory**   26
- **Keeping Up With The Times**   27
  - Postmodernism   27
  - The 'risk' society   30
  - 'Late' modernity   30
  - Globalisation   31
- **Conclusion**   32
- **Chapter Summary**   32
  - Further Reading   33
  - Useful Websites   33
  - Bibliography   34

Tony Sweeney is a Senior Lecturer in Social Sciences at Glasgow College of Nautical Studies and an Associate Lecturer with the Open University in Scotland. He is an Executive Director, Scottish Organiser and Newsletter Editor with the Association for the Teaching of the Social Sciences (ATSS) and regularly contributes book reviews to the ATSS journal, *Social Science Teacher*. He is an SQA External Examiner and Vetter for NQ Sociology and has produced curriculum resources for the Scottish Qualifications Authority (SQA), the Higher Still Development Unit (HSDU) and Learning and Teaching Scotland (LTScotland). Teaching and research interests include sociology and social theory.

Dr Alex Law currently teaches sociology at the University of Abertay Dundee and has taught with the Open University in Scotland. He was awarded a Masters and a Doctorate from the University of Edinburgh. An accomplished author, he has written in fields such as culture and the sociology of Scotland and is currently working on a book-length monograph entitled *The Social Geometry of Nations*, Nove Science. Previous publications include: co-editor of *Boundaries and Identities: Nation, Politics and Culture in Scotland* (2001), University of Abertay Press, Dundee and numerous articles in recognised journals. He is a member of the National Executive of the BSA.

John Lewis is Section Leader/Senior Lecturer in Sociology and Politics at Cardonald College, Glasgow and Associate Lecturer with The Open University in Scotland. He is an SQA External Examiner and Vetter for NQ Sociology and External Moderator for HNC/HND Social Sciences. He has been actively involved in several Scottish curriculum development initiatives, including producing curriculum materials for the HSDU, LTScotland, the Colleges' Open Learning Exchanges Group (COLEG) and the SQA, with whom he remains involved in the development of the new HNC/HND Social Sciences award. He has previously taught in a number of Scottish FE colleges and HE institutions.

Neil McPherson teaches part-time in the Division of Sociology, School of Law and Social Sciences at Glasgow Caledonian University. He currently teaches on the Introductory Sociology and Environmental Sociology modules in the BA (Hons) Social Science programme. He is also involved in teaching the sociology of health modules on the Nursing, Midwifery and Community Health programmes. He is currently writing up his PhD thesis, the focus of which is the sociological deconstruction of the discursive networks that legitimise the practice of vivisection in contemporary society.

Dr Gerry Mooney is Staff Tutor in Social Sciences and Senior Lecturer in Social Policy with the Open University in Scotland. He has written widely on issues relating to urban studies and social policy and is co-editor of *Unruly Cities*, Routledge (1999), co-editor of *Class Struggle and Social Welfare*, Routledge (2000) and co-author of *Rethinking Welfare*, Sage (2000).

Susan Regnart is an experienced Lecturer in Social Sciences and Social Care at Stevenson College, Edinburgh. Research interests include feminist and 'egalitarianist' issues in contemporary sociology.

Neil Etherington is a doctoral student in the Department of Human Resource Management at the University of Strathclyde, where he also teaches, and is an Associate Lecturer with the Open University in Scotland. His background is in the further education sector where he has taught social sciences across all levels, in various colleges in England and Scotland since 1989. He has participated in a number of curriculum initiatives, and the production of curriculum support materials, more recently with the SQA and LTScotland. His involvement in further education continues in various capacities at Langside and Cardonald Colleges, Glasgow and at Stevenson College, Edinburgh.

Maria Feeney is a Lecturer in Sociology in the School of Social Studies at Bell College, Hamilton. Her teaching interests include the Sociology of Health, both to the BA Social Sciences and nursing and midwifery students in the School of Health. She is module co-ordinator for Introductory Sociology and Sociology of the Mass Media, and joint module co-ordinator in the Sociology of Health on the BA Applied Social Science programme.

Linda Gray graduated from the University of Abertay Dundee in 2001, having made the transition from a long-established career in the banking industry. She has maintained her association with the University through the role of teaching assistant, and is particularly interested in historical and cultural changes to the structure of households and families, and the potential implications for social relationships. She is also committed to the concept of lifelong learning and has been involved in the University's part-time programme, delivering classes on contemporary issues and social identities.

Tony Holman is a training specialist in the private sector and has extensive experience of teaching in the FE sector from Aberdeen College. He has produced curriculum resources for the SQA, for whom he is also an External Examiner and Vetter for NQ Sociology.

Dr David Inglis holds degrees from the Universities of Cambridge and York. He is currently a Lecturer in Sociology at the University of Aberdeen and writes in the areas of social theory and the sociology of culture. He is an executive member of the British Sociological Association (Scotland) (BSA). He is the author of several publications, including (with John Hughson) (2000) *Confronting Culture: sociological vistas*, Polity Press, and (a co-edited 5 volume set) *The Body: Critical Concepts in Sociology*, Routledge (2003).

Notes on Contributors

Jason Annetts is a Lecturer in Sociology at the University of Abertay Dundee, specialising in areas such as Youth in Modern Society, Sex and Sexuality, and Social Movements and Political Protests. His research interests include class and sexuality, analyses of gay social movements, HIV and sexual health, and related government policy. He has been contributing to publications and conferences since 1990, and has authored and co-authored a number of reports for Health Authorities in London, Brighton and Hove, and Berkshire.

Dave Brown is a highly experienced Lecturer in Sociology at Bell College, a HE institution in Hamilton, Lanarkshire, and previously taught in the FE sector for many years. Teaching and research interests include differential achievement and truancy in secondary education, on which he has published articles in recognised academic journals. He is also the author of two books on climbing and the social and cultural life surrounding that activity; the award winning *A View from the Ridge*, Ernest Press, with Ian Mitchell, and the bestseller, *Mountain Days and Bothy Nights*, Luath Press.

Professor Hazel Croall is Chair of Criminology at Glasgow Caledonian University and was formerly Head of Division of Sociology at the University of Strathclyde. She is an accomplished author and widely recognised expert in the field of Criminology. Her main research interests lie in the area of White Collar and Corporate Crime, including its conceptualisation, its status within criminology and aspects of victimisation, regulation and sentencing. Recent publications include *Understanding White Collar Crime* (2001), McGraw-Hill and *Crime and Society in Britain* (1998), Gaunt, Inc. Other publications include Croall, H. and Ross, J. 'Sentencing the Corporate Offender' in Tata, C. and Hutton, N. (eds.) (2002) *Sentencing and Society: International Perspectives*, Ashgate, and is co-author (with Malcolm Davies and Jane Tyrer) of *Criminal Justice in England and Wales*, 2nd Edition (1999), Longman. She is an associate member of the Centre for Sentencing Research.

Brian Dunn is Curriculum Manager in Social Sciences at Aberdeen College, where he teaches Sociology. Research interests include race and ethnicity in modern Scotland. He is actively involved in a number of Scottish curriculum development initiatives, including COLEG and the SQA, where he is involved in the development of the new HNC/HND Social Sciences award.

Acknowledgements

The authors and editors of this Book would like to thank *The Society Guardian*, for allowing the use of material in this publication. The publishers have made every effort to trace and contact copyright holders of copyright for materials used in the production of this text. However, if any material has been incorrectly acknowledged, the publishers would be pleased to correct this at the earliest available opportunity.

The Editorial Team, and Neil Etherington, in particular, would like to extend an acknowledgement of thanks to Peter Bain, Lecturer in the Department of Human Resource Management at Strathclyde University, for comments on call centres.

The Editorial Team would like to extend thanks to the writers and others who helped in the production of this book. Particular thanks go to our families, who have been exceptionally patient and understanding and to Gerry Mooney, Consultant Editor, for continued advice, guidance and support. Without the co-operation of these individuals, this book could never have been written.

We would like to dedicate this book to Scottish sociology students past, present and future and hope that this book contributes in some way to the development of their 'sociological imagination'.

Tony Sweeney
John Lewis
Neil Etherington

Editorial Team
Glasgow, August 2003

when investigating a particular issue. These summary points, besides providing a useful bullet-point summary of a particular chapter, like 'Triggers', help provide a useful platform for investigation into the topics covered in other chapters and beyond.

Each chapter also contains a list of useful Website addresses, which, for those with Internet access, allows for an almost up-to-the-minute opportunity to utilise what is going on in the world of politics, for example. This should also serve to enhance the student's knowledge-building experience, as well as provide appropriate IT Core Skills enhancement opportunities for the 'technophobes' among us. The specified further reading and comprehensive bibliography at the end of each chapter are also intended to remind students that an enormous wealth of resources exist beyond the pages of this Book and to encourage them to seek them out, wherever possible.

Why 'Sociology *and* Scotland'?

The focus of this project was to make an introductory level provision whereby Scotland, and various examples of Scottish daily life, economically, politically, institutionally, socially and culturally, could be directly compared with such aspects of social life in the *wider* social environment, be that nationally, regionally or globally. Each of the chapters contained within these pages seeks to address this to varying degrees, as appropriate.

This Book does not attempt to provide an exhaustive comparative sociological account of all things occurring this side of Hadrian's Wall with that occurring immediately south of it and the near and far reaches of the four points of the compass beyond it. Nevertheless, the intention of the book is to encourage students to examine their own social reality, of life in Scotland, and in doing so develop the skills of interpretation and application in relation to the materials presented. The development of the aforementioned skills will further provide students with the confidence to engage more actively with the social sciences.

What the student or other reader will be aware of, is that the considerable number of writers for a text of this ilk, 16 in total (though a number of chapters are jointly written), produces as might be expected a number of different styles. This represents a particular strength, in that each contributor, or co-contributor, emphasises different aspects of Scotland and Scottish society in different ways, with some providing a little more, some a little less coverage of Scotland and Scottish issues. This is particularly important in terms of generating an understanding of where Scottish society fits into the economic, political, social and cultural 'jigsaw' that is the UK, Europe and the rest of the world.

Sociological Development in/and Scotland

McCrone (2001a) suggests that a sociology that focuses primarily on Scotland in particular and not just the UK in general, is important, as the UK, he argues, has never really been, in the strictest sense of the term, a nation-state. Often, in sociology, have we been prepossessed by a sociology that focused primarily on England, though generally couched in terms of a *British* sociology. Experiencing what, to all intents and purposes, appeared to be 18 years of social and economic policy imposed on Scotland by a Conservative government, which latterly could not even win a Westminster parliamentary seat here, would have provided, one would think, plenty of ammunition for a whole plethora of Sociology *of* or *and* Scotland textbooks.

Besides McCrone's (1992; 2001b) two editions of *Understanding Scotland*, which *do* address a sociology *of* Scotland, the shelves of the bookshops from Aberdeen to Auchtermuchty remained relatively barren of Scotland-focused sociological brain fodder.

However, a substantial number of topic-specific books did appear (Philo *et al*, 1982), though even these tended to address Scotland by reference to specific Scottish studies among studies relating to other parts of the UK, valuable though they were. Many academic books and journals also produced a whole host of studies on specific areas of life in Scotland (Philo *et al*, 1982; Payne and Abbott, 1990), or even addressed issues of social life in Scotland as a whole (the journal, *Scottish Affairs*, for example).

The dearth of more Scotland-focused sociology was rather unfortunate, considering the fact that it was within this 'region' of the UK that the 'Scottish Enlightenment' emerged (1707-1830), spreading with it, as it did, *enlightenment* as to the importance that should be attached to empirical ('positivist') rather than individualistic ('interpretivist') accounts of social life (see Chapter 2: Sociological Theory and Chapter 3: Sociological Methods). This Enlightenment, which, according to Abercrombie *et al* (1988: 216), allowed Scotland to:

> [E]xperience considerable economic growth which was associated with a flowering of Scottish culture, particularly moral and social philosophy and political economy. The Scottish Enlightenment [..] in many respects anticipated the development of sociology by [August] Comte and [Herbert] Spencer in the nineteenth century.

During that period the Scottish universities of Glasgow and Edinburgh were, "unlike their English equivalents Oxford and Cambridge, [seen as] centres of innovation" (Jary and Jary, 1995: 580), fuelled by contributions from Scottish 'greats' such as the philosopher, David Hume, and the economist, Adam Smith. This suggested spur for

6

two of sociology's 'founding fathers', Comte and Spencer, leaves McCrone's (2001a) claims that Scotland is the 'home' of sociology with some considerable foundation.

Further, claims McCrone (2001a), this historical legacy of Scotland's, allied to the value of investigating the ongoing societal development of this 'stateless nation' (McCrone, 1992; 2001b), particularly in an apparently globalising world where the traditionalist notions of nation statehood are arguably being eroded, makes the focus of sociology on Scotland particularly relevant. Thus:

> [G]iven the Scottish bedrock to sociology and the social sciences more generally[,] Scotland, far from being some kind of sociological anomaly best left to one side, or treated as a part of a homogeneous state, seems to me to become a particularly useful example of the fissiparous tendencies in the modern world, a world in which the correspondence of states, societies and nations is far less clear cut.
>
> (McCrone, 2001a)

We hope that you enjoy *Sociology and Scotland*, and that your 'sociological imagination' continues to develop, both throughout your studies in particular, and lives in general.

Good luck!

Useful Websites
The following websites should be of use to you:

General
Social Policy Information Service (SPIS) (British Library): www.bl.uk/services/information/social.html

Sociology
Social Sciences Information Gateway (SOSIG): www.sosig.ac.uk
An excellent site with free resources: http://www.sociology.org.uk/cload.htm
Association for the Teaching of Social Sciences: http://www.le.ac.uk/se/centres/ATSS/atss/html
Sociology Central: http://www.sociology.org.uk

Government
HMSO (Her Majesty's Stationery Office): www.hmso.gov.uk/
National Statistics and Regional Trends: www.statistics.gov.uk
New Policy Institute: www.npi.org.uk
Scottish Executive www.scotland.gov.uk
Social Trends www.statistics.gov.uk
The Stationery Office: Official Documents: www.official-documents.co.uk/index.html
UKonline.gov.uk: www.ukonline.gov.uk/

Bibliography

Abercrombie, N. et al (1988) *The Penguin Dictionary of Sociology*, Second Edition, Harmondsworth: Penguin

Abbott, P. and Payne, G. (1990) 'Women's social mobility: the conventional wisdom reconsidered', in Payne, G. and Abbott, P. (eds.) *The Social Mobility of Women, Basingstoke*: Falmer Press

Homer (1996) *The Odyssey*, Translated by Robert Fagles with an Introduction and Notes by Bernard Knox, Bath: TSP

Jary, D. and Jary, J. (1995) *Unwin Hyman Dictionary of Sociology*, Second Edition, Glasgow: HarperCollins

McCrone, D. (2001b) Stateless Nations in the 21st Century: the Case of Scotland, Henry Duncan Prize Lecture given at the Royal Society of Edinburgh, 29 October (accessed at: http://www.institute-of-governance.org/onlinepub/mccrone/RSElecture29Oct2001.html

McCrone, D. (1992) *Understanding Scotland: The Sociology of a Stateless Nation*, London: Routledge

McCrone, D. (2001a) Understanding Scotland: the sociology of a nation, Second Edition: London: Routledge

Mills, C. Wright (1959) *The Sociological Imagination*, New York, NY: Oxford University Press

Payne, G. and Abbott, P. (eds.) (1990) *The Social Mobility of Women, Basingstoke*: Falmer Press

Philo, G. et al (1982) *Really Bad News*, Glasgow University Media Group, London: Writers and Readers

Scottish Affairs, Various

Chapter 2   Sociological Theory

David Inglis

Introduction: Why Theory?

This chapter provides an introduction to some of the most influential sociological theories. It will examine the different types of sociological theory, setting out their major characteristics and examining the differences between them. It will also explore some of the strengths and weaknesses of each type of theory. However, at the outset it must be stressed that this Chapter is not an exhaustive attempt to cover all theories, but will provide some foundation and reference point for subsequent chapters.

Before beginning to set out what each type of theory looks like, two key questions need to be addressed. The first is: what is 'theory' in sociology? The second is: why do we need to know about theory when studying sociology?

In terms of the first question, theory in sociology involves explanations. A sociological theory is a set of claims about how a particular part of the social world works. A theory allows us not just to *describe* a particular aspect of society, but to *explain* it too. Different types of theory provide different types of explanation, but all of them are meant to show us *why* a particular aspect of society is the way that it is. The job of the person who constructs sociological theories – the theorist – is to provide explanations that help us to better understand what a particular aspect of society is, what its characteristics are, and how it effects the people connected with it.

In terms of the second question – why someone studying sociology has to know about theory – there are a number of answers.

First, theory allows us to go from the *part* to the *whole*. By this we mean that theory can 'unlock' the wider significance of the particular aspect of society being studied. A theory can show us how the particular aspect of society we are looking at 'fits' with the other parts of the same society. This insight can allow us to better comprehend the particular part of the society we are looking at, perhaps revealing aspects of it that could not be spotted at first glance. By relating the *particular* (the part of society we are studying – i.e. crime) to the *general* (the whole society) we can see more clearly the specific part we are looking at (i.e. whether crime is influenced by certain aspects of society, such as poverty). By examining the parts of society in this way, we can get a clearer picture of what the whole society looks like, too.

9

Although there are many different types of sociological theory, almost all of them agree on one fundamental assumption. This is that society is 'greater than the sum of its parts'. What this means, is that there *is* such a thing as society (unlike Margaret Thatcher's infamous claim, when British prime minister) and that it can be studied in its own right. Society is more than just a collection of individual persons. Instead, these individuals are subjected to forms of 'social organisation'. Whether they like it or not, or whether they are fully aware of it or not, individuals cannot just do as they like. There are certain demands that society makes of them, and certain rules and regulations it imposes upon them. How loose or tight these social regulations are varies from context to context (e.g. political system, laws, etc.), but almost all versions of sociological theory agree that we must look at the individual person in terms of his or her place in a wider context, that is, his or her place in society. Only by having a theory as to what society looks like and how it works can we locate the individual in this way, and see him or her as truly a 'member of society'.

Second, another reason why the student of sociology needs to know about theory is that theory can be used to understand the *hidden* aspects of the thing we are looking at. One of the central ideas of most versions of sociology is that there is more to social life than meets the eye. Theory allows us access to the more covert and subterranean aspects of the social world, aspects that the people in society themselves are possibly not fully aware of. For example, Marxist theory argues that societies are fundamentally based around the oppression of other social classes by a dominant ruling class (see Chapter 4: Social Class). Sociologists using Marxist theory might look at a specific aspect of society, such as government and politics. According to Marxist theory, the political system in modern Western societies is only 'democratic' in a very superficial way. Underneath the surface, politics operates in the interests of powerful social classes, which have an interest in keeping the other classes subordinated to their rule. It is only through the possession of *theory*, in this case a Marxist one, that the sociologist can try to get beyond the surface appearance of things, and see what is really happening at a more profound level below the surface. It is theory that allows the sociologist to see aspects of society that other people cannot, or at least are not fully aware of. Theory is an essential tool in the sociologist's endeavour to provide knowledge about society that goes beyond the ideas about how society works held by people in that society themselves. If sociology is to be more than just 'common sense', theory is required.

Third, someone studying sociology needs to know about theory because otherwise the sociological knowledge he or she has would just be a random and disjointed collection of 'facts' about society. These would not illuminate the nature of society if they were not joined together in some way. Being in possession of theories allows us to make our knowledge of society more *systematic* and *coherent*. Without theory we could potentially have a great collection of facts about the social world, but we would have no way of fitting them together with each other, or of understanding their significance. Theory allows us to make sense out of the observations we collect about society. Without theory, sociology as the 'systematic study of social life' would be impossible.

Trigger

In what ways are sociological theories useful tools for studying society?

Now that we have set out why theory is crucial for sociology, we will now begin to set out the main types of theory. We will begin with functionalist theory, then move on to 'conflict theory', such as Marxist and feminist theories, and then look at theories of 'social action' and 'interaction'. We will end with a description of some of the ways in which sociological theory is developing today.

Beginnings: 'Classical' Sociological Theory

Any account of the nature of sociological theory has to begin with the 'classical sociologists'. These are the thinkers who first pioneered the sociological way of understanding human life, in the late eighteenth and nineteenth centuries.

These classical sociologists were faced with a very pressing issue – how to understand the new society that was emerging in Western Europe before their eyes? The older, more traditional society of the past, where most people lived in the countryside, was fast being replaced by a society that was primarily urban, was centred around industrial production in factories rather than agricultural production on farms, and was characterised by a very rapid growth in the population. The questions that faced the classical sociologists were: what was the essence of this new society? How was it going to develop? What problems was it going to create, and what were the best ways of solving them? The new type of society that was appearing in the lifetimes the classical sociologists referred to as 'modernity'. Sociology since that time has primarily been, in one way or another, the study of modernity (Nisbet, 1967).

Most of these early sociologists were French or German. Indeed, the very word *sociology*, was coined by the Frenchman, Auguste Comte (1798-1857). However, *the* central sociological idea, that society is 'greater than sum of its parts' was used by several influential Scottish thinkers of the later eighteenth century, such as Adam Smith and Adam Ferguson. They argued that there really *was* such a thing as society, and that it was more than just a collection of individuals. Thus, although most sociological theory was developed in the classical period in France and Germany, the roots of sociological theory are, in part, Scottish too.

In classical sociological theory, there is a central dividing line between the different thinkers involved. On the one hand, there are thinkers who develop theories based on the idea that societies can only operate if there is, on the whole, cooperation and consensus among people in that society. On the other hand, there are other thinkers who see societies as marked more by conflict than consensus, and who see social life as a series of struggles between different groups.

Society as 'Consensus'
Functionalist theory
In this section we will look at the ideas of those who emphasise that societies are fundamentally based around cooperation between different social groups. The classical sociologist most associated with a consensus perspective is Emile Durkheim (1958-1917). Durkheim is generally regarded as a key founder of the functionalist school of thought within sociology. Durkheim's central question was how complex modern societies, made up of a diverse set of different parts, do not collapse into anarchy and chaos.

In the first book he wrote, *The Division of Labour in Society*, Durkheim (1984 [1893]) argues that it is actually the complexity of modern society itself that ensures that there is 'social order' rather than chaos. Durkheim sees modern societies as being characterised by a very complex and sophisticated 'division of labour'. This means that modern societies are made up of a whole series of different social institutions. These include:

- **The economic system:** the ways in which people work
- **The political system:** where politicians decide what policies their country should be governed by
- **The education system:** where children are educated into the 'norms' of the society
- **The religious system:** where people are taught and think about the highest, most sacred values of that society
- **The family system:** inside which parents rear children and bring them up to respect social values.

All of these systems are interconnected with each other. For example, each of them either socialises people into accepting certain moral values, or relies upon the other systems having done so. Children are brought up within the family system, and learn the values that society places a high regard on, such as law-abiding behaviour. Getting children to respect society's values is also carried out by the religious system and the education system (see Chapter 9: Education). In addition, it is the political system that defines what laws are, and thus decides what law-abiding behaviour involves. Once children have entered adulthood, they live their lives according to the sense of right and wrong they have taken from the various social systems they have been exposed to. They bring this moral sense with them into their various activities, such as working in a job (that is, operating within the economic system). This allows them to realise that certain behaviours – such as stealing from their place of work – are morally unacceptable. The conclusion Durkheim (1984 [1893]) draws from this way of looking at society is that because all of society's systems work *with*, rather than *against*, each other, social order is made possible and chaos is avoided. Moreover, everyone in that society adheres to the society's values and norms. By accepting the values of society, everyone is willing to contribute in their own way to its continuing functioning and well-being.

Even *within* the particular systems that make up modern societies, Durkheim argues, there is order and co-operation rather than anarchy. For example, the modern economic system is characterised by a complex division of labour. This means that there are many different types of jobs and occupations. In modern societies, there are literally hundreds of different types of job, each with its own special contribution to make to the overall running of society: fire brigade personnel put out fires, shopkeepers sell goods, coalminers dig coal, teachers teach children and so on, and so on. Each occupation relies either directly or indirectly on the others. For example, the teaching of children could not happen if there was no electricity in the schools to power the lights. The lighting is made possible by electricity plant workers who in turn, are dependent on coal miners providing the coal that drives the electricity turbines. In the complex division of labour that modernity has, everyone is dependent on everyone else. They all work together with each other, and that is what keeps society functioning (see Chapter 10: Work and its Organisation).

Functionalism can be defined as the idea that the particular parts of a society have certain tasks to fulfil in keeping the overall society functioning effectively. We can see this occur both at the level of particular types of job and at the level of the social systems described above. Society requires everyone to fulfil a particular 'role' that contributes towards the continued functioning of the society. The people who have the job of being teachers are charged with fulfilling the social requirement – the role – that they teach children what their society defines as *right* and *wrong*. Teachers are part of the education system. It is the *function* of this system to ensure that young members of society are socialised into accepting the values of the society. Without this system providing this function there would be a lack of shared values and thus a serious lack of cooperation amongst people in the society.

The outlook of functionalist sociology can be grasped very clearly if we consider the central metaphor that functionalist sociologists, such as Durkheim, like to understand society through. For functionalists, a particular society is like the body of an animal. Each of the organs that make up the body has a role to play in keeping the body, not only alive, but healthy too.

Functionalists living after Durkheim who were inspired by his work, such as the American sociologist, Talcott Parsons (1903-1979), developed this idea. Parsons (1951) is well known as the advocate of structural-functionalist theory. This asserts that each social structure (system) is like the organ of the overall *body* of society, and has a certain function to fulfil in keeping the body healthy.

For example, the political system of a modern society is like the brain, which makes the decisions as to how the other parts are going to work. The economic system is like the body's digestive organs, ensuring that the body has enough material resources (such as food) to keep it working. The family, education and religious systems are like the heart. In an animal or a human being, the heart pumps the blood the body requires around it. In a similar fashion, the systems just mentioned pump the moral values of *right* and *wrong*, *good* and *bad*, around the overall body of the society. These moral values are just as vital for society as blood is for the physical body, because they need to be accepted by the people in the society such that people's thoughts and activities are in line with what society demands of them.

If people could just act in any way they wanted, according to functionalists, there would soon be chaos and social order would collapse. Thus, the overall society is like a body in that it needs to be fed (economic system), guided (political system) and regulated (family, education and religious systems). When these systems work in harmony with each other, there is a situation of 'social consensus': all the people in the society are working together for the common benefit of the society. However, if these systems were not contributing to the overall life of the society, the social *body* would *die* – that is, there would be chaos and the society would fall apart.

Trigger

1. How might modern Scottish society fit with the functionalist analogy of the body?
2. Is modern Scotland characterised by consensus?

14

Society as Conflict
Karl Marx, Marxism and neo-Marxism

Many criticisms have been made of the functionalist perspective. For example, it seems to suggest that individuals are like 'puppets' of society, enacting the roles that society requires of them without much thought or resistance (Wrong, 1961). Moreover, struggles and antagonisms between people, and between systems, are downplayed or ignored, in favour of an emphasis on how every aspect of society runs smoothly and harmoniously. Critics who make these kinds of assertions are often part of the broad camp in sociological thought known as conflict theory. This type of sociological theory sees sociology as essentially the study of *social power*. The sorts of questions sociologists in this school of thought ask are these: Which groups in society have power and which do not? What types of power do the powerful groups have? How do the powerful groups exercise and make use of their power? How can less powerful groups challenge the more powerful groups, and how successful might they be in doing this?

Karl Marx (1818-1883) is often taken as the founder of this type of sociological theory. The influence of Marx has not just been limited to sociology. Instead, Marx's ideas have come to figure as some of the most influential ideas produced in the last two hundred years. Whole societies such as the former Soviet Union and communist China have arguably represented attempts to put into practice Marx's ideas about social revolution and the building of a freer, fairer social order. Marx's study of modern society was never intended just as an academic exercise. Instead, it was meant as a call to action, showing those people Marx felt were oppressed by contemporary society both that they were *oppressed*, and that they should rise up in order to sweep away the social conditions that kept them in this situation. Marx's analysis of society is therefore explicitly *political* in that it seeks to guide the oppressed towards revolution and thus ultimately towards creating a better society.

While Marx was a revolutionary, Durkheim was a reformist, who saw his sociology as way of identifying problems within contemporary society that could then be fixed, primarily through the intervention of government. Durkheim believed that modern society was, in principle, a sound society and that its problems could be rectified. By contrast, Marx thought that modern capitalist society was fundamentally flawed, and that it should be abolished in favour of a completely new form of social organisation.

The different political views Marx and Durkheim have effect how each sees the nature of modern society and how it works. We saw above that for Durkheim, society is like a body, each of the parts being like organs, working for the overall health of that body. Marx, by contrast, sees the different parts of society as being in conflict with each other, either in open and direct ways, or in more hidden and covert fashions.

For Marx (1977 [1859]), the most *fundamental* type of social power is economic power. What Marx argues is that the group (or groups) that controls the economic system of a society will control that society overall. If a certain group controls the economy, it will have power within all the other social systems – family, education, religion, politics, and so on – too. Thus, if we want to know which is the most powerful group in a society, we must ask which group controls the economy.

According to Marx, there are always two main groups in any society's economic system. These are the owners and the non-owners. The owners are the powerful group who control what goes on in the economic system (e.g. in an industrial economy, they own the factories, the machines and the raw materials used to make goods). The non-owners are under the control of the owners. The non-owners are the group of people who actually do the work in the economy (e.g. the people who operate the machines that make goods). The owners are a particular social class, as are the non-owners. For Marx (1981 [1844]), the fundamental division of labour is always between a powerful class of owners and a relatively powerless class of non-owners. The owner class is the 'ruling class', which has power over the class of non-owners.

Marx's sociology can be seen as part of conflict theory because it emphasises that in all societies these social classes are in fundamental conflict with the other. This is because it is in the interests of the owners to control and exploit the non-owners. Likewise, it is in the interests of the non-owners to resist this control, and try to end the rule of the owner class. For Marx, all human history is the result of struggles between the two classes, the owners and non-owners. Marx's sociology is fundamentally a study of class conflict.

If we want to understand how a society works, says Marx, we must identify who the ruling class are, how the economy works in their interests, and how they are in control of all the other social systems in that society. Modern society is essentially a capitalist society for Marx, because the economic system of this society is a capitalist one. The ruling class of owners is the 'capitalist class', which is sometimes also referred to as the 'bourgeoisie'. This class possesses monetary resources (*capital*) that allow them to control what goes on in the economic system. The class of non-owners are the group who carry out work for the capitalists. This is the *working class*, whom Marx refers to as the 'proletariat', and individual members of which he calls proletarians.

In modern capitalist society, the capitalist class always benefits from the work of the proletariat, while the workers themselves get very little back in return for their efforts. Marx's vision of a better society in the future is based on his belief that such a society would not have classes at all. If all property was owned in common by everyone, not just by an elite class, then everyone would share in the wealth created in the economic system. This future society Marx calls 'communism', and it is the desire to abolish the unfair and exploitative capitalist society, and to create a more egalitarian communist society, that is the driving force behind Marx's sociology. Marx's sociological analysis is a *critical theory* because he compares the ideal society of communism against the currently existing capitalist society, and finds the latter lacking, because it is based around class oppression rather than allowing individuals freedom of expression. Marx's sociological theory looks to a better future and in so doing criticises and rejects the present form of society.

We noted above that Marx argues that the class in control of the economy in any society will be in control over all the other systems in that society too. He claims that this is the case in capitalist society – the other social systems operate in the interests of the capitalist class. Despite appearances to the contrary, the laws of a society and its government are not unbiased or working for the benefit of all members of that society. Instead, the laws are formulated and the government works in ways that benefit the ruling, owner class. The laws are written in ways that justify that the capitalist class are entitled to control the economy. The government enforces these laws through institutions such as the police and the armed forces. These are groups of people who can ultimately use physical force to enforce the continued rule of the ruling class. Thus, the government has these tools at its disposal to ensure that the working class do not step too out-of-line, and do not seriously disrupt the workings of an overall society that is based on maintaining the interests of the ruling capitalist class. This view is in quite stark contrast to Durkheim's functionalist idea of the government as the beneficial *head* of society's *body*, making sure that all the parts of the society work harmoniously together for the benefit of everyone.

Marx also identified another more subtle way in which the ruling class can maintain its grip on power. The ways of thinking in a society tend, in generally unintentional ways, to benefit the ruling class. This is because they reflect the ruling class' way of seeing the world, and in a disguised way promote the interests of the ruling class. Marx (1991 [1845-6]) describes the dominant ways of thinking in a particular society as 'ideologies'. An ideology can be defined as a way of thinking that passes itself off as representing the interests of everyone, but actually represents only the interests of the ruling class. One of the main aims of Marx's sociological theory is to expose these ideologies for what they are – as partial and biased ways of thinking that help to maintain the social *status quo*.

In modern capitalist society, ideologies have the role of getting the working classes to accept the rule of the capitalist class. Indeed, Marxist sociology sees the power of the capitalist class being at its height when the oppressed do not realise they are oppressed, and when they do not even see themselves as being ruled by a dominant class. The 'dominant ideology' of capitalism involves ways of thinking in which capitalist society is seen to be a free, fair and democratic society, rather than one fundamentally based around the exploitation and domination of the proletariat by the capitalist class. According to Marx's view, capitalist society remains stable not because of the interdependence of all of its parts, as Durkheim claims, but because it produces ideologies which get the working class to accept their own oppression.

Trigger

How could Marx's ideas be used to understand situations of conflict, such as strikes, in Scottish society?

Many criticisms have been made of Marx's ideas over the years, from people both sympathetic and unsympathetic to his revolutionary stance. For critics who reject Marx's politics, his social analysis is simply a series of highly biased statements, rather than a theory based on good, solid evidence. Every aspect of society is related back to, and explained in terms of, class struggle, even when this might not be appropriate (Popper, 2002). In a similar vein, many critics argue that Marx is a 'determinist', in that he sees all aspects of society as ultimately shaped by the nature of that society's economic system. Thus, Marx is too prone to regard all the social systems of a society as being shaped by the economic system, and therefore working in the interests of the class of owners, the ruling class (see Inglis and Hughson, 2003). This point has ramifications for Marx's ideas on ideology. In a complex modern society there may be more ideologies than that propagated by the dominant class. This opens up the possibility that there is no 'dominant ideology' at all, just a series of competing ideologies and systems of ideas, some of which are more powerful than others, but none of which is totally dominant (Abercrombie *et al*, 1980).

One of the most famous criticisms of Marx was made by another 'classical' sociologist, Max Weber (1864-1920). For Weber (1947), Marx places far too much emphasis on class as the main type of group in society. In modern societies there are other groups beyond classes, such as 'status groups'. These are social groups that are made up of individuals who share a certain sense of identity with each other. Membership of such groups can be more important to the individual than the class they are part of. For example, a person can see themselves primarily as the member of a sports organisation such as a football club, rather than as a member of the working class. Their identity, their sense of themselves, is more bound up with being a member of the club than in being part of a class. Weber sees status groups as cutting through and across class boundaries. He argues that it is only in relatively rare situations where individuals do see themselves first and foremost as members of a class; generally other identities take priority in how they understand themselves.

Marxism 'today': neo-Marxists

Marx developed his theory of society in the mid-nineteenth century. Sociologists and others who have tried to extend Marx's ideas to fit the social conditions of the twentieth and twenty-first centuries are known as 'neo-Marxists'. On the whole, they have been especially concerned to rework Marx's views on ideology, retaining the idea that the powerful groups in society tend to have a great deal of influence in shaping the way other groups in society think, but acknowledging that this situation is not completely guaranteed or fixed. A particularly influential thinker here is the Italian Communist, Antonio Gramsci (1891-1937), who died while imprisoned for his political beliefs and activism by Benito Mussolini's Fascist regime. Gramsci (1971) replaced Marx's notion of ideology with the term 'hegemony'. This is meant to capture the notion that there is always some give-and-take between the rulers and the ruled in any society. For Gramsci, there is not just a ruling class, rather there is a *power bloc* made up of different social elites. From this perspective, the power bloc in Scottish or British society is made up of groups such as the chief executives of large companies, top-level politicians and civil servants, and high-ranking military officers. Although there are occasional conflicts between them, the groups in the power bloc generally co-operate with each other in order to maintain the social order in ways that best suit their own interests.

Gramsci, however, sees this domination of the power bloc over other groups in society as never being guaranteed or certain. The power bloc has to constantly struggle to maintain their authority. They need to win the *consent* of the wider population, so that the latter regard the society they live in as *free* and *democratic*. This means that the rulers have sometimes to give certain concessions to the interests of *the ruled*, for example, providing a minimum wage or restricting the amount of hours a week it is legal to work for. Gramsci's view of hegemony as a constant process of *negotiation* between the rulers and the ruled also opens up the possibility of seeing the ways in which ordinary people might resist or contest the ideas and activities of groups in positions of social authority (de Certeau, 1984). In essence, the notion of hegemony is meant to encompass the idea of struggles between classes as involving *both* the power exercised by the powerful, *and* the resistance to power sometimes exhibited by the relatively powerless. This prevents Marxist theory seeing capitalist society as always automatically and successfully repressing the lower classes.

Trigger

Some sociologists argue that Marx's views are now outdated.

1. What do you think?
2. Which, if any, of his ideas do you think are no longer relevant?
3. Which do you feel are still useful for understanding our society?

Feminist thinking

Marxist theory is a conflict theory in that it is centrally concerned with what it sees as the subordinate position of the working classes in modern society. Feminist theory is also part of the family of conflict theories as it seeks to examine what it sees as the subordinate position of women in society. However, feminist theory differs from all other sorts of sociological theory in that it criticises them for not paying sufficient attention to women in particular and issues of 'gender', of femininity and masculinity, more generally. Feminist theory is intended as a remedy to the relative blindness of other forms of sociological theory to the gendered aspects of social life (see Chapter 5: Gender for a more in-depth discussion on the family).

There are various types of feminist theory, but they all agree that men are in a dominant position over women in Western society. The dominance of men over women is generally described by feminist theorists as a system of 'patriarchy' (Walby, 1990). This literally means 'rule by the father'. In a more general sense, it refers to forms of social organisation that operate on the basis of men dominating and exploiting women.

Feminist theory, like Marxism, both seeks to identify the nature of oppression – in this case, of men over women – and sees the knowledge it develops as a tool in the struggle for overcoming that oppression. Feminist theory is therefore not just a purely academic exercise, as it seeks to *change the nature* of society itself. Feminist theory in its various forms is allied to the women's movement, the coalition of groups in wider society that seek to challenge patriarchal social relations. The differences between various groups in the women's movement are reflected in the fact that there are several different types of feminist theory, such as *liberal* feminism, *Marxist* feminism, *socialist* feminism, *'dual system's'* feminism, *black* feminism, *postmodernist* feminism and *radical* feminism (see Chapter 5: Gender for explanations of these different theories).

It was noted above that sociological theory could help us reveal aspects of social life that often remain somewhat hidden. Feminist thinking in sociology would claim to do just that. A good example of this is Ann Oakley's (1974) study of housework. This draws upon feminist theory to illuminate the covert aspects of this everyday activity. The category of women this society defines as 'housewives', Oakley argues, are in a disadvantaged position, because they are expected to work without being paid. Their labour is not paid for in money, as it would be if they were working outside the home in a 'job'. This means that their contributions not just to the running of the particular household they are part of, but to the economy as a whole, are not recognised. Without husbands and children being looked after by the housewife, the society overall would run much less smoothly than it does. Thus, the housewife is absolutely pivotal in keeping the whole society working. However, she remains un-rewarded for her labours and unappreciated by society as a whole. From this perspective, modern society is fundamentally based around a 'gendered division of labour', which keeps women in positions of economic subordination to men.

The fact that it is *women* who are the unheralded backbone of society is identified and criticised by sociology informed by feminist theory. In so doing, an aspect of how society works that might otherwise not have been dwelt upon becomes a topic for discussion and debate, and is made into a political issue. Highlighting such hidden aspects of female oppression is one of the primary aims of feminist sociological theory.

Trigger

1. What areas might feminist theorists critique in Scottish society today?
2. How would you defend feminist theory from those who do not agree with its conclusions about our society?

Individuals and Interactions: Micro-sociology

In our review of functionalist and conflict perspectives we have looked at versions of macro-sociological and 'structuralist' forms of theory. These are the types of sociological theory that begins by looking at large-scale social institutions – *structures* and *systems* – and then turns to examine how these effect the behaviour and ideas of individual people. Perspectives in this type of theory attempt to reveal the ways in which the actions of individuals are shaped by social forces. However, according to critics of such perspectives, they focus too much on the demands that social systems make on individuals, and do not take into account enough how individuals may negotiate and creatively respond to such demands. Such critics tend to hold to perspectives within 'micro-sociology'. This is made up of a series of related perspectives that insist on seeing *individuals* as in certain ways creating society, rather than society merely creating *them* and determining their behaviour. In this view, society is not a given that confronts people, but instead is the achievement and product of individuals interacting with each other. Society on this view should be seen as the *outcome* of individuals interacting with each other, rather than only as the structures that constrain their actions (Dawe, 1971).

Weber and 'action theory'

One of the first versions of micro-sociology was action theory as defined by Max Weber. We noted above that most versions of sociological theory agree that society is more than just a collection of individual people. Both Marx and Durkheim agree that 'social structures' have an existence of their own, beyond the lives of the individuals who are involved in them. Weber rejects this idea by insisting that society is nothing more than *patterns of interactions* between individuals. In other words, society is made up of individuals interacting with each other. If these interactions did not happen, there would be no society at all. For Weber, we must start with the individual and how he or she interacts with other people. We start at this basic level, and work out towards looking at more general factors, towards what macro-sociologists call social structures or systems.

Weber (1947) was interested in studying the different types of actions individuals engage in, and why they do so. This allows the sociologist to reconstruct *why* particular individuals act as they do. This is the main aim of sociology: the explanation of why certain people act in certain ways. Sociology studies actions that are *meaningful* to the person carrying them out. A person carrying out the action – the actor – attaches some kind of meaning to what they are doing. For example, in Scotland a person nodding their head has the intention of signifying agreement to something. The point of sociology is to try to reconstruct what the meaning of the action was for the person who carried out that action. The sociologist tries to 'get inside the head' of the person, to see how the world looks from *their* point of view, and why they acted as they did in light of this perception. Sociology, on this definition, is the study *not* of social structures, but of the 'actor's point of view'. For macro-sociologists, however, this type of sociology does not give enough attention to how social structures constrain the activities of individuals, and how these structures do indeed have a 'life of their own' beyond the individuals who operate within them (Campbell, 1996).

Phenomenology

An important twentieth century development in this type of sociology, which tries to reconstruct how people understand the social world they are part of, has been *phenomenological sociology*. The pioneer of this type of sociology was Alfred Schutz. In philosophy, phenemonology is the study of how people perceive things. Schutz (1967) adapted this notion for sociology. Sociology, for Schutz, is the investigation of how particular individuals, or groups of individuals, make sense of the world they are part of. The mundane, everyday world in which people operate is called the 'lifeworld' by Schutz. This is made up of the ways in which individuals view the world they are in, and the manners in which they act within it. The lifeworld is formed by the *culture* of the particular society in question. The culture creates the *commonsense* ways in which people experience the world. Most human actions are, says Schutz, carried out in *practical* rather than *reflective* ways. That is to say, people act on the basis of taken-for-granted, commonsense assumptions, rather than having fully thought through the ultimate reasons for their actions. What sociology has to investigate is how people act in particular, mostly taken-for granted, ways, as a result of living within a particular cultural context, namely a 'lifeworld'.

Ethnomethodology
Schutz sees phenomenological sociology as getting at the *details* and *particularities* of how particular people live their lives. This is also the aim behind a type of micro-sociology first pioneered in the 1960s called 'ethnomethodology'. This is a style of sociology associated particularly with figures such as Harold Garfinkel and Harvey Sacks. The word, ethnomethodology, refers to sociology as the study of the methods people use to make sense of the social world they are part of. Ethnomethodologists would claim they are not doing 'theory' at all, but are instead reconstructing what goes on in particular 'lifeworlds'. Like Schutz, ethnomethodologists are interested in describing in detail the actual ways in which people perceive and act upon the social world they live in. However, ethnomethodology adds to this focus a stress on how social actors (who are referred to as *members* of particular social realities) are constantly in the process of actively achieving the sense of reality that they have. In other words, society is not something that exists *outside* people's everyday thoughts and activities, and imposes itself on them, as structural sociology can tend to suggest. Rather, society is constantly being 'made' by people in their everyday actions (Garfinkel, 1967).

Ethnomethodologists are particularly interested in how *members* create the sense of reality they operate with through the means of certain social competencies. These are the resources that members deploy, generally in practical rather than fully reflective ways, in order to make their relations with other people comprehensible and meaningful. A particular form of social competence ethnomethodologists focus on is how conversations are managed between two or more people (Sacks *et al*, 1974). In order for a conversation to *work*, the participants must have a practical sense of how to conduct conversation. This involves knowing how to judge when it is appropriate for them to start speaking, knowing when the other person has finished speaking, and knowing what the appropriate response is to the other person's words.

Ethnomethodologists claim that other types of sociology miss these subtle aspects of social interaction and thus remain abstract and too theoretical. For phenomenological sociology and ethnomethodology, sociology is fundamentally about *describing* how real people perceive the world and act in it, and this description is to be as neutral and non-judgmental as possible. This marks a major difference with Marxism and feminism, which see sociology as about analysing and *criticising* the social world. This difference in styles of sociology has often meant that sociologists in the macro-sociological, structuralist camp often regard phenomenology and ethnomethodology as politically conservative, because they are not interested in drawing attention to the issue of power – should be about the analysis of large-scale social systems and the criticism thereof, or about describing particular people in particular forms of interaction with each other, is one of the great controversies in sociological thought that continues to this day.

Symbolic interactionism

A form of micro-sociology that arguably has some capacity to deal with macro-structures, *is* symbolic interactionism. In its early days, at the beginning of the twentieth century, this perspective was developed by American scholars, such as George Herbert Mead (1863-1931), Charles Cooley (1864-1929) and Herbert Blumer (1900-1987).

The title, symbolic interactionism, gives a fair idea of what this view of social life involves. First, it is an account of society as being made up of the interactions of different persons. Second, this interaction is seen to be dynamic in nature; that is, social life can be transformed as well as reproduced by people's interactions. Third, interaction is always 'symbolic'. This means that when people are interacting with each other, they each try to discern the meanings of the actions of the other person(s) involved. Each person responds to another person's actions in a particular way, the meaning of which is then interpreted by the first person, and he or she then acts in light of that interpretation, which is in turn interpreted, and so on. In other words, interaction is a never-ending stream of interpretation and attempts at understanding.

If society is essentially made up of an infinite number of interactions, society itself should not be seen as rigid and unchanging, but as made up of activities, flows and flexible processes. Social actors are constantly negotiating, manipulating and innovating upon the social reality they are part of. This is what gives interaction its dynamic character – it is never totally predictable where interaction will lead. For some symbolic interactionists, like Blumer (1969), social structures are not determining of interaction, as most forms of macro-sociological structuralism maintain. Instead, social structures are best seen as *frameworks* within which interaction is shaped and guided, but not fully determined in advance. People can, and do, modify the social situations they find themselves operating inside. This position has come under fire from structuralists, who argue that Blumer does not adequately take into account the ways that social institutions can compel people to act in certain ways, even if they do not want to act in those ways. For example, teachers do not have complete freedom in how they deal with pupils, because the education system has rules and regulations, and those who do not follow them can be subjected to sanctions and punishments.

A more 'structuralist' version of symbolic interactionist theory, that perhaps can better deal with the *rigid* nature of social institutions, was offered by Erving Goffman (1922-1982) in his 'dramaturgical model' of social relations. Goffman (1959) sees social life literally in terms of *actors acting*, that is, all of us are like actors on a stage, presenting a play. The 'audience' is made up of other social actors. We are all constantly *play-acting* all the time with each other. Thus, when we are interacting with each other, we adopt strategies to try to ensure our acting is seen by the audience (other people) in a way that reflects well on us. Essentially, Goffman sees social interaction as involving 'impression management'. A social actor wants to feel that he or she is performing the *role* that he or she is playing well. This is the more symbolic interactionist element in Goffman's theory. The more structuralist element is that each actor is playing a role given to them by the social institution or system they are operating within. The institution or system demands that the 'role' be played in certain ways and not others.

For example, doctors go to great lengths to seem *professional* to their patients. This is because the social system of medicine demands that doctors play out their *role* of doctor in certain ways that are deemed to be professional. The social system of professionalised medicine has defined the role of doctor as involving a serious tone and a sober look. Thus doctors, if they are to live up to this ideal, must give off the impression, must act, as if they are like that. This may involve adopting a serious tone when on duty rather than a 'jokey' one. The doctor-actor may also use props such as wearing a stethoscope and a white coat, for in Western societies these are taken as symbols of what a 'proper' doctor ought to have around his or her person, whereas, for example, a dirty pair of jeans and a T-shirt would seem too casual and thus not becoming of a professional doctor. Not acting in such socially approved ways will result in various sanctions. For example, a doctor turning up to a hospital for work in a dirty pair of jeans will probably neither be respected by the patients nor tolerated by his or her superiors.

Goffman's version of symbolic interactionism is an attempt to reconcile this perspective, which looks at micro-level interactions, with a more structuralist focus on the demands that social systems make on individuals to conform with their requirements. His sociology can be seen as an attempt at a structuration theory. This is a type of sociological theory that seeks to unite the micro-sociological focus on an individual's actions and his or her interactions with other people, and the structuralist focus on social systems and the demands they make on actors to behave in certain ways.

Trigger

Use the following types of micro-sociology to analyse and discuss in groups your social relationships:
- Weber's action theory
- Phenomenology and ethnomethodology
- Symbolic interactionism
- Goffman's dramaturgical model.

Giddens' Structuration Theory

The most prominent recent figure to formulate such a theory is the English sociologist, Anthony Giddens, who is well known for what he calls structuration theory. His central aim is to provide a set of terms that reflect his main contention: that social action and social structure are not different things, but are parts of an overall process. Giddens wants us to see how, simultaneously, social structures are generated by social actions, and social actions are shaped by social structures.

Giddens (1984) suggests we drop the term 'action' and replace it with 'practices'. This term captures better how people's behaviours are partly intended by them and partly unintended. Here, Giddens draws on the idea first produced by phenomenological sociology that people generally act in *practical* ways: they know what they are doing, but they generally do not fully reflect on what they are doing. Furthermore, the practices of individuals often lead to consequences not intended by those people themselves. It is in this way that 'social structures' are reproduced. Whilst people may have no conscious intention of doing things beyond their day-to-day activities, their practices may nonetheless unintentionally be part of the reproduction of wider social patterns. For example, when someone goes shopping, they may be *intending* only to go to the supermarket to buy groceries; but the *unintended* effect of their shopping practice is to help contribute to the profitability of supermarkets and thus to the development of the economy of the country in which they live. For Giddens (1984: 2), society should be seen as being made up of "social practices ordered across time and space." This means that what most macro-sociology sees as social structures outside of the individual, Giddens sees as 'patterns of practices'. For Giddens, then, *structure* is not a thing in itself, but is made up of practices that are ordered in certain ways, and which are reproduced in practical rather than reflective ways by the people involved in the social world.

How successful Giddens has been in reconciling macro-sociology and micro-sociology takes us to the heart of what one might think about the different types of sociological theory in general. Your assessment of Giddens depends on what you think the prime purpose of sociology should be. If, like Schutz (1967), the symbolic interactionists and others, you believe that sociology must look at micro-level interactions first and foremost, there are good reasons for arguing that Giddens has provided an effective way of linking these micro-level activities with more macro-level structures, by defining the latter as the outcome of the former.

However, if you believe in line with Durkheim, Marx and the Marxists and certain types of feminist, that sociology is primarily about studying the big structures of society, such as the political system, the capitalist economy or patriarchy, the ideas of Giddens can be said to be less satisfactory. From this point of view, he puts too much emphasis on the *action* side of the action-structure equation, and is blind to the ways in which *structures* are indeed more than just the practices of individuals involved with them. From this perspective, Giddens' analysis is quite superficial, seeing only the surface-level of what people *do*, rather than investigating the deeper reasons why they are constrained to act as they do (Craib, 1993). From a structuralist point of view, he gives too little attention to how structures do largely determine the practices of actors (Bourdieu, 1992).

Trigger

1. Which style of sociology do you find more useful - macro-sociology or micro-sociology? Why?
2. Do you think sociologists can successfully blend together micro-sociology and macro-sociology?

Keeping Up With The Times

The debates about structure and action that sociologists engage in concern the basic workings of all human societies. However, sociological theory has from its beginnings also been crucially concerned with understanding the nature of contemporary society. Marx, for example, provided his analysis of capitalist society because of what he saw as a pressing need to understand, criticise and change contemporary social conditions. Sociologists today also seek to understand – if not also to change – the world we live in.

Postmodernism

Perhaps the most major debate between different types of sociologist in recent years has concerned the controversy as to whether we live in a 'modern' or a 'postmodern' society. The latter view is put forward by the type of theorists known as 'postmodernists', who are often philosophers and literary critics as much as sociologists.

One of the most well-known of these is the French philosopher, Jean-Francois Lyotard. His book, *The Postmodern Condition* (1984), outlined some of the key themes of postmodernist theory. His central claim is that a postmodern society is one characterised by 'incredulity towards metanarratives'. What this means is that people today are on the whole sceptical about types of knowledge that claim to explain *everything* about the social world. Examples of these would be science, Marxism and Christianity: they all claim to possess the key for truly understanding the nature of life. As a society, modernity was characterised by belief in 'big stories' (metanarratives) like these, but we are now living in a new type of society that came *after* modernity. This is postmodernity, and it is based around people recognising that no one form of knowledge has a monopoly on the truth. There are different opinions and viewpoints, and there is no way of saying which of these is better or more truthful. They are all as good in their own particular ways.

This 'relativist' argument of Lyotard's has two important ramifications for the study of society. First, it suggests that society today is postmodern because it is much more fragmented and dispersed than hitherto. There is no general agreement on what is good or bad, right or wrong, moral or immoral. In other words, postmodernity is a society where there is no certainty or agreement, made up of multiple different groups each with their own ideas and agendas. These groups, according to postmodernists, are increasingly not class-based but are centred around issues of gender, race and other forms of lifestyle (Featherstone, 1991). Whereas modernity was a society centrally based around class conflict, as Marx claimed, postmodernity is seen by postmodernists as one based around new forms of dispute and struggle, such as over the environment and gay and lesbian rights. In general, we now live in postmodernity because the issues that are important to us are no longer those that were important in modernity.

The second implication of Lyotard's argument concerns sociology itself. If every form of knowledge is just as good as any other, and no particular knowledge, no matter how scientific it claims to be, is more accurate or truthful than any other, then the whole idea of what sociology is, and how it should operate, is thrown into jeopardy. Sociology can longer claim to be 'scientific'. It can no longer see itself as knowing more about social life than the people it studies. In other words, the sociologist is no longer someone with the authority to say "this is how society works" (Bauman, 1987). If sociology can no longer plausibly claim to be a better form of knowledge about society than rival forms of knowledge, then what is to be done? Another well-known postmodernist, Jean Baudrillard (1983), argues that we should abandon the old ways of doing sociology – seeking to give accounts of the general dynamics of social life, and carefully gathering empirical evidence to generate or back-up theories – and write about social matters in a loose, impressionistic way, throwing out musings and opinions as we see fit. Baudrillard's (1983) postmodernist social analysis often reads like a cross between journalism, poetry and science fiction. This is a deliberate strategy on his part – he wants us to reject the older, modernist view of sociology as science and embrace what he sees as the fact that the world today is so complicated no single story (metanarrative) can grasp it fully. Instead, we need to loosen up and "go with the flow", making particular comments about particular things, but not seeking to give an overarching account of the way a whole society works.

Nonetheless, Baudrillard (1983) does seem to think that one social institution above all seems to dominate in postmodern society. This is the mass media, which he sees as having become the most important part of people's lives in postmodernity. The media no longer report and reflect reality. Instead, they now shape it. Our sense of what is true and false comes increasingly from one source: the media, especially television. How we think about the world, what we understand as important and relevant, all come from media sources. Baudrillard (1983) calls this situation 'hyper-reality'. This is where media images seem more real than everyday life, and where the latter is increasingly taken over by the former. Hyper-reality describes a situation where audiences in the West know about wars in places such as the Persian Gulf only through television news, and thus experience such events not as 'real' wars but as entertainment and spectacle; real death and slaughter are transformed by the media into, and are experienced by audiences as being like, Hollywood movies or computer games. So powerful are the mass media in postmodernity, so much information do they pump out to us twenty-four hours a day, that we no longer have a sense of what is 'real' or 'unreal' any more. We have truly become creatures of a *mass-mediated* world.

How we assess the claims of Baudrillard (1983) as to the dominance of the mass media in an allegedly postmodern situation depends on what we think of postmodernist thinking as opposed to (modernist) sociology. For postmodernists, it does not matter if Baudrillard's claims are highly speculative and more akin to philosophy than sociology, because the idea of collecting empirical data to prove theories is just an old-fashioned belief based in the idea that some forms of knowledge are more truthful than others. In postmodernity, we recognise that no view is better than another, so Baudrillard's ideas cannot be criticised for lacking proof. On the other hand, if one retains a belief in sociology, and its ability to provide theories about social life that are based in evidence, then Baudrillard's (1983) claims look very suspect indeed. Sociologists of the media (e.g. Morley, 1992) who collect empirical information about how media audiences think and act are highly sceptical about Baudrillard's (1983) claims that the media influence so thoroughly what people believe and do. Sociologists who are not postmodernists argue that postmodernist ideas are often unconvincing, precisely because they are just asserted, rather than being proven in any way.

Trigger

Do you find arguments that claim we live in postmodernity convincing or not? Why?

The 'risk' society

Sociologists who are not postmodernists also argue that the postmodernists are wrong to claim that we live in a wholly new society called 'postmodernity', that is, totally different from what came before it, namely 'modernity'. Instead, these sociologists are of the view that today we live in a *deepened* version of modernity, one that *extends* and *develops* the characteristics of modernity first identified by thinkers like Marx and Durkheim. Ulrich Beck (1992), for one, argues that contemporary life in the West is best described under the heading risk society. This is a version of modernity where things are less certain than before, and more and more problems are being created that in turn have to be dealt with. Beck particularly has in mind the fact that Western societies have a great tendency to pollute the natural environment and to meddle with the natural world. For example, current forms of intensive farming have solved one problem – feeding millions of people relatively cheaply, but the ways in which cattle and other animals are reared and kept has generated further problems, such as BSE ('mad cow disease'). What was a solution to one problem becomes a new problem in itself. Beck argues that the risk society is one which is caught in an endless paradox – the more we try to mend things, the more problems we create. Although this happened in early forms of modernity, it is the risk society version of modernity that truly brings this dilemma to the fore.

Trigger

What sorts of problems face people living in a 'risk society'?

'Late' modernity

In a similar vein, Anthony Giddens (1990) argues that we live not in *post*modernity but in late modernity. This is a society that retains many of the features of modernity, such as a political system based around parliamentary democracy, and a capitalist economic system. However, late modernity changes the nature of these institutions.

It does so in particular by means of *disembedding* social relations out of their original contexts and into new ones. What Giddens means by this is that social relations are now no longer primarily located within the boundaries of a particular country, but are spread over many parts of the world. For example, when we go shopping we are in some kind of relationship with people in far-away places who have provided the things that we buy, such as the workers in Singapore who sew the shirts that we wear or the farm workers in the Caribbean who harvest bananas and the other fruits that we eat. It is no longer the case that the people who grow good for us or provide services are located locally. They can be situated in a completely different part of the world. By pointing to the fact that there is now an *international* – rather than merely national – *division of labour*, Giddens points out that in late modernity, our social relations are transformed from being primarily *local* to potentially being *global*.

Globalisation

Not only Giddens, many other sociologists have argued that it is better to characterise our contemporary situation not as postmodernity but as a *globalised society*. This entails looking at processes of globalisation. A globalised society is a situation where social relations are no longer bounded within a particular country. In particular, electronic forms of communication, such as email and the internet, are seen to be changing the nature of social relations, such that we can have often intimate contacts (such as that with an email penfriend) with spatially-distant others in very far-off parts of the globe. This situation is sometimes argued to be diminishing the power of particular country's governments, as people in one country can increasingly get access to information produced outside that country's boundaries, through email, internet and satellite television, even if their government does not wish them to have such access. Moreover, it is also often argued that today governments have much less control over the nation's economy than they did previously, because now capitalism is truly global in scope. Large transnational corporations (TNCs) now are the institutions that possess economic power, *not* individual states (Held, 1999).

There is some controversy as to what the effects will be of such processes of globalisation. According to some (e.g. Latouche, 1996), globalisation will make almost every part of the world similar in character, in that every country will be dominated by the culture of large transnational corporations – there will be no escape from Coca-Cola, Nike and Gap, wherever you are in the world. On the other hand, globalisation is taken by other's, such as Roland Robertson (1992), as fostering new forms of social and cultural 'hybridity'. This is a condition where the culture of a particular society becomes more and more influenced by the cultures of other countries. For example, in Scotland and the rest of the UK today, the favoured foods are no longer just 'traditional' fare like fish and chips, but pizzas and pasta (originally from Italy), kebabs (originally from Greece and Turkey) and curries (originally from the Indian subcontinent). Globalisation has brought these foods into the mainstream of culinary tastes, perhaps indicating that a globalised society is one characterised by cultural multiplicity and eclecticism, rather than uniformity and sameness.

Trigger

1. What are the ways in which processes of globalisation affect the way you live today?
2. Does contemporary Scotland have a 'hybrid' culture?

Conclusion

In this chapter we have looked at the variety of theoretical perspectives available today to the student of sociology. Within contemporary sociology, there is no consensus as to what sociology *is* or *should be*, or what makes a *good* theory or a *bad* one. Controversies over whether micro- or macro-sociological perspectives are to be adopted continue, as do debates over whether functionalist or conflict perspectives are more useful for understanding the nature of contemporary society. Whether we live in some form of modernity, or in a very different sort of society called postmodernity continue to provoke much argument and controversy. It is certainly true to say that sociology continues to be a discipline marked by disagreements between different theoretical perspectives, rather than by general agreement and unanimity of outlooks.

However, this is not a situation to be lamented. It shows that the student of sociology today has many different theoretical perspectives to hand for explaining individuals, groups and the society they live in. By coming to grips with these various ways of analysing social life, your sociological imagination will be enriched, and your capacity to understand your own society and your place within it, will be greatly enhanced.

Chapter Summary

- Theory is essential for the sociological study of society. Without it, we would not be able to offer explanations of how parts of society operate, or to uncover how they really work.
- The central idea of sociology is that individuals are members of a 'society' and that there is such a thing as society that can be studied.

- Sociology was founded by the 'classical sociologists' of the eighteenth and nineteenth centuries. They initiated the sociological study of 'modernity'.
- 'Macro-sociology' is the study of large-scale social structures and systems. It is divided into two main types: 'consensus' ('functionalist') theory and 'conflict' theory.
- Functionalist theory, such as that developed by Durkheim, examines the ways in which particular parts of a society contribute to the functioning of the society as a whole.
- Conflict theory, such as that developed by Marx, examines the ways in which different social groups, such as social classes, are often in antagonistic relations with each other.
- 'Feminist' theory looks at the nature of 'patriarchy', and identifies the ways in which women are oppressed in particular societies
- 'Micro-sociology' looks at the social relationships that pertain between particular individuals. Types of micro-sociology include 'action theory', 'phenomenology', 'ethnomethodology', 'symbolic interactionism' and the 'dramaturgical model'.
- Sociologists seek to use theories to understand the nature of the society in which we live. Ideas such as 'postmodernity', 'risk society', 'late modernity' and 'globalisation' have been developed to understand the world we currently live in.
- Sociology is a discipline marked by many rival theoretical perspectives. These provide us with a range of ways of understanding our own place in society and in the world more generally.

Further Reading

Cuff, E.C., Sharrock, W. and Francis, D. (1990) *Perspectives in Sociology: Classical and Contemporary*, Fourth Edition, London: Routledge

Hughes, J.A., Martin, P.J. and Sharrock, W.W. (1995) *Understanding Classical Sociology: Marx, Weber, Durkheim*, London: Sage

May, T. (1996) *Situating Social Theory*, Milton Keynes: Open University Press

Miles, S. (2001) *Social Theory in the Real World*, London: Sage

Ritzer, G. (2000) *Sociological Theory*, New York, NY: McGraw Hill

Sharrock, W.W., Hughes, J.A., Martin, P.J. (2003) *Understanding Modern Sociology*, London: Sage

Useful Websites

A very useful gateway to a wide range of resources on sociological theory:
http://www.mcmaster.ca/socscidocs/w3virtsoclib/theories.htm

A site that contains a map detailing the relations between different types of sociological theory:
http://www.hewett.norfolk.sch.uk/curric/soc/theory.htm

The site of the 'Dead Sociologists' Society', it contains a wide range of materials on the classical sociologists: http://www2.pfeiffer.edu/~lridener/DSS/INDEX.HTML

A wide range of Marxist writings are available at this site: http://www.marxists.org/

A site that contains useful sources for Durkheim and functionalist theory:
http://www.relst.uiuc.edu/durkheim

This site contains many useful materials for understanding the ideas of Max Weber:
http://www.faculty.rsu.edu/~felwell/Theorists/Weber/Whome.htm

This site contains a host of information on feminist thinking: http://www.feminist.org/

A site that contains an abundance of information on contemporary social theory:
http://www.theory.org.uk/main.htm
A very useful site for learning more about postmodernism:
http://www.as.ua.edu/ant/Faculty/murphy/436/pomo.htm
A site that contains lots of information on the issues surrounding globalisation:
www.globalisationguide.org

Bibliography

Abercrombie, N. *et al* (1980) *The Dominant Ideology Thesis*, London: Allen and Unwin

Baudrillard, J. (1983) *Simulations*, New York, NY: Semiotext(e)

Bauman, Z. (1987) *Legislators and interpreters: on modernity, post-modernity and intellectuals*, Cambridge: Polity Press

Beasley, C. (1999) *What is Feminism? An introduction to feminist theory*, London: Sage

Beck, U. (1992) *Risk society: towards a new modernity*, London: Sage

Blumer, H. (1969) *Symbolic Interaction*, Englewood Cliffs, NJ: Prentice-Hall

Bourdieu, P. (1992) *The Logic of Practice*, Cambridge: Polity Press

Campbell, C. (1996) *The Myth of Social Action*, Cambridge: Cambridge University Press

Craib, I. (1993) *Anthony Giddens*, London: Routledge

Dawe, A. (1971) 'The Two Sociologies' in K. Thompson and J. Tunstall (eds.) *Sociological Perspectives*, Harmondsworth: Penguin

de Certeau, M. (1984) *The Practice of Everyday Life*, Berkeley, CA: University of California Press

Durkheim, E. (1984 [1893]) *The Division of Labour in Society*, Basingstoke: Macmillan

Featherstone, M. (1991) *Postmodernism and Consumer Culture*, London: Sage

Garfinkel, H. (1967) *Studies in Ethnomethodology*, Englewood Cliffs, NJ: Prentice-Hall

Giddens, A. (1984) *The Constitution of Society*, Cambridge: Polity Press

Giddens, A. (1990) *The Consequences of Modernity*, Cambridge: Polity Press

Goffman, E. (1959) *The Presentation of Self in Everyday Life*, Garden City, NY: Anchor

Gramsci, A. (1971) *Selections From the 55
Prison Notebooks*, London: New Left Books

Held, D. (1999) *Risk society: towards a new modernity*, Cambridge: Polity Press

Inglis, D. and Hughson, J. (2003) *Confronting Culture: sociological vistas*, Cambridge: Polity Press

Latouche, S. (1996) *The Westernization of the World: the significance, scope and limits of the drive towards global uniformity*, Cambridge: Polity Press

Lyotard, J-F. (1984) *The Postmodern Condition: a report on the condition of knowledge*, Minneapolis, MN: University of Minnesota Press

Marx, K. (1977 [1859]) *A Contribution to the Critique of Political Economy*, Moscow: Progress Publishers

Marx, K. (1981 [1844]) *Economic and Philosophic Manuscripts of 1844*, London: Lawrence and Wishart

Marx, K. (1991 [1845-6]) *The German Ideology*, Arthur, C.J. (ed.), London: Lawrence and Wishart

Morley, D. (1992) *Television, Audiences and Cultural Studies*, London: Routledge

Nisbet, R. (1967) *The Sociological Tradition*, New York, NY: Basic Books

Oakley, A. (1974) *Housewife*, London: Allen Lane

Parsons, T. (1951) *The Social System*, London: Routledge and Kegan Paul

Popper, K. (2002) *The Open Society and Its Enemies: Hegal and Marx*, London: Routledge

Robertson, R. (1992) *Globalization: social theory and global culture*, London: Sage

Sacks, H., Schegloff, E. and Jefferson, G. (1974) 'A Simplest Systematics for the Organisation of Turntaking for Conversation', *Language*, Vol. 50, pp. 696-735

Schutz, A. (1967) *The Phenomenology of the Social World*, London: Heinemann

Tong, R. (1989) *Feminist Thought: a comprehensive introduction*, London: HarperCollins

Walby, S. (1990) *Theorizing Patriarchy*, Oxford: Blackwell

Weber, M. (1947) *The Theory of Social and Economic Organization*, Talcott Parsons (ed.), New York, NY: Free Press

Wrong, D. (1961) 'The Oversocialized Conception of Man in Modern Sociology', *American Sociological Review*, Vol. 26, pp. 183-93

Chapter 3   Sociological Methods

Tony Holman

Introduction

The purpose of this Chapter is to provide an introductory explanation of many of the research methods used within the field(s) of sociological research. In so doing, it employs a number of specific and speculative examples (including those relating to Scotland) to illustrate the usefulness and effectiveness, or otherwise, of pursuing an understanding of social life through the application of testable, verifiable and even interpretive methods of research. For this reason, this Chapter can be seen, like Chapter 2: Sociological Theory, as a 'tool' with which to understand the processes that sociologists navigate in the pursuit of 'answers'.

Sociologists and other social scientists have at their disposal a range of *methods* that serve the purpose of generating the data required to investigate a selected topic. Since several research methods are available to the researcher, there is usually an element of choice involved and, typically, a combination of available research methods may be selected, taking into account factors such as time, cost, funding, ethical considerations and resources. Crucial to the selection of particular research methods is the *methodology* influencing the researcher, and it is here that we will begin.

Theoretical Underpinnings to Sociological Research

There are three main theoretical approaches to research: the 'positivist' approach, the 'anti-positivist' ('naturalistic') approach and the 'realist' approach. Each approach makes fundamental assumptions about the nature of knowledge and thereby influences the choice of method of obtaining such knowledge (see Chapter 2: Sociological Theory).

The positivist approach

The positivist approach uses similar principles to those of the natural sciences, such as biology and physics, in the sense that it aims to be *scientific*. It is based on a range of assumptions, such as:

- Social 'facts' exist that can have explanatory power about the laws upon which societies are based
- Only *observation* and *experience* can lead to valid knowledge claims
- Objective, scientific 'truths' can be established using rigorous, systematic and controlled research techniques

- Much of human behaviour is *determined*, or is caused by *environmental* stimuli
- Social life is ordered and can therefore be explained and predicted.

Sociologists influenced by this methodological stance tend to use rigorous, systematic and controlled methods such as structured interviews, questionnaires and surveys, all of which will be examined later. These methods can generate 'quantitative' data, that is, 'numerical' data that can be translated into statistics in the shape of trends and patterns that, it is assumed, can reveal facts or laws about the topic under investigation. The results of such research can provide 'generalisations' that can be applied to the wider social world.

The anti-positivist (naturalistic) approach
This approach developed in opposition to the positivist assumption that the social world operates in a similar way to the natural world. It arose from the discipline of social anthropology and makes the following claims:

- Human behaviour cannot be explained by the 'cause and effect' relationship used to study inanimate objects
- Theorising at a structural level overlooks the fact that social reality comes from within
- No independent, universal and objective truths exist
- The social world and, therefore, knowledge of it, is in a state of flux
- Human behaviour can best be understood by influencing factors such as culture, norms, values and the way in which individuals interpret the social world around them.

Sociologists influenced by this methodological stance tend to focus on how individuals experience the world and how they derive meaning from their relationships and social contexts. They tend to use methods of data collection that can be used in the individual's *natural setting,* such as unstructured in-depth interviews, participant observation, personal documents and diaries. The data they generate are *non*-numerical or *qualitative*, i.e. the data will take the form of words, rather than numbers.

The realist approach
This approach attempts to find a middle ground between positivism and anti-positivism. It seeks to reconcile the stark differences between the approaches by synthesising elements from each. Like positivism, it considers the objective, scientific method of analysis as useful in explaining some aspects of the social world. Like anti-positivism, it considers human behaviour as arising from the conscious and

intentional communication of individuals who engage, actively, in the creation of their own social worlds. The realist approach is, however, distinct in the sense that it focuses on:

- Structural aspects of society as a whole
- How influences on behaviour at the institutional level interact with influences at the individual level
- The underlying and often hidden causal processes of social phenomena such as ideology, oppression and discrimination.

Sources of Data

Researchers derive information from sources that can be categorised as 'primary' and 'secondary'. Primary sources of information are being employed when the researcher makes direct contact with people in order to collect the relevant data. When, for example, the interview method is being used, the sociologist must communicate with a number of respondents, who, it is hoped, will provide the information required. In this case, the research *method* is the interview and the *primary source* refers to those people (e.g. professional criminals) who are in a position to respond to the interviewer's questions. The data are original, therefore, and they relate to a particular research process undertaken by the sociologist. Primary sources of information are employed, then, in situations where the researcher makes use of methods such as participant observation, interviews and questionnaires because, in each case, some sort of contact with people is needed in order to generate the data.

Secondary sources of data are used when information is being gathered without making contact with people. The data already exist and the sociologist simply decides to examine them for his or her own research purposes. Secondary sources include official statistics, government reports, existing sociological literature and archived records.

Types of Data

The two main types of data are *quantitative* and *qualitative*. Quantitative data are normally presented in the form of numbers or statistics and are often used to measure quantities such as suicide rates or divorce rates. Researchers may use this type of data to make generalisations after establishing trends, patterns and correlations. Structural or positivist sociologists prefer this type of data as they provide scientific measurements of phenomena at a macro level. Quantitative data are seen to have a tendency to be reliable, as they can be easily replicated by other researchers. Asking respondents in a questionnaire what age they are, for example, would presumably produce the same results if the same respondents were asked a month later, assuming that they had not had a birthday in the interim. Quantitative data are often considered factual, although this is not necessarily the case, as some people may lie about their weight, for example, if asked.

Qualitative data provide more detailed, in-depth information on the subject under investigation. The *quality* of the information is preferred over the *quantity*, for anti-positivists and action theorists, who tend to focus on subjective analyses at a micro level (see Chapter 2: Sociological Theory, for further discussion on micro approaches). Qualitative data tend to be low on reliability, as they cannot be replicated so easily. However, they can be high in terms of validity as they often reveal detailed, complex information in relation to individuals and may provide sufficient information to explain as well as describe.

Choosing a Research Method

Whatever the topic of the research, the nature of those individuals or groups being researched (or even the possible political/ideological bent of the researcher), it is important that the researcher takes careful consideration of the methodology and methods that they will employ in conducting their work. The method(s) for obtaining data that they use may be based on a variety of factors – what is important is that they make an appropriate and educated choice, as this will make a significant contribution to the final product of their research efforts. The main methods of research used by sociologists, along with some examples, are discussed in the pages below.

Official statistics

Official statistics can take several different forms, including numbers, percentages, averages, graphs, rates, and so on (see Box 3.1 below).

Sometimes, official statistics may also take the form of *projections*. An example of this would be predicting divorce rates over the next decade. The type of data to be found in official statistics is *quantitative*; that is, the data are predominantly of a numerical nature. Official statistics are also a clear example of a *secondary* source of data.

By referring to available official statistics, a sociologist may wish to establish trends and patterns, rather than leaving the data in their raw state. Official statistics can provide information that is both interesting and relevant to the researcher. It can tell the researcher *what* they want to know. For example, a researcher may want to determine unemployment rates amongst construction workers in the west of Scotland. Statistics can provide this kind of information, but they cannot *explain why* such an occurrence can be seen. Therefore, the use of official statistics is usually just the first step in the research process for the sociologist.

> **Box 3.1 Examples of Official Statistics**
>
> - With regard to *numbers*, the Home Office (2001) informs us that 29 murders occurred in Edinburgh during the period 1997-1999.
> - In relation to *percentages*, total recorded crime in Scotland fell by 8 per cent, according to a Home Office report published in 2001.
> - Regarding *averages*, the Office for National Statistics (a fertile secondary source of data) discovered in 2001 that the average number of occupants in British households was 2.3, compared with 2.9 in 1971.
> - *Graphs* can be produced, which will illustrate, for example, annual increases in the number of couples obtaining a divorce in Scotland, or year-on-year changes in the number of crimes recorded by the police.
> - Looking briefly at *rates*, the Home Office (2001) tells us that the number of murders per 100,000 of the population was 2.1 for Scotland, compared with a European Union (EU) rate of only 1.7.

Official statistics can also be of limited validity, in that they may fail to indicate accurately what is occurring in society. This is particularly true in the case of official crime figures, which do not provide an accurate portrayal of the volume of crime that *really* exists (see Chapter 11: Crime and Deviance). The main reason for this is that many crimes, in particular minor offences, are not reported to the police, in which case they are not represented in the official figures. Those crimes that do not appear in the official statistics are known collectively as the 'dark number' or 'dark figure'. It would not be reasonable to claim, however, that official statistics can *never* provide us with an adequate portrayal of events occurring in society. In the case of divorce, for example, all divorces will be recorded in the official figures, with the result that, in this case, there is *no* dark area. Thus, the two main drawbacks of using official statistics as a research method are that:

- They describe but *do not* explain
- Data generated are often *incomplete* and *inadequate* as a result.

Using official statistics does have certain advantages, however:

- They are usually easily and quickly accessible
- They can constitute the basis or the 'trigger' for further research
- They often have a powerful visual impact
- They can reveal trends occurring within society
- They can enable us to identify important links or statistical connections between different variables

- They can allow for comparative analyses of societies.

Alternative secondary sources

Alternative secondary sources can provide the basis for sociological research, such as films, televised documentaries, personal diaries, photographs, newspaper articles, novels and existing sociological literature. Songs may also embody imagery that may inspire debate and further research.

Trigger

What are some of the main advantages and disadvantages of using secondary sources of data?

It could be said, then, that the data derived from secondary sources are, in a sense, 'second hand' or unoriginal. In order to pursue originality therefore, sociologists will often move beyond the use of such sources when they are conducting their research. For primary sources of data the following research methods are often employed:

- Interviews
- Questionnaires
- Observation
- Sampling
- Surveys
- Experiments
- Case studies
- Documentary and content analysis.

These methods can be used either alone or in combination, in order to provide a much greater depth and complexity of information. Each method involves the sociologist in gathering new or original data, instead of data that have been gathered by someone else and which exist in some shape or form already. Also, these research tools will normally entail making some sort of contact with people directly (though not always necessarily face-to-face), in order to collect the information. In simple terms, the data are obtained by talking to, listening to, or watching, people.

Interviews

An interview always involves 'direct' contact between the researcher and the interviewee, or *respondent*. In the past it tended to be conducted in the presence of the interviewee, but telephone and e-mail interviews are becoming increasingly more popular. The interviewer tends to play a fairly active role in putting a series of questions to the respondent in a specific sequence. Responses to these questions will then be encouraged. The respondent's role, by comparison, tends to be more passive. A distinct advantage of this method is that the list of possible topics that can be covered by the interview is almost endless. Respondents may be asked questions on practically any subject of sociological interest, from attendance of formal and organised religious service to the consumption of illegal drugs.

Interviews can be either *structured* or *unstructured* (the latter often being referred to as 'non-directive'). Both types are widely used by sociologists. In the case of the structured interview, the sociologist uses pre-set questions. Restricted responses are encouraged by the fact that the questions tend to be closed, i.e. they do not encourage the respondent to elaborate. An example might be asking high school pupils in their sixth year at an Ayrshire school, "Do you intend to go to university when you leave school?" The expected answer would come in the form of 'Yes', 'No' or 'Don't Know'.

Structured interviews
Some of the *advantages* of the structured interview:

- All respondents are asked the same questions, with the result that the same topics or issues will be covered in respect of each respondent
- Answers to questions will tend to be relevant
- The data can be organised and collated fairly easily, given that respondents can offer brief answers only
- It tends to be less time-consuming than the unstructured interview (see below)
- It is fairly easy to keep the interview 'on track'.

Some of the main *disadvantages* of the structured interview:

- The data may appear rather thin and superficial, given that the respondents can provide brief answers only
- The interviewer may be unable to probe responses and it might not be possible for him or her to request elaboration and clarification
- This type of interview does not really suit talkative respondents, who may feel frustrated with the process.

Unstructured interviews
In the case of unstructured interviews, there are no pre-set questions as such. Instead, the actual questions asked and their sequence will tend to reflect the general flow of

the conversation. Also, the questions will tend to be more open-ended. To take an example, a sociologist might ask an adolescent living in a council estate in Dundee, the question, "Can you tell me how you spend your time at the weekend?" This type of question invites a fairly elaborate response and the respondent is more or less at liberty to answer at length if he or she so wishes.

The main *advantages* of the unstructured interview:

- A large volume of data can be gathered and information on related topics may arise from the responses
- The interviewer has an opportunity to probe the respondent's answers and to request both clarification and elaboration
- In some respects, the atmosphere may seem more relaxed and informal from the point of view of the respondent, which can have the effect of creating rapport.

The principal *disadvantages* of the unstructured interview:

- The data may become difficult to organise and collate
- A large volume of irrelevant data may be generated
- It tends to be time-consuming and, therefore, costly.

Structured and unstructured interviews may be represented as opposite extremes on a continuum, as the diagram below indicates.

STRUCTURED  UNSTRUCTURED

However, in practice, the technique selected will tend to mix the two types with a predominance of one type rather than its exclusive use. This can mean that some pre-set, closed questions will be combined with a few open-ended questions, which will enable the respondent to elaborate and to provide more detail. In reality, then, those interviews labelled structured will be those that occupy a position somewhere to the *left* of the mid-point on the continuum and those labelled unstructured, somewhere to the *right*.

Trigger

What are some of the principal differences between structured and unstructured interviews, and what impact might these have on research?

Interviews can generate a large volume of often complex, detailed and personalised information that might never have been available to the researcher while using other methods. Despite these fairly obvious advantages of the interview as a research method, it is not without its limitations.

- Some respondents may be unwilling to participate for a number of reasons, such as lack of time or apathy. Also, the topic under investigation may be quite delicate or personal and the respondent might not wish to reveal anything that could produce feelings of shame or embarrassment
- Respondents may exaggerate (in order to try to impress the interviewer), or facts may be concealed, if the respondent suspects that his or her responses will not be kept in the strictest confidence
- Respondents may find it hard to explain events, or even their own behaviour patterns, clearly and coherently, due to a general lack of communication skills and/or lack of recall
- The interview can be very time-consuming, particularly in the case of the unstructured interview
- It can be difficult trying to organise and collate the accumulated data – particularly, again, in the case of the unstructured interview
- Interviewers may use leading questions in the hope or expectation of receiving particular answers
- The respondent may be influenced in their responses by the presence of the interviewer
- It may become difficult for the researcher to remain objective if rapport is established, or if they begin to empathise with the interviewee.

Questionnaires

In its simplest form, the questionnaire consists of a list of questions on a particular issue or topic. It is used frequently for gathering data when a survey is being conducted. A survey involves the collection of the same type of information from all members of the chosen sample. All the respondents may be given identical sets of questions and are then asked to provide answers to them. Essentially, the questionnaire makes use of a primary source of data, as people are contacted in order to provide the information. However, the questionnaire differs from the interview in that it need not involve *direct* communication between the researcher and the respondent. In the case of postal questionnaires, for example, lists of questions can be sent out by post to large numbers of people, or the questions can be handed directly to the respondents in a variety of possible locations, such as in the street, in shops or at the workplace. Completed questionnaires are returned by post, again avoiding *direct* (including verbal) contact. The questionnaire constitutes a relatively cheap, quick and efficient method of obtaining large amounts of information from relatively large numbers of people. The data that are generated are often quantified fairly easily, which means they can be presented numerically. For example, a questionnaire completed by factory workers in Falkirk might show that 58 per cent of them belonged to trade unions and that, of these trade union members, 80 per cent of them supported the Labour Party. When data are presented in this way, it is possible to gauge the strength of the connection between different variables – in this example, trade union membership and allegiance to the Labour Party.

Those who support the use of questionnaires argue that they produce comparable data. Since all respondents answer exactly the same questions, it is claimed that different responses will reveal real differences between the respondents, with a greater degree of clarity than the interview, particularly the unstructured type. In the interview situation, different responses to questions may reflect differences in terms of how they were phrased, or they could reflect different reactions to the interviewer and the type of person he or she is. This is known as *interviewer bias*.

There are, however, a number of disadvantages associated with the use of questionnaires. With regard to postal questionnaires, the response rate is frequently very low. Often, only a small percentage of the sample actually return postal questionnaires and those who do may have a special reason for doing so and may, therefore, be untypical of the sample as a whole. In 1977, a nationwide survey of the sexual behaviour of American women, known as the Hite Report, was published. One hundred thousand postal questionnaires were sent out, but only 3,000 were returned, which means that a mere 3 per cent of the sample responded.

Sometimes, popular magazines produce questionnaires and readers are invited to complete them. To illustrate, in the mid-1970s in Britain, *Woman's Own* magazine produced a questionnaire on the subject of love and marriage, which was completed and returned by some 10,000 women. Generally, though, non-response rates for questionnaires are high, which causes serious problems when the sociologist is attempting to generalise about people's behaviour patterns, beliefs and attitudes in the wider social world. However, because postal questionnaires tend to be distributed to large numbers of people, what response there is, is usually seen as reasonably representative.

Another problem with regard to the questionnaire is that the questions will tend to be closed, with the result that the respondents are unable to elaborate or to provide interesting, relevant detail. In this sense, the assembled data may appear rather superficial. Great care must be taken with the actual wording of the questions. It is important that the questions convey the same meaning to the respondents as that intended by the researcher who designed the questionnaire. The following example will illustrate this point.

A Gallup poll survey in 1939 (http://www.gallup.com/) found that 88 per cent of the US population described itself as middle class, a result that surprised the researchers. Members of the sample had been offered a choice of three alternatives, namely – 'upper', 'middle' and 'lower' class. The survey was repeated shortly afterwards and the phrase, 'lower class', was replaced by the phrase, 'working class'. When repeated, 51 per cent of the sample described themselves as working class.

Sampling
When interviews and questionnaires are being conducted, the research will be more rigorous if the social scientist has knowledge of sampling procedures and of some of the main sampling techniques.

Prior to dealing with this issue, however, the term *population* must be defined. A statistical population refers to every member of a social group or category, all of whom are in possession of the same feature(s) or characteristic(s). Here are some examples of populations:

- Pakistani people living in Glasgow
- The elderly in Scotland
- Unemployed people in Aberdeen
- Students at Perth College.

In each of these populations, all the members of the group in question will share certain qualities. In the first example, all those people who belong to this group are of Pakistani origin and they all live in Glasgow. Therefore, references to population(s) can have varied meanings.

Sampling means to select a representative smaller group from a wider and larger population, in order to make studying them more practical and manageable. A representative sample will be one whose members' characteristics are similar to those in the wider population. In order to achieve this, the researcher draws up a list of individuals who fall into the target population. This list is known as the 'sampling frame'. Social scientists will also often employ 'random sampling' in order to achieve this match. This technique attempts to ensure that the chance of any one member of the population being included in the sample should be the same as that for any other member. Random sampling techniques include: 'manual selection', such as pulling names out of a hat; 'random number tables', where names are allocated numbers that are then selected randomly; and computer generated samples, where computer programmes choose the research sample randomly. These techniques have the effect of guarding against the inadvertent construction of a *biased* sample. A biased sample is one that is not typical of the statistical population as a whole and which is, therefore, unrepresentative.

Within a statistical population there will also often exist distinguishable sub-groups that differ from each other in terms of important characteristics. In order to accommodate this, the researcher may use 'stratified sampling', which entails selecting individuals from each stratum of the sample population. If our statistical population is composed of ScotRail employees, for example, then this large group of people can be broken down according to sub-categories, such as age group and ethnic origin. If, for example, it is the case that 70 per cent of these employees are aged 40 or over and only 30 per cent of them are aged 16-39, then such proportions should be reflected in the sample chosen. This would mean ensuring that 70 per cent of those in the sample are aged 40 or over and only 30 per cent aged 16-39. If the researcher was interested in levels of industrial militancy amongst the workforce, for example, then stratifying the sample by age might be necessary, as there could exist a connection between age and militancy. Let us assume, for the sake of illustration, that younger employees are generally more militant than older employees. If, by purely random methods, a sample is constructed that includes mainly older workers, then the impression may be created that typical ScotRail employees are non-militant. The use of stratified sampling is designed to prevent this problem arising.

Other sampling techniques include:

- *Quota sampling*, where categories based on similar characteristics in the population are established and sampling stops when the quota has been reached. If in a population of students at St. Andrews University, 50 males and 50 females are required, then data collection will cease once those numbers have been obtained
- *Snowball sampling*, which is used when the required sample cannot be easily identified, for example non-convicted car thieves. The sample is created by individuals persuading other individuals to contact the researcher and volunteer their services
- *Self-selecting sampling*, where the sample is comprised of respondents to an advertisement that requests volunteers to take part in the study.

Surveys

The survey is often mistakenly described as a research method, when it is actually a *tool* for data *collection*. A survey, then, is something conducted by the researcher in order to collect data. The actual research method(s), however, relate(s) to the tool(s) which will be used in order to generate the information required for the survey. Thus, research methods such as the interview or questionnaire, or a combination of both, may be used so that the survey can be conducted.

Observation

Many sociologists claim that an effective study of human behaviour requires as full and complete a picture as possible of people's behaviour patterns. It is often argued that the best way of obtaining such a picture is by observing people directly as they engage in their normal, routine, day-to-day activities. Observation can be used in those situations where people are unlikely to co-operate with an interviewer, or to take the time to complete a questionnaire. There may even be something quite appealing about observing people's behaviour patterns at first hand. As an observer, the sociologist need not rely upon people to respond to questions, or to answer honestly and truthfully in relation to how they tend to behave, or about events that may have occurred some time ago. Instead, the researcher is physically present when events occur. All forms of observation are similar in that they generate *qualitative* data from *primary* sources. There are, however, several different types of observation.

Participant Observation

When using participant observation, the researcher actually participates in the activities of those being studied. For example, the sociologist may decide to join a team of workers in a factory, a group of unemployed youths on the street corner, or a delinquent gang, in order to obtain data in relation to the typical behaviour patterns of their members. Participant observation offers the sociologist the opportunity to see life as it is actually lived and he or she is 'on the scene' when events happen. It becomes possible, then, to observe a range of phenomena directly.

The participant observer has to participate on the one hand and observe on the other. This research tool tends to involve *covert* observation, which means that the observer attempts to conceal his or her identity. Those people being studied believe the researcher to be 'just one of them'. As an example, the researcher could literally pretend to be an assembly-line worker in a car plant, a delinquent, and so on. This technique can be very difficult or awkward, as the researcher has to put on a convincing performance in order to avoid being exposed, which will entail much in the way of careful preparation. The sociologist may have to alter his or her physical appearance, speech patterns and so on, in order to blend in with the group.

A very clear example of the use of covert participant observation is presented in James Patrick's (1973) study, *A Glasgow Gang Observed*. Patrick was a teacher at an approved school in Glasgow. He was asked by a juvenile offender in his care to experience gang life first hand. In order to become a gang member without blowing his cover as an impostor, Patrick had to adopt a similar dialect, speech pattern and dress code as the other gang members. This required meticulous preparation and high levels of concentration at all times, as Patrick sought to play the role of gang member and of *covert* observer. He put himself in a position of considerable risk, as he had to engage in street battles in order to make his performance convincing to other gang members. He ran the constant risk of being found out by other gang members. However, because of his direct involvement in the group, Patrick was able to witness the typical behaviour patterns of the gang and to gain very valuable insights into the values, attitudes and beliefs of its members. This type of research facilitates a greater understanding of crime and deviance in society and Patrick's study has become a classic in its own right.

Covert participant observation has a number of strengths and weaknesses.

Strengths:

- Valuable insights can be provided into aspects of social life that might never be revealed using other methods
- Behaviour is witnessed in its natural state, unaffected by those being observed *knowing* that they are being observed.

Weaknesses:

- Participating researchers may begin to over-identify with the participant role, making it difficult for them to remain unbiased, impartial and objective. The researcher may actually begin to think and act like those being studied. This phenomenon is known as 'going native'. This is often also referred to as the 'Hawthorne effect', after a study by Roethlisberger and Dickson (1939; cited in Rose, 1988), where those being studied knew they were being observed, thus effecting their behaviour. The researchers also developed friendly relations with those being studied, thus affecting the outcome of their research
- Researchers engaged in covert participant observation run considerable risks, as Patrick (1973) referred to in his study
- Participant observers may be able to record and describe behaviour, but not necessarily explain it. Experiencing a situation is not the same as understanding why it is occurring
- Consequently, covert participant observation may be insufficient on its own and may have to be complemented by the use of the interview technique, in order to try to bridge the gap between description and explanation
- There are significant ethical issues concerning covert observation, since those studied are not aware that they are being observed.

It is possible for the participant observer to use *overt observation,* which means that he or she participates in the activities of those being researched, without them realising they are being observed by a researcher. This approach will reduce the likelihood of the researcher 'going native', but on the other hand, he or she might gain a distorted impression of the participant's typical behaviour patterns, as it is common for people not to act normally when they realise they are being observed. Some of the reasons for this are as follows:

- Members may try to impress or shock the observer in order to create a powerful impression, resulting in an exaggerated display of behaviour
- Those observed may fail to display certain patterns of behaviour, out of fear that the observer might inform someone in a position of authority, or 'grass them up', in colloquial parlance.

Additionally:

- The actual participation of an observer (whether overt *or* covert) in the activities of those he or she is researching can, in itself, be said to affect the outcome of the research.

Non-participant observation

Another type of observation is known as *non-participant observation*. With this technique, the activities of the participants being investigated are monitored without any direct involvement or participation on the part of the researcher, who tends to remain fairly detached or distant from the action. The group or individual being investigated may be aware of the fact that they are being studied, in which case the observation is overt, or alternatively the participants may be unaware that they are the object of study, in which case the observation is covert. An example of the latter could be a situation where a researcher decides to observe, from a safe distance, the activities of a group of notorious football hooligans in or around a major stadium in Glasgow or Edinburgh. If, however, a researcher sits in on a class of sixteen-year old school pupils in Inverness, then the type of observation would probably be overt, as everyone involved can be expected to be aware of the true identity of the researcher (see Willis, 1977, for his work of this ilk in a Midlands comprehensive school).

One of the dangers inherent in non-participant observation is that the researcher becomes, in a sense, too detached from the group being studied and begins to place a subjective interpretation on the behaviour that can be seen. This interpretation may be distorted or inaccurate. To illustrate, a sociologist using non-participant observation as a research tool to study the phenomenon of industrial sabotage in a factory in Paisley may misinterpret worker behaviour. Workers metaphorically 'dragging their heels' on the completion of tasks may be interpreted as laziness or boredom, when the actual reason might be more closely related to attempts to seek revenge against the management, for perceived or actual grievances. In this scenario, the non-participant observer has committed an error, in that he or she has begun to impose a subjective interpretation upon the activities of the group. This fault is referred to as 'ethnocentricism', but its effects can be minimised by combining observation with the interview technique.

Additional problems inherent in using observation as a research tool:

- It can be exceedingly time-consuming
- The researcher can spend long periods of time observing a group, without witnessing anything of significance
- Some situations or locations will be inaccessible to the sociologist, e.g. covert participant observation would be very difficult in a hospital operating theatre – a lack of knowledge or technical expertise would render it impossible for the researcher to assume this type of role
- Factors such as race and ethnicity and age and gender can prove to be major obstacles, e.g. covert participant observation in a monastery on Barra would probably preclude female researchers; and a sixty year old female researcher may find it difficult convincing gangs in Edinburgh that she was a genuine contender for membership.

> **Trigger**
>
> What problems might be associated with the use of observation as a research tool in understanding classroom participation on your course of study?

Experiments

The experiment, particularly the laboratory experiment, is used sparingly in sociology. It is much more likely to be used as a research tool in various branches of psychology. More common in sociology is the 'field experiment'. This is conducted in everyday locations, such as schools, factories, hospitals and so on, rather than laboratories. As an example, a field experiment could be conducted whereby disruptive pupils are placed in smaller class groups in which they are permitted to engage in joint decision-making with members of staff, in order to ascertain whether such innovations can have a beneficial effect on pupil behaviour.

Sometimes, 'participants' can be deliberately placed in a real setting, where the objective is to observe their patterns of behaviour. Zimbardo (1973) conducted a well-known experiment using a group of his students in a simulated prison in California. One group of students, selected at random, was instructed to play the role of prison guard and the other group were told to play the role of inmate. Zimbardo's aim was to discover to what extent the acting out of these sharply contrasting roles would influence the students' attitudes and behaviour. Interestingly the 'guards' became very authoritarian and they displayed much in the way of hostility towards the 'inmates', who were treated with utter contempt. The 'inmates', for their part, displayed the rebelliousness and apathy considered typical of actual prisoners. The animosity that existed between the two groups became so intense that Zimbardo was forced to terminate the experiment prematurely!

Recently, as part of the current television craze to create 'real life' or 'docu*dramas*', Zimbardo's concept was used by the BBC (with the collaboration of two psychologists) for the recently screened, *The Experiment.*

Notice that this type of research uses a primary source of data and that the data produced will be qualitative, because the experimenter will produce a written report summarising the main research findings.

Another form of experiment in sociology is the 'naturally occurring experiment', where, for example, organisations introduce major changes on their own initiative, sometimes gradually. The sociologist can, in a sense, just 'wait in the wings' to see whether these changes will have the effect of altering people's behaviour patterns and attitudes. A pertinent example of this is the Volvo experiment of the early to mid-1970s in Sweden (Kohler, 1997). Up to this point, the company had been using the traditional assembly line method of production, which is often seen as the root cause of low morale, dissatisfaction, stress, de-motivation and conflict among workers, all of which were in evidence at Volvo, due to the endless repetition and resulting monotony. In addition, rates of absenteeism and staff turnover were very high and the company was finding it difficult to recruit new, especially young, employees to the organisation. These problems were also attributed to the assembly line system used at the plant. Volvo decided to invest £8.7 million in the creation of a new car plant at Kalmar in south-east Sweden, which replaced the assembly lines with a series of work bays in which teams of workers enjoyed the benefits of job rotation, increased decision-making in relation to such things as working methods, pace of work and opportunities to learn and apply a much wider range of skills. The

reduction in monotony and the increased variety were accompanied by major improvements at Volvo. Rates of absenteeism and staff turnover declined sharply, conflict between workers and management was minimised, output rose and quality improved. Other, similarly 'naturally occurring' experiments have since been carried out elsewhere in the motor industry, at Renault, Saab and Fiat, amongst others.

Trigger

Beyond the examples provided, how much scope is there for experimentation in sociological research?

Case studies

The case study allows the researcher to gather qualitative, in-depth data by focusing closely on an individual or group. Examples might include examining the life history, or current circumstances of individuals, such as a notorious soccer hooligan living in Aberdeen, a drugs dealer based in Dunfermline, or groups such as homeless people living on the streets in Stirling. Subjects are often chosen on the basis of how well they fit the researcher's notion of what a 'good example' of the particular phenomenon under investigation might be. A central aim of the case study is to arrive at a comprehensive understanding of the group under investigation. Case studies may be carried out over relatively short periods of time or, in the case of longitudinal studies, may be repeated over longer periods, in order to assess the impact of time on the variables under investigation. Although the case study will tend to make use of primary sources of data, this is not always the case, as secondary sources, such as police and school records, may also be used. The data provided will tend to be qualitative, rather than quantitative. In sociology, case studies are often used in order to explore issues and topics in the area of crime and deviance.

Case studies may focus on groups of varying sizes, as well as individuals. A relatively small group of people may be targeted, such as the 'Norton Street gang' from the Italian slum neighbourhood of Boston, Massachussets, which features prominently in Whyte's (1955) work entitled *Street Corner Society*. Alternatively, a whole community may be examined. Ken Pryce's (1979) study of a single West Indian community in St. Paul's, Bristol, attempted, at one level, simply to understand the main features of that particular community. In some cases, an in-depth study will be made of an unusual phenomenon, such as a bitter and protracted industrial dispute. A recent example would be the long-running industrial dispute at Timex in Dundee.

Referring to a case study as a research method is problematic, however. This is because it actually makes more sense to say that a range of research methods can be employed in order that a case study can be carried out. Many case studies, then, will employ a mixture or variety of research methods (see methodological pluralism below). A convenient illustration of this point is Ball's (1981) work, entitled *Beachside Comprehensive: A Case Study of Comprehensive Schooling.*

If we examine the methodology used by Ball (1981), then we can discover the following:

- Interviewed pupils and teachers – therefore, primary sources of data were used in order to produce qualitative data
- Carried out several small-scale questionnaires using primary sources, again in order to produce *both* qualitative and quantitative data
- Worked through and analysed school records and registers, which entailed employing secondary sources, in order to generate *both* qualitative and quantitative data
- Used participant observation to try to find out more about the workings of the school, and so primary sources were used to generate qualitative data.

Case studies – the advantages:

- They can provide us with a richer and more detailed picture of an individual or a small group than research based upon large samples
- They can provide us with fresh insights into human behaviour. For example, Paul Willis' (1977) study of an English secondary school provides an insightful account of the main reasons for educational failure on the part of working class boys
- They can be used to refute a general theory in relation to human social behaviour. For example, Gough's (1952) study of Nayar society demonstrated that family structures based upon a marital bond are not, in fact, universal
- They can be useful in terms of generating new hypotheses, which can then be tested against other data and subsequent studies. For example, a case study of one homeless person may generate a hypothesis on the main reasons for homelessness in Scotland, which can then be tested against a larger or wider study of homeless people
- They can be used during the initial stages of a research project. Ideas and hypotheses can be generated and then they can be analysed later, using a large, representative sample of the population. In other words, the case study can be used as a 'pilot study'

- They can be useful in terms of providing information for a larger research project. The experiences of one prisoner of war could be used to produce a questionnaire which could be designed to examine the extent to that these experiences apply to other prisoners of war

- A single case study can challenge or contradict the findings of a larger study and call into question the conclusions drawn from previous findings.

Case studies – the disadvantages:

- The evidence produced may only be useful to one particular researcher and is unlikely to be representative of people in general
- They may be limited and unrepresentative, since they focus on specific examples and cannot, therefore, be used as a basis for generalisation.

Documentary and content analysis

This method employs secondary analyses of research, information or data banks. With the rapid growth in new computer technologies, it is being used with greater regularity in sociology. The method analyses both qualitative *and* quantitative data. Qualitative documents such as diaries, personal records, newspapers and mass media products (such as video footage and advertisements) may be analysed, as well as quantitative documents, such as official crime statistics, Home Office reports and United Nations statistics. Researchers using this method essentially evaluate recorded information and data. This has the advantage of providing further valuable sociological criticism and comment on already published works, but the disadvantage that the secondary research is only as good as the initial data. Analysing recorded data may reveal trends and patterns hitherto unnoticed. However, the success of this method depends on the quality of the data available, access to such data and the degree of mathematical and technological competence of the researcher.

Methodological Pluralism or 'Triangulation'

We have considered each research method in turn, which might create the impression that researchers tend to use one single method in any study undertaken. This would be a false impression. In order to gather as much in the way of accurate data as possible, several different research methods may have to be employed in combination. Pure reliance on one particular method may fail to provide sufficient depth and detail in relation to the chosen topic. We can refer to the use of more than one research tool as 'methodological pluralism' or, alternatively, 'triangulation'. A clear example of this strategy can be seen in Ellen Barker's (1984) study, *The Making of a Mooonie*. Barker studied members of the religious sect known as the Moonies, with a particular focus on who made up the membership, how they came to be members of the sect and their reasons for joining. In carrying out the study, Barker employed three methods of gathering data, including in-depth interviews, questionnaires and participant observation. Her aim was to obtain information on a number of different levels, and the multi-faceted approach she adopted allowed her to glean information on the thoughts, background and values of individual members, the families and friends affected and how members behaved in the context of the movement.

The Research Process

Any chapter devoted to research methods in sociology would be incomplete, however, without providing an account of the various steps that combine to form the research process. Below is a brief explanation of how this process is generally employed.

There are *five* main steps or stages that can be identified:

1) **Theory**: Before embarking on any piece of research, the sociologist will conduct a literature review of other research carried out in the relevant area and of related sociological concepts, debates and theories.

2) **Hypothesis**: An hypothesis is the formulation of a particular idea, concept or phenomenon that the sociologist wishes to investigate. It is normally presented in the form of one, or more, statement(s). Thus, a sociologist may decide to investigate the apparent link between unemployment and youth crime. The hypothesis could be that, in areas where the unemployment rate is high, youth crime will be both more prevalent and more serious than in areas of the country where unemployment rates are comparatively low. Another possibility is that if unemployment rises in a particular area, then so too will the incidence of youth crime. Research can then be conducted in order to test these hypotheses.

3) **Operationalisation**: This stage consists of *four* sub-stages, which are:

   - Choice of research method: after constructing and defining the hypothesis, the sociologist decides on a suitable method, or combination of methods, to investigate the chosen area
   - Definition of concepts: terms and concepts used or referred to in the study are defined (e.g. what definitions of social class are to be used)
   - Setting measurements: whether the study will use quantitative or qualitative measurements, or a mixture of both and how they will be deployed in the study
   - Sampling: which sampling procedures will be used and how the sample(s) will be constructed.

4) **Fieldwork**: Fieldwork entails actually conducting the research, using a selected methodology. Prior to launching the study, however, the sociologist

may conduct a 'pilot study', which means that a questionnaire, for example, may be administered to a small group of people in order to gauge whether or not the actual questions are reasonable or appropriate in this context. Any necessary adjustments can be made at this stage. The same type of exercise can be carried out in relation to the interview, if required.

5) ***Processing and presentation of results***: Once the research has been completed, attention turns to analysing the data and presenting the findings. Results are often presented in the form of journal articles, books or pamphlets. A consideration of the main research findings may allow the sociologist to confirm or refute the initial hypothesis. Alternatively, the data may be inconclusive, indicating that further research may be required. Researchers will often provide evaluative comment on all aspects of the study, including the effectiveness and suitability of the method(s) used, the validity and reliability of results and to what extent the hypothesis has been proven.

Conclusion

To conclude, then, this Chapter has demonstrated a range of research methods and processes that sociologists are able to avail themselves of, which can be employed in order to gather data as scientifically and systematically as possible. Essentially, it is the sociologist's rigorous approach to data collection that distinguishes the sociological perspective from common sense ways of analysing and understanding the social world in which we live.

Chapter Summary

- Sociologists select from a range of research methods in order to generate the data required to investigate a selected copy.
- Crucial to the selection of particular research methods is the methodology influencing the researcher. There are three main theoretical approaches to research: the 'positivist' approach, the 'anti-positivist' (naturalistic) approach and the 'realist' approach.
- Researchers derive information from sources that can be categorised as 'primary' and 'secondary'.
- The two main types of data are 'quantitative' and 'qualitative'.

- A range of research methods were described and evaluated including: the use of secondary sources of data such as 'official statistics', research methods that use primary sources of data such as the 'interview', the 'questionnaire', 'observation', the 'experiment' and the 'case study'.
- Researchers often combine research approaches in an attempt to more fully analyse the topic under investigation. This is known as 'methodological pluralism' or 'triangulation'.
- There are five main stages to the 'research process': theory, hypothesis, operationalisation, fieldwork and processing and the processing and presentation of results.

Further Reading

Churton, M. (2000) *Theory and Method* (Skills-based Sociology Series, London: Macmillan
Kumar, R. (1996) *Research Methodology*, London: Sage
Langley, P. (1993) *Managing Sociology Coursework*, Lewes: Connect Publications
Lee, R. (1993) *Doing Research on Sensitive Topics*, London: Sage
Layder, D. (1993) *New Strategies in Social Research*, Cambridge: Polity Press
McNeill,P. (1990) *Research Methods*, London: Routledge
Walsh, M. (2001) *Research Made Real: A guide for students*, Nelson Thornes

Useful Websites

For examples of current research in the social sciences: http://www.esrc.ac.uk/
A free Internet tutorial on research methods is available at:
http://sociology.camden.rutgers.edu/main.htm
An excellent site with free downloads on research methods:
http://www.sociology.org.uk/cload.htm

Bibliography

Ball, S.J. (1981) *Beachside Comprehensive: A Case Study of Secondary Schooling*, Cambridge: Cambridge University Press
Barker, E. (1984) *The Making of a Moonie*, Oxford: Blackwell
Gough, E.K. (1952) 'Changing Kinship Usages in the Setting of Political and Economic Change among the Nayars of Malabar', *Journal of the Royal Anthropological Institute*, LXXXII
Home Office (2001) http://www.homeoffice.gov.uk/crimpol/index.html
Kohler, H. (1997) *Economic Systems and Human Welfare: A Global Survey*, Cincinnati, OH: South-Western (at http://www.hbcollege.com/business_stats/kohler/resources/applications/app22_3.doc)
Office for National Statistics (2001) http://www.statistics.gov.uk
Patrick, J. (1973) *A Glasgow Gang Observed*, London: Eyre Methuen
Pryce, K. (1979) *Endless Pressure*, Harmondsworth: Penguin
Rose, M. (1988) *Industrial Behaviour*, Second Edition, Harmondsworth: Penguin
Roy, D. (1960) 'Banana Time: Job Satisfaction and Informal Interaction', *Human Organisation*, Vol. 18
Whyte, W.F. (1955) *Street Corner Society*, 2nd Edition, Chicago, IL: University of Chicago Press
Willis, P. (1977) *Learning to Labour: how working class lads get working class jobs*, Farnborough: Saxon House
Zimbardo, P.G. 'A Study of Prisoners and Guards in a Simulated Prison', *Naval Research Review* (Sep 1973), Washington, DC: Office of Naval Research, Department of the Navy

Chapter 4   Social Class

Tony Sweeney, Neil Etherington and John Lewis

Introduction

This chapter introduces you to some of the key issues surrounding social class in sociology. Rather than attempting to be an exhaustive account, it attempts to encourage you to think about the various uses (and abuses) of the term and to be able to incorporate the concept into your way of thinking about the world sociologically. An overview of problems of defining and measuring class is provided, followed by an introduction to theoretical explanations of social class. From this, you will see that social class is an area of political as well as sociological debate, since class is often linked with ideology. More recent debates on changing class structure are then examined before considering whether or not Scotland is a class society. This chapter should be read alongside other chapters that focus on types and forms of social stratification, since class, as an analytical tool, cannot explain all aspects of human behaviour. The 'sociological imagination' (see Chapter 1: Introduction) is better served by taking a holistic approach.

The Uses and Abuses of 'Class'

Social class is one of the most significant, yet hotly contested, concepts in sociology. Since the earliest days of sociology as an academic discipline, sociologists have debated issues surrounding social class. Theoretical traditions, such as Marxism, place class at the very heart of theoretical analysis, while in other traditions, such as that identified with Durkheim, class features only vaguely. In recent years, class has become the topic of ever more rigorous debate both within and out with sociological circles. Politicians, for example, have become increasingly keen to pronounce on class. On becoming prime minister in 1979, Margaret Thatcher promised to strive to make everyone in Britain middle class. Her successor, John Major, went so far to claim that Britain had become a 'classless society'. More recently, Tony Blair pronounced that "the class war is over" (Labour Party Conference, October 1997) and "slowly but surely the old establishment is being replaced by a new, larger, more meritocratic middle class" (Blair, 1999). Contemporary sociologists continue to debate the continuing relevance of class. For Kingston (2000), class as a concept has been replaced by inequality as a useful tool of sociological analysis. Pahl (1989) argues that 'class as a concept is ceasing to do any useful work in sociology' while Pakulski and Waters (1996) venture so far as to proclaim 'the death of class'.

Despite such claims, the last fifteen years or so has seen a resurgence in class analysis in sociology, albeit uneven and tentative, with many commentators insisting on the continuing, indeed, ever increasing relevance of class. McNall *et al* (1991), for example, calls for a return to traditional class debates in light of the recent deepening of material inequalities in capitalist societies. He claims that whilst class is still a useful tool of analysis, it must be modified and adapted to adequately explain contemporary societies. Goldthorpe (1995) argues for the concept of class to be retained as a sociological *problematik*, since the continued existence of class in modern societies *can* be empirically demonstrated. For Clark and Lipset (1991), social class still forms a fundamental aspect of contemporary societies, despite its inability to explain all modern social and political processes. Ferguson, Lavalette and Mooney (2002: 52) claim that:

> [C]lass analysis remains crucial to understanding the social situation of the vast majority in the modern world [and] the working class [...] is not merely an oppressed, suffering class, but has the potential to re-shape society anew.

Despite this recent resurgence of interest in the impact of social class in modern societies, no single definition of class as a concept exists. As Ralph Miliband (1991:19) notes, "an extraordinary degree of confusion and obfuscation attends the discussion of class in relation to capitalist societies."

Defining Social Class

Social class is a wide-ranging concept and has a number of related dimensions that determine how sociologists measure it. Some commentators focus on the *political* dimension of class and measure it in terms of indicators such as power and status. Others view class as *cultural* and use measurement indicators such as norms, values, expectations, attitudes and lifestyle. However, it is the *economic* dimension of social class that is used most by sociologists, using indicators such as income, wealth and occupation. Social class can thus be defined both *subjectively* and *objectively*.

Subjective definitions

Subjective definitions of class focus on people's shared subjective understandings over how they and others rank in systems of structured inequality. This approach has been used to establish how individuals *locate* their own class position alongside other social categories such as ethnicity, gender and occupation. This approach may be useful for comparing how individuals see themselves in relation to class position and when survey results are considered it is clear that class still *matters* to people. In a 1996 survey, two-thirds of respondents agreed that "there is one law for the rich and one for the poor" (Adonis and Pollard, 1998: 11) and in a Gallup Poll in 1995, 81 per cent of respondents said 'yes' to the question: 'Do you think that there is a class struggle in this country?', representing a significant increase from 56 per cent in 1961 and 70 per cent in the 1980s (cited in Adonis and Pollard, 1998: 3). Subjective interpretations of class might, on the one hand, be presented as evidence that the effects of class are very real to people's lives. On the other hand, however, they may be seen as problematic and subject to change over time and place. It may be the case that respondents believe that it is no longer cool to be middle class and that identifying with the working class, regardless of personal level of affluence to the contrary, is more desirable now. Cultural icons such as the pop singer, Robbie Williams, and the rock band, Oasis, deliberately make a play of their working class roots. Even the American pop singer and actress, Jennifer Lopez, sings "don't be fooled with the rocks (*diamonds*) that I've got, I'm still Jenny from the block (*working class neighbourhood*)," despite a reported lifestyle that would contradict the sentiment expressed in the lyrics. Regardless of the reasons behind these results, subjective definitions of class remain problematic, as there is often a mismatch between subjective and objective class location.

Trigger

1. How would you define your own class position?
2. What has influenced your view?

Objective definitions

Class can be objectively defined in *four* key ways:

- *As position in distributional hierarchies*: Here, class is defined as position within systems of material inequality and is often measured by indicators such as income or wealth. Class is used as a *gradational* concept where class location is determined within structured hierarchies, such as the common sense notion of a three-class model of upper class, middle class and working class. In this case, 'upper class' is defined as the highest category of income distribution and working class; the lowest

- *As determinant of life chances*: Class is used here as a means of explaining economic inequalities such as material standard of living and economic life chances. In this case, class is viewed as a *relational* concept, that is, class position is objectively defined in relation to an individual's capacity to generate income and wealth and how this impacts of life chances

- *As an explanation for historical variations in class structure*: Here, the focus is on class structures and how they vary across time and place. It is a macro-level of analysis that focuses on historical variations in class inequality and how they come about

- *Class as oppressive and exploitative*: This definition is both sociological and political and is most associated with Marxist theorists. It is embedded in normative judgements over the undesirability of economic inequality, oppression and exploitation and how class can be instrumental in emancipating projects of social change.

Once social class is defined, it can then be *operationalised*. That is, it can be classified and measured using specific indicators. This further determines how class is measured. We will see that how class is defined greatly influences how it is measured and therefore choice of method of measurement is, in itself, politically and ideologically (i.e. *subjectively*) underpinned.

Objective Measurement of Social Class
Official social classification in the UK

Official social classifications in the UK tend to group individuals by occupation and industry. The Registrar-General's Classificatory Scheme (RGCS) has been historically based on the assumption that class in British society can be assessed using a graded hierarchy of occupations (Rose, 1995). This assumption is, in fact, distinctly Weberian in origin (see Theoretical Approaches to Social Class, below). Raw data for the scheme is derived from the ten-yearly population census and individuals are assigned to social classes by occupation and employment status, measured as 'relative standing in the community'. There are *five* such classes in this model, as indicated in Box 4.1, below.

Box 4.1 The Registrar-General's Classificatory Scheme

I	Professional, etc., occupations
II	Management and technical occupations
III	Skilled occupations:
	(N) non-manual
	(M) manual
IV	Partly-skilled occupations
V	Unskilled occupations

The scheme was based on a two-class model of middle and lower class (the upper class often do not work!) where the middle class was defined, in simple terms, as non-manual workers and the lower class as manual workers. This classificatory system ranks groups hierarchically and is, therefore, an example of a gradational system.

Strengths of the Registrar General's Model:

- The model has been extensively used in census reports, longitudinal studies and surveys but is, perhaps, most notable in sociology for its use in research into health inequalities
- The system is relatively simple to interpret and use notwithstanding the problematic nature of the categories
- The data derived allow for comparison of changes over time.

Weaknesses of the Registrar General's Model:

- Individuals who do not hold occupations are excluded such as: the wealthy, the unemployed, those too young to be employed and home makers who work, but are not formally employed. These individuals make up around 40 per cent of the population (Rose, 1995)
- The measurement, 'relative standing in the community', is essentially vague, undefined and *subjective*
- The categories used were too broad to allow for status differences within occupations
- The scale assumes broad consensus over occupational status and does not cater for changes in occupational classifications over time, such as the blurring of distinctions between manual and non-manual work and between the old industrial and service sectors
- It effectively measures social status rather than social class
- It overlooks the role that income levels have on determining life chances, grouping together, as it does, occupations that have widely ranging levels of income
- Feminists critique such classificatory systems as they are based on the male head of household model.

The Registrar General's Socio-economic Groups (SEG) model

This alternative method of official classification was devised in recognition of the inadequacies of the RGCS in providing for the diversity of occupational structures brought about by the shift from manufacturing to service sector industries (see Chapter 10: Work and its Organisation). This model, originated by the sociologist, David Glass (1950), contains 17 classifications measured by employment status as opposed to skill level and is favoured by many sociologists, as it appears to be *more* social scientific. Following a review by the Economic and Social Research Council (ESRC), a new model of classification was introduced in 2001 entitled the National Statistics Socio-economic Classification (NS-SEC). This system replaces the models mentioned above and is based on an eight-class model (see Box 4.2, below).

Box 4.2 National Statistics Socio-economic Classification Analytic Classes

1	Higher managerial and professional occupations	
	1.1	Large employers and higher managerial occupations
	1.2	Higher professional occupations
2	Lower managerial and professional occupations	
3	Intermediate occupations	
4	Small employers and account workers	
5	Lower supervisory and technical occupations	
6	Semi-routine occupations	
7	Routine occupations	
8	Never worked and the unemployed	

NB: An additional category, 'not classified', includes students, occupations not described or stated and those not classifiable for other reasons.

Other classificatory systems for measuring social class include:

- The 'advertising industry standard', which measures disposable income
- The 'Hope-Goldthorpe scale', which was developed as a result of John Goldthorpe's social mobility research (Goldthorpe, 1980). This model endorses *seven* classes into *three* groups, labelled the 'service class', the 'intermediate class' and the working class
- The 'Surrey Occupational Class Scheme' (Arber, Dale and Gilbert, 1981), which incorporates women
- Neo-Weberian (see the Weberian approach, below and in Chapter 2: Sociological Theory) models such as Will Hutton's (1995) '30:30:40 model' (see Chapter 10: Work and its Organisation), which suggests that modern UK society is characterised by *three* main classes: the top 40 per cent – 'the advantaged', the intermediate 30 per cent – the 'newly insecure', and the bottom 30 per cent – the 'disadvantaged'. This model is heavily influenced by Weber's definition of class as determined by an individual's market and work situation.

Trigger

In what ways is choice of measurement linked to how class is defined?

Theoretical Approaches to Social Class
The functionalist approach
Functionalist theories view class as a naturally occurring form of stratification and that class position reflects natural, often biologically based, differences in levels of skills, talent, application and ability. While social class *origin* is ascribed, social class *destination* is meritocratically achieved (see Chapter 9: Education). Inequality is 'functional' for society in that it helps to meet 'functional pre-requisites' – societies' basic needs. They do not explicitly focus on class other than its function as a form of social stratification in complex societies. Durkheim, for example, wrote little explicitly on class. Talcott Parsons (1964) defined class along the lines of 'general standing in society', which is a measure of a number of factors, including economic position, schooling, neighbourhood and family background. As we shall see, this description overlaps with Weber's notion of 'social honour'. For Parsons, stratification systems derive from common values – 'value consensus'.

The American functionalists, Davis and Moore (1945), viewed social stratification as inevitable, functional and, even, desirable. In order for society to meet basic requirements, top positions must be filled by those individuals most talented and able. Adequate rewards must be institutionally established in order to encourage individuals to undergo the specialist training required to qualify for these positions. Therefore, occupations should be rewarded in terms of the importance of their role to the functioning of society – 'functional importance'. This would mean that doctors, lawyers and judges would command high salaries and high social rank, while cleaners and manual labourers would be paid low wages and occupy low social rank. Although cultural variations exist over the status attached to roles, reward systems are universal.

Melvin Tumin (1967) claims that this position is untenable. It is unclear that some occupations are more functionally important than others. For example, while doctors tend to citizen's health, cleaners help ensure that fatal disease is not spread through the proliferation of dangerous bacteria. There is no necessary link between high status, high level of reward and talent and ability as the example of the British Royal Family might illustrate. Ultimately, the functionalist approach overlooks the apparently inherent conflict in capitalist societies, assuming that societies naturally tend towards order, or 'homeostasis'.

The Marxist approach
Karl Marx (1818-1883) placed class struggle at the heart of his analysis of social change (see Chapter 2: Sociological Theory). All complex societies have been characterised by various modes of production, which is, for Marx, fundamental to the human condition. This notion, that production is the most fundamental human

activity is known as 'historical materialism'. Marx refers to *three* main modes of production historically:

- The **Asiatic**, found in ancient societies where production barely meets the subsistence requirements of producers and non-producers. Consequently, in such simple societies there is virtually no economic surplus, little social division of labour and an absence of private property. Such societies are effectively classless as there is no material basis for antagonistic division between groups who commonly consume all forms of production
- The **feudal**, found in North-West European societies in the middle ages, where a clear division of labour between the nobility and peasantry and developments in the technical forces of production enable non-producers (the nobility) to expropriate economic surplus from producers (the peasantry)
- The **capitalist**, where the 'ruling class' – the 'bourgeoisie' or owners of the means of production – expropriate economic surplus from the non-ownership subject class, the 'proletariat'. These "two great warring and hostile camps" (Marx and Engels, 1848: 49) are inherently conflictual.

For Marx, the significance of social class can only be understood in a framework of economic production and how it is expropriated, distributed and consumed (Scase, 1992). In capitalist societies, labour is not defined by occupation; rather, it incorporates both mental and manual production. He defines the working class as *all* those who sell labour power and the ruling class as those who own the conditions of production. Capitalist employment relations dictate that workers receive a wage for their labour while owners appropriate profit, or *surplus value*, from the products of their labour. This Marx saw as exploitative. Crucial to the maintenance of class relations in capitalist societies is state support for the extraction of surplus value in the employment relationship.

For Marx, then, class membership is *objectively* defined by relationship to the means of production, regardless of whether members of a particular class subjectively define themselves differently. This is not to say that Marx did not advocate identification with class position and the exploitative nature of class relations in capitalist societies. Rather, he uses the distinction 'class in itself' to describe the quantity of workers in the subject class, but claims that only when this class becomes a 'class in itself', that is, when members develop awareness of their subordinate position to capital and the state, that the overthrow of capitalist relations of production may come about. Such awareness Marx refers to as 'class consciousness' (see Chapter 10: Work and its Organisation), which, when fully realised, will bring about conditions ripe for radical social transformation through proletarian revolution. Marx was confident that class-consciousness would develop in the working class in capitalist societies. This was because he believed capitalism to be an essentially contradictory system where conflict is endemic to this system that "sows the seeds of its own destruction." As workers become concentrated in large workplaces they are able to organise effective resistance. Although the relationship between the two warring classes is antagonistic, without the working class, the bourgeoisie has no one to exploit and so they develop the *superstructure* (law, ideology, culture, values, and beliefs) to legitimate their exploitation and conceal the source of exploitation, which is the material *base* of production-capitalism (see Chapter 2: Sociological Theory).

A key point, here, is that this 'deterministic' relationship between economic base and superstructure is not an inevitable one. Neither is the increased polarization of classes, immiseration (see Chapter 10: Work and its Organisation) and pauperisation that accompany capitalist development, inevitable consequences of the laws of nature. Rather, they are the result of how social institutions have been specifically designed under capitalism and they are, therefore, able to be socially transformed through class struggle. In the *Communist Manifesto*, Marx and Engels (1962 [1848]: 34) describe the history of class struggle, thus:

> Free man and slave, patrician and plebeian, lord and serf, guild-master and journeyman, in a word, oppressor and oppressed, stood in constant opposition to each other, carried on an uninterrupted, now hidden, now open fight, a fight that each time ended, either in a revolutionary reconstruction of society at large, or in the common ruin of the contending classes.

The approach developed by Marx and Engels (1962 [1848]), and those who followed in that tradition, such as Kautsky, Lenin, Trotsky and Luxembourg, has come to be known as 'Classical Marxism'. This can be contrasted with the heavily 'structuralist' strand of thought developed in Western societies since the second world war, by those such as Adorno, Althusser and Marcuse, known as 'Western' or 'Academic' Marxism (Anderson, 1976). This latter strand has done much to obscure the essence of Marx's thought and was characterised by:

- A focus on the philosophical aspects of Marxist thought rather than the political
- Support for Western Communist parties and an ambivalance to Stalinism
- A level of abstraction and obscurity that distanced their writings from the ordinary lives and struggles of working class people (Rees, 1998).

Evaluating the Marxist approach
Marx's theory of class has received qualified praise from a number of unlikely sources. The postmodernist, Pakulski (1996: 181-182), for example, states:

On the one hand, the capacity of [Marxist class theory] to span the domains of structure *and* action, to explain social inequality *and* division, social stability *and* social change, has always constituted its major attraction. [...] The downside of the conflation has been a tendency for a conceptual stretch and a theoretical blur [...] resulting in almost infinite plasticity of the class concept.

The 150th anniversary of the publication of *The Communist Manifesto* in 1998 saw a revival of interest in Marx from the broadsheet press. *The Financial Times* (25 March 1998) argued that "Marx was not only the harbinger of revolutionary hatred, but a shrewd, subtle analyst of capitalist society," and *The Independent on Sunday* (7 December 1997) asked "Was he right all along?," touting Marx as "the next big thinker" (cited in Ferguson, Lavalette and Mooney, 2002: 8).

Strengths:

- His analysis is able to explain how classes form and develop historically and provide the dynamic for social change
- The theory is relational and therefore explains relationship between classes
- His class theory has had a major impact on sociology since and has greatly influenced the development of so-called Marxist societies in the twentieth century
- It highlights possible causes of increasing inequalities in capitalist societies
- It is, within its own criteria, consistent and coherent with considerable analytical and explanatory power.

Weaknesses:

- Marx has been criticised for adopting a 'two-class' model of capitalist society. In actual fact, however, Marx recognised societies as having a multiplicity of classes. In *The Eighteenth Brumaire of Louis Bonaparte* (1962 [1852]), for example, he describes eight classes! What Marx meant was that all societies have two *major* historic classes and the struggle between them is instrumental to social change
- The 'problem' of the middle class – it would appear that a large middle class has arisen in contemporary class societies, which Marx did not account for. However, it is unclear that this group exist independently as a class. Modern Marxists state that there are many in the middle class who are oppressed and exploited and in reality, therefore, are working class while others in higher ranges of the middle class often have ownership stakes in the form of shares. Wright (1979) refers to the middle class as occupying 'contradictory class locations'

- It may be seen as an example of 'economic determinism' by those who argue that social life emanates from factors other than the economic (see the Weberian approach, below)
- Proletarian revolution, as Marx understood it, has not occurred, as yet
- His belief that 'class consciousness' would develop may have been at best exaggerated and at worst mistaken
- Marx's account has been criticised for being 'gender blind' and neglecting other forms of stratification such as age and ethnicity. He focuses mainly on those in formal production relationships who tended to be men at the time of his writing
- The growth of new social movements that cut across class lines and form around 'single issues', such as environmentalist groups or the gay movement, may suggest that class struggle does not adequately explain contemporary forms of conflict
- Relatively low strike rates in Britain in the late 1990s and early years of the new millennium might suggest that class struggle is a thing of the past. However, Marx argued that class, and class struggle, were not static concepts and that conflict can resurface when conditions allow. Also, Moody (1997: 21) notes that, in the period 1994-1997, mass or general strikes occurred in no fewer than twenty countries worldwide.

The Weberian approach

Max Weber (see Chapter 2: Sociological Theory) wrote little explicitly on class, but what he did write greatly influenced the development of an approach to class analysis associated with his name. In *Economy and Society* (1978 [1924]), he writes:

> We may speak of 'a class' when (1) a number of people have in common a specific causal component of their life chances, insofar as (2) this component is represented exclusively by economic interests in the possession of goods and opportunities for income, and (3) is represented under the conditions of the community or labour markets. This is 'class situation'. [...] [T]he kind of chance in the *market* is the decisive moment which presents a common condition for that individual's fate, Class situation is, in this sense ultimately market situation.   (Weber, 1978 [1924]: 927-8)

Weber, therefore, defines class as market-determined life chances, where owned resources determine opportunities for income generation through market transactions. No essential relationship exists between economic processes and political power and, whilst no common interests exist between buyer and seller, no systematic conflict exists either. A central contrast in Weber's approach can be found in his distinction between 'class', 'status' (and their relation to 'party') and 'authority' as key dimensions of stratification. 'Classes' are determined by the economic resources individual members bring to market transactions whereas membership of 'status' groups is determined by estimations of 'social honour'. Status groups comprise individuals who derive common identity from perceived similarities in status. The term, 'party', has less relevance to his overall perspective, but adds to what might be viewed as his *pluralist* approach to social stratification. Groups organise around 'party' lines for the taking and/or exercising of political power. Such groups draw membership from within and out with social classes and status groups. Authority relations comprise the third dimension of Weber's approach to social stratification. As industrial societies become increasingly more complex, they develop sophisticated and hierarchical bureaucracies in order to administer capitalist relations of production. Location in the chain of command, in the hierarchical structures found in formal organisations such as states and business enterprises, determines the level of individual power and influence, and thereby impacts on 'life chances'.

For Weber, then, the process of industrialisation creates a more complex division of labour that has the effect of increasing the number of classes and of creating cross-class alliances and internal class conflicts. The *three* main institutional forms of social stratification represent how power in society is distributed. The economic aspect of social class co-exists alongside the other forms – status groups and (positions of) authority. Whilst class can be *objectively* defined by 'market situation', status and party are *subjectively* defined by the individual.

Although Weber agreed with Marx that a fundamental determinant of social class position was derived from the ownership or non-ownership of property, he disagreed with Marx's focus on two main classes as agents of social change and the notion that systemic conflict between the two was inevitable. For Weber, *four* main classes can be identified:

1. The class privileged in terms of occupation and ownership
2. Technicians and lower level management
3. The petty bourgeoisie
4. The (manual) working class.

Significantly, Weber categorises the above classifications in terms of economic power, social status and political influence in keeping with his multidimensional approach to class analysis. Weber asserts that capitalist societies are predominately class societies but are only so because technical and economic transformation are fundamental to its reproduction. This is not true of all societies, as "when the bases of the acquisition and distribution of goods are relatively stable, stratification by status is favoured" (1978 [1924]: 938).

Evaluating the Weberian model

- Weber's approach has been used to account for the development of a middle class in contemporary capitalist societies
- His approach recognises that an individual may derive identity from across class, status groups, party interests and positions of authority. Some individuals may be working class in occupational terms, but vote Conservative. Others may have high social status such as a priest or minister, but little wealth
- Marxists argue that Weber's approach overlooks the oppressive and exploitative elements of class relations in capitalist societies
- Perhaps ironically, Weber's assertion that economic classes are predominant in times of technical and economic transformation might suggest that social class is ever more relevant in contemporary societies undergoing radical structural transformations.

There are certain crucial similarities and differences between Marx and Weber on class, as seen in Box 4.3.

Box 4.3 Marx and Weber Compared

Similarities include:
- Both viewed class as related to economic factors and as significant forms of inequality.
- Both recognise the key class division as related to ownership of property.

Differences include:
- For Marx, class relations derive from relationship to the means of production and are exploitative and oppressive. For Weber, class situation is derived from market-determined life chances.
- Marx argues that class is an agent for social change whereas Weber claims that social change determines class structure.
- Marx claims that class struggle is inevitable and endemic to capitalism, whereas Weber sees class conflict as merely possible alongside other forms of protest.

Trigger

Which of the theoretical approaches do you find more convincing, and why?

Debating Class Structure Today: Continuity and Change

Although the sociology of social class – from the 1960s to the onset of postmodern approaches in the 1980s and 1990s – was predominantly influenced by the Marxist and Weberian traditions, approaches developed before then have largely been overlooked (see Chapter 2: Sociological Theory). Sorensen (2000) notes that before the resurgence of interest in Marxist and Weberian traditions, class was variously associated with different mentalities, lifestyles, and the daily lives of individuals and communities. It is also worth noting that debates over class are rarely neutral and are often linked to political orientation. Debates on class since the 1960s have been based on the assumption that Western capitalist nations underwent a period of rapid social, economic and political change that has had major consequences on the class structure of advanced societies. It may be useful to note that a considerable amount of continuity exists in contemporary class structure as well as change.

The upper class

There are *four* main theoretical approaches to analysing the upper class in Britain:

1. The Marxists, Westergaard and Resler's (1975), view that a ruling class still exists in Britain
2. The New Right (presented by Peter Saunders (1990)) view that this class represents an economic elite rather than a ruling class
3. John Scott's (1991) predominantly Weberian view that Britain has an upper class, but one that has significantly changed over the course of the twentieth century
4. The neo-Marxist, Leslie Sklair's (1995), position that a 'transnational' capitalist class has emerged as a result of the increased globalisation of production (see Chapter 1: Sociological Theory for further discussion on globalisation).

First, Westergaard and Resler (1976) claim that (at the time of their publication) British society was still dominated by a ruling class, determined by ownership of capital. For them, the main class division in contemporary British society was between the ruling class and the working class and that this gap had significantly widened. They claim that wealth is concentrated in the richest five per cent of the population and ownership of industry remains highly concentrated due to increased monopolisation of industry. Wealth distribution had, to some extent, spread to the middle and upper working classes thorough the expansion of share ownership and private housing. This did not, however, significantly impact on the existence of a powerful and influential ruling class. This class is made up of higher professionals, company directors and senior civil servants who all tend to have large shareholdings in private companies and can therefore be classed as owners of the means of production.

Second, Peter Saunders (1990) rejects this claim and contends that the spread of ownership of private homes, shareholdings, private pensions and savings schemes means that a great many more people own capital than before and no distinct property-owning ruling class exists.

Third, John Scott (1991) notes that ownership of shares does not mean control over them and he points to the fact that the value of shares can go up and down. The effects of this are much more damaging to individuals than major companies who can handle one-off losses. A small elite maintains control over financial capital in the UK and it is they who form the upper class today. They are comprised of directors of large companies, inheritors of substantial wealth and entrepreneurs.

Fourth, Leslie Sklair (1995) argues that global production has become increasingly dominated by the power of wealthy, powerful and influential transnational corporations (TNCs) such as Microsoft, McDonalds and Sony. TNCs now wield more power over capitalist relations of production than individual nation states and their influence extends to poorer, less developed countries that provide pools of cheap labour. While ruling classes retain power within individual nation states; the transnational capitalist class is able to override their power by switching investments to countries that support their interests.

The middle and working classes
A number of contemporary theoretical explanations of the middle and lower strata are considered including:

- The 'embourgeoisement' thesis
- The 'service class'
- The 'professionalization' debate
- 'Proletarianisation'
- The 'contradictory class location' argument
- A 'radical middle class'.

Embourgeoisement
The rapid social, economic and political transformations of the late 1950s and 1960s, brought forth the claim that Western capitalist societies were witnessing the transition from industrial society to post-industrial society (Bell, 1973). Central to this transition is the gradual disappearance of the working class and an expansion of the middle class – a process known as embourgeoisement (Zweig, 1961). This essentially functionalist/neo-liberal notion claims that, due to rising affluence in the late twentieth century, many workers from the lower strata are becoming middle class in terms of income and lifestyle. Goldthorpe *et al* (1968) investigated this notion in a study of car plant workers in Luton, in the 1960s. They selected this

group of workers as they had been geographically mobile in the search of employment and had secured significantly higher income levels than previously. It was assumed that if embourgeoisement was occurring at all in UK society, it would be impacting on their subjects. Their findings include:

- The workers had achieved affluence in terms of matching middle class income levels, but only through working overtime and meeting rigid production targets. They also faced much more job insecurity than their middle class counterparts
- They were no less likely to vote Labour, but had developed an 'instrumental collectivism' in that they would only strike if it might raise wages
- The workers being studied, in common with their middle class counterparts, become more 'privatised' in the sense that they associated mainly with immediate family out with the workplace. They did not, however, see themselves as middle class, nor did they seek to associate socially with those workers they viewed as middle class
- Most workers took a *gradational* view on social class, linking class position to levels of income. However, they denied that the levels of income they were receiving at the time made them middle class, as they saw their current levels of remuneration as temporary and subject to change.

Goldthorpe *et al* (1969) concluded that embourgeoisement had not taken place among their subjects and was, therefore, unlikely to be occurring in wider society. Instead, they claimed that the subjects of their study formed part of a 'new working class' who should be viewed as situated between the traditional working classes and the middle class. This new group of individuals were characterised by 'privatised instrumentalism'.

A number of critical comments could be made about the study and the Goldthorpe *et al's* (1969) conclusion:

- At is ambitious, to say the least, to create theoretical concepts form a study of workers in one workplace
- The subjects were all male
- Complex concepts were used, which would have had to be interpreted by the researchers from answers to simpler questions
- Respondents may have been influenced by 'Hawthorne Effects' (see Chapter 3: Sociological Methods) and fear of reprisal from management
- Marshall *et al* (1988) found further evidence of 'instrumentalism' and 'privatism' in studies of the workplace, but concluded that these characteristics have always existed in the working class.

The service class

Goldthorpe *et al* (1987) later claimed, however, that a privileged and homogenous service class of salaried employees had arisen. This had come about, he claimed, due to the expansion of professional and managerial occupations coupled with upward social mobility. The new service class had begun to develop a sense of class solidarity as it became clear to them that they formed a distinct group in the labour market. Lash and Urry (1987) agree that a service class has developed, but claim that they do not form a homogenous group, rather they are fragmented like other institutional forms in 'disorganised capitalism'. They have developed a new class situation due to the expansion of welfare professional and bureaucratic positions. Roberts *et al* (1977) also argue that the middle class does not constitute a single, homogenous group. Rather, the middle class has fragmented into *four* distinct groups with differing lifestyles and 'images' of their own class position. Although this approach could be criticised for adopting a subjective definition of class it does highlight the fact that the middle class is a wide-ranging and disparate group. Abercrombie and Urry (1983) argue that the middle class is increasingly polarising, with routine white-collar workers such as clerical workers at the lower end, and professionals and managers moving towards the higher ends in terms of status and reward.

There are a number of difficulties associated with the classification of jobs in the service sector. First, many of the 'new' jobs in the service sector, in call centres, hotel and catering and in the electronics industry, for example, are low paid, temporary, poorly unionised, unskilled and routine, which is a far cry from the notion of the 'independent practitioner' associated with the service sector. Second, jobs like refuse collectors, bus drivers and postal workers that would better fit the description 'traditional' working class, are classified as service occupations. Third, the so-called rise of the service sector at the expense of a declining manufacturing sector has been largely confined to advanced capitalist societies (see Chapter 10: Work and its Organisation). This has come about mainly due to Trans-National Corporations (TNCs) shifting manufacturing production to Africa, Southeast Asia, China and Latin America rather than as a result of technological development.

Professionalisation

Closely related to the embourgeoisement thesis is the notion that the UK labour market has undergone a massive growth in the number of professional occupations since the 1980s. A good deal of debate surrounds what actually constitutes a 'professional'. Neo-liberals, such as Daniel Bell (1973), have claimed that professionals are more moral and ethical beings who possess specialist knowledge and are community-orientated. They, therefore, deserve high status and reward in recognition of their contribution to society.

Neo-Weberians, such as Parry and Parry (1976), claim that professionals are those who define their own market position as such, in order to secure high level of status and reward and to close off similar benefits to other groups. Professional bodies, such as the Institute of Chartered Accountants, for example, serve to protect the interests of, and maximise the levels of reward attached to, membership.

Others have questioned the notion that professionals constitute a separate class. The neo-Marxists, Ehrenreich and Ehrenreich (1979), claim that professionals are *not* distinct from other members of the middle class in that their role and function is to serve the needs of the ruling class through organising and controlling the production process. The status of professionals is also open to question, as they may be seen as the mass ranks of salaried welfare professionals, an image more associated with the traditional working class rather than the middle class.

Proletarianisation

The Marxist, Harry Braverman (1974; see also Chapter 10: Work and its Organisation), argues that routine white-collar workers such as clerical workers, hotel and catering staff and shop assistants are increasingly joining the ranks of the traditional working class. This is coming about due to a process of 'deskilling'. The shift from manufacturing based industries to service sector from the 1960s on in Western capitalist societies has had the effect of replacing (human) skill with technology. Computerisation means that office work begins to resemble the assembly line production process common to traditional industries. The spread of comprehensive education in post-war Britain has meant that the skills required for jobs previously seen as professions, such as clerical work, have become commonplace with the effect that the bargaining position of these workers diminishes greatly. There are around 14 million UK workers in office, administrative, retail and service sector occupations such as call centres compared to 60,000 in 1851. These jobs are often low paid, temporary, part time and are increasingly filled by women. They are often tedious, routine and highly controlled, which leads some to claim that they resemble jobs that should be considered part of a non-manual working class rather than middle class (see Chapter 10: Work and its Organisation).

Blom *et al* (1992) define proletarianisation as a process whereby the labour power of the new middle class becomes devalued. This trend has been accompanied by a polarisation of classes and a growing number of individuals are becoming economically, if not culturally, defined as working class. Blom *et al* (1992) predict the further polarisation of wealth in the US and UK placing millions of 'secure' jobs in jeopardy and steadily reducing the disposable income of middle income groups. The middle class is increasingly characterised by a number of distinct heterogeneous groups possessing varying levels of job security and status. Mann (1991) warns that sectionalism, social closure, sexism and racism are likely to increase in the workplace as formerly middle class workers battle to reclaim losses in wages and conditions. Miliband (1991) does, however, propose a solution to this problem. He views the process of proletarianisation as an inevitable consequence of capitalism and indicative of the growing power of international capital. As the balance of power in employment relations shifts evermore towards capital and away from labour, a resurgence of radical socialist tendencies in the workplace would be required to improve the plight of workers.

Contradictory class locations

The Marxist author, Erik Olin Wright (1990), has claimed that no separate middle class exists in contemporary class societies. Members of what he terms the 'intermediate strata' – managers, supervisors and semi-autonomous workers like professionals – function in the interests of the ruling class and partly benefit from this in the form of higher levels of reward and prestige. However, in other ways, workers in these strata have no real independent control and share common characteristics with the working class as they are subject to oppressive and exploitative employment practices. They, therefore, occupy a 'contradictory location' in the class structure. For Wright (1994), the bourgeoisie are those who control the process of capital accumulation and the middle class is split into two camps. At one end are those with a contradictory location between capital and labour and at the other end are those with a contradictory location between labour and the 'petit-bourgeoisie'. Callinicos and Harman (1987) use Wright's definition to claim that the working class contains the vast majority of workers in advanced economies, the bourgeoisie remain a relatively small proportion of the population and around 20 per cent of the population occupy 'contradictory locations'.

A radical middle class

Alvin Gouldner (1979) argues that in contemporary class societies, radical political action is more likely to arise from a newly forming middle class than the traditional proletarian working class. This new middle class would be comprised of left-wing intellectuals who would aspire to radical social reform by means of critical debate. This approach is heavily influenced by Pierre Bourdieu's (1984) concept of 'cultural capital' (see Chapter 9: Education). Members of this new class possess the necessary linguistic, intellectual and social skills to "win the argument" on the need for radical social reform. To some extent, this position echoes Marx's claim that intellectuals would, together with the 'petty bourgeoisie', join forces with the proletariat when conditions were ripe for revolution.

A similar theme is taken by Savage *et al* (1992), who include the ownership of 'cultural assets' in their assertion that the middle class holds *three* main advantages that help secure middle class positions for their offspring. These are:

1. 'Property assets' through the ownership of property
2. 'Organisational assets' acquired through occupational status
3. 'Cultural assets', through higher levels of educational achievement, and the possession of social and linguistic skills.

Trigger

How do the debates outlined above illustrate continuity as well as change in the class structure of modern Scotland?

Social Exclusion and the Underclass

In the 1980s/early 1990s the term 'underclass' resurfaced in sociological debate (see Chapter 8: Poverty and Chapter 6: Race and Ethnicity). The concept itself is highly emotive and politically charged and has been used by both sides of the political spectrum, albeit in different ways. The term refers to a group of people who have formed a class below the lower reaches of the working class – hence *under*class. This notion is not a new one and has had a 'disreputable' history (Moore, 2001). Marx referred to the section of society who are poor, irresponsible and of no revolutionary potential, as the 'lumpenproletariat'. Marx's solution would be to round up this "scum of the depraved elements of all classes" (Marx and Engels, 1950 [1848]: 267) and ship them off to a desert island! Other derisory terms such as 'the pauper class,' 'the residuum' and 'the relative stagnant poor' have been used in the past to refer to a group that could most obviously be described as 'the poor' (Mann, 1992: 2). Contemporary right wing theories of 'the underclass' have taken a similarly less than sympathetic view of this group.

The American New Right theorist, Charles Murray (1984; 1989; 1990), claimed in serialised articles in *The Sunday Times* (26 November 1989) that Britain was witnessing the development of an underclass similar to the one that had developed in the US. This group consisted of lone mothers, minority ethnic groups, the old, the unemployed and the sick and were becoming increasingly detached from the rest of society in terms of political and social participation and behaviour. Murray's approach is characteristic of the New Right tendency to distinguish between the 'deserving' and 'non-deserving' poor (Morris, 1994). He suggests that the latter group had developed a 'culture of poverty' and a 'culture of dependency':

- ***Culture of poverty***: the norms, values, attitudes, expectations, lifestyle and behaviour of this group has effectively caused their poverty and reinforces it for them and their offspring

78

- ***Culture of dependency***: members of the underclass become reliant on state benefits and develop lack of incentive to find employment.

The poverty experienced by this group is a *type* rather than *extent* for Murray. The underclass is to blame for their poverty and should be held responsible for changing their situation. Murray (1984; 1989; 1990) argues that his group also exhibit loutish, amoral and criminal behaviour. He advocates social policy measures such as the reduction of benefits to encourage those who lack incentive to work, re-education on the benefits of the traditional family, and increased surveillance of areas where the underclass are concentrated.

Murray's (1984; 1989; 1990) theory has been criticised on a number of fronts. Some have argued that consistent with other authors from the New Right, he seeks to advance an individualistic level of explanation for something that has structural roots. The high levels of poverty, inequality, unemployment and reliance on welfare support stems from the social and economy policies of New Right governments in the 1980s/1990s, such as the Republican administrations in the USA and the Conservative administrations the UK rather than the actions of individuals. Others have suggested that the underclass that Murray (1984; 1989; 1990) speaks of is not a homogeneous group and cannot be considered to be a class at all. There are only tenuous links between members of this group. The sick and the old may have very little in common with young lone mothers, for example. Also, lone mothers are not a homogenous group, and many do not necessarily remain lone mothers for long periods.

Pilkington (1984) criticised the very use of the term 'underclass' as a sociological concept. He claims that the terms is used pejoratively and infers that poverty is pathological. He also notes that the term is used as a scapegoat for structural dysfunctions such as increasing polarisation of income, rising crime levels and lone parenthood. He disputes the claim that a culture of dependency exists noting the lack of evidence to back this claim. Gallie (1994) found little evidence of different norms, values and behaviour among the long term unemployed, rather he found a strong commitment to securing employment, citing examples of many individuals going to great lengths to retrain and undergo academic qualifications in an attempt to escape their situation, rather than resign to it. Ruth Lister (1991: 194) states that the term underclass: "is the language of disease and contamination [...] it stigmatises," and Moore (2001: 324) concludes that:

> The idea of an underclass lacks conceptual clarity, it has the most tenuous empirical basis and has been part of a rhetoric of domination and exclusion. It is time sociologists stopped using the term except when they need to discuss the problem of the people who do use the term.

Murray's (1984; 1989; 1990) theory did, however, greatly influence the development of social policy in the UK under successive Conservative administrations in the period 1979-1997. John Major's ill-fated 'Back to Basics' campaign was an example of the moralistic approach taken by Murray. Whilst the term underclass has almost disappeared from sociological and political discourse in the new millennium, the individualistic and authoritative approach it embodied may have found new form from the late 1990s on, in the guise of New Labour's focus on the 'socially excluded' (Levitas, 1998). Sociologists from left-of-centre political persuasions such as Anthony Giddens (1991) had previously adopted the term social exclusion as a sociological concept in order to emphasise structural causes of poverty (see Chapter 8: Poverty, for further discussion on social exclusion).

Giddens (1991) notes that a growing number of individuals have experienced a lack of employment opportunities. This has arisen through labour market restructuring and the need for re-skilling amongst sections of the labour force who have witnessed the demise of the occupations they had trained for. Possible solutions advanced were 'Welfare to Work' programmes advanced in United States and which eventually led to the introduction of the 'New Deal' programme in the UK. This policy could arguably be seen to have been influenced by Durkheimian functionalism. Indeed, Levitas (2000) claims that the New Deal represents a form of 'punk-Durkheimianism'. In *The Division of Labour in Society* (1947 [1893]), Durkheim claims that in complex industrial societies, human fulfilment can be met through finding one's niche in the occupational structure (see Chapter 10: Work and its Organisation). Natural expressions of talents and abilities are embodied in the class structures of 'advanced' societies. In other words, the route to a more ordered and stable society is through the world of work for Durkheim, a notion reflected in New Labour's obsession with moving people off benefits and into work, even if it is low paid and of a temporary nature.

Social Mobility

The claim that UK society is 'meritocratic' is based on the assumption that it has an open system of stratification, or, in other words, there is high potential for individual social mobility. Social mobility may be upward or downward and high degrees of social mobility would mean that position in the social hierarchy is *achieved* rather than *ascribed*. An entirely open and meritocratic society would demonstrate social mobility based solely on individual achievement rather than on class background, inherited wealth, gender, ethnicity or 'who you know' (see also Chapter 9: Education, for a discussion on educational meritocracy).

Social mobility studies

Sociologists distinguish between *absolute* and *relative* social mobility. Absolute mobility is the overall, or total rate of mobility that includes mobility brought about by occupational changes, such as professionalization. Relative mobility is the amount of, or potential for, movement out of one's social class of origin (as defined by the class of the head of household). Relative mobility might, then, be a useful indicator of the extent of equal opportunities in the labour market. Relative mobility might be interpreted as the likelihood of class destination of offspring as against that of class origin.

The first major British study of social mobility was carried out by David Glass (1949). He and his colleagues found little evidence of absolute social mobility and what mobility there was tended to be short range. This would seem to suggest that Britain was very much a class-ridden, closed society in the immediate post-war years.

A study conducted in Oxford in 1972, known as the 'Nuffield Study', found a rather different picture emerging. Rates of absolute mobility had increased significantly. The proportion of people in the top two classes had increased and the traditional working class (as measured by the Hope-Goldthorpe classification) had decreased to around two-fifths of the workforce.

Goldthorpe *et al* (1987) revisited the data from the Nuffield Study (1983) and found further evidence of upward, absolute mobility. In the 1972 study, around 48 per cent of respondents were in manual occupations, whereas in Goldthorpes's study the number was around 34 per cent. Around eight per cent more respondents had service sector jobs in 1983, than in 1972. Despite these results, it should be noted that changes in the occupational structure were beginning to have the effect of changing how occupations were classified. The massive shift from manufacturing jobs to service sector jobs may have had an impact on responses. Notably, Goldthorpe *et al* (1987) considered the evidence from the 1983 study as indicative of Britain *not* becoming a more open society. He pointed to the fact that relative chances upward mobility differed greatly according to social background.

Peter Saunders (1990a) claims that we should not be surprised that relative mobility levels remain low since humans have *natural* differences in level of ability. Adopting a somewhat neo-functionalist stance he claims that the class structure inevitably reflects natural difference:

> In the idealised world of John Goldthorpe and other 'left' sociologists, people's destinies should be randomly determined because talents are randomly distribute, British society is thus found wanting because people of working-class origin are not in the majority in all the top jobs. This argument is ludicrous, yet in modern sociology it is all too rarely questioned.   (Saunders, 1990a: 83)

Saunders (1990) goes on to argue that greater meritocracy will not come about through state regulation, in the form of equal opportunities policies, for example. Rather, he combines a functionalist theoretical stance with a neo-liberal economic argument that competition 'incentivises' people to perform best. He asserts that education is still the best means to improve rates of relative social mobility. Marshall and Swift (1993) dispute this claim, reporting that the results of their study showed that social class of origin had a far higher influence on relative mobility than educational qualifications.

Trigger

To what extent do the range of mobility studies outlined above prove that Britain/Scotland is becoming a more meritocratic society?

Class Structure in Scotland: Classless or Class-ridden?

A 'myth' of egalitarianism has long existed in Scotland similar to the 'American Dream' in the United States. The notion that, in Scotland, ability combined with effort determines one's chances of 'getting on' has roots in a selective memory of the past. These notions are embodied in two forms of Scots' vernacular. The common saying "we're a Jock Tamson's bairns," has no known source in literature, but is defined in the *Scottish National Dictionary* (Murison, 1986, cited in McCrone, 2001: 91) as "the human race; common humanity; also with less force, a group of people united by a common sentiment, interest or purpose." Another common saying appealing to the notion that Scots have an identity aligned to common humanity derives from the poet, Rabbie Burns: "A man's a man for a' that." Burns claims that all men are equal, but his claim is ambiguous. It is not clear that he proposes equality at all, but rather that all men should be *seen* as equal regardless of wealth and status.

Such mythical notions nevertheless serve to provide an identity for Scots and, regardless of their validity, in reality can provide legitimation for inequality in contemporary society (McCrone, 2001: 91). With this notion that Scottish society is more egalitarian in mind, we will turn to an examination of the class structure in Scotland. If Scottish society is indeed more meritocratic, then we need not be surprised that inequality exists, but we could expect to find that such inequality has been randomly and meritocratically distributed. In other words, then, we should find that Scotland is *not* a 'classless society'.

Is there a ruling class in Scotland?

Whilst it would be misleading to overlook the impact of the British ruling class, evidence may exist over the existence of a distinct propertied upper class in Scotland.

Land ownership in Scotland is characterised by gross inequality. Of Scotland's 19 million acres of land, 16 million acres are privately owned. Almost two-thirds of the land in Scotland is owned by just 0.025 per cent of the population and two-thirds of this land is concentrated in the hands of just 1252 landowners (Wightman, 1996, cited in Sheridan and McCombes, 2000). The landed aristocracy also tend to hold positions of influence within the establishment such as the clandestine band of the Queen's honorary institution "The Queen's Household in Scotland" (Rosie, 2000).

Evidence for the existence of an upper class in Scotland might also exist in Edinburgh's network of exclusive dining and golf clubs. Edinburgh's Speculative Society, founded in 1764, attracts members from legal and literary circles for dinner and debating sessions. The 'New Club' is one of the most exclusive and expensive to join and is made up from members from senior social and professional backgrounds. The Honourable Company of Edinburgh Golfers has 550 members who also come from highly privileged backgrounds, and who were educated in a cluster of schools at the heart of the Edinburgh educational establishment. Architects, businessmen, investment managers and lawyers, tend to make up the Society of High Constables of Edinburgh, which provides a networking forum for its members as well as fulfilling ceremonial duties for the Lord Provost.

Private wealth in Scotland, as in other parts of Britain, tends to be concentrated in the hands of a relatively few individuals. Brian Souter and his sister Ann Gloag own the transport company, Stagecoach, and have a combined wealth of £565 million (*Sunday Times* 'Rich List', 2000). The previous owner of the Sports Division chain, Tom Hunter, comes second in the list of wealthy Scots, with a personal fortune of £400 million. Irvine Laidlaw, the Scottish Conservative Party's largest donor, shares third place alongside David Murray, ex-Rangers Football Club chairman. Each can dine on personal fortunes of £300 million.

The middle and working classes in Scotland
Scotland's class structure has been measured using a variation of the RGCS (see Box 4.4, below).

In recent years the class structure of the Scottish middle and working classes has shown remarkable convergence with that found in England. This is not what we might expect to find in an apparently 'more meritocratic country'. McCrone (2001: 83-84) states that:

> While Scotland has marginally fewer routine non-manual workers, its salariat or 'service class' is slightly bigger in proportional terms. In like manner [...] it has a bigger manual working class, but somewhat more skilled manual workers. What these data show is the growth in non-manual employment in all parts of Great

Britain, especially in the white-collar labour force (class III). There are, of course, important gender effects in these changes, such that white-collar work is the largest occupational category for women [...]. It is difficult to escape the conclusion that the considerable divergence in political behaviour between Scotland and England since the 1970s cannot be explained by the fact that the two countries have distinctly different class structures.

Trigger

Look at the Box 4.4, below, and consider the following questions:

1. By using the Weberian manual/non-manual distinction, what percentage of the Scottish working population are: a) middle class b) working class?
2. If we use a Marxist interpretation, what percentage of the Scottish working population are working class?

Box 4.4 Social Class of Working Age Population, 2000, (%)

- Professional   6.4
- Management and Technical   29.2
- Skilled non-manual   22.3
- Skilled manual   20.8
- Partly skilled   15.3
- Unskilled   5.1
- Other   0.9

(Source: Adapted from 'Total Working Age Population, 2000', *Scottish Key Facts* at: http://www.scottishdevelopmentinternational.com/uploads/Scotland-key-facts-June-2003.pdf)

Evidence for a sizeable working class in Scotland may be present if income levels are used as a measure of class position. Over 90 per cent of Scots earn less than £30,000 per year and 75 per cent earn less than £20,000 per year. Less than 0.5 per cent earn more than £90,000 per year (*Inland Revenue Statistics 1999*, cited in Sheridan and McCombes, 2000: 155). The organisation, 'Scottishpolicynet.org', claims that Scotland has become a society of 'three nations' – 'Excluded Scotland', 'Insecure Scotland' and 'Settled Scotland', with the second of the groups making-up the larger part of the population.

Social class also plays a large part in determining individual life chances in Scotland, as Box 4.5, below, demonstrates.

Box 4.5 Social Class and 'Life Chances' in Scotland

- Scots kids born into unskilled manual families are seven to eight times less likely to go to university than kids born into the families of professionals.
- Residents of Bearsden can expect to live on average eight years longer than residents of neighbouring Drumchapel.
- Children in Easterhouse are five times more likely to die in the first year of life than the UK average.
- Members of Social Class V in Scotland are more than twice as likely to die before the age of 65 than those in Social Class I.
- Obesity is more common to poor Scottish households due to high fat, high sugar, lower cost diets.

(Source: Adapted from The Scottish Council Foundation Website: http://www.scottishpolicynet.org.uk/scf/publications/paper_3/chapter3.shtml#different#different

---

Social Mobility in Scotland

The Scottish Mobility Study (SMS) conducted by Payne (1987), noted that age and region greatly determined the potential for social mobility in Scotland. Payne predicted that mobility patterns evident in the study may lead to a number of significant developments in class structure:

- High rates of upward mobility among the young in central belt urban areas
- Low rates of mobility for older adults, particularly in the rural North of Scotland
- A growth of a heterogeneous middle class
- A growth of an increasingly homogeneous working class and underclass
- An increasing dissatisfaction among the young, particularly in the underclass, which would threaten the 'safety-valve' function of social mobility through engagement in disruptive behaviour such as inner-city rioting.

Payne (1987) notes that whilst the study showed little evidence of movement between broad class groupings, there were generally high rates of upward mobility through occupational mobility. In other words, relative rates of mobility were low, but this was, to some extent, compensated for by higher rates of absolute mobility. Looking at patterns of recruitment, Payne (1987: 65) concludes that:

> Although this is not to say that Scotland is an 'open' or egalitarian society, it does show that direct inheritance of occupations is relative.

Inter-generational social mobility data for 1997 (McCrone, 2001) in Scotland shows higher levels of upward social mobility into the middle class than in 1975, but again the *similarities* are more notable than the *differences* between Scotland and England.

While social mobility patterns and the class structure of Scotland and England largely converge, the populations of each country have a different perception of individual location. In other words they 'subjectively' define class differently. This difference is most transparent among Scottish professionals who had been upwardly mobile from working class origins. This group were much more likely to identify themselves as 'working class', than those from the English sample. McCrone (2001: 90) argues that:

> Put simply, we should not expect that social class in Scotland will be interpreted and explained in the same way as in England, because key institutions such as the legal system, religion and the education system will evidently mediate structures and experiences to produce different political and social outcomes.

Trigger

To what extent can Scotland be viewed as a class-ridden society? Give examples.

Conclusion: The Continuing Relevance of Social Class

As noted in the introduction to this chapter, some sociologists, along with other commentators, have claimed that class as a tool of analysis has lost its explanatory power and relevance to contemporary Western capitalist societies. For Pakulski and Waters (1996: 4), however, modern Western societies are characterised by a:

> [W]ide redistribution of poverty, the proliferation of indirect and small ownership; the credentialistion of skills and the professionalisation of occupation; the multiple segmentation and globalisation of markets; and an increasing role for consumption as a status and lifestyle generator.

For them, we have witnessed the "death of class" as a tool for sociological analysis, with class being replaced by a "new gender, 'eco' – and 'ethno' – centred politics" (Pakulski and Waters, 1996: 3). New cultural differences have created 'status conventional' divisions that have supplanted traditional divisions based on class. Fukuyama (1992: 20) claims that the collapse of the Soviet-dominated Eastern bloc nations, near the end of the twentieth century coincided with what he calls the 'end of history', which has heralded the defeat of all alternatives to the neo-liberal ideology that underpins capitalism – "the world's only viable economic system."

Zweis (2000) argues that this notion is mythical and, if it were true, would be very bad news indeed for the working class in Western nations that make up around two-thirds of the working population, in his estimation (2000). He claims that authors such as Fukuyama attempt to legitimate exploitative and oppressive class relations in capitalist societies, by suggesting that no alternative form can exist. Domhoff (2000) concurs with this view, arguing that the shift in power from labour to capital in recent years has *furthered* the exploitation of the working class, rather than bringing about the death of class.

If, in actual fact, the death of class has come about, many sociologists seem unaware of this. John Scott (2002) argues that the 'death of class' thesis has brought forth a recognition that class as a concept does not embrace all forms of division, but that it does not mean that it should be abandoned. Thus, "class relations still exist and exert effects on life chances and conditions of living" (Scott, 2002:1).

Perhaps ironically, social class is one of the fasted growing areas in sociology in the early years of this new millennium. Claims to the contrary have been made because, historically, class theorists have tended to reduce all forms of inequality to class relations. Modern class theories must engage with explanations of how age, disability, gender and ethnicity, for example, generate inequality in modern Britain.

Chapter Summary

- Social class is a form of social stratification that has been variously defined by classical and contemporary theorists.
- Various measurements of social class were considered, and they can be seen to be influenced by how class is defined.
- Classical theoretical explanations were outlined and shown to have had considerable bearing on how the sociology of class has developed since.
- Debates on changing class structure appear to imply considerable continuity as well as change in the class structure of modern Britain.
- Social class is linked to many aspects of social life and theoretical explanations of the relationship between class and culture and identity and voting behaviour were examined.

- The concepts 'social exclusion' and the 'underclass' provide examples of applications of modern class analyses. Both terms can be seen as problematic, emotive and politically charged.
- Studies of social mobility were examined in light of the claim that Britain is an open and 'meritocratic' state.
- The prevailing existence of class in contemporary Scotland suggests that Scotland is *neither* a classless society, *nor* more meritocratic than its southern neighbour, England.
- Notions that class is no longer a useful tool in sociological analysis are disputed by those who claim the continuing relevance of class in capitalist societies.

Further Reading

Crompton, R. (1998) *Class and Stratification* 2nd Edition, Cambridge: Polity Press
Crompton, R., Devine, F., Savage, M., Scott, J. (eds.) (2000) *Renewing Class Analysis*, Oxford: Blackwell Publishers/The Sociological Review
Kirby, M. (1999) *Stratification and Differentiation*, Basingstoke: Palgrave
Payne, G. (ed.) (2000) *Social Divisions*, Basingstoke: Palgrave

Useful Websites

Sociology Central provides excellent resources at: http://www.sociology.org.uk/cload.htm
Sociology Online has a user-friendly introduction to class at:
http://www.sociologyonline.co.uk/soc_essays/Class.htm
Extracts from original works can be found at: http://www.spc.uchicago.edu/ssr1/PRELIMS/theory.html
Information related to class in Scotland can be accessed at: http://www.scottishcouncilfoundation.org/

Bibliography

Abercrombie, N. and Urry, J. (1983) *Capital Labour and the Middle Classes*, London: Allen and Unwin
Adonis, A. and Pollard, S. (1998) *A Class Act*, Harmondsworth: Penguin
Anderson, P. (1976) *Considerations on Western Marxism*, London: New Left Books
Arber, S., Dale, A. and Gilbert, N. (1981) 'The limitations of existing social classifications of women' in Jacoby, A. (ed.) *The Measurement of Social class*, Guildford: Social Research Association
Bell, D. (1973) *The Coming of the Post-Industrial Society*, New York, NY: Basic Books
Benyon, H. (1989) 'Politics: the Thatcher phenomenon' in Haralambos, M. (ed.) *Developments in Sociology*, Volume 5, Ormskirk: Causeway Press
Bendix, R. and Lipset, M. (eds.) (1967) *Class, Status and Power*, 2nd Edition, London: Routledge and Kegan Paul
Blair, T. (1999) Speech to Institute of Public Policy Research, January 14, 1999, London
Blom, R., Kivenen, M., Melin, H. and Rantalaiho, L. (1992) *The Scope Logic Approach to Class Analysis*, Oslo: Avebury
Bourdieu, P. (1984) *Distinction: A Social Critique of the Judgement of Taste*, London: Routledge and Kegan Paul
Braverman, H. (1974) *Labour and Monopoly Capitalism*, New York, NY: Monthly Review Press
Burgess, R.G. and Murcott, A. (eds.) (2001) *Developments in Sociology*, London: Pearson
Butler, T. and Savage, M. (eds.) (1995) *Social Change in the Middle Classes*, London: UCL Press
Callinicos, A. and Harman, C. (1987) *The Changing Working Class*, London: Bookmarks
Clark, T. and Lipset, S.M. (1991) 'Are Social Classes Dying?' in *International Sociology*, Vol. 6, No. 4.

Davis, K. and Moore, W.E. (1967 [1945]) 'Some Principles of Stratification' in Bendix, R. and Lipset, M. (eds.) *Class, Status and Power* 2nd Edition, London: Routledge and Kegan Paul

Domhoff, G.W. (2000) *Who rules America: power and politics in the year 2000*, 3rd Edition, Mayfield: Mountain View

Durkheim, E. (1947 [1893]) *The Division of Labour in Society*, New York, NY: The Free Press

Ehrenreich, B. and Ehrenreich, J. (1979) 'The professional-managerial class' in Walker, P. (ed.) *Between Labour and Capital*, Sussex: Harvester Press

Ferguson, I., Lavalette, M. and Mooney, G. (2002) *Rethinking Welfare: A Critical Perspective*, London: Sage

Fukuyama, F. (1992) *The End of History and the Last Man*, Harmondsworth: Penguin

Gallie, D. (ed.) (1994) 'Are the unemployed an underclass? Some evidence from the social change and economic life initiative', in *Sociology*, Vol. 28, No. 3, pp.737-757

Giddens, A. (1991) *Modernity and Self Identity: Self and Society in the Late Modern Age*, Cambridge: Polity Press

Glass, D.V. (ed.) (1954) *Social Mobility in Britain*, London: Routledge, Kegan and Paul

Goldthorpe, J.H. (1980) *Social Mobility and Class Structure in Modern Britain*, Oxford: Clarendon Press

Goldthorpe, J.H. (1995) 'The Service Class revisited' in Butler, T. and Savage, M. (eds.) (1995) *Social Change in the Middle Classes*, London: UCL Press

Goldthorpe, J.H., Lockwood, D., Bechhofer, F. and Platt, J. (1968) *The Affluent Worker: Industrial Attitudes and Behaviour*, Cambridge: Cambridge University Press

Goldthorpe, J.H. (1969) *The Affluent Worker in the Class Structure*, Cambridge: Cambridge University Press

Goldthorpe, J.H., Llewellyn, C. and Payne, C. (1987) *Social Mobility and Class Structure in Modern Britain*, 2nd Edition, Oxford: Clarendon

Gouldner, A. (1979) *The Future of Intellectuals*, Basingstoke: Macmillan

Haralambos, M. (ed.) *Developments in Sociology*, Volume 5, Ormskirk: Causeway Press

Hutton, W. (1995) 'High-risk strategy is not paying off', *Guardian Weekly*, 12 November 1995

Jacoby, A. (ed.) *The Measurement of Social class*, Guildford: Social Research Association

Kingston, P. (2000) The Classless Society, Stanford, CA: Stanford University Press

Lash, S. and Urry, J. (1987) *The End of Organised Capitalism*, Cambridge: Polity Press

Levitas, R. (1998) *The Inclusive Society? Social Exclusion and New Labour*, Basingstoke: Macmillan

Lister, R. (1991) 'Concepts of Poverty', in *Social Studies Review*, Vol. 6, No.5

Mann, K. (1991) *The Making of the English Underclass? The Social Divisions of Welfare and Labour*, Milton Keynes: Open University Press

Mann, K. (1992) *The Making of an English Underclass*, Milton Keynes: Open University Press

Marshall, G., Newby, H., Rose, D. and Vogler, C. (1988) *Social Class in Modern Britain*, London: Hutchinson

Marshall, G. and Swift, A. (1993) 'Social class and social justice', in *British Journal of Sociology*, June

Marx, K. and Engels, F. (1950 [1848]) 'Manifesto of the Communist Party' in Marx, K. and Engels, F. *Selected Works*, Vol. 1, Moscow: Foreign Languages Publishing House

Marx, K. and Engels, F. (1962 [1852]) 'The Eighteenth Brumaire of Louis Bonaparte', in Marx. K. and Engels, F. *Selected Works*, Vol. 1, Moscow: Foreign Languages Publishing House

McCrone, D. (2001) *Understanding Scotland: the Sociology of a Nation*, 2nd Edition, London: Routledge

McNall, S.G., Levine, R.F. and Fantasia, R. (1991) *Bringing Class back in*, New York, NY: Westview Press/Praeger

Miliband, R. (1991) *Divided Societies: Class Struggle in Contemporary Capitalism*, London: Oxford University Press

Moody, K. (1997) *Workers in a Lean World*, London: Verso

Moore, R. (2001) 'Rediscovering the Underclass' in Burgess, R.G. and Murcott, A. (eds.) *Developments in Sociology*, London: Pearson

Morris, L. (1994) *Dangerous Classes*, London: Routledge

Murison, D, (ed.) (1986) *Scottish National Dictionary*, Aberdeen: Aberdeen University Press

Murray, C.A. (1984) *Losing Ground*, New York, NY: Basic Books

Murray, C.A. (1989) 'Underclass', *Sunday Times Magazine*, 26 November

Murray, C.A. (1990) *The Emerging British Underclass*, London: IEA Health and Welfare Unit

Pahl, R.E. (1989) 'Is the Emperor naked? Some questions on the adequacy of sociological theory in urban and regional research', *International Journal of Urban and Regional Research*, Vol. 13, No.4, pp.709-720

Pakulski, J. and Waters, M. (1996) *The Death of Class*, London: Sage

Parry, N. and Parry, J. (1976) *The Rise of the Medical Profession*, London: Croom Helm

Parsons, T. (1964) *Essays in Sociological Theory*, New York, NY: The Free Press

Payne, G. (1987) *Mobility and Change in Modern Society*, Basingstoke: Macmillan

Payne, G. (ed.) *Social Divisions* (2000), Basingstoke: Palgrave

Pilkington, A. (1984) *Race Relations in Britain*, Slough: UTP

Rees, J. (ed.) *Essays on Historical Marxism,* London: Bookmarks

Rees, J. (1998) 'Revolutionary Marxism and Academic Marxism' in Rees, J. (ed.) *Essays on Historical Marxism,* London: Bookmarks

Roberts, K., Cook, F.G., Clark, S.C. and Semenoff, E. (1977) *The Fragmentary Class Structure*, London: Heinemann

Rose, D. (1995) 'Official Social Classifications in the UK', *Social Research Update*, Issue 9, University of Surrey, Department of Sociology

Rosie, G. (2000) 'All the Queen's Men', *The Sunday Herald*, 10 December 2000

Saunders, P. (1990a) *Social Class and Stratification*, London: Routledge

Saunders, P. (1990b) *A Nation of Home Owners*, London: Unwin Hyman

Savage, M., Barlow, J., Dickens, A. and Fielding, T. (1992) *Property, Bureacracy and Culture: Middle Class Formation in Contemporary Britain*, London: Routledge

Scase, R. (1992) *Class*, Milton Keynes: Open University Press

Scott, J. (1991) *Who Rules Britain?* Cambridge: Polity Press

Scott, J. (2000) 'Class and Stratification' in Payne, G. (ed.) *Social Divisions* (2000), Basingstoke: Palgrave

Scott, J. (2002) 'Social Class and Stratification', in Special Issue of *Acta Sociologica*, Vol. 45, No. 1

Sheridan, T. and McCombes, A. (2000) *Imagine: A Socialist Vision for the 21ˢᵗ Century*, Edinburgh: Rebel Inc

Sklair, L. (1995) *Sociology of the Global System*, 2ⁿᵈ Edition, Hemel Hempstead: Prentice Hall

Sorensen, A.B. (2000) 'Employment relations and class structure' in Crompton, R., Devine, F., Savage, M. and Scott, J. (2000) *Renewing Class Analysis*, Oxford: Blackwell/The Sociological Review

Sunday Times, The (2000) 'Rich List', available at http://www.sunday-times.co.uk/richlist2000.html

Tumin, M. (1967) *Social Stratification: The Forms and Functions of Social Inequality*, Englewood Cliffs, NJ: Prentice-Hall

Walker, P, (ed.) *Between Labour and Capital*, Sussex: Harvester Press

Weber, M. ([1924] 1978) *Economy and Society*, Berkeley, CA: University of California Press

Westergaard, J. and Resler, H. (1976) *Class in a Capitalist Society*, Harmondsworth: Penguin

Wightman, A. (1996) *Who Owns Scotland?* Edinburgh: Canongate

Wright, E.O. (1979) *Class, Crisis and the State*, London: Verso

Wright, E.O. (1990) *The Debate on Classes*, London: Verso

Wright, E.O. (1994) *Interrogating Inequality*, London: Verso

Zweig, F. (1961) *The Worker in an Affluent Society*, London: Heinemann

Zweis, M. (2000) *The Working Class Majority: America's Best Kept Secret*, Ithaca, NY: ILR Press

Chapter 5   Gender

Susan Regnart

Introduction

Within the field of Sociology an understanding of gender is integral to appreciating forms of stratification in society. Historically, the sociology of gender found its roots due to the invisibility of women in society and as a consequence of this, previous sociological research and theories failed to take into account gender differences. Prior to the 1960s, empirical sociology focused on men and boys and a great deal of the research regarded women's economic role as unimportant (see Chapter 2: Sociological Theory).

A change to this approach developed in the 1960s with the rise of the Women's Movement, which had a major impact on the discipline of sociology at all levels, from the topics chosen, to methods used for investigation and theoretical perspectives. Early feminist research emerged out of women's direct experience of, and response to, sexual oppression and exploitation, with the study of *gender* in recent times focusing primarily on women. 'Gender Studies' is now a degree programme in its own right, though more common at postgraduate rather than undergraduate level.

This chapter is first and foremost not an exhaustive study of gender, feminism, and empirical research associated with this topic. With this in mind, the sentiments of this Chapter are not only to introduce you to a variety of competing explanations and theories of gender and feminism that compliment Chapter 2: Sociological Theory in this Book, but also provide links to other areas such as education or working patterns (see Chapter 9: Education and Chapter 10: Work and its Organisation).

Today, women make up around 67 per cent of the UK workforce, but 43 per cent of these jobs are part-time. Despite gains since the Equal Pay Act of 1970, women in full-time work across the UK can still expect to earn 18.8 per cent less than the average hourly earnings of men (Equal Opportunities Commission, 2003: 1) and are more likely to be employed in industries that are low paid. Women have not broken through to top jobs in anything like the numbers we are led to believe by popular films, TV programmes and adverts. Significantly, in the field of employment, Scotland has a *widening gap* between male and female pay (IDS, 2003: Report 873), despite around 40 per cent of the Scottish Parliament being made up of women MSPs who have a direct influence on legislation and policymaking (Engender, 2003c). Such a scenario leads to questions about the impact that women, in positions of power, can have on society.

This Chapter, then, is intended to introduce you to ideas surrounding gender and act as a spur for you to link to other areas of social life, in doing so you are encouraged to examine issues of power and inequality. Such a route will enable you to consider the comprehensiveness and coherence of feminist theories.

However, *men* have gender, too! Many young men are under-achieving in education (see Chapter 9: Education) and suicide rates among young men in Scotland are increasing at alarming rates. Nevertheless, this Chapter's main focus is on gender and how it impacts upon women.

Why, then, do men and women occupy such different social roles? To begin to answer this question, we must consider the *differences* between sex and gender.

The Distinction Between Sex and Gender

Although Ann Oakley (1972) is credited with being the first to introduce this distinction into the social sciences, it was Dr Robert Stoller (1968) who first observed that while *sex* referred to external genitalia, internal genitalia, gonads, hormonal states and secondary sex characteristics, *gender* refers to cultural conceptions of 'masculine' or 'feminine' behaviour, which are passed on to children by the society in which they live. Interestingly, although this distinction is now the cornerstone of gender studies, it has been eroded in popular language to the extent that application forms sometimes ask for a person's 'gender' rather than their 'sex'. The blurring of these terms in popular language has occurred because people want to avoid any confusion between 'sex' as male/female and 'sex' as sexual intercourse. However, this coyness has resulted in a much greater verbal confusion.

Sex

A person's sex is not inherited in the same way as other physical characteristics, such as hair colour. We inherit 23 pairs of chromosomes. When the twenty third pair are identical (XX) the foetus becomes female. When the pair are different (XY), the foetus becomes a male. Embryo's start off with undifferentiated gonads (glands), but if the Y chromosome is present the gonads develop into testes. If the Y chromosome is absent, the gonads develop into ovaries. The Y chromosome also acts as a switch that triggers the release of the male hormone, testosterone, in the womb.

Sociobiology and gender

Sociobiology is the view that men and women have developed different characteristics and abilities due to evolution. For example, because men can spread their genes widely they are motivated to have sex with a variety of women, whereas women, who only produce one egg a month, are motivated to find one man to support them whilst pregnant, breastfeeding and rearing children. However, human behaviour is much more complicated than this view implies. Many men are monogamous, and many women are promiscuous. Some people remain 'child-free' and, therefore, never pass on their genes by having children, whilst others are homosexual.

Gender role socialisation
Although male and female babies are difficult to tell apart, parents tend to adopt common sense explanations of gender, expecting boys to be strong, boisterous, and active and girls to be delicate, quiet, and caring. Such expectations shape the socialisation process through which children learn to adopt gender appropriate behaviours. Gender role socialisation does not stop at childhood, however, but continues throughout life.

Masculinity and femininity
Definitions of masculinity and femininity are socially constructed and change over time and place. In the past, women who worked, wore trousers or drank pints of lager, Guinness or 'heavy', were seen as alarmingly unfeminine, and men who spent too much time with their children or did any domestic labour were dismissed as *effeminate*. Such views on gender-appropriate behaviour can be seen to be culturally specific. Anthropologists report that in the Polynesian Island of Tahiti, men are expected to ignore insults and be co-operative and passive. However, in the East African Samburu tribe, males have to demonstrate their bravery over a period of around twelve years, in a process called 'Moranhood'. The first test for these males at the age of 14 or 15 is to undergo a circumcision ritual without anaesthetic. If the boy flinches he is shamed as a coward. Thus, sociologists argue that definitions of what constitutes masculine or feminine behaviour change in emphasis over time and place and are, therefore, different from biological sex differences. Table 5.1, below, highlights a number of masculine and feminine 'ideals'.

Table 5.1 Masculine/Feminine Ideals

Masculine	Feminine
Active	Passive
Assertive	Softly spoken
Competitive	Cooperative
Dominant	Yielding
Leadership	Team players
Independent	Dependant on others
Aggressive	Caring
Ambitious	Un-ambitious
Interested in *things*	Interested in *people*
Sexual instigators	Sexually passive/coy

Trigger

Consider the following questions, preferably in pairs or groups:

1. Using Table 5.1, above, how far do you agree that men and women exhibit these traits?
2. Do you think that these notions of masculinity and femininity have changed over time? If so, explain why?

Table 5.2 The Gendering of Sexual Behaviour

Female	Male
Slut	Stud
Slag	Gigolo
Prostitute	Rent boy
Whore	
Harlot	'Jack the Lad'
Jezebel	
Flirt	
Floozy	
Tart	
Slapper	
Strumpet	
Trollop	
'Bike'	

Trigger

Consider the following questions, which relate to Table's 5.1 and 5.2:

Why do you think there are more negative words in the English language to describe women's sexual behaviour when compared to men's?

The Sexual Division of Labour

The anthropologist, George Peter Murdock (1949), studied the activities assigned to men and women in 224 societies, ranging from hunting and gathering bands to modern nation states. He found hunting, lumbering and mining to be predominantly male roles and water carrying, cooking, repairing clothes and gathering wild vegetables to be predominantly female roles. Murdoch (1949) attributed this to the fact that women are tied to the home through childbearing and breast-feeding and that their weaker physique ruled out more strenuous tasks. He concluded that the 'sexual division of labour' is a *universal* phenomenon based on physical sex differences.

Ann Oakley (1974), however, rejects this biological view and claims that there is no evidence that a given task is performed exclusively by one sex (except childbearing). She points out that there are 14 societies in Murdock's sample where lumbering is done either exclusively by women or shared by both sexes, 38 societies where cooking is a shared activity, and 36 societies were women are solely responsible for land clearance. Oakley (1974) also cites a number of societies where sex seems to have little bearing on women's roles, such as the Mbuti Pymies living in the Congo rain forest, who have no division of labour by sex, but who hunt and gather together and *share* responsibility for the care of children.

The Marriage Contract

The traditional (and still frequently used) marriage ceremony in Western societies transfers a daughter from the 'legal ownership' of her father to her husband, replacing her father's surname with her husband's surname. Whilst a man is always 'Mr' as an adult, women have two legal titles – Miss and Mrs. The term 'Miss' (i.e. miss-*ing* a man) is supposed to indicate that she is a virgin and that her father must be asked for *his* consent to *her* marriage. The term 'Mrs' (i.e. *Mr's*) indicates that she is now the *property* of a husband. The marriage ceremony ends by pronouncing the couple 'Man and wife' and only women are asked to love and 'obey'. Feminists have attempted to change this hangover from the past by inventing the word 'Ms' as an equivalent of 'Mr'. They have also campaigned for the phrase 'man and wife' to be replaced by 'husband and wife' to reflect our changing values. Today, in Western religious ceremonies references to 'husband and wife' are more likely, whilst demands for 'obedience' from the bride-to-be have generally been dropped.

Feminism

What is feminism?

Feminism (see Chapter 2: Sociological Theory) is both an *academic* body of knowledge and an ongoing *political movement*, both elements of which influence each other. The term, 'feminist', describes someone who believes that women are treated differently and unequally from men, and that this must be changed through political activism. The term itself conjures up many different 'common sense' images, many of which are less than complementary to women. Some feminist theories look at women's experience from a conservative stance, such as that taken by functionalists (see Chapter 2: Sociological Theory). Some align themselves with the political left, whilst others wish to distance themselves from traditional political viewpoints altogether. This section begins with an historical overview of the development of feminism as a political movement. It then considers the main approaches to explaining gender inequality, with an analysis of the strengths and weaknesses of each.

The Historical Development of Feminism
The 'first wave'

> Women are much more like each other than men: they have, in truth, but two passions, vanity and love; these are their universal characteristics.
> (Earl of Chesterfield, in a letter to his son, 19 December 1749)

Modern feminism began with Mary Wollstonecraft's (1975 [1792]) book, *A Vindication of the Rights of Women*, which emerged in the aftermath of the French Revolution (1789). In response to criticisms like those in the quote above, Wollstonecraft argued that it should be no surprise that women preoccupied themselves with trivia and their appearance, when they were confined to domestic roles and were barred from education. However, such debates were less irrelevant to working class women who could not take up the option of being 'a lady' of leisure. Despite Wollstonecraft's plea for equality, women and children were still regarded as the property of men in the mid-1800s. Whilst a husband could divorce on the grounds of adultery, wives had to prove incest or bigamy in addition to adultery. After having her children abducted by her husband, Caroline Norton researched the legal situation herself and wrote several pamphlets attacking the law. Her campaigning resulted in the Infant Custody Act (1939), which permitted wives of 'good character', against whom adultery had not been proven, to have custody of children under the age of seven. It was not until 1873 that women were given custody of children up to 16 and not until 1973 that mothers were given the same legal authority over children as fathers (in Sanders in Gamble, 2001).

In 1856, 25,000 women signed a petition in favour of married women's property ownership and limited legal rights were introduced with the Matrimonial Causes Act of 1857. Eighteen further Acts followed and, by 1870, married women were allowed to keep their earnings and inherit personal property, with everything else going to their husband. If the 1850s was a decade of marriage reform, the 1860s became a time of educational reform. When the first schools for girls were eventually opened, they were mainly to train middle class girls to be governesses, but the curriculum slowly broadened out, and calls for entry into higher education soon followed. However, it was not until 1948 that women at Cambridge University could be awarded degrees on equal terms with men.

Within a matter of 30 years, individual women had shown that they could mobilise to campaign for specific reforms in matrimonial law, property ownership, child custody rights and education. However, the last challenge for first wave feminists was the vote. In 1862, John Stuart Mill (1806-1873) was the first British MP to propose giving women the vote, but was defeated in the House of Commons by 196 votes to 73. After decades of resistance, the 'Suffragettes' eventually won the vote in 1918 for women over thirty (whose political choices could be guided by their husband), but younger single women were regarded as too irrational to make political choices. It was not until 1928 that women could vote on the same terms as men. Feminist activity slowed down during the First World War (1814-1818) and beyond, but by the 1970s a new society was taking shape.

The 'second wave'
The second wave of feminist activity was a continuation of the movement toward sexual equality. Whilst first wave feminists believed that the vote would be followed by full equality with men, women of the second wave knew this optimism was unfounded and that more radical measures would need to be taken to secure social and cultural equality. For some, nothing short of revolution would rid women of patriarchal structures. The second wave began in the late sixties when the success of the Black Power movement created a climate where all forms of discrimination could be challenged and gave many women valuable experience of political activism. However, women's participation in male dominated left-wing movements often consisted of food making and clerical work, and men were sometimes openly sexist towards women. Once it became clear that female subordination was endemic in all social relations with men and spanned areas like the workplace, home, media and education system, women set up non-hierarchical, local women's liberation groups.

The year, 1968, also marked fifty years since women's suffrage in Britain. In the intermediate period they had been enthusiastically and officially drawn into the workforce during World War II (1939-1945) as a 'reserve army of labour', but after the war the government quickly shifted to a renewed attack on working women, encouraging them to give up work to free-up jobs for the men returning from the Front. However, in the United States, the publication of Betty Friedan's (1964) best seller; *The Feminine Mystique*, re-kindled feminist activism by arguing that the home could never be the place of fulfilment for women, because the romanticised image of the contented homemaker disguised the dull drudgery of domestic labour. The success of this book was in its resonance with white, middle class women – the very group who would become most active in the feminist movement of the 1960s. Inspired by Friedan, the demonstration at the 1968 'Miss World' pageant in Atlantic City in the United States, became a hallmark event. The protesters set up a 'freedom trash can' outside the venue and threw in girdles, make up, stilettos and bras as symbols of constraining beauty norms imposed on women by men. However, the event was distorted in the press and led to the urban myth about feminists 'burning their bra's'. In fact, the authorities had not allowed the protesters to have a fire, but the media accounts of 'crazy bra burner's' helped to undermine the credibility of this subversive new movement.

The second wave spread quickly throughout Europe and many groundbreaking books appeared in this period including, Germaine Greer's (1970) *The Female Enuch*, Kate Millet's (1971) *Sexual Politics* and Shulamith Firestone's (1979) *Dialectic of Sex*. Although feminists were never fully united in their views, they exerted their collective strength and many successful campaigns were waged throughout this period. In Britain, the Women's National Coordinating Committee tabled four basic demands:

1. Equal pay
2. Free contraception and abortion on demand
3. Free 24-hour nurseries
4. Equal education and job opportunities.

A 'third wave'?

The second wave succeeded in gaining important changes in legislation that made discrimination against women illegal, although many of the initial demands are ongoing concerns. Present day campaigners point out that feminism is experiencing a media backlash that seeks to reassert patriarchal values, and that beauty norms are now stronger than they were in the 1970s. Some predict that a third wave of feminist activism will be necessary in the new Millennium to fully realize the four conditions of equality tabled by women of the second wave.

Trigger

Outline the main differences between the 'first', 'second' and 'third' waves of feminism.

Feminist Perspectives
Liberal feminism

> Love a woman? You're an ass!
> 'Tis a most insipid passion
> To choose out for your happiness
> The silliest part of God's creation.
> (John Wilmot, Earl of Rochester, English poet, *Song*, 1680)

Liberal feminism is one of the oldest forms of feminist thought. It comes out of a tradition of liberal philosophy, which is concerned with liberty, individual rights, equal opportunities and legal equality. Liberal feminists believe that societies should treat people according to merit and ensure fair competition for jobs and other resources. However, they claim that the treatment of women in contemporary society violates all of liberalism's core political values, because cultural stereotyping leads to the creation of economic, legal and political obstacles to equality.

Liberal feminists of the second wave, such as Betty Freidan, continued Mary Wollstonecraft's (1792) emphasis on the importance of equal educational opportunities. In *The Feminine Mystique*, Freidan (1971 [1963]: 1) wrote:

> Each suburban housewife struggled with it alone. As she made the beds, shopped for groceries, matched slip cover material, ate peanut butter sandwiches, chauffeured Cub Scouts and Brownies, lay beside her husband at night, she was afraid to ask even of herself the silent question: is this all?

The main aim of liberal feminism is to gain changes in legislation and to eradicate sexist stereotypes in the media, education, the workplace and the family. In short, liberal feminists believe that women should be free to be as *unequal* as men are in a capitalist society. Liberal feminist's argue that gender inequality can be overcome by grass root campaigns and high-level political pressure. Betty Friedan (1971 [1963]) was a founder member of the National Organisation of Women (NOW), which continues to exert political pressure in America.

A critical evaluation of liberal feminism:

Liberal feminism probably enjoys greater public popularity than other feminist perspectives, as it conveys the sense that existing social structures in liberal democratic societies are fundamentally adequate, but need to be gradually changed from within. However, it is this very adherence to a liberal philosophy that has attracted criticism on the following counts:

1) ***A bourgeois theory?*** Liberal feminists often fail to recognise that working class or black women experience more barriers to social mobility than white middle class women. This has led some to dismiss liberal feminism as a white, bourgeois movement

2) ***Add women and stir***: Liberal feminists claim that existing social structures in liberal democratic societies are not *inherently* sexist or elitist, so their solution lies in simply reforming legislation and practice in order to make possible the admission of women to male-dominated institutions, such as medicine, senior business levels, etc. However, research has revealed that the

recent 'feminisation of the workforce' has done little to change their situation, since domestic labour and childcare do not easily fit around long working hours designed for men

3) ***The Biological origin of stereotypes***: Liberal feminists do not explain where discriminatory laws and stereotypes come from in the first place, because they discount the impact of biology on gender roles. Thus, liberal feminists cannot explain why the overwhelming majority of world cultures (notwithstanding the notable exceptions outlined above), tend to develop similar interpretations of masculinity and femininity.

However, despite its flaws, liberal feminism has made an enormous contribution to the emancipation of women, and is still considered radical in countries that do not afford basic rights to women. Rosemary Tong (1989: 38) argues that:

> We owe to liberal feminism many, if not most, of the educational and legal reforms that have improved the quality of life for women. It is doubtful, that without liberal feminists' efforts, so many women could not have attained their newfound professional and occupational stature.

Trigger

Sexist jokes – are they innocent fun?
Each time a sexist joke is passed on it reinforces gender stereotypes and keeps prejudice alive. Read the following 'joke' and answer the questions that follow:

Yesterday scientists suggested that beer contains female hormones. To test the theory 100 men were fed 6 pints of larger. It was observed that 100 per cent of the men gained weight, talked excessively without making any sense, became overly emotional, couldn't drive, failed to think rationally, argued over nothing and refused to apologise when wrong. No further testing is planned.

1. Identify *four* negative stereotypes about women in this piece.
2. Would the joke make sense if the sexes were reversed? Explain your answer.
3. Suggest *two* reasons why these stereotypes continue to be in popular use?
4. Do you think that Scotland is a sexist society? Why?

Marxist feminism
Marxist feminists believe that capitalism is the main cause of women's oppression. In *The Origin of the Family, Private Property and the State*, Freidrich Engels (1972 [1884]) argued that women are 'proletarianised' within the marriage arrangement (see Chapter 2: Sociological Theory and Chapter 4: Social Class, for further

discussion on proletarianisation). His solution was for women to join men in the labour market to overthrow the capitalist system that oppresses both sexes.

Productive/reproductive labour

Later Marxist feminist's built on the work of Karl Marx (1818-1883) and Engels (1820-1895), distinguishing between *productive* and *reproductive* labour. Productive labour takes place in the public sphere where workers produce 'things' that create surplus value (profit) for employers. Reproductive labour is carried out in the home and involves providing food, shelter, emotional warmth and the socialisation of children. However, this is unpaid and undervalued in society and because it is not concerned with creating surplus value.

Services to capitalism

Marxist feminists claim that the oppression of women benefits capitalism. Women service their husband and perform labour, freeing him to work long hours for his employer (in return for a share of his wages); women also bring up the next generation of workers free of charge to employers. Although men benefit from free domestic labour and childcare, they are forced to work long hours and rarely get to spend quality time with their children. Borrowing a term from Marx, Bruegel (1979) argues that women are used as a 'reserve army of labour', who are moved in and out of the labour market in times of need. An additional benefit of this flexible labour force is that groups with low status (like women and ethnic minorities) can then be paid less for their labour (see Chapter 6: Race and Ethnicity). Contemporary Marxist feminists focus on the lack of value attached to women's work generally, both in paid employment and outside. For example, women are relegated to the most low paid, routine jobs as well as going home to carry out domestic work and childcare, which is *still not* regarded as 'real work'.

Marxist feminists claim that in a socialist society, the state will provide childcare and gender inequality will fade away. Marxists argue that as women join the ranks of the proletariat they will gain more equality with men, but only with the overthrow of capitalism can they secure complete equality.

A critical evaluation of Marxism feminism:

1) **Men as oppressors**: In her article, 'The unhappy marriage of Marxism and feminism', Heidi Hartmann (1981) claims that Marxism fails to explain why it is specifically women who occupy low status employment and are allocated responsibility for domestic labour and childcare, as capitalism would benefit just as much from low paid male workers and house-husbands
2) **Sexuality**: Michelle Barrett (1988) argues that Marxist feminists say very little about issues of sex compared with the world of work. Marxism's heavy

reliance on economic analysis cannot explain the existence of things like foot binding, chastity belts, female infanticide, female circumcision, domestic abuse and rape being inflicted on women and young girls in many parts of the world. Sexist ideology plays an important role alongside economics

3) ***Gender-free socialism***: There is no guarantee that women's oppression would come to an end with the advent of a socialist society. Although the lives of women in Eastern Europe and the Soviet Union improved a great deal under socialism, sexual violence and reproductive freedom were as low on the list of priorities as they are in capitalist countries. Marxist feminists would tend to stress that by entering paid employment women end up carrying a double workload.

Marxist feminism has nevertheless contributed greatly to our understanding of women's work in capitalist societies. It has evolved a great deal since these criticisms were made and has moved much more in the direction of what some term 'socialist feminism'. We will shortly discuss this approach after looking at radical feminism.

Radical feminism

Radical feminism emerged during the late 1960s and can be characterised by the belief that women were historically the first oppressed group, that this oppression is present in virtually all known societies, and that it is one of the most difficult of all forms of inequality to eradicate. Radical feminists believe that cultural stereotypes and economic inequalities are based on the biological fact that men and women have different bodies. They differ from liberal and Marxist feminists, by focusing on the way that men control women's bodies in the form of contraception, abortion, sterilisation, pornography, rape, women battering and sexual harassment, and focus on the private sphere rather than the world of work. Their slogan, 'The Personal is Political', captured the idea that private lives and relationships can also be oppressive.

'Patriarchal' ideology

One of the key concepts used by radical feminists to explain women's inequality is 'patriarchy', which can be translated as 'rule by the father'. This describes a male dominated culture, where women have less power, lower social status, and less opportunity for economic advancement. In *Sexual Politics*, Kate Millet (1970) argues that patriarchal ideology exaggerates differences between men and women, bringing boys up to be dominant and girls as submissive. This is done through institutions like the family, church and education system, so that most women *internalise* their inferiority to men. Although Millet's (1970) book has been criticised by some feminists, the coining of the term 'sexual politics' and Millets' call for a 'revolution in consciousness' helped shape radical feminism.

Reproduction

The radical feminist, Shulamith Firestone (1970), argues that the sexual division of labour is the most important form of inequality. Women constitute a 'sex class' because they are dependant on men for physical survival whilst pregnant, breastfeeding and rearing infants. Firestone's (1970) solution is to free women from childbirth through reproductive technology that would enable babies to be conceived and developed outside the womb. Thus, 'man-the-producer' and 'woman-the-reproducer' would be eliminated, allowing people to achieve a state of androgyny in a more equal society.

Sexuality

Susan Brownmiller (1975) argues that because all men have the biological capacity to rape, and because some men *do* rape, *all* women must police themselves on a daily basis to avoid it. Rape is, therefore, a means of social control, because women cannot go out alone at night, must be alert to which area of town they are in, and must dress 'respectably'. Although this biological inequality will always exist, Brownmiller (1975) argues that it is the cultures in which we live that allow rape to happen, by socialising men to be dominant and aggressive (see Tables 5.1 and 5.2, above). This threat could be averted in a more equal society.

Radical feminists formed 'consciousness-raising' groups in the 1960s to increase women's awareness of gender issues and campaigns for political change. This is still their preferred form of action, though some radical feminist's believe that male dominance is so endemic that 'separatism' is the only answer, where women live in non-hierarchical communities separate from men. Radical feminist analyses have stimulated much debate and helped raise women's consciousness of their own exploitation. However, there have been some common criticisms arising from this school of thought, as indicated below.

A critical evaluation of radical feminism:

1) *Patriarchy*: Radical feminists do not analyse the way social class interacts with patriarchy. For example, there is a big difference between the degree to which sexism is experienced by bourgeois women compared with working class women. Equally, black and lesbian feminists have argued that the radical feminist call for 'sisterhood' seems to ignore the fact that heterosexual white women often oppress black and lesbian women. Barbara Ehrenreich (1983) notes that sexism has different impacts in different societies. While in one society (i.e. China, though this is not an official policy), sexism is expressed in female infanticide, in another it manifests itself in unequal representation (most Western states, not least in Britain and Scotland). The difference, she insists, *is* worth dying for

2) ***Biological essentialism***: Although radical feminists claim that sex roles are a product of socialisation, they often imply that sex roles are rooted in biology. Using such a model may, however, reinforce patriarchal ideology rather than challenge it. Ultimately, many critics feel that biological arguments are self-defeating, because if sexism is shown to be biologically based, there would be little hope in overcoming it.

Radical feminists have helped to make women's work visible and have enlarged the political domain by showing how women's bodies and labour are exploited. Thus, Rosemary Tong (1989: 138) writes:

> What feminists owe to radical feminism is the conviction that what women share is their sexuality and that even if this sexuality has been a source of danger for women in the past, it can become a locus of pleasure and power for each and every woman in the future.

'Dual-systems' feminism

Given that Marxist feminists are accused of focusing too much on economics, and that radical feminism does not explain how capitalism exploits women, many writers have moved towards a synthesis of these theories, taking the best from each. Dual-systems theorists (or socialist feminists) argue that women are oppressed by *men* and *capitalism* and that the two cannot be separated. For example, we cannot understand the million dollar beauty industry that encourages women to pour time and energy into staying thin and making themselves attractive, unless we consider the way that both men and big businesses benefit from this. Many feminist writers, such as Alison Jagger (1983), now take a dual-systems approach.

Black feminism

> 'Woman is the nigger of the world.'
> (Yoko Ono)

Black women are doubly disadvantaged in that they face both *sexism* and *racism*. However, mainstream feminists have tended to overlook such concerns and, indeed, have been openly prejudiced against them. Suffragettes of the first wave appealed to white men by arguing that it would be immoral for black men to be given the vote before they achieved it. Historically, black women have had to prove that they should be included in the category, 'woman', to qualify for some of the opportunities afforded to white women. As Imelda Whelehan (1995: 117) states:

> The black woman was characterised as unfeminine, promiscuous, as a woman who cannot be raped because she herself is indiscriminately sexually voracious; this is set against the view of black men as the rapist incarnate.

The myth of 'sisterhood' in second wave feminism

In a similar gesture to the political activist, Malcolm X, the black feminist, bell hooks, spells her name in *lower case* to remind readers that black Americans lost their roots when slave owners imposed their own surname on slaves. Thus, hooks argues that second wave feminists made the mistake of believing that oppressed people could not themselves be oppressors, and that one of the main problems with second wave writing was the continual analogies drawn between women and blacks, where sexism was ranked as a more important problem than racism. For example, Firestone (1979) states that "racism is sexism extended." In addition, many of the platform issues pursued by white women had quite different meanings for black women. While white women wanted to fight for better contraception and access to abortion, black women were suspicious of reproductive technology, which had been used against them by the 'eugenics' movement in the United States. Given these differences, hooks proposed that the notion of 'sisterhood' should be replaced with the word 'solidarity'. Alice Walker (1983), author of the book (later made into a blockbuster movie), *The Color Purple*, about the racism and sexism experienced by its main character, prefers to call herself a 'womanist', as the word 'feminist' is so narrowly associated with white women's interests.

A critical evaluation of black feminism:

1) ***Are we so different?*** The writings of black feminists have illuminated important differences between women and served as a crucial corrective to the ethnocentric nature of second wave feminism. However, many white writers maintain that their analyses are equally applicable to black women and that differences between women can be exaggerated. Barrett and McIntosh (1995), for example, argue that they have yet to hear any evidence of racial differences that would lead them to modify their stance on the family

2) ***Who speaks for whom?*** One problem with all-inclusive terms, like 'black', is that some black writers speak for others without any experience of their subject position. For example, Kanneh (1998) points out that Alice Walker sometimes speaks for black women in the Third World, generalising her middle class, black American perspective. Thus, like white feminists, black feminists have learned to be sensitive to divisions and tensions within their own community.

There is now a wide literature by black feminists, which explores the history of black women in the US, Europe and the 'Third World'. Although black feminists are themselves divided in terms of ethnic origin, social class and sexuality, they continue to remind mainstream feminism of the importance of considering *difference*.

However, to this day there is a distinct shortage of black female academics, which means that black voices are still under represented.

Postmodernist feminism

Feminist theory from the 1980s onwards has had to explain the commonality of women's oppression, whilst taking account of differences *between* women in terms of class, race, ethnicity and sexuality. Alongside these tensions within traditional feminist theory, came a growth in the popularity of a new perspective, namely 'postmodernism' (see Chapter 2: Sociological Theory) in the social sciences. Some feminists proposed that a synthesis between postmodernism and feminism would offer a completely new form of feminist theorising that could accommodate differences between women.

It may not be obvious why some feminists are attracted to a position that holds that no objective analysis of 'women's' situation is possible, but feminism has always shown that there are multiple versions of history and that 'objective' accounts of the world are usually written from a white, Western, middle class, male perspective. Nancy Fraser (1995) makes the claim that feminist theory is riddled with 'metanarratives', which attempt to identify the ultimate cause of women's' oppression, or find the single activity (or 'practice') that all women share. Examples of this are Shualmith Firestone's (1979) view of women as a 'sex-class'. However, the most obvious metanarrative that feminism holds on to is the concept of 'woman', which is regarded as having universal significance. In her book, *Gender Trouble*, Judith Butler (1990) claims that the word 'woman' is a signifier with no substance, because there are no universal characteristics that make the word meaningful. Thus, postmodernist feminists urge mainstream feminists to abandon their project to find the 'truth' about gender.

A critical evaluation of postmodern feminism:

1) ***The category 'Woman'***: Many feminists have expressed reservations about jettisoning the categories of man and woman. Sylvia Walby (1988) points out that while there is nothing essential in being male or female, and that gender takes many forms, there are enough historical and cross-cultural similarities to warrant the use of such categories. Similarly, Christine Di Stephano (in Nicholson, 1990: 75-76) is suspicious of postmodernist writers, given that they tend to be white, middle class, male academics, whose own work has been "remarkably blind and insensitive to questions of gender."

2) ***Political action***: Many feminists have raised concerns over the political cost of ditching categories like 'woman' or 'patriarchy'. Although the word 'patriarchy' disguises differences in the degree of domination experienced, feminists have found it to be useful for rallying women to engage in political

action. Some feminists may fear that engagement in postmodern debates would marginalize feminist politics.

Postmodernism throws up some interesting possibilities for those feminists who have always been suspicious of 'objective' grand narratives and large categories like male/female. However, this is an ongoing debate, and as Barrett (1998) asserts, *later* theory is not necessarily *better* theory.

Trigger

1. What are your views on the feminist perspectives?
2. Which of these perspectives do you most closely agree or identify with, and why?
3. Which of these perspectives do you think portrays the most accurate image of contemporary Scottish society?

Challenges to Feminism

Despite having won considerable legislative and attitudinal changes in UK society, feminism is no stranger to conflict, ridicule and criticism. The continuing, indeed, renewed, recent backlash may be seen as a reaction to both the significant gains achieved by second wave feminism and/or an attempt by some to return us to a world before the 1970s, where differences between men and women were seen as natural and women's role was primarily domestic. This backlash has taken many forms. Historically, it has come from the male-dominated media, from politically conservative politicians (men *and* women) and, significantly, from within the feminist movement itself.

Backlash and the media
'Feminism is now obsolete'

In *Overloaded: Popular Culture and the Future of Feminism*, Imelda Whelehan (2000) points out that the media attempts to undermine feminism, by promoting the idea that feminism is obsolete because women now have full equality with men. Women are even depicted as power-hungry vixens who dominate men, although 'action babes' like 'Zena: Warrior Princess', 'Lara Croft', and 'Charlie's Angels', are always slim, semi-clad, white, and conventionally attractive, designed more to titillate, rather than frighten the male viewer. In *Backlash: The Undeclared War against Women*, Susan Faludi (1991) argues that depictions of women like Demi Moore's character in the film, *Disclosure*, are particularly worrying. Here, Demi Moore's character is portrayed abusing sexual harassment legislation to get back at a male colleague who has rejected her sexual advances; in reality, however, sexism in the workplace is overwhelmingly directed *at* females, though there appears to be a shortage of Hollywood movies covering that genre.

'Feminism has made women unhappy'

The media also promote the contradictory view that feminism is too powerful and has made women unhappy. This view has gained ground in North America, particularly within right wing Christian politics and has filtered across the Atlantic via programmes and films like *Sex in the City*, *Ally McBeal*, *Bridget Jones Diary* and *One Fine Day*. Career women are depicted as stressed, hardened and unloved, lurching from one emotional crisis to the next and incomplete without a man and the benefits of children and a family life. The happy ending is to 'get the guy', which the career has been a substitute for, and retire to domestic bliss. These images are tapping into a very real situation, as women do feel that they have tried to have it all, but are left simply exhausted and unfulfilled. The real problem may be that women with childcare and domestic responsibilities cannot easily fit into work patterns designed for men without childcare and domestic duties.

Post-feminism

The word, 'post', suggests that this approach supersedes feminism, rather than being a rejection of it, but many feminists have explicitly linked post-feminist critiques to a betrayal of feminist struggle. In *The New Victorians: A Young Woman's Challenge to the Old Feminist Order*, Rene Denfield (1996) claims that feminism has lost all credibility with the younger generation due to its belief in female victimisation and the insatiable male libido. This is echoed in Naomi Wolf's (1993) *Fire with Fire*, where she is greatly critical of what she calls 'victim feminism' and distinguishes this from her own brand of 'power feminism', which 'hates sexism without hating men'. In *The Morning After*, Katy Roiphe (1994) also blames second wave feminists for exaggerating the power of patriarchy and claims that the fear of 'date rape' on US university campuses has led to a puritanical atmosphere leading some women to abuse the term and refer to any sexual encounters that go wrong as date rape.

A critical evaluation of post-feminism:

The problem with post-feminist work, according to Sarah Gamble (2001), is that it takes a simplistic view of feminism and portrays it as a monolithic structure stifling dissent. The reality is much more complex, as feminism has always been a hotbed of discussion where no one point of view is allowed to dominate. Gamble (2001) observes that Denfield's (1996) view of feminism holds Victorian notions of femininity, dismissing an entire history of complex struggle from the first wave onwards. Like Whelehan (2000), Gamble (2001) argues that of great seriousness is the post-feminists' uncritical incorporation of the media backlash arguments into their work, without examining these assumptions for their 'truth value'.

Standing up to the challenge?

As a political movement, feminism will always face challenges, whether from the media, 'new Feminists', or from men. The dialogue with 'new feminism' can be seen as a clash between younger feminists and the 'founding mothers' of the second wave, but the feminist movement has shown itself to be a broad church, and continues to value constructive criticism, while remaining suspicious of attempts to undermine it. Although some challenges are plainly anti-feminist, they have stimulated debate by opening up discussions on the popular image of feminism today.

Trigger

1. To what extent has the mass media played a role on undermining the progression of women in the late 2oth and early 21st centuries?
2. Does the mass circulation of pornography and 'Lad's Mags' (e.g. *Loaded*, *Front*, FHM, etc.) indicate a 'backward step' for women?

Gender and Employment

Although women form an increasingly large proportion of the labour market, employment patterns in Britain are deeply gendered. To reiterate an earlier discussion in this Chapter, UK figures in 2001 show that 67 per cent of women aged 16-64 are in employment compared with 79 per cent of men. Forty three per cent of these women work part-time compared with only 9 per cent of men (Equal Opportunities Commission, 2003; see also Chapter 10: Work and its Organisation).

The dispersion between male and female workers is also accounted for by the rise of female employees and the acute drop in male employment, with job growth in Scotland almost exclusively female – 46 per cent of total employees. However, much of this work remains part-time and accounted for 38 per cent of the total hours worked in 2001 (Miller, Scottish Further Education Unit, 2002). Despite the growing presence of women in the workforce, UK figures illustrate women's wages still lag behind males and represent a source of inequality symptomatic of that noted by Hutton (1996), where he suggests that they are still marginalized and insecure employment-wise (see Chapter 10: Work and its Organisation). The New Earnings Survey (IDS, 2002: Report 869) in April 2002, illustrated that full-time male workers earned £513.80 per week, which was up 4.8 per cent from 2001, and part-time male workers £165.30 per week, up 15.1 per cent. On average, all male workers enjoyed a 4.7 per cent rise, with a weekly wage average of £484.10. By comparison, women in full-time work earned £383.40 per week – up 4.5 per cent, with their part-time counterparts earning an average gross weekly pay of £145.80 (up 6.2 per cent). The total average for all women workers was £283.50 per week, representing an increase of 4.3 per cent.

The largest widening of the pay gap across the UK can be found in Wales and Scotland as a consequence of the faster earnings growth at the higher end of the male earnings distribution, mainly in occupations such as marketing and sales management (IDS, 2003: Report 873).

Employment segregation
Employment segregated between the sexes can be seen in *two* distinct ways:

1) *'Horizontal segregation'*
This refers to the extent to which men and women do different types of jobs, while 'vertical segregation' refers to the way that men tend to command higher status and higher paid jobs, such as in management and the professions. From the 2002 New Earnings Survey (IDS, 2002: Report 873) it is possible to illustrate the following:

- Figures for a top non-manual occupations (i.e. General Managers in large companies and organisations) shows that 79.8 per cent of this group are males, compared to 20.2 per cent for women. Average salaries in this group are £2,079 per week
- For a top earning manual occupation, such as rail signal operatives, the workforce figures are 97.1 per cent males, compared to 2.9 per cent female, with weekly earnings averaging £599.50
- A bottom earning non-manual occupation (i.e. retail cash desk and check out operatives) has the proportion of females employed as 79.6 compared to 20.4 of the staff being male. Weekly average earnings total £205. However, more starkly contrasted, in terms of the weighting for those employed, are receptionists with females making up 100 per cent of the workforce with average weekly earnings of £246.10
- A bottom earning manual occupation (e.g. kitchen porters/hands) has a balance of staff at 69.7 per cent women, 26.2 men, with average weekly earnings of £209.20.

In August 2000, the Equal Opportunities Commission asked Dr Damian Grimshaw and Professor Jill Rubery (2001) of the School of Management, University of Manchester Institute of Science and Technology (UMIST), to provide a review on the cause and consequences of the gender pay gap in Britain. They identified the explanations identifies in point *2) Individual choices* for this trend:

2) *Individual Choices*

Mainstream economists argue that women spend less time investing in education and are attracted to more low-paid work or work concentrated in the public sector. However, the problem with this argument is that women's employment prospects may be more constrained than men's, and that also there is evidence that when women move into an occupation there is often a decline in pay. This suggests that it is not the jobs themselves that deserve low pay, but the fact that women are doing them. For example, when clerical work was performed by men it was associated with high social status and good pay and conditions, but when women became clerks all three declined rapidly. The trend can also be seen in the opposite direction, for example, when men moved into catering and became chefs, the pay and status of the position improved greatly.

Range of professions

A second, more plausible, explanation for gender inequality, according to Grimshaw and Rubery (2001) is that women are concentrated in a narrow range of occupations. They found that more than 60 per cent of women's employment is concentrated in just 10 out of 77 occupations they looked at.

Public sector work

Women are concentrated in public sector occupations, which are relatively low paid in Britain by international standards. For example, in 1998, women working as full-time qualified nurses in the UK earned six per cent less than the average earnings of full-time male employees, whereas nurses in Australia earned 18 per cent more than the average earnings of male full-time employees. Current trends in the public sector are also damaging to pay, for example, by replacing high skilled employees with low skilled workers and sub-contracting services to the private sector.

Part-time work

However, the fact that 44 per cent of women work part-time is one of the most important factors, as few high paid jobs allow for part-time work. Indeed, part-time workers are often marginalized in organisations, with fewer promotion prospects and limited access to training. In addition to having lower hourly pay, female part-timers have reduced entitlement to benefits like pension contributions and unsocial hours payments.

Since the Equal Pay Act of 1970, women's pay has steadily increased in proportion to men's. However, as *The New Earnings* survey indicates (IDS 2003: Report 873), women in full-time work still earn on average only 81.2 per cent per hour and 74.6 per cent per week of male wages, which is one of the widest gender gaps in earnings in Europe.

Trigger

In October 1999, the Equal Opportunities Commission set up the employer-led Equal Pay Taskforce to look at factors behind, and ways of closing, the gender pay gap. The Taskforce published its report 'Just Pay' in February 2001, identifying discrimination in pay systems, occupational segregation and the unequal impact of women's family responsibilities as three main factors leading to the gap between men's and women's average earnings (IDS, 2002:Report 856).

Discuss why, despite the fact that today there are more women in employment, male wages are increasing more rapidly than women's.

The Sexualisation of Women's Work

Adkins and Lury (1992) argue that unlike their male counterparts, women have to provide 'sexual serving' to customers as well as their economic function. They found that women working in bars and hotels were required to be young and attractive and make male customers feel good as part of their job. This can take the form of smiling frequently and laughing off sexual harassment from colleagues or customers. Women who will not perform these services are rarely employed or may even be sacked.

Women and Political Careers

For women, jobs associated with positions of political power would appear to be no more accessible than those in other areas of social life (although the Scottish Parliament provides an interesting example that appears, in some ways, to contradict this trend, with a movement towards 50:50 representation). Women are under-represented in all of the higher domains of decision-making in UK (and Scottish) society and greatly over-represented in social positions wielding little power, influence, status and low economic reward. This is symptomatic of both *horizontal* and *vertical* segregation.

In recent years, there has been a growing concern about the under representation of women at the Westminster Parliament. In 2002, 18 per cent of Westminster MPs in were women (House of Commons Weekly Information Bulletin, 2002). Since women make up over half of the UK population at any one time, however, women are still considerably under-represented in the Westminster Parliament. Reasons for this tend to fall into two main categories. First, a lack of supply of candidates – a shortage of interested or experienced women putting themselves forward, and second, a lack of demand and problems in the nature of the job itself, such as long hours away from home. The Scottish Parliament's attempt at addressing this is discussed below.

Supply and demand of candidates

Vicky Randall (1982) suggests that because political institutions have historically been male dominated, behaviour patterns associated with men, like aggressiveness (the 'Opposition' benches at the Westminster Parliament are still positioned at one sword's length apart) become normalised, so that 'feminine' qualities like a willingness to compromise disadvantage women selected by males using male-oriented criteria. Discrimination against women in parliamentary selection procedures may be a crucial factor in women's under-representation. Male-dominated selection committees have been reluctant to adopt women for winnable seats, despite the fact that there is no evidence that women are less likely to be elected (see Box 5.3, below).

Box 5.3 'Revealed: How Labour Sees Women'

The Fawcett Report, which covers all the main political parties, was written by Laura Shepherd-Robinson, the Fawcett Society's campaigns officer, and Professor Joni Lovenduski of the University of London. It is based on focus groups and face-to-face conversations with 'well qualified female candidates who had tried but failed to be selected by a safe or winnable parliamentary constituency. It makes grim reading. One woman told the Fawcett researchers: 'It was said to me, 'We do enjoy watching you speak, we always imagine what your knickers are like. We picture you in your underwear when you are speaking'. Another was asked: 'I suppose you are one of the women we have got to look at?' Two of the women questioned were told: 'Your children are better off with you at home'. Another was introduced to someone in the constituency as 'one of these here radical militant feminists'.

(Source: Adapted from the *New Statesman*, 4 February, 2002)

Trigger

Read the passage in Box 5.3 and answer the following questions:

1. What kind of barriers do female parliamentary candidates face, according to the Fawcett Report?
2. What would be the *advantages* and *disadvantages* of 50:50 representation in parties and parliament's?

The Scottish Parliament
The creation of the first Scottish Parliament since 1707, gave the Women's Movement in Scotland a vital opportunity to shape a new institution. Political institutions have traditionally been very difficult to transform once they are well established and parliamentary seats occupied. On 12 May 1999, the number of women taking their seats at the first meeting of the Scottish Parliament was 37.2 per cent (48 out of 129 in total). This figure was similar to that of the Welsh Assembly (40 per cent) (Engender, 1999), but both overshadow the most recent Westminster figure of 17.9 per cent (118 seats from a total of 659) at the May 2003 General Election (Inter Parliamentary Union, 2003).

The proportion of female MSPs in the Scottish Parliament means that Scotland now ranks among the top countries in the world in terms of top-level female political representation. The percentage of female representatives in the Scottish Parliament actually increased to 39.5 per cent after the May 2003 Scottish elections (Engender, 2003c). This figure compares with the Welsh Assembly at 50 per cent (Engender, 2003c) and countries like Sweden (45.3 per cent), Denmark (38 per cent), Finland (37.5 per cent) and Norway (36.4 per cent). Wider global comparisons include Cuba, at 36 percent, New Zealand, 28.3 per cent and Australia at 25.3 per cent (Inter Parliamentary Union, 2003).

The '50:50 Campaign'
Campaigns for gender balance attracted public and political party support due to a perceived history of a 'democratic deficit', whereby successive Conservative governments seemed to have no mandate to govern in Scotland, returning as that party did, few Conservative MPs to the House of Commons (in the 1997 General Election they held no seats in Scotland). In 1989, the Women's Committee of the Scottish Trades Union Congress (STUC) proposed the radical measure of 50 per cent male and 50 per cent female representation. The proposal quickly gained the support of the Scottish Labour Party who passed it overwhelmingly at their 1990 conference. In June 1992, the Women's Co-ordination Group was established, which was made up of volunteers from the STUC Women's Committee, Women's Forum Scotland, the Scottish Joint Action Group, Engender, and the Church of Scotland's Women's Guild.

The '50:50 Campaign' is ongoing and seeks for Scottish women an increase in access to powerful and influential key institutions and decision making bodies (Engender, 2003b). Indeed, to quote Julie Mellor, EOC Chair (Parliamentary News release 9 August 2001, cited in Engender, 2003b), who stated:

> [W]here women have reached critical mass in terms of representation, there is clear evidence of policy impact. Sex Equality issues have become part of the mainstream

debate in Scotland, so that, for example, the potential impact on women of social and economic issues is always taken into consideration. That should be the case in all our institutions.

However, despite recent gains in the number of women in representative positions in the Scottish Parliament, as well as recent legislation (Sex Discrimination (Election Candidates) Act 2002) passed by the UK government permitting political parties to use positive action to improve levels of women's representation, only two of the six political parties used specific measures, the Labour Party and the Scottish Socialist Party (SSP) (Engender, 2003c).

Although not the 50 per cent campaigned for, the increase in women's representation to nearly 40 percent at 2003 (Engender, 2003c) is more than many think of as the 'critical mass' of 25-30 per cent necessary for women to make an impact on the political agenda. The Scottish Parliament has made a commitment to mainstreaming equality throughout all policy areas. A cabinet post and Deputy Minister for Equalities has been created and the parliamentary day has been set within the more family-friendly times of 9.00am-5.00pm, and not until the possible wee small hours, as is the case at Westminster. Scottish school holidays are also recognised. Even the seating is designed in a horseshoe shape rather than along the lines of Westminster's highly confrontational opposing benches. This was made possible by the co-ordinated efforts of various women's groups and by cross-party alliances that maintained pressure throughout the consultation process and beyond.

Trigger

Consider how more women taking up political careers in the Scottish Parliament could have an impact on issues of equality in other workplaces?

Conclusion

Feminism has often come under attack from a wide variety of sources. British society is fairly typical of the contradictory nature of the backlash, in that women are declared as fully equal by the media, although a glance at employment statistics clearly contradicts this view.

Many writers have found the liberal feminist approach merely continues to perpetuate deep-seated inequalities in society and fails to address notions of class and ethnicity. Equally, both radical feminism and Marxist feminism could be considered as incomplete in trying to explain gendered employment patterns in Britain. Radical feminist approaches are correct in arguing that women are often exploited because they are women, but the interests of capitalism and their desire to maximise profits are also important to consider. Equally, Marxist approaches are correct in arguing that women are functional for capitalism as a reserve army of cheap labour, but tend to ignore the role of men in limiting women's employment opportunities. This has led some writers to propose that only a combination of these approaches will provide the best way forward for understanding horizontal and vertical segregation in Britain today.

Recent challenges to feminism and a growing awareness that men have genders, too, may strike a fatal blow at feminism, as we know it, but the '50:50 Campaign' for the Scottish Parliament illustrates what a 'third wave' of feminist activity *might* look like.

Chapter Summary

- Sociologists distinguish between 'sex' – a biological classification, and 'gender' – a social construction that varies across time and place.
- Feminism is both an *academic* body of knowledge and an ongoing *political movement*, comprised of sociologists and political commentators who believe that women are treated differently and unequally compared to men, and that this must be changed through political activism.
- The historical development of feminism has produced a 'first' and 'second wave' of literature and activism. Debate continues as to the emergence of the 'third wave'.
- The main feminist perspectives considered were 'liberal feminism', 'radical feminism', 'Marxist feminism', 'black feminism', 'dual-systems (socialist) feminism' and 'postmodern feminism'. Each branch focuses on women's oppression and exploitation in society, but interpret it differently and offer different solutions to the problem.
- Challenges to feminism as a movement have arisen from a number of sources including the mass media and, from within the movement itself, in the form of 'post-feminism'.
- Although women form an increasingly large proportion of the labour market, employment patterns in Britain are deeply gendered and a considerable gender pay gap remains despite recent gains for women.
- For women, positions of political power are no more accessible than those in other areas of social life. Women are grossly under-represented in all of the higher domains of decision-making in UK society and greatly over-represented in social positions wielding little power, status and low economic reward.
- The creation of the Scottish Parliament may, however, provide women with greater opportunities for political representation and comparisons with the Westminster Parliament are encouraging for those in favour of a 50:50 balance at Holyrood, the home of the Scottish Parliament.

Further Reading

Abbott, P. and Wallace, C. (1997) *An Introduction to Sociology: Feminist Perspectives*, Second Edition, London: Routledge

Garret, S. (1987) *Gender*, London: Tavistock

Lovell, T. (ed.) (1990) *British Feminist Thought: A Reader*, Oxford: Blackwell

Useful Websites

The Equal Opportunities commission: http://www.eoc.org.uk/

The World Health Organisation: http://www.who.int/en/

UNICEF: http://www.unicef.org/

The government's women and equality unit: http://www.womenandequalityunit.gov.uk/

Engender: http://www.engender.org.uk/

Excellent resources on sex and gender: http://www.sociology.org.uk/cload.htm

Bibliography

Adkins, L. and Lury, C. (1992) 'Gender and the Labour market: old theory for new?' in Hinds, H., Phoenix A. and Stacey, J. (eds.) *Working Out: New Directions for Women's Studies*, London: Falmer Press

Barrett, M. (1988) *Women's Oppression Today: Problems in Marxist Feminist* analysis, London: Verso

Brownmiller, S. (1975) *Against Our* Will, Harmondsworth: Penguin

Bruegal, I. (1979) 'Women as a reserve army of labour: a note on recent British experience', *Feminist Review*, No.3

Butler, J. (1990) *Gender Trouble: Feminism and the Subversion of Identity*, London: Routledge

Dawson, G. (2000) 'Work: from certainty to flexibility?' in Hughes, G. and Fergusson, R. (eds.) *Ordering lives: family, work and welfare* (DD100: Introduction to the Social Sciences: Understanding Social Change), London: Routledge/Open University

Denfield, R. (1996) *The New Victorians: A Young Woman's Challenge to the Old Feminist Order*, New York, NY: Warner Books

Ehrenreich, B. (1983) *The Hearts of Men*, London: Pluto

Engels, F. (1972 [1884]) *The Origins of the family, Private Property and the State*, London: Lawrence and Wishart

Engender (1999) *Women elected as MSP's in the Scottish Parliament* (accessed at: http://www.engender.org.uk/scotparl/wip/msp.html)

Engender (2003a) *Women and the Scottish Parliament* (accessed at: http://www.engender.org.uk/)

Engender (2003b) *The 50=50 Campaign* (accessed at: http://www.engender.org.uk/5050.html)

Engender (2003c) *Election results for 2003: new records for women's political representation* (accessed at: http://www.engender.org.uk/Election%20results%202003.htm)

Equal Opportunities Commission (2003) *Facts About Women and Men in Great Britain*, Manchester: Equal Opportunities Commission

Faludi, S. (1992) *Backlash*, London: Chatto and Windus

Firestone, S. (1979) *The Dialectic of Sex*, London: The Women's Press

Fraser, N. (1995) 'Politics, culture and the public sphere: towards a postmodern conception', in Nicholson, L. and Seidman, S. (eds.) *Social postmodernism: Beyond Identity Politics*, Cambridge: Cambridge University Press

Friedan, B. (1971[1963]) *The Feminine Mystique*, London: Gollancz

Gamble, S. (2001) *Feminism and Post-feminism*, London: Routledge

Greer, G. (1971) *The Female Eunuch*, St Albans: Paladin

Grimshaw, D. and Rubery, J. (2001) *The Gender Pay Gap: a Research Review*, Equal Opportunities Commission Research Discussion Series, Manchester: Equal Opportunities Commission

Hartmann, H. (1981) 'The unhappy marriage of Marxism and feminism', in Sargent, L. (ed.) *The Unhappy Marriage of Marxism and Feminism*, London: Pluto Press

Hinds, H., Phoenix A. and Stacey, J. (eds.) (1992) *Working Out: New Directions for Women's Studies*, London: Falmer Press

Hooks, B. (1981) *Ain't I a woman? Black women and Feminism*, Boston: South End Press

House of Commons (2002) *Weekly Information Bulletin*, 12 January

Hughes, G. and Fergusson, R. (eds.) (2000) *Ordering lives: family, work and welfare* (DD100: Introduction to the Social Sciences: Understanding Social Change), London: Routledge/Open University

Hutton, W. (1996) *The State We're In*, London: Vintage

Income Data Services (2002) *The Equal Pay Challenge*, Report 856, May, pp.14-27, London: Income Data Services

Income Data Services (2002) *New Earnings Survey*, Report 869, November, pp.2-3, London: Income Data Services

Income Data Services (2003) *The gender pay gap*, Report 873, January, pp.11-16, London: Income Data Services

Inter Parliamentary Union (2003) *Women in Parliaments: World Classifications* (accessed at: http://www.ipu.org/wmn-classif.htm)

Jackson, S. and Jones, J. (eds.) (1998) *Contemporary Feminist Theories*, Edinburgh: Edinburgh University Press

Jagger, A.M. (1983) *Feminist Politics and Human Nature*, Hemel Hempstead: Harvester Press

Kanneh, K. (1998) 'Black feminisms', in Jackson, S. and Jones, J. (eds.) *Contemporary Feminist Theories*, Edinburgh: Edinburgh University Press

Marx, K, Engels, F. (1964[1844]) *The Economic and Philosophical Manuscripts*, New York: International Publishers

Mill, J.S. (1869) *The Subjection of Women*, Oxford: Oxford University PressMiller, M. (2002) 'The Scottish Labour Market', Briefing and Information Services Briefing Paper, September, Stirling: Scottish Further Education Unit

Millet, K. (1970) *Sexual Politics*, New York, NY: Doubleday

Murdoch, G.P. (1949) *Social Structure*, New York, NY: Macmillan

New Statesman, The (2002) 'Revealed: How Labour Sees Women', 4 February

Nicholson, L. (ed.) (1990) *Feminism/Postmodernism*, New York, NY: Routledge

Nicholson, L. and Seidman, S. (eds.) (1995) *Social postmodernism: Beyond Identity Politics*, Cambridge: Cambridge University Press

Oakley, A. (1972) *Sex, Gender and Society*, London: Temple Smith

Oakley, A. (1974) *The Sociology of Housework*, Oxford: Martin Robertson

Randall, V. (1982) *Women and Politics*, Basingstoke: Macmillan

Roiphe, K. (1994) *The Morning After*, London: Hamish Hamilton

Sargent, L. (ed.) (1981) *The Unhappy Marriage of Marxism and Feminism*, London: Pluto Press

Scottish Parliament (2003) *A young person's guide to the Parliament*, (accessed at: http://www.scottish.parliament.uk/educationservice/young.html)

Stoller, R. (1969) *Sex and Gender: On the Development of Masculinity and* Femininity, New York, NY: Science House

Tong, R. (1989) *Feminist Thought, a Comprehensive Introduction*, Boulder, CO: Westview Press

Walby, S. (1988) 'Gender Politics and Social Theory', *Sociology*, Vol.22

Walker, A. (1983) *The Color Purple*, London: The Women's Press

Whelehan, I. (1995) *Modern feminist Thought: From the Second Wave to 'Post-feminism'*, Edinburgh: Edinburgh University Press

Whelehan, I. (2000) *Overloaded: Popular Culture and the Future of Feminism*, London: The Women's Press

Wolf, N. (1993) *Fire with Fire*, London: Chatto and Windus

Wollstonecraft, M. (1975 [1792]) *A Vindication of the Rights of Women*, Harmondsworth: Penguin

Chapter 6   Race and Ethnicity

Brian Dunn

Introduction

Social stratification refers to a system of socially structured inequalities between particular groups and individuals. Societies are viewed as social hierarchies when groups and individuals are ranked according to certain attributes. Arguably one of the most controversial attributes by which people have been stratified, is the on the basis of skin colour or by reference to a group's 'culture'. In an increasingly multi-cultural society the study of 'race' and 'ethnicity' has become a complex but highly important area for sociological investigation. This Chapter seeks to provide an overview of issues associated with race and ethnicity. However, at the outset it must be stressed that this is far from exhaustive and is intended as an introduction to encourage the inquisitive reader to explore issues further.

The themes of the chapter are traced initially through the competing definitions of 'race' and 'ethnicity'. Both terms are the focus of current research and analysis in the social sciences. Indeed, in everyday terms, there is a common sense understanding of 'race' and 'ethnicity', although this generally leads to a simplification of issues through basic stereotypes. Notions of 'institutional racism' allows for an illustration of how racism can manifest itself in the institutions of a society.

The embedding of theoretical insights within the chapter provides a vehicle for understanding some of the underpinning reasons why ethnic minorities are stratified, and allows students to interpret and apply issues through particular frameworks. There follows a discussion about the historical nature of immigration in relation to both the British Empire and also post-war immigration and the legislation that has accompanied and shaped such movements of people. In the context of this section, attention is paid both to the overall British context and also the Scottish experience of immigration. The concept of a multi-ethnic Britain is explored in the context of legislation and aspects such as employment.

The changing nature of how sociologists are examining race and ethnicity, illustrates that Britain/Scotland is part of global context whereby racial and ethnic issues are becoming more profound. Often these issues arise as a consequence of conflict. The 'asylum issue', for example, demonstrates how Britain/Scotland are greatly affected by global events, which are symptomatic of both an imperialistic history and reflects the emergence of Britain/Scotland as part of a European order or system.

Race as a Concept
Non-sociological definitions

Identifying a clear definition of the term race is exacerbated by the fact that politicians, biologists, geographers, historians and sociologists have used the term in a number of ways. A further problem of definition derives from the fact that the term race has historically been defined in different ways. Definitions in the 19th century focused on the idea of 'race' as a distinct or discrete group of people who could be classified like fossils, butterflies, or rocks; each of which have different physical appearances and behaviours and come from different parts of the globe. 'Race' was based primarily on physiological and biological characteristics such as skin colour, facial type, cranial profile, texture, colour and amount of hair.

Three main race 'types' were classified, accordingly, in the 19th-century:

- *Caucasoid* (or Caucasian): White Europeans and those of European descent
- *Mongoloid* (or Mongolian): So called 'red' or 'yellow' Native American Indians and Asians
- *Negroid* (or Negroes): Black African and African-Americans (slaves).

Trigger

Smelser (1994: 274) argues that the legitimacy of such physical or biological grounds is confounded by historical migration across many centuries, together with mixing and inter-procreation among the groups identified as race types.

Can you think of other problems with defining 'race' biologically?

This idea that ethnic and racial groups can be defined on the basis of biology was linked to ideas about the inherent superiority of white people and was tied to slavery, colonialism and imperial expansion. The eminent 19th century French scientist, Georges Cuvier (1769-1832), derived definitions of race from fields such as geology, palaeontology, and comparative anatomy. He insisted that 'factual' evidence proved the existence of separate racial groups, but, more controversially, his fascination with anatomy led him to collect information on different peoples from around the globe and to classify them in a hierarchy of superiority. Other 19th century race theorists, such as Joseph Arthur Comte de Gobineau (1853-1855) in his *Essay on the Inequality of the Human Races*, believed that there existed a hierarchy of races and that white people were the most 'important' followed by 'yellows' and then 'blacks'. He popularised the idea of the so-called 'Aryan race', through his publicly stated fear of 'racial degeneration' and belief in the racial 'purity' of the Aryan race. This concept was later taken up by Hitler and the Nazis and, in Britain, extreme right-wing factions, such as the National Front (Kivisto, 2002: 17) and is evident in another form in the white supremacist ideology of 'Apartheid' as practiced by the South African State prior to 1994.

Much of the reasoning behind notions of a superior 'white' race has tended to ignore important facts about historical settlement and achievement and has centred on the high levels of economic development and scientific advances, particularly in Europe and North America as proof of white superiority. However, many of the advantages that the 'white' race has enjoyed may be seen as a consequence of *imperialism*, which has resulted in exploitation and domination of other groups and the plundering of resources (both human and non-human) in other parts of the world.

Most scientists today favour the idea that we all share a common ancestry from the same geographical area (interestingly, in Africa) and they therefore reject biological ideas of race. The biologist, Steven Rose (1998), has pointed to the fact that there is as much genetic variation *within* a so-called 'race' as there are *between* groups of people classified as being of different race.

The myth of 'race', however, continues to be a powerful ideology that attempts to account for the origin of a particular group of people (white) in a way that justifies the social position and needs of that group to the exclusion of others. In so doing, vast inequalities in wealth and power between groups have become *naturalised*, that is, come to be understood as a 'natural' component of human life.

Trigger

Carefully consider how dominating social meanings of race allow some groups to wield power over others.

Sociological Explanations of Race
Race and/or ethnicity?
We have seen then, that the term 'race' is problematic for sociologists. Significantly, much of the scientific community has, in modern times, rejected 'race' as a real biological difference between human beings. However, 'common sense' understandings of 'race' are very real in their consequences, as evidenced by the legacies of apartheid in South Africa and the many other cases of racism that have been a conspicuous aspect of American, British and European history. Sociological definitions of race differ from biologically based definitions in *two* main ways. First, race is viewed as culturally and socially constructed. Therefore, common sense

references to physical and biological characteristics are seen as social categories rather than statements about physique or biology. Second, leading to racism *proper* is the notion that some races are superior. Although the scientific basis of such a claim is greatly disputed in sociology, the term 'race' remains sociologically significant. Smelser (1994: 281-282) argues that "it becomes the structural basis for human interaction, stratification and domination." In other words, regardless of whether race exists or not, there are social consequences for the meanings associated with the term. In this sense, sociologists consider race to be a social construct that has no real scientific validity, but which has very real consequences, as summed up by the American sociologist, W.I. Thomas (1923), when he suggested that "if men define situations as real, they are real in their consequences."

Evidently, there are no distinct biologically defined races but equally clear is the fact that a great many people believe and act as if there were. Other sociologists have further argued that the term, 'race', is best understood as the means by which perceived differences are expressed in cultural practices and beliefs (Anthias and Yuval-Davis, 1993). A 'New Racism' has emerged from the political right that has replaced the old racism based on biological factors and focuses instead on perceived differences between groups based on culture and religion (Manne, 2002). Examples of this New Racism may be the growing 'Islamophobia' (distrust of all things Islamic), particularly since the attack on New York's World Trade Centre on 11 September, 2001; and the rejection of notions of multi-culturalism and diversity by groups such as the right-wing Ayn Rand Institute. Some sociologists have, therefore, argued that race should continue to be used as a justifiable concept for sociological investigation and analysis. David Mason (1995: 9) suggests a more restricted use of the term. He argues that the only acceptable sociological usage is when 'race' is considered as a particular form of social relationship, constructed through social processes that are based on racist reasoning. Others, such as Miles (1989), however, reject the use of the term race completely, arguing that the term has been invented in order to obscure the true nature of capitalist economic relations and thereby fragment the working class. Pilkington (2003) claims that notions of racial difference in the form of a 'black/white divide' are no longer of use to social scientists and should be replaced with a framework that considers material disadvantage between and within ethnic groupings and which considers how individuals (often deliberately) hold on to ethnic identities in the face of globalising tendencies.

Trigger

1. Do you think by continuing to use the term 'race', sociologists are in fact helping to perpetuate the perception that race exists?
2. In what ways might 'New Racism' be potentially more socially divisive than old racism?

Whilst the concept of biological racial difference may not be considered to be a credible social science concept, it is still very evident that people associate differences between groups as being associated with features such as skin colour. In this way, the concept of race is still viewed according to the biological and physical as a source for distinguishing the identity of groups. As such, this understanding of race tends to negate the social, political, historical and economic factors, as race becomes a powerful cultural and social fact. This is due to people feeling that racial differences existing between groups are important. The terms, 'multi-racial' and 'multi-ethnic' society, by definition, imply differences between groups both in terms of *appearance* and *culture*. Indeed, 'ethnicity' focuses more on the cultural differences between groups such as kinship and language. This perhaps leads to some confusion, since being part of the same kinship group could be considered in a social scientific sense as a *natural* belonging, and in some ways, then, blurs the distinction between ethnicity and race. Despite this confusion it will become clear that ethnicity is more explicitly *cultural*.

What is 'ethnicity'?

Ethnicity is defined as "a shared racial, linguistic or national identity of a social group" (Jary and Jary, 1995: 206). Ethnicity unites people through particular kinship and shared cultural experiences and interests that identify the group, while also marking them as different from other groups. Arguably, the most important feature is that this concept focuses on the notion of a shared culture, so that ethnic groups are defined (equally important, *self defined*) on the basis of language, religion, customs, traditions, values, or nationality. The sociologist, Steve Fenton, (1999: 891) argues that:

> The term 'ethnic' has a much greater claim to analytical usefulness in sociology because it is not hampered by a history of connotations with discredited science and malevolent practices in the way the term 'race' is.

Ethnicity has become a popular area of investigation for sociologists, as debates about globalisation and multiculturalism have become increasingly prevalent in sociological discourse and theorising. For instance, social scientists have tracked the patterns of migration as people move about the globe to become new members and citizens of various nations. Although no precise figures exist, estimates of the amount of international immigrants have been put at between 80 million and 125 million (Castles and Miller 1993; Faist, 2000, cited in Kivisto, 2002). However, in his book, *Multiculturalism in a Global Society*, Kivisto (2002) argues that the vast majority of people choose not to leave their country of origin and refers to Thomas Faist's (2000, cited in Kivisto, 2002) claim that the migrant population forms approximately two per cent of the world's population. However, the migrant population tends to be concentrated in a comparatively small band of nations, and Kivisto (2002) indicates that countries such as Mexico and Turkey have experienced relatively large-scale emigration, while many poorer countries have experienced relatively small-scale emigration. The countries of Europe and North America have traditionally been the destination for these migrants, along with Australia and Middle East countries like Bahrain, Kuwait, and Saudi Arabia, which can also attract migrant labourers from poorer neighbouring countries and Asia (Kivisto, 2002).

Despite the debate over a distinction between race and ethnicity it is evident that discrimination can take place on two general grounds. First, through race in the form of 'biological racism', discrimination because of skin colour. Second, discrimination based on ethnicity, due to an intrinsic association with particular cultural beliefs and language.

It is clear that any notions of racial superiority and the subsequent racism that flows from such standpoints stand discredited. It is also evident, by contrast, that ethnicity has resulted in a celebration of culture. Although it is possible to suggest that whilst ethnicity tends to allow positive identities to be nurtured by smoothing out some of the harshness associated with race, there are still issues to consider. Indeed, when terms such as race and ethnicity become rigid in definition, both the biological and the cultural become 'racialised', and genetic imprinting becomes a feature of both concepts. Hence, viewing a group negatively is due to innate factors, which influence perceptions of that group.

The sociologist, Neil Smelser (1994), believes that there are various good reasons for separating race and ethnicity because of the uncertainty between the racial and the ethnic:

- First, negative biological attributes associated with race such as one group being ugly, dirty, stupid, and aggressive are enshrined in their culture and used as stereotypical, negative, reference points. This shift from biology to culture does little to diminish the social force of racism
- Second, stereotypes prove to be particularly resonant in their association with race. Smelser (1994) points to the United States and the example of blacks being stereotyped as hypersexual (oversexed). This persistence of stereotypes and the harbouring of prejudice as a consequence of this across all groups can result in simplistic frameworks for understanding reality. Certainly, the stereotype of blacks as hypersexual has been used to as a basis for lynching or jailing blacks in cases of rape or sexual harassment of white women
- Third, the racial mentality in defining groups often means that 'part-black' categories, i.e. 'mulatto' become legalised and provide examples where notions of race still override notions of ethnicity. The transformation of groups from racial to ethnic, Smelser (1994) feels, is possible although it is

easier if a group is regarded as ethnic to begin with and then assimilated through the vehicles of religion, language and lifestyles

- Fourth, race and ethnic identification can be intersected. Some ethnic groups can be tagged as belonging to the same 'race' although they are culturally different and recognised as such, e.g. Haitian and West Indian blacks are recognised as culturally different although from the same race

- Fifth, being a member of an ethnic group and considering status or social distance between grounds is important. Smelser (1994) uses the example of the social distance between a white Christian and a black Muslim is greater than black Christian and white Christian, due to the basis of distinctions being attributional in the form of a membership category

- Sixth, stereotyping groups as a shorthand device in the same category, i.e. black ignores national differences amongst groups and can be considered as an 'aggregative' form of racism. Hence, African, Afro-Caribbean, South Asian can find themselves being placed in the category of 'black' exemplifying the racial thinking which dismisses the differences among groups. In doing so, an understanding of notions of racism across groups remains obscured and is simplified

- Seventh, the realities of race remain in everyday life. The stereotyping of national and ethnic groups by immigration officials, for example, those who look 'Arabic' or 'Islamic', does little to remove race as a dimension with which to understand discrimination in everyday life

- Eighth, the power of race in conditioning responses both to, and by, groups differs according to how they are identified, i.e. in racial or ethnic terms. Hence, some groups may be more sensitive to suspected injustice in, for example, the context of an educational institution where some minorities may suspect discrimination by teaching or administrative staff.

Trigger

Discuss whether being discriminated against due to ethnicity is just as discriminatory as that of race. Do you feel that it is more acceptable to talk of *ethnicity* rather than *race*? Why?

Institutional Racism

Institutional racism can be defined as a particular form of racism that arises from the unintentional actions of members within an institution to disadvantage a group because of colour, culture and ethnic origin. Significantly, however, institutional racism can exist independently of overt, conscious or individual prejudice. Whilst institutional racism may present itself in many deliberate or avoidable forms, some accounts examine how the ramifications of policy making are sometimes unintended (see Box 6.1).

BOX 6.1 Institutional racism – The Stephen Lawrence Enquiry

The Stephen Lawrence Inquiry and subsequent Macpherson Report (1999) noted that despite the availability of valid evidence regarding the stabbing and death of Stephen Lawrence in April 1993 by a group of white youths in London, there was a failure to convict. Both the Inquiry and the Report illustrate how deeply ingrained the problem of institutional racism is in areas of London and the issues raised have relevance across Britain. The Macpherson Report 1999, defined institutional racism as:

"The collective failure of an organisation to provide an appropriate and professional service to people because of colour, culture or ethnic origin. It can be seen or detected in processes, attitudes and behaviour which amount to discrimination through unwitting prejudice, ignorance, thoughtlessness and racist stereotyping which disadvantages minority ethnic people."

The Report, therefore, suggested that the Metropolitan Police Force may have been racist in that they failed to properly investigate the case with the consequence that those allegedly responsible were released without charge. Whilst the report stops short of suggesting that all Metropolitan Police Officers can be labelled as racist, institutional practices at all levels in the force could well lead to the unconscious and, therefore, unintended consequence of institutional racism. A further problem may be the lack of police officers from ethnic minority communities, a situation replicated throughout the UK at the time of the Report (1999). At Strathclyde Police, 37 officers out of 7,159 came from an estimated ethnic population of around 21,000. The police forces of Grampian had two out of 1,240 and Central region also had two from 705, Fife had three officers out of 688, whilst Northern had one from 6,304. The Dumfries and Galloway force had no ethnic officers in its employment at the time.

(Source: Adapted from *The Sunday Herald*, 28 February 1999)

What the Macpherson Report (1999) did was to exemplify that perhaps many other institutions in the UK were culpable of practices that led to disadvantages for those from ethnic communities. Significantly, the Race Relations (Amendment) Act 2000 became a key part of the Labour government's implementation of the Stephen Lawrence Inquiry's recommendations, adding a new enforceable duty on public bodies to promote race equality with an onus on making procedures and practices fair.

Theoretical Approaches to Understanding Ethnic Stratification in Britain

Theoretical understandings of race and ethnicity make it possible to examine how minorities are stratified in terms of wealth and employment, education, culture and the machinations of the legal system. Theories of racial and ethnic stratification can be accommodated under four distinct headings: Marxist, Weberian, a hybrid of functionalist/pluralist and New Right (see Chapter 2: Sociological Theory).

Marxist theory – racism and capitalism

Marxists view capitalist relations of production as superseding any link between class and race (see Chapter 4: Sociological Theory). The driving force in creating social identity is the relationship of the individual or group to the means of production. This means that even within and across minority groups there can be divisions along class lines. Racist beliefs are considered by Marxists to be intrinsic to a capitalist social system. Marxist theories are particularly useful in an examination of capitalist exploitation and how the state promotes racism through policy making.

One of the earliest theories of racism was developed by Oliver Cox (1970), who thought that racism was directly related to capitalism and colonialism. He saw racism as being determined by the economic system and as a feature of ruling class domination. Whilst many Marxists have agreed with this early premise of Cox, some feel that the theory is perhaps simplistic in the context of the contemporary development of capitalism as the development of racism can be located in the rise of capitalist society through slavery, colonialism and imperial expansion. There are several strands of development in Marxist thought on racism.

Miles (1989) and Castles and Kosack (1973) depict migrant labour as part of a 'reserve army of labour'. For Miles (1989), racism is integral to capitalism, being a social construct that obscures economic relationships and fragments the working class. Indeed this notion of 'reserve army' cuts across ethnic gender and age categories, the key being the flexibility of such a cheap workforce able to serve the needs of capitalism in times when it is needed but having few employment rights and therefore easy to dispose of when this group has outlived its usefulness. This notion accords with the earlier work of Castles and Kosack (1973), who depict the reserve army of labour as supplementing the indigenous subject class. This theory differs from Weberian analysis (see Weberian Theory – a racial underclass, below) in that the Marxists do not see the reserve army as an underclass, but concentrate more on how the needs of capitalist economies serves to subjugate those such as ethnic minorities. Such groups are seen as part of the working class but are more likely to be among its poorest element. This, of course, raises the matter of cross-cutting dimensions of identity, i.e. gender, age, poverty, etc., although Marxists would envisage such factors as obscuring the raising of class-consciousness. Nevertheless, Miles (1982) believes that 'race' as a construct serves to divide and confuse the working class and in doing so becomes a construct that compounds stratification. Race, therefore, operates as a strategy for 'divide and rule'

Sivannadan (1982) presents race as a concept that obscures the realities of class and in doing so serves to divide the working classes. To adequately conceptualise race, it is necessary to move towards an understanding of institutionalised racism and to note that social and political policy is underpinned by the state. Therefore, post-war British immigration policy is fundamentally flawed due to its inherent institutionally racist nature.

Stuart Hall and his colleagues at the Centre for Contemporary Cultural Studies (CCCS) (1982), in *The Empire Strikes Back*, developed an approach from a neo-Marxist position that offers a contemporary insight into 'race' and 'ethnicity'. They note that there may be some limited use in conceptualising racism, and responses to it, as being separate from those of class. However, this is only of limited use because such independence is, in the final analysis, overshadowed by class/economic factors, which, are of greater significance to explaining race and racism. This theoretical strand of thought illustrates that a variety of historical, cultural and economic factors have combined to produce racism and it emphasises cultural differences as opposed to biological superiority as a way of exposing notions of what 'Britishness' is, and means, to sections of society.

Critique of Marxist understanding:

It is argued by some that the structural foundations of Marxist theories lead to a kind of determinism, which propels progress through a future characterised by revolution. Indeed, such determinism could be accused of ignoring the agency of 'social actors' who are instrumental in the construction of the social fabric of society. Perhaps more emphasis needs to be placed on the role of the individual actor in the social system.

There appears to be a tendency to underplay social impact of concepts of race and ethnicity due to an inherent emphasis on the primacy of economic factors, such as class. Neo-Marxists in some ways accept other historical and political and cultural factors as being important in an understanding of race and ethnicity, although ultimately they, too, stress that *economic* factors outweigh all else.

The claim as to the class location of ethnic groups is also subject to dispute. Not all members of minority ethnic groups are working class. Weberian theorists agree to some extent with Marxists that conflict may increase in capitalist societies, but place emphasis on factors other than class. By incorporating other elements such as 'status' into a theory of stratification, they show that it is possible to identify other forms of power within groups. This might illustrate that not everyone is disadvantaged by social class alone.

Weberian theory – a racial underclass

The basis of this approach is the claim that a black underclass develops due to discrimination and racism in wider society. The key concepts of Weber's theory of stratification (see Chapter 4: Social Class) are evident when analysing the position of various ethnic groups across the UK. To begin with, class is associated with market position. The black underclass have a distinct lack of upward social mobility, which tends to be illustrated by the inter-generational reproduction of this groups' occupational position. The labour market position of the black underclass has been exacerbated due to economic crisis and subsequent recession in various industries. Status is demonstrated as a consequence of social prestige, as the black underclass is located in a position that is very different from the white working class. Although undertaken over thirty years ago, Rex and Tomlinson's (1979) study of Handsworth, Birmingham, does much to illustrate the notion of a dual labour market and establish that the job situation of the black underclass is far less desirable and more insecure than that of whites. 'Dual labour markets' exist when there are two distinct possibilities for employment, one that is secure and consists of desirable jobs and the other being less desirable and insecure (see Chapter 10: Work and its Organisation).

The black underclass would therefore be considered as a group forming lower elements of the working class or more significantly below this group. According to the Registrar General's Classification System (RGCS) (see Chapter 4: Social Class), the black underclass would generally be located in Class 7 (either in a partially skilled or unskilled position, with job insecurity a feature of employment prospects) but more likely to be found in Class 8 (unemployed, unemployable and never worked). The position of this group would be envisaged as worse than that of the white working class as a direct consequence of racism. To a large extent, the asylum issue in the UK could provide rich fertile ground for research and contribute to the underclass debate.

The main assumptions of the black underclass theory centres on racism as the main cause, and finds its origins in the 1970s through the work of its key proponent, John Rex, who suggests that there are differences between and within black groups in terms of mobility and position. Rex determines the structural nature of conflict being the fight over resources and the conditions under which occupational segregation takes place. The divisions in the context of black groups are primarily evidenced by separation from white class stratification. Therefore, Weber's notion of status is centred on a distinction based on 'race'. The later study of Handsworth by Rex and Tomlinson (1979), demonstrates that the marginal position of the black underclass resulted in the development of their own self-help groups as a tool for political action to raise the profile of racism.

Critique of Weberian understanding:

The multi-dimensional nature of Weberian stratification theory leads towards an emphasis on the notion of status as being more important than class. This tends to obscure the real issues of economic exploitation in the sense that the black underclass is separate from the rest of the working class. Marxists would see this as dividing the working class with the underclass merely forming part of the working class; albeit the poorest section. Therefore, it is questionable that race be seen as a real category of analysis in the same way that class is. Indeed viewing race as a separate category (Rex and Tomlinson, 1979) may leads to notions of separatism.

The problem of treating a black underclass as a separate group in their own right, overlooks the fact that many members of other ethnic groups (including white) are also severely economically disadvantaged. The problems of using the term 'underclass' are explored further in the social class and the poverty chapters.

The tendency to concentrate on discrimination against black workers results in viewing them as a group out with the working class when in fact they may be objectively defined as such. Whilst discrimination is part of their lives, so is being working class. This is seen as more important by Marxists because of the economic position black workers find themselves in.

There may be an over-emphasis on individual social actions; albeit in the context of material constraints. The structural or 'conflict' aspects of Weberian theory do reflect structural realities, but there is a tendency to relate racism to individual perceptions and in doing so privileging the social action approach. It would also suggest that racism could be eradicated through understanding the interests of individuals and groups in society. Empirical evidence would point to the existence of a significant degree of institutional racism, which cannot easily be wished away.

Functionalist/pluralist theory – 'host-immigrant'

This almost hybrid approach to understanding ethnic stratification assumes at the outset that it *is* possible to achieve a value consensus in wider society regardless of cultural variations between ethnic groupings within societies. Ethnic groupings need become *assimilated* into mainstream or dominant culture. It is a case, therefore, of *absorption* rather than *division*.

A key assumption behind this approach is that although societies undergo a period of *adaptation* with an influx of immigrant groups, they *naturally* re-stabilise as these groups are absorbed. Immigrant groups become like their hosts and in doing so can participate in the benefits of the host society, such as upward social mobility. This may not occur immediately, but is often experienced by second and third generations as they become more assimilated into the host culture.

The 'host-immigrant framework' is most clearly demonstrated in an early study by Sheila Patterson (1965), *Dark Strangers*, which was conducted in the 1950s amongst first generation Afro-Caribbean immigrants in Brixton, London. Patterson (1965) assumed that the immigrants would have more of an onus placed on them to adapt to British society involving, for them, considerable changes in lifestyle. Patterson (1965) likens this to a reconciliation and realignment of values. She outlined *three* stages of adaptation: first, *accommodation* in relation to lifestyle across employment, housing and social and family mores. Second, *integration* would eventually take place in economic and civil life. Finally, *assimilation* would lead to complete adaptation by the immigrants and acceptance by the hosts as full citizens. O'Donnell (1991) notes that pluralists also emphasise the need for a strong system of multi-cultural education and more liberal elements of this theory believe that it is necessary for state intervention in the form of anti-discrimination laws.

Critique of functionalist/pluralist understanding:

- Patterson's (1965) host-immigrant framework assumes that the gradual move towards assimilation is inevitable. It indirectly assumes that immigrant groups would want to give up their own cultural identity in favour of 'Britishness'. Such thinking denies choice to retain culture traits, which may be fundamental to personal and collective identity. There is an overwhelming tendency in the theory to underplay both racism and conflict in favour of a model that assumes an already existing consensus
- The Weberian notion of underclass is uncritically accepted by supporters of a liberal/pluralist position, when they assume that racism is an obstacle to integration (O'Donnell, 1991)
- Marxists, such as Castles and Kosack (1973), would advocate that the capitalist international system of domination and exploitation more adequately explains migration and claim that the host immigrant model is too simplistic. Tracing cultural differences that can be overcome as immigrants adapt to the hosts way of life is often embedded within a racist ideology of superiority.

New Right theories
Such theories tend to concentrate on more fixed cultural differences between groups rather than some of the older debates centred on notions of biological superiority. They tend to link 'race' with concepts surrounding nationalism and common identity and prefer to avoid tackling the real meanings behind using 'race' as a term, preferring instead to retain notions of poor 'cultural fit' for some groups, due to a lack of a clearly 'British identity'. Racism, according to this perspective, is reinforced institutionally through, for example, immigration legislation and particularly in its application to refugees and asylum seekers.

The notion of *culture* as a by word for racism is encapsulated in the concept of a 'black underclass' by Charles Murray who has had long associations with the New Right having been an adviser to the Reagan administration in the United States. Charles Murray (1984), in his book, *Losing Ground: American Social Policy (1950-80)*, explains the underclass in terms of a group with particular cultural deficiencies. Such cultural traits include a lack of moral responsibility. These overtones are manifested due to an increase in black single parents and the withdrawal of blacks from the labour market, compounded by an unwillingness to work. For Murray, such scenarios are not about a lack of opportunities but more significantly a dependence on welfare benefits. Murray's (1984) views and predictions of a dangerous class developing in America's inner-cities have been adapted and accumulated popularity with regard to welfare spending by successive American and British administrations.

More recently, Murray (1984) has sparked further controversy by claiming a racial basis to intelligence. In *The Bell Curve: Intelligence and Class Structure in American Life* (Murray), he (with Herrnstein, 1994) claims that inequality is rooted in natural and fixed differences in inherited intelligence. *The Bell Curve* presents an alleged correlation between Intelligence Quotient (IQ) test results, income and race and is used by Murray and Herrnstein (1994) to claim that the failure of American blacks to close the income gap is not due to discrimination but to having lower than average intelligence, as measured by IQ tests. Despite having lower IQs, they claim, black individuals actually have a better chance of obtaining a degree and securing 'high IQ occupations' than whites when IQ is held as constant. Such adjustment to take into account lower tested IQ is considered by Heartfield (1994: 26) as a device for Murray to support the position that "the real discrimination is in favour of blacks, through affirmative action."

Critique of New Right understanding:

- The emphasis on capitalist free enterprise becomes almost hegemonic in such approaches, but it may be possible to use the notion of cultural incompatibility to the capitalist system as a tool to explain the failure in the marketplace of some groups
- The definition of underclass lacks the explanatory potential provided by the Weberian structural multi-dimensional model. Therefore, the group labelled as a 'black underclass' would in a sense be subject to multiple deprivations; only some being as a consequence of racism
- Marxists refute the use of the term 'underclass' in any form preferring the notion of 'lumpenproletariat' (see Chapter 4: Social Class). They might also point out that usage of the term ignores the fact that race is often used as a tool to obscure the real nature of economic exploitation

- Whilst conflict theorists have differing views about the notion of a developed underclass they tend to view structural factors as being at the heart of inequality. They disagree with those on the New Right, who blame the welfare system as a consequence of lenient social policies and the cultural traits of welfare claimants

- Heartfield (1994), in a critique of Murray and Herrnstein's work, argues that those who focus on research such as *The Bell Curve*, do so in an attempt to justify the status quo in the face of a failing free market economy with its concomitant affect on blacks, the poor and the privileged

- The work of Murray and Herrnstein (1994) linking IQ, income and race is imbued with the notion of failing cultural traits that are a consequence of inheritance. This is a return to biological racism and the idea of white superiority. The 'scapegoating' of particular groups by the privileged (who have social power in society), therefore, fails to acknowledge the economic failure of the system.

Theoretical understandings and debates on race and ethnicity then, help us to unravel issues surrounding the usage of the terms and contribute an understanding of the material impact of racism and ethnic differentiation. In order to interpret the application of theoretical understandings to Scotland, it would be pertinent to appreciate more fully issues of race and ethnicity in Scottish history.

A Brief History of Immigration to Scotland

The history of immigration to Scotland shows a historically multicultural and ethnically diverse nation. The writers of the 'Declaration of Arbroath (1320)' were in no way confused about the origins of the Scottish people:

> This nation having come from Scythia the greater, through the Tuscan Sea and the Hercules pillars, and having for many ages taken its residence in Spain in the midst of a most fierce people, and can never be brought into subjection by any people, how barbarous soever."   (Cited in Harvie, 2002: 11)

Moreover, that great symbol of the Scottish nation, the 'Stone of Scone', had, according to a Norman-French ballad of 1307, been taken from Egypt by the Gaelic King Gadelaus and Scota the daughter of Pharaoh to be set down in Scone (Harvie, 2002: 48-49). Though we are partly dealing with myth here, it is interesting to think that Scotland gets its name from a black Middle Eastern woman, Scota, the daughter of Pharaoh and perhaps, even, the mother of Scotland.

From the sixteenth century, Scotland's history shows that the nation's role with regards to migration has been primarily one of being a 'donor' for other nations (Ascherson, 2002:66). Scotland experienced waves of emigration to nations as far away and diverse as Poland and the Baltic countries, Canada, United States,

Australia, New Zealand, South Africa, and of course England. Writers such as Ascherson (2002), are quick to remind us that emigration from Scotland has been interpreted in a positive light when it represented Scottish enterprise, invention and drive, but also more depressingly as the result of dispossession, as in the Highland Clearances of the late eighteenth and nineteenth centuries (Ascherson, 2002: 67). The clearances resulted in people from throughout Scotland being forced from the land, but nowhere were this more noticeably apparent than in the Gaelic speaking North West of Scotland. Here, landowners and clan chiefs effectively made refugees of many Highland Scots and administered the clearances. Added to this is the fact that Gaelic culture and tradition was virtually outlawed by Westminster government following the 1745 Jacobite Rebellion. It is for this reason that the highland clearances are often viewed as one of Europe's earliest examples of ethnic cleansing.

The Scotland of the early centuries prior to the middle ages was, according to the historian Tom Devine (1999), on the whole a heterogeneous society made up of a mix of different ethnic groups such as Gaels, Picts, Scandinavians, Britons and Angles. Scotland was essentially a multi-ethnic country. By the nineteenth century, Scotland had developed a more clear and consistent national identity and culture, and with that an increasing suspicion of immigrants and cultures that Scots perceived as different. People from many different cultures arrived in Scotland during the nineteenth and twentieth centuries; most significant were the Irish, Italian, Lithuanian, Polish, Jewish, Asian, and English migrants (Devine, 1999: 486). There is a commonly held perception that Scotland has tended to be less prejudiced and racist towards newcomers than its neighbours south of the border. However, the arrival over the centuries of different ethnic groups to Scottish daily life has tested the self-image of Scots as tolerant and welcoming to strangers, offering hospitality and an inclusive community. However, as we might expect with commonly held perceptions, the reality is often a different matter.

The Lithuanian migrants who came to work in the coalfields of Lanarkshire between 1870 and 1914 experienced a great deal of hostility on arrival, mainly because the locals considered them as cheap labour that would keep miners wages down. Similarly the Italians who opened the cafes and fish-and-chip shops in many small towns in Scotland faced anti-Italian riots as Scots anger towards Mussolini's Fascist axis with Hitler spilled onto the streets of towns and cities (Ascherson, 2002: 67). The recent increase in asylum seekers and refugees coming to Scotland at the end of the twentieth century also provides us with an example of conflict due to perceived prejudices within Scottish society. Arguably though, the ethnic group to have had the biggest impact on Scottish society is the Irish (see Box 6.2, below).

Trigger

How can Weber's theoretical concepts of 'Class, Status, and Party' help to explain the position of the Scottish Catholic community in the nineteenth and twentieth centuries?

Box 6.2 Irish in Scotland: 1850-1920s

The mass emigration from Ireland that took place in the nineteenth century saw only 8 per cent of that total arrive in Scotland (Devine, 1999). However, the Catholic Irish represent the main migrant group to arrive in Scotland in modern times. By the middle of the nineteenth century Irish immigrants numbered 250,000 and the flow of immigration did not begin to tail off until the 1920s. Friedrich Engel's had, in 1843, commented on the crucial role Irish immigrants had made to the British industrial revolution, but as the Scots historian, Tom Devine, points out, their role was even more significant in Scotland when it is noted that compared to England and Wales, where the population of Irish born accounted for only 2.9 per cent of the population in 1851, the figure was 7.2 per cent of the population in Scotland (Devine, 1999).

The Irish immigrant population was concentrated in particular parts of the country, namely in and around Glasgow, Dundee, and the mining areas of Lothian and Ayrshire. Like the Lithuanians, the Irish were often accused by the Scottish workers of being cheap labour and as a threat to Scottish working class trade union solidarity. However, the Irish continued to do many of the semi and unskilled manual jobs Scots found unattractive but were in fact crucial to Scotland's economic and industrial development. Devine (1999) provides an excellent account of the complexity of the Irish experience in Scotland, he points to the fact that most Irish immigrants were from Ulster, the area of Ireland least affected by the blight of the Great Famine. Though there were many thousands of impoverished refugees arriving from the Irish province, the most destitute refugees from Southern and Western Ireland were to be found going to England through Liverpool (Devine, 1999).

More significantly, Devine points out that between a quarter to a fifth of the Irish immigration to Scotland was not Catholic, but Ulster Protestant. These descendents of the seventeenth century Scots Presbyterian's, who migrated to Ulster, had a cultural and religious heritage that helped them integrate and assimilate to Scottish society better than the Catholic Irish. Devine writes: "The regional origin of the migrant streams was deeply significant because it meant that the tribal hatreds of Ulster were transformed to the industrial districts of Scotland and faction fighting between Orange and Green sympathizers became a routine feature of life in several communities in Lanarkshire and Ayrshire in the nineteenth century" (Devine, 1999: 487).

Writers, such as Ascherson (2002), have argued that as time passed the everyday discrimination and hostility toward Irish Catholics, particularly in the West of Scotland, became institutionalised in the sphere of employment. As a response to this, the Catholic community retreated into a cultural enclave of Catholic parish care, the segregated Catholic schools that continue within the present state education system, and Catholic football teams. Moreover, the Labour Party can claim to have its roots in many of the socially excluded Catholic areas of Greater Glasgow in the early twentieth century (Ascherson, 2002).

(Source: Adapted from Devine, T. (1999) The Scottish Nation 1700-2000, London: Penguin; and Ascherson, N. (2002) *Stone Voice: The search for Scotland*, London: Granta)

One answer to the above 'Trigger' question may be that Max Weber's theory of stratification is multi-dimensional, in that it accommodates various attributes in an understating of divisions in society. Weber, therefore, sees 'class' as being tied to market position, whilst 'status' refers to prestige or the social position that is attributed to a group to which individual may belong. 'Party' refers to the political power that results from the bringing together of people with common goals. This can be facilitated by membership of a political party or voluntary organisation. Given Weber's view of how society is stratified now consider this above question using this framework and also think about how we can examine the position of asylum seekers in Scottish society.

United Kingdom Immigration, 1950s-2002
To perhaps understand contemporary Scotland in the context of the UK, it is necessary to understand that Scotland played a major role in the development of the British Empire, with Glasgow commonly known as the 'Second City of the Empire' behind London. Indeed, it is with this in mind that we can explore the nature of more recent immigration to Britain.

The 1950s are often viewed as a 'Golden Era' in British history, with full employment and record low levels of unemployment. This was complemented by rising incomes and living standards, supported by better health and education through the formation of the NHS in 1948 and the Educations Acts of 1944 (England), 1945 and 1947 (Scotland).

This period of apparent prosperity and economic change attracted new immigrants from Britain's former colonies in Africa, the Caribbean, and the Indian subcontinent, to fill the multitude of unskilled and low-paid jobs that were surfacing in large-scale manufacturing and the expanding service sector. According to Devine (1999), the response from Indian, Pakistani, and Bangladeshi immigrants in Scotland was to seek employment in the jute mills, building sites, bakeries, and with the transport departments. By 1960, there were 4000 Asians in Scotland, and by the time Chinese immigrants from Hong Kong arrived in 1970, the Asian population had reached 16,000 (Devine, 1999). The British Nationality Act of 1948 allowed citizens of Commonwealth status the right to freely stay and work with their families in the UK. The demand for labour saw the government and employers (such as London Transport) openly encourage the recruitment of Commonwealth migrants throughout the 1950s. Commonwealth migrants became concentrated in those areas that required labour, the main ones being Greater London for service and transport employment, the West Midlands for manufacturing industries and the North West of England for textiles (Mason, 1995).

For the remainder of the twentieth century, various governments have implemented a number of immigration policies (see Box 6.3, below) to manage the flow of immigrants from the Commonwealth countries. However, some writers have argued that immigration legislation has pandered to racist assumptions that views black, or immigrants of colour as a problem. For instance, Solomos (1993) states that the Immigration Act 1971 essentially put an end to the right of black Commonwealth immigrants to settle and live in the UK, and that this "represented an important step in the institutionalisation of racist immigration controls" (Solomos, 1993: 70).

Immigration legislation since 1948 has been overwhelmingly negative in that it uses measures that consistently restrict entry into the United Kingdom. This provides us with an insight into the structurally racist features apparent in the legislation (see Box 6.3).

Trigger

Search the Internet for information on each of the pieces of legislation indicated in Box 6.3, below.

1. To what extent do these measures ensure that the UK becomes a more inclusive society?
2. To what extent are the measures structurally racist in orientation and implementation?

Box 6.3 UK Immigration and Anti-racism/Discrimination Legislation Post-1948

UK Immigration legislation since 1948
- British Nationality Act 1948
- Commonwealth Immigrants Act 1962
- Commonwealth Immigrants Act 1968
- Immigration Act 1971
- British Nationality Act 1981
- Immigration Act 1988
- Asylum and Immigration Act 1993
- Asylum and Immigration Act 1995

Anti-racism/discrimination legislation:
- Race Relations Act 1965
- Race Relations Act 1968
- Race Relations Act 1976
- Race Relations (Amendment) Act 2002

Race, Ethnicity and Differentiation

Whilst immigration has always been a feature of British/Scottish society, it is the scale and consequence of post-war immigration (and its problematic political identification) that has been different due to it being much larger and more visible. Different communities have grown leading to an increasing internal diversity in culture, although the main concentrations of ethnic groups have tended to be in particular cities in England. Such diversity has also led to significantly different economic experiences between different groups with the notion of 'black' often used as a category to distinguish certain ethnic groups from the European majority. This internal diversity has also been connected to specific inequality around power and opportunity, which has resulted in differences that are marked by exclusion and racism in areas due to inferior life chances combined with the systematic nature of inequality.

Therefore, it is useful when looking at a continually changing British/Scottish society to consider race and ethnicity in the context of inequality, because such an analytic device through the vehicles of wealth and power enables the critic to establish the multi-dimensional facets of inequality.

The most significant outcomes from post war immigration are that immigrants tended to stay in the worst housing, been employed in the lowest paid jobs and were increasingly becoming identified as scapegoats for many of the social problems of the day (Pilkington, 2003). The picture today shows that the socio-economic position of some ethnic groups is improving. However, many from ethnic minorities still experience a range of social inequalities (see Table 6.1, below). One significant area of inequality is income, which of course, has a direct bearing on the living standards and quality of life people experience, education; health and life chances generally can all be dependent on household incomes.

Table 6.1 Households Below Average Income (percentages)							
Income	White	Caribbean	Indian	African/Asian	Pakistani	Bangladeshi	Chinese
Below half average	28	41	45	39	82	84	34
Between half and one and a half times average	49	47	43	46	17	15	44
Above one and a half times average	23	12	12	15	1	2	22

(Source: Adapted from Berthoud, R. (1997) 'Income and standards of living', in Modood, T. *et al* (ed.) *Ethnic Minorities in Britain: Diversity and Disadvantage*, London: Policy Studies Institute, p.160)

It is clear from Table 6.1 that the ethnic groups experiencing the lowest average incomes come from the Pakistani and Bangladeshi communities. Richard Berthoud (1997) has analysed the then Department of Social Security's Family Resources Survey (FRS), and discovered that even if adults in a family are working, Pakistani and Bangladeshi households are more likely to be experiencing poverty than white, non-pensioner households where no one has a paid job. These two ethnic groups also record high unemployment among men and low levels of economic activity among women, which would invariably contribute to poverty. Overall, the poverty rate in Pakistani and Bangladeshi communities is four times the rate found in the white population (Joseph Rowntree Foundation, *Findings*, November 1998 – Ref. N48).

In terms of health, the death rates from coronary heart disease (CHD) for males from the Indian sub-continent are 36 per cent higher than the average for the UK population; the figure for women is 46 per cent higher, whilst the lowest rates were among African-Caribbeans (Balarajan and Bulusu, 1990). When we look at mental illness we find that the admission rates are highest in the African-Caribbean population and there is a much greater chance of schizophrenia being diagnosed (Skellington, 1996: 113-121). It appears that the minority ethnic population experiences the same illnesses as the white working class because of similar employment and unemployment indicators but with higher rates of illness.

Employment is an important indicator of position in society and is a central feature in both the Marxist and Weberian schemas of analysis. For Marxists the relationship to the means of production is the crucial factor, although for Weber it is a more multi-dimensional scenario, whereby market position, status and party are all elements that contribute and can feature in notions of occupation. Indeed, employment becomes a significant factor in the monitoring of social and economic success and disadvantages that incorporates other indicators alongside ethnicity such as class and gender. Other prominent factors include age and disability.

Many ethnic groupings across Britain tend to be disproportionately featured in patterns that reveal disadvantage in relation to occupational groupings, the pay they receive discrimination in both the attempts to obtain employment and whilst in a job combined with higher levels of unemployment. However, a more recent study of ethnic minorities in *Britain, Ethnic Minorities in Britain: Diversity and Disadvantage* (Modood *et al*, 1997), illustrates that the picture for ethnic groupings is complex in relation to the labour market. Whilst those of African, Asian and Chinese descent are virtually on a par with indigenous earnings and unemployment, others from for example Bangladeshi backgrounds are more likely to feature in unemployment statistics and less likely to occupy professional jobs.

A Cabinet Office report commissioned by the Labour government of Tony Blair and implemented by the Performance and Innovation Unit, demonstrates the heterogeneous nature of ethnic groupings but also that "the odds of being unemployed do vary with religion" (*The Guardian*, 2002). Even after considering factors such as education and residential area, the study found that Pakistani Muslims are three times more likely to be jobless than Hindus. Also, Indian Muslims are twice as likely to suffer unemployment as Indian Hindus. Anthony Heath (1992), the Oxford sociologist, submitted papers as part of the aforementioned study describing 'a continuing story of disadvantage', whereby educational qualifications gained by ethnic minorities should, but often do not, lead to better jobs. It is also evident that there are differences on gender and class lines, most clearly identified with the fact that Caribbean women are more 'professionalised' than white women, although Caribbean men remain somewhat marginalized, with them earning £115 a week less than their white counterparts. The study also noted that racist attitudes are a feature of UK life although more likely to be 'concentrated in the north and among older, poorer and less educated white people – 'Old' Labour's constituency'.

In the field of education, various statistics show that there appear to be barriers to career progression for ethnic minority staff. Statistics gained from the Higher Education Statistics Agency and presented by the Association of University Teachers (*Education Guardian*, 21 February 2003), illustrated the position of ethnic minority academics. Out of 11,000 university professors in 1999/2000 academic year there were only 29 black academics and 179 Asian academics showing that despite a population of 6.5 per cent professors classified as non-white, ethnic minorities have a representation of less than two per cent. Such scenarios indicate that institutional racism in the academic workplace is a feature of working life for many amongst the ethnic minorities of Britain and that social divisions such as race, class and gender inter-relate.

The Asylum Issue

From the 1990s, the focus of legislation has been primarily on the British government's response and obligation to refugees and asylum seekers, many of who are coming from parts of the world experiencing ethnic conflict, such as the Balkans. Over the last few years, the plight of refugee and asylum seekers has become a fiercely debated issue for the British press. In particular, the tabloid press has tended to use 'asylum' in coded terms and have created a perception in the public eye that Britain is being 'swamped' by 'an invasion' of 'beggars', 'criminals', and 'bogus' refugees wishing to access the UK benefits system. Some have suggested that 'asylum' has become synonymous as a code word in the media for 'race', which in effect means that the asylum issue can be used as "'a respectable vehicle' for the expression of otherwise socially and politically unacceptable racist sentiments" (Diboll, 2000: 9).

Banner headlines have tended to focus attention on the 'asylum issue' illustrating the increased numbers of those seeking asylum. *The Daily Record* (1 March 2003) carried the headline 'Asylum Figures Record', detailing that the amount of asylum seekers had increased by a fifth and that in 2002, 110,000 people had asked to live in the UK. Politicians assisted the nurturing of a moral panic (see Chapter 11: Crime and Deviance) amongst the British public, with rises in the numbers seeking asylum being described by Home Secretary David Blunkett as 'bad news' because Prime Minister Tony Blair had sought to halve the number of asylum seekers in seven months. Figures for Scotland reported that 'refugees rose from 4,990 to 6,000'.

In response to the negative press on asylum seekers the Refugee Council and other groups in the context of Scotland (e.g. Scottish Asylum Seekers Consortium (SASC)) has set about dispelling many of the myths about refugees by trying to establish facts behind the arrival of asylum seekers and refugees (see Useful Websites). For example, the immense vulnerability of asylum seekers is requires to be stressed, as many of those arriving in Scotland are families with children fleeing violence and persecution in their own country. Central government meets the costs of care; hence local services do not suffer additional burdens. Limited numbers are posted to each of the locations and length of stay is limited while the Home Office looks at each case for asylum. The point such organisations also try to establish is that refugees are nothing new and have be coming to the UK for centuries, often making significant contributions to British society.

Legislation has had an affect on the living conditions of such people, an example being that asylum seekers are not permitted to access mainstream welfare benefits; instead they must apply to the National Asylum Support service (NASS), which is the government body responsible for helping asylum seekers. Those asylum seekers possessing skills and qualifications that may be beneficial to the economy cannot take up employment until after six months. Given such cases, a single adult will have to get by on the £37.77 a week provided by NASS, an amount that puts them firmly below the accepted poverty line in Britain.

The many inaccuracies and particularly racist language used by the British media has led to the Council of Europe proclaiming that the UK is the most racist country in Europe with regards to refugees (*The Guardian*, 3 April 2001). The negative media portrayals and amplification of a 'moral panic' (Cohen, 1980) have coincided with increased tension between local populations and asylum seekers, resulting in many incidents of racial harassment and physical violence.

Racially motivated violence
Familiar tales in the press depict the plight of refuges and asylum seekers. The headline 'Scotland Plagued by Racial Violence' (Linsay McGarvie, Political Editor, *Sunday Mail*, 20 February 2002), refers to the fact that racist violence and harassment is still a major problem in Scotland. Racial abuse made up half of the complaints made to ethnic minority advice groups such as Positive Action in Housing. Complaints ranged from 'name calling and stone-throwing to physical attacks'. Such racial conflict is encapsulated in the headline, 'Asylum seeker in hospital after Glasgow stabbing' (Hugo Macleod, *Scotland on Sunday*, 1 December 2002), where an asylum seeker (Masood Gomricki, a 32 year-old Iranian) was attacked and stabbed by a gang of white youths. The attack happened in Sighthill, Glasgow, where many of Scotland's asylum seekers are housed. This followed in the wake of the death in 2001 of a 25 year-old Kurdish asylum seeker, Firsat Yildiz (known also as Firsat Dag), who was stabbed to death in Sighthill Park while walking home from the city centre with a friend. The death of Firsat Dag provoked outrage in the local and ethnic communities of Glasgow, leading to a solidarity march in the city three weeks after the tragic event. Hundreds of residents from Sighthill, including locals, asylum seekers and politicians marched on Glasgow's George Square to demand better police protection for refugees, better education and information on the asylum issue,

but also to highlight the extent of poverty and deprivation in housing schemes such as Sighthill.

Such cases prompted severe criticism of the way that asylum seekers were being dispersed in high concentrations to postcodes in deprived urban areas, such as Sighthill and subjected to stigmatisation, abuse and attacks. Sighthill is one of Glasgow's many housing 'schemes' experiencing a number of the problems associated with social deprivation and poverty (see Chapter 8: Poverty). As with many other deprived areas of the UK, it has attracted media attention over asylum issues. Significantly, "today it bears a set of unenviable tags: poorest constituency in Scotland; second most unhealthy in Britain; highest male unemployment level in Scotland; lung cancer rate twice the national average" (*The Guardian*, 9 August 2001). Those in work tend to be in low skilled, low paid jobs, while a great number, especially young people, are unemployed and on benefits. As part of the Home Office dispersal programme, Glasgow City Council was asked to house 8,000 asylum seekers and many were moved from the south of England to the vacant flats in Sighthill. The media generated stories of how generous benefits being handed out to refugees had acted as a catalyst for trouble between the local population and the refugees, with at least 70 racist attacks being reported during 2000-2001 (*The Guardian*, 7 July 2001).

Conclusion

This chapter has introduced some of the important issues involved in the study of race and ethnicity, issues that are imbued with complexity. Race and ethnicity can be examined as concepts in their own right, although it is necessary to be aware of the multi-dimensional nature of inequality and disadvantages due to the cross cutting effects of 'race', gender, class and disability.

Certainly, by understanding some of the theories that emphasise the structural impacts of inequality, the sociologist is better equipped to examine issues of power in relation to societal position. This is not to underplay the importance of agency or action, but allows an understanding of how cultural and economic structures can determine the position of groups and individuals in society, hence providing a framework to understand the constraints placed on the individual. The emphasis suggests that the problems of race and ethnicity cannot be overcome by an encouragement of toleration (of different cultures), but is more deeply engrained in the infrastructure and institutions of a society. To understand inequality from this position is to gain a more profound understanding race and ethnicity. The aim of the Scottish Executive to attract immigrant workers in an attempt to reverse a falling population must be accompanied with anti-racist and anti-discriminatory policy and practice if Scotland is to become a *truly* more inclusive society.

Chapter Summary

- Defining race on the basis of biology has been used as a powerful tool of domination as it can justify social position and naturalise inequalities.
- Sociologists consider race to be a 'social and cultural construction'.
- Ethnicity focuses on shared culture as a way of distinguishing groups with language, religion, customs, traditions, values or nationality being defining characteristics.
- Institutional racism has various forms from being deliberate, as a consequence of state policy making, with the effects of policymaking sometimes being unintended.
- Theoretical approaches enable us to work within frameworks and include: Marxist ('reserve army of labour'), which sees capitalism as the driving force linking class and race; Weberian ('underclass') where a black underclass develops with the main cause being racism; functionalist/pluralist ('host-immigrant') belief that a consensus is possible with assimilation of ethnic groups into mainstream society; New Right theories focus on 'fixed cultural differences'.
- Scottish immigration is marked by a historically multicultural and ethnically diverse nation.
- Despite a cultural diversity, British immigration and race relation's policy making is structurally racist in its orientation and implementation portraying ethnic groups as a problem to be legislated for.
- Britain has been transformed by the presence and fusion of different ethnic groups.
- Ethnic groups across Britain tend to be disproportionately featured in patterns that reveal disadvantages. However, patterns of inequality are complex and ethnic groups are not homogeneous some groups fair better than others.
- The recent focus for British legislation has tended to be as a response and obligation to asylum seekers displaced by conflicts around the world.
- Negative press reporting has often fuelled many incidents of conflict on a community level and pressure groups like the Scottish Asylum Seekers Consortium try to dispel the common myths that are socially constructed as part of a stereotypical common sense view of asylum seekers often amplified by large sections of the media.

Further Reading

Kirby, M. (1999) *Stratification and Differentiation*, Basingstoke: Palgrave
Pilkington, A. (2003) *Racial Disadvantage and Ethnic Diversity in Britain*, Basingstoke: Palgrave
Skellington, R. (1996) *Race in Britain Today*, London: Sage

Useful Websites

The following are examples of links that can be found at the Channel Four History site:
http://www.channel4.com/history/microsites/B/blackhistorymap/index.html
http://www.historytoday.com/index.cfm?Articleid=11007
A Scottish Executive Central research unit site on researching ethnic minorities in Scotland:
http://www.scotland.gov.uk/cru/kd01/red/ethnic-00.htm

A Joseph Rowntree Foundation 'Findings' site focusing on the incomes of ethnic minorities:
http://www.jrf.org.uk/knowledge/findings/socialpolicy/sprN48.asp
An excellent site on the 'Asylum Issue':
http://www.scottishrefugeecouncil.org.uk/Documents/Facts.PDF
A series of myths surrounding asylum seekers are dispelled by the Scottish Asylum Seekers Consortium
(2003) at: http://www.asylumscotland.org.uk/mythsfacts.html
Social Science Information Gateway links site to for articles on the sociology of race and ethnicity:
http://www.sosig.ac.uk/roads/subject-listing/UK-cat/socrace.html

Bibliography

Anthias, F. and Yuval-Davies, N. (1993) *Racialised Boundaries*, London: Routledge

Ascherson, N. (2002) *Stone Voice: The search for Scotland*, London: Granta

Asylum Briefing (2001) *New era for race relations dawns in Glasgow*, Autumn (accessed at: http://www.asylumscotland.org.uk/briefing02/cases.html)

Balarajan, R. and Bulusu, L. (1990) 'Mortality among immigrants in England and Wales, 1979-83', in Britton, M. (ed.) *Mortality and Geography. A Review in the mid-1980s, England and Wales*, Decennial Supplement, London: HMSO

Black, I. (2001) 'UK 'most racist' in Europe on refugees', *The Guardian*, 3 April (accessed at: http://www.society.guardian.co.uk/asylumseekers/story/0,7991,467684,00.html)

Bright, M. (2003) 'Welcome to Immigration Central. Please join the queue: your number is 110,001 . . ', *The Observer*, 2 March (accessed at: http://www.observer.co.uk/focus/story/0,6903,905708,00.html)

Britton, M. (ed.) (1990) *Mortality and Geography: A Review in the mid-1980s, England and Wales*, Decennial Supplement, London: HMSO

Bulmer, M. and Solomos, J. (ed.) *Ethnic and Racial Studies Today*, London: Routledge

Cox, O.C. (1970) *Caste, Class and Race*, New York, NY: Monthly Review Press

Castles, S. and Kosack, G.C. (1973) *Immigrant Workers and Class Structure in Western Europe*, Oxford: Oxford University Press

Carvel, J. (2001) 'Minority groups grow by 15 per cent', *The Guardian*, 21 September (accessed at: http://www.guardian.co.uk/racism/Story/0,2763,555360,00.html)

Daily Record, The (2003) 'Push for Asylum Seekers to Join Scot Life', 20 February (accessed at: http://www.dailyrecord.co.uk/news/newspage.cfm?objectid=12657823&method=full&siteid=89488)

Diboll, M. and Heffernan, E. (2000) 'Labour's racism: the last straw', *Socialist Review*, June

Devine, T. (1999) *The Scottish Nation, 1700-2000*, London: Penguin

Donnelly, B. (2003) 'Immigration is McConnell's solution to population fall', *The Herald*, 26 February (accessed at: http://www.theherald.co.uk/news/archive/26-2-19103-0-29-42.html)

Elliott Major, L. (2002) '2 per cent of UK professors from ethnic minorities', *Education Guardian*, 21 January (accessed at: http://www.guardian.co.uk/racism/Story/0,2763,636906,00.html)

Fenton, S. (1999) *Ethnicity: Racism, Class and Culture*, Basingstoke: Macmillan

Flockhart, S. (1999) 'Young, Black...and Angry', *The Sunday Herald*, 26 February

Goldblatt, D. and Woodward, K. (2001) *Mid Course Review* (DD100: An Introduction to the Social Sciences: Understanding Social Change), Milton Keynes: Open University

Gould, S.J. (1993) *The Mismeasure of Man*, New York: Norton

Hall, S. *et al* (1982) *The Empire Strikes Back*, London: Hutchinson

Haralambos, M., Holborn, M. and Heald, R. (2000) *Sociology Themes and Perspectives*, Fifth Edition, London: Collins

Harvie, C. (2002) *Scotland a Short History*, New York, NY: Oxford University Press

Heartfield, J. (1994) 'An unintelligent argument', *Living Marxism*, December

Heath, 1992) 'The attitudes of the underclass', in Smith, D.J. (ed.) *Understanding the Underclass*, London: Policy Studies Institute

Hill, A. (2001) 'Racism has turned the good people here bad', *Society Guardian*, 12 August (accessed at: http://society.guardian.co.uk/asylumseekers/story/0,7991,536078,00.html)

Howe, D. and Worsthorne, P. (1998) 'What is a true Brit?' *The Guardian*, 25 April

Jary, D. and Jary, J. (1995) *Unwin Hyman Dictionary of Sociology*, Second Edition, Glasgow: HarperCollins

Kivisto, P. (2002) *Multiculturalism in a Global Society*, Oxford: Blackwell

McCrum, M. (2002) 'We must act now to avert identity crisis', *The Herald*, 18 February

McGarvie, L. (2002) 'Scotland Plagued by Racial Violence', *Sunday Mail*, 20 January (accessed at: http://www.sundaymail.co.uk/news/breakingnews/page.cfm?objectid=11552056&method=full&siteid=86024)

MacLeod, M. (2002) 'Asylum seeker in hospital after Glasgow stabbing', *Scotland on Sunday*, 1 December (accessed at: http://www.scotlandonsunday.com/index.cfm?=1339782002)

MacPherson, Sir W. (1999) *The Stephen Lawrence Inquiry*, London: Stationery Office

Manne, R. (2002) 'Beware the New Racism', in *The Age* (accessed at: http://www.theage.com)

Mason, D. (1995) *Race and Ethnicity in Modern Britain*, Oxford: Oxford University Press

Miles, R. (1989) *Racism*, London: Routledge

Miles, R (1993) *Racism after Race Relations*, London: Routledge

Modood, T., and Berthoud, R. *et al* (1997) *Ethnic Minorities in Britain: Diversity and Disadvantage*, London: Policy Studies Institute

Murray, C. (1984) *Losing Ground*, New York, NY: Basic Books

Murray, C. and Herrnstein, R. (1994) *The Bell Curve: Intelligence and Class Structure in American Life*, New York, NY: Basic Books

Parreira, F. (2003) 'Britishness course structure unveiled', *The Guardian*, 31 January (accessed at: http://politics.guardian.co.uk/homeaffairs/story/0,11026,886545,00.html)

Patterson, S. (1965) *Dark Strangers*, Harmondsworth: Penguin

Pilkington, A. (2003) *Racial Disadvantage and Ethnic Diversity in Britain*, Basingstoke: Palgrave

Rose, S. (1997) *Lifelines: Biology, Freedom, and Determinism*, Harmondsworth: Penguin

Rex, J. and Tomlinson, S. (1979) *Colonial Immigrants in a British City: A Class Analysis*, London: Routledge and Keegan Paul

Seenan, G. and Scott, K. (2001) 'A dream turned sour', *Society Guardian*, 9 August (accessed at: http://society.guardian.co.uk/asylumseekers/story/0,7991,534302,00.html)

Skellington, R. (1996) *Race in Britain Today*, London: Sage

Smaje, C. (2000) *Natural Hierarchies: The Historical Sociology of Race and Caste*, Oxford: Blackwell

Small, S. (1994) 'Black People in Britain', *Sociology Review*, April

Smelser, N.J. (1994) *Sociology*, Oxford: Blackwell

Smith, D.J. (ed.) (1992) *Understanding the Underclass*, London: Policy Studies Institute

Smith, I. (2003) 'Asylum Figures Record', *The Daily Record*, 1 March (accessed at: http://www.dailyrecord.co.uk/news/news/page.cfm?objectid=12689712&method=full&siteid=89488)

Guardian, The (2001) 'He fled from hell in a Turkish prison only to die a bloody death in Glasgow', *Society Guardian*, 7 August (accessed at: http://society.guardian.co.uk/asylumseekers/)

Thomas, W. I. (1923) *The Unadjusted Girl*, Boston: Little, Brown and Co

Walker, D. (2002) 'Study reveals jobs plight of Muslims', *The Guardian*, 20 February (accessed at: http://www.guardian.co.uk/racism/Story/0,2763,653116,00.html)

Woodward, K. (ed.) (2000) *Questioning Identity: Gender, Class, Nation*, London: Routledge/Open University

Wrench, J. and Solomos, J. (1993) *Racism and Migration in Western Europe*, Oxford: Berg

146

Chapter 7   The Family

Jason Annetts and Linda Gray

Introduction: Defining the 'Family'?

We are all familiar with the concept of 'the family' and the majority of us have differing personal experience of family life. Our experience of the family and the way in which it is represented by the church, government, the mass media and schools, helps to shape our understanding of it. However, although we are all familiar with 'the family', defining it is problematic since there does not exist one definitive family form. Diana Gittins (1993: 70) argues that the very "notion of there being such a thing as 'the family' is thus highly controversial and full of ambiguities and contradictions." This ambiguity stems from the constantly evolving structure of the family and the numerous different ways in which the family can be organised.

Organisation and Structure of the Family

How the family is organised, or structured, is dependent upon longitudinal (see Chapter 2: Sociological Theory, Chapter 3: Sociological Methods and Chapter 5: Gender) and cross-cultural factors (see Chapter 13: Culture). In the UK and most western industrialised societies, the family is typically described as consisting of parents and their biological children. This is what has been widely referred to as the 'nuclear' or 'conjugal family'. Muncie and Sapsford (1995: 10) define the nuclear family:

> [A]s a small unit derived from the relationship between a man and a woman legally bound together through marriage as husband and wife. The nuclear family is created when a child is born to this couple. The unit shares a common residence and is united by ties of affection, common identity and support.

Many families, however, do not conform to this pattern. Some families may also include other members of the extended kinship network, such as, grandparents, uncles, aunts, and/or cousins. These families are normally referred to as 'extended families'. It had been widely believed that before industrialisation households that comprised of extended family members were common while after industrialisation the modern nuclear family became the dominant family form. However, research by Peter Laslet (1972) seems to indicate that even before industrialisation households were relatively small and "corresponded roughly to nuclear families" (Gittins, 1993: 6). This has led some writers to claim that the nuclear family was not an outcome of industrialisation but rather facilitated the growth of industrial society (Berger and Berger, 1983).

This is not to suggest that the extended family is of no importance in modern western societies and that in some communities they do not continue to have a central role in family relationships. For example, Wilmott and Young's (1960) classic study of working class families in Bethnal Green during the 1950s, entitled *Family and Class in London,* found that numerous households contained three generation of kin organised around the relationship between mothers, daughters and grandchildren. The continuing importance of the mother-daughter relationship has also been highlighted "as a crucial variable in understanding patterns of sociability among kinsmen" (Farmer, 1970: 37). Furthermore, in some ethnic minority communities extended kinship networks remain particularly important, such as those from Asian and Chinese communities. People in these communities are more likely to live in households that include members of their extended family, while those from the Afro-Caribbean community are more likely to live in lone parent households (Dallos and Sapsford, 1995).

Even when the family conforms to the nuclear pattern, it would be wrong to suggest that the extended kinship network has no role to play in the modern family. A number of different studies have demonstrated the continuing importance of the extended family, even when they do not live in a single household. For example, Litwak and Szelenyi (1977) argue that through modern technology the extended family, even when geographically separated, remain an essential support network. Similarly, Finch and Mason (1993), in *Negotiating Family Responsibilities,* argue that kinship ties remain an important source of support and assistance for many people in society. This support can take many forms including the lending of small amounts of money, helping to look after someone who is ill, offering practical help with household chores, or simply giving emotional support. They also note that many of the people they interviewed had shared a residence with a member of their extended kinship network for part of their life. Although Finch and Mason (1993: 168) found that most people do not attribute specific duties and responsibilities to kinship, family relationships are characterised by a 'developing commitment', by which they mean "responsibilities are a product of interactions between individuals over time."

There has been a sharp rise in the number of *lone parent families* both in Scotland and throughout the UK. Lone parent families can be described as households comprising of "one parent, frequently the mother, living alone with her children, with a greater proportion of responsibility for caring for children financially and emotionally" (Dallos and Sapsford, 1995: 128). The phrase, 'lone parent family' covers a wide variety of family configurations. Haskey (1992), for example, has identified *five* types of lone-parent families, including: single lone mothers, divorced lone mothers, separated lone mothers, widowed mothers and lone fathers. However, the vast majority of such families comprise of a mother and her children with only about nine percent of lone-parent households being headed by a man (Popay, Rimmer and Rossiter, 1983).

Despite the increasing number of divorces and children born to lone mothers, the majority of children are still raised in nuclear style households consisting of two adults and dependent children (Dallos and Sapsford, 1995). However, it is increasingly common for families to consist not just of the biological parents and their children but stepparents, biological siblings, stepsiblings and half-siblings. These *reconstituted families* can be considerably more complex than the traditional nuclear family, depending upon whether one or both partners bring children from previous marriages into this 'reconstituted' arrangement. This complexity can place such families under considerable strain, as relationships between stepparents and stepchildren can often be fraught and lacking clear expectations and responsibilities (Elliot, 1986).

Trigger

To what extent is the changing family form an indication of the continued strength and adaptability of the family?

Alternatives to marriage

Diversity of family life is as evident in Scotland as elsewhere in the United Kingdom, and as *Social Trends* (2002: 40) confirms, compared to previous times, people today tend to live in a greater variety of household types. Many factors contribute to this present-day pattern, for example, the structure of the family changes according to the particular stage of the life cycle that family members are in. Furthermore, marriage, cohabitation, separation or divorce, the creation of second or subsequent families, the increasing numbers of people choosing to live alone and the relaxation of social conventions or 'rules' have all contributed to the widening variety of family structures.

Until relatively recently, marriage and children had been assumed to be at the very heart of family life. However, an increasing number of couples are choosing *cohabitation* over marriage. Although marriage remains popular, the relaxation of attitudes among young people to cohabitation, marriage remains 'very' popular. For many couples, cohabitation is simply "an experimental stage prior to marriage" (Giddens, 2001: 192). Therefore, couples today are more likely to live together for a number of years before getting married, but, statistically speaking, the majority will still get married.

However, families do not necessarily need to be based upon kinship ties. Weston (1991) uses the phrase 'families of choice' to describe 'families' of unrelated individuals who have chosen to constitute themselves as a family, despite not having any blood or legal ties to each other. An example of this is the growing number of gay male and lesbian couples who do not have the opportunity to legally and/or religiously formalise their partnerships through the institution of marriage. It should, perhaps, be noted that the perceived increase in homosexual relationships does not necessarily indicate a relatively new phenomenon. Though we can find evidence that such relationships have existed throughout human history, it is only in relatively recent times in western societies that laws forbidding or restricting homosexuality have been relaxed or removed.

There is an increasing acceptance of lesbian and gay partnerships as families, which has been demonstrated by a Scottish court's April 2002 ruling giving a lesbian couple joint parental rights over each other's children, rights that had only been previously given to heterosexual couples (*Scotland on Sunday*, 7 April 2002). This decision, among others, is extending the legal definition of the family to include homosexual couples.

Furthermore, in a number of countries such partnerships have already become legally recognised. In 2001, the Netherlands became the only country in the world to allow gay male and lesbian couples to marry which followed the introduction of a civil registered partnership scheme in 1998. Both heterosexual and homosexual Dutch couples can now choose one of three options: cohabitation, registered partnership or marriage. Although no other country has yet to legislate for gay and lesbian marriages, countries such as Denmark, France, Germany and Iceland, have opted for legally recognised partnership schemes giving gay and lesbian couples the same legal protection in law as married heterosexual couples (Waaldijk, 2001).

Although at the time of writing we have not seen a concerted move in this direction by either the British government or the Scottish Executive, both in London (2001) and in Manchester (2002) there have been pioneer schemes that enable gay male and lesbian couples to register their relationships. The first of these registration schemes was set up following the victory of the politically left-leaning former Labour MP, Ken Livingstone, in the London Mayoral election and, although it is not legally binding, they do have a symbolic value. Furthermore, these city-based schemes could be important in winning public support for the creation of a legally binding partnership registration scheme. In Scotland, the gay and lesbian lobby organisation,

The Equality Network, has already begun to campaign for the Scottish Executive to create such a scheme. This has followed an extensive consultation between the Equality Network and the Scottish gay and lesbian community, which found that the majority of gay men and lesbians preferred legally binding partnerships to simply allowing gay male and lesbian couples to marry (The Equality Network, January 2002).

Trigger

Outline the arguments for and against:

1. Allowing gay male and lesbian couples to marry
2. Establishing a legally binding partnership scheme
3. The continued denial of any official recognition of gay and lesbian relationships.

Which of these options do you prefer and why?

Relationships and adoption

The growing acceptability of non-traditional relationships, including cohabiting couples and gay and lesbian partnerships, can be demonstrated through the current debate on adoption. In Britain both Prime Minister Tony Blair and Health Secretary Alan Milburn, have supported moves to enable both unmarried heterosexual and homosexual couples to jointly adopt children (*The Guardian*, 8 May 2002).

Although this amendment to the Adoption and Children Bill (2002) was criticised it does seem to indicate a growing belief that unmarried couples, regardless of their sex and sexuality, can provide a healthy environment for raising children. Furthermore, the changing rules on adoption, and the growing acceptance of cohabiting couples as families demonstrate the extent to which what we define as 'the family' has changed in recent years; it also reflects the socially constructed nature of the *definition* of the family.

The Family in Scotland

This section will explore some of the data that helps us to examine 'the family' in its Scottish context. Scottish Executive publications provide a wealth of statistical information relating particularly to the situation in Scotland, while publications such as *Social Trends* encompass information related to the whole of the United Kingdom, and often include comparative European Union data. You should find these sources useful, not just as a means of collecting 'facts and figures', but also as a tool for cross-referencing information you may find elsewhere. Since we have already suggested that in the UK 'the family' is typically described as consisting of parents and their children, we will be principally concerned with household types which are inclusive of children.

Scottish statistics tend to bear out the claim that marriage remains highly popular in Scotland. The majority of Scottish adults (56 per cent) are in a marriage relationship, while an estimated 6 per cent are 'living together' without being married (cohabiting), 21 per cent are single, 8 per cent are either separated or divorced and 10 per cent are widowed (Scottish Household Survey (SHS), 1999/2000: 20).

According to SHS (1999/2000: 13), less than one-third (around 28 per cent) of Scottish households contain children under the age of 16. Four per cent of households have three or more children, 11 per cent have two children and 13 per cent have one child. Immediately, it can be seen that the *general* trend is towards smaller family units comprising of one or two children, with only a comparatively small proportion of households containing more than two children. The majority of Scottish households (in many cases forming the extended kinship network) do not contain children under the age of sixteen. However, some caution has to be exercised when interpreting statistics. As Moore (1987: 93) notes: "the statistics refer to the number of *households*, not the number of *people*." Therefore, it needs to be borne in mind that the majority of *people* live together in a family structure.

Box 7.1 Scottish Facts

- In 2000, there were 30,367 marriages in Scotland, an increase of 427 from 1999
- Nearly, 30 per cent of people marrying in 2000 had been married previously
- The average age at first marriage was 30.5 years for men and 28.6 years for women
- There were 11,143 divorces in Scotland in 2000, the lowest number since 1981

(Source: General Register Office for Scotland (2002))

The cities of Dundee, Aberdeen and Edinburgh have the lowest proportion of households with children (22 per cent, 23 per cent and 24 per cent, respectively) while the Shetland Islands, West Lothian and East Renfrewshire have the highest with 36 per cent, 34 per cent and 34 per cent respectively (SHS, 1999/2000: 15 and Table 1.18 of that source]. In Scotland as a whole, the majority (53 per cent) of households with children under 16 are classified as small family households.

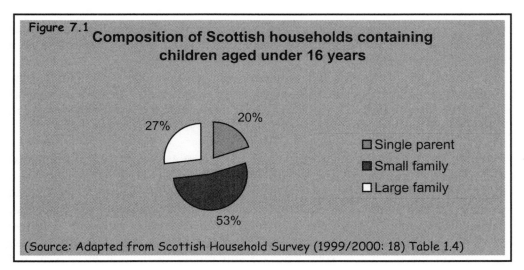

Figure 7.1

Composition of Scottish households containing children aged under 16 years

27% 20% 53%

☐ Single parent
■ Small family
☐ Large family

(Source: Adapted from Scottish Household Survey (1999/2000: 18) Table 1.4)

NB: The SHS classification of household is: **Single parent**: 1 adult of any age and 1 or more children. **Small family**: 2 adults of any age and 1 or 2 children. **Large family**: 2 adults of any age and 3 or more children, or 3 or more adults of any age and 1 or more children.

Figure 7.1 (above) shows the composition of family households with children (aged under 16 years). Fifty three per cent are small families, 27 per cent are large families, and 20 per cent are single parent families. However, in terms of overall figures, 8 per cent of Scottish households are composed of large families, 15 per cent of small families and around 6 per cent of single parent families, with children under 16 years making up about 21 per cent of all Scottish household members (SHS, 1999/2000).

Further to the SHS (1999/2000) report, although lone adults with children account for only 6 per cent of all households in 1998, this figure is projected to increase to 8 per cent by 2012, while one-person households are projected to increase from 32 per cent in 1998 to 38 per cent by 2012 (Factfile Scotland, 2002). Whether such projections indicate evidence of the 'growing crisis' in 'the family' or whether they indicate a progressive change in family form is, of course, a matter of opinion and debate.

Economic and material dependence of 'older' children
Before we examine the statistical information in greater detail, take some time to consider the implications of the arguments and evidence presented above. For

example, you may already have noted that defining 'children' as being those aged under-16 years is problematic. Given the nature of extended educational opportunities, many young people are economically and materially dependent upon the family structure beyond that particular age. Indeed, a report in *The Evening Times* (Glasgow, 4 April 2002) indicated that, as a result of the Family Law (Scotland) Act 1985, parents are responsible for the provision of financial support for their children until the age of 25, provided their children are still participating in further education or training.

Jones (1992: 27) suggests that social class (see Chapter 4: Social Class) is influential in the nature of dependency and independence in the parent-child relationship, with middle class children more likely to maintain economic parental dependence than working class children, usually because of the continuance of education. Paradoxically, Jones (1992: 35) also found evidence from the *Scottish Young People's Survey* (1987) to suggest that: "In practice it is mainly working-class parents and the parents of sons who are still providing their nineteen year old children with permanent homes, rather than holiday bases." Recent research has gone one step further by revealing that there is now a growing tendency in Britain for 'children' to stay at home well into adulthood and "refuse to cut the apron strings even when they do leave." Financial benefit was one of the main reasons given for the reluctance to leave the family unit (*The Daily Telegraph*, 21 March 2002).

Trigger

In what ways might you expect the economic relationships between parents and children to have an influence on family structure and dynamics?

Lone Parent Households

The term, *lone parent household*, is carefully chosen, because, as Crow and Hardey (1992) explain, many 'lone parent families' involve a parent who has involvement in family relations though not living under the same roof. Nevertheless, as Rodger (1996: 121) comments:

> It is in the area of single parenthood, which has become a particular public issue in the 1990s, that the family has become the centre of a broader debate about social and moral behaviour.

Since the vast majority of lone-parent households are headed by women (Macionis and Plummer, 2002) it would seem that it is the issue of the 'absent father' that prompts the social and moral debates.

Crow and Hardey (1992) discuss the diversity and ambiguity amongst lone parents that effectively limits the collective strength they might otherwise experience as part of a significant social structure, and thus their ability to challenge the negative attitudes that often surround their status. Crow and Hardey (1992: 147) also argue, that while some "routes into lone-parenthood" are clearly channelled by events such as a partner's death or a birth to a single mother; others – such as separation, divorce, or an end to cohabitation – are much less clearly delineated. Furthermore, lone parenthood is not, of course, the *exclusive* remit of women. Indeed, it has recently been indicated that approximately five-to-ten per cent of the total number of single parent families in Scotland are headed by males (*The Sunday Herald*, 22 July 2001).

Challenges for lone parent families
There is substantial evidence to suggest that single parent households are disadvantaged across a range of areas, including income and standard of living, housing, education and training and employment (One Parent Families Scotland (OPFS), 2001). As a measure of income, for example, OPFS (2001) report that in 1999, while 25 per cent of small two parent families and 29 per cent of large two parent families had a net annual income of less than £10,000, 70 per cent of single parent households in Scotland experienced this level of income. Furthermore (or, perhaps, consequently), single parent households in Scotland tend to be much more dependent on rented housing compared to two parent families, with 25 per cent of single parents living in owner occupied housing compared to 71 per cent of two parent families.

In the area of education, lone parents again appear to be disadvantaged with 76 per cent of unemployed lone parents possessing no vocational training. Interestingly, there are marked differences in the working arrangements for lone mothers in Scotland compared to some of their European counterparts: while 38 per cent of lone mothers in Scotland in 1999 were in employment, these figures shrink in comparison to French and Swedish lone mothers, where 82 per cent and 70 per cent, respectively, were working (OPFS, 2001). Low employment rates among the Scottish lone mothers are often attributable to a lack of good childcare facilities, and this may well be the case. However, the differences in social, political, and fiscal policies between European countries cannot be ignored, and like Rodger (1996: 127), you might find that: "Accepting that caution must be taken when comparing statistics compiled in different ways and relating to different factors that may not be comparable, general trends in childcare provision and family policy emerge." For example, if we look at the places available in publicly funded childcare services, "a good index of government commitment to assisting lone-parent employment" (Rodger, 1996: 127), we can see the differences between some of the European countries (see Table 7.1 below).

We can see from the information in Table 7.1 that Britain does not compare very favourably with some other European countries in the provision of publicly funded childcare services. Denmark is by far the most prolific provider of childcare services, catering for 48 per cent of under-threes and 85 per cent of under-sevens (when school education begins), while for the same period Britain provides just 2 per cent of under-threes and 35-40 per cent of under-fives with a similar service. To emphasise Britain's paucity in such provision, a 1999 survey commissioned by the Scottish Office Education and Industry Department found that, in Scotland, grandparents were the most commonly used providers of childcare (Hinds and Park, 2000). While this was largely true also for England and Wales, grandparents were not used quite so extensively as in Scotland. Furthermore, the study revealed that lone parents faced more difficulties than couples in meeting the demands for childcare. It is interesting to note that, despite having already undertaken parental duties for their own children, grandparents are being increasingly expected to undertake a range of such 'parental' responsibilities for their children's children. For those affected, such a development might be variously construed as a welcome activity to help fulfil their own lives, or a necessary chore that restricts their own desires to enhance their family's livelihood.

According to the Scottish Office Education and Industry Department (SOIED) (1999) survey, grandparents are favoured *very* strongly in Scotland as providers of childcare, with nursery centres or schools also featuring among Scotland's families' 'ideal providers'. In delivering its Social Justice Annual Report Scotland (Scottish Executive 2001: 7), the Scottish Executive declared that: "Childcare services to support working parents are recognised as critical to the success of economic development as well as social inclusion policies." (See Chapter 8: Poverty.)

Nevertheless, the pressures which lone parents experience may turn out to be more complicated than a policy proposal can engage in. The Policy Studies Institute (1996), for instance, found that other things besides the cost or lack of childcare contributed to lone parents' inability to take paid jobs. Having young children who needed their mother at home, an adjustment to a new 'single' situation, a lack of confidence in skills and ability to compete in the labour market, and some perceptions of employer discrimination were also given as obstacles to employment (Policy Studies Institute (PSI) press release, 3 December 1996).

Table 7.1 Places in Publicly Funded Childcare Services as a Per Cent of All Children in the Age Group

Country	Year of Data	Under 3	3 – compulsory school	
France	1988	20	95+	(school begins 6 years)
Belgium	1988	20	95+	(school begins 6 years)
Italy	1986	5	85+	(school begins 6 years)
Germany	1987	3	65-70	(school begins 7 years)
Denmark	1989	48	85	(school begins 7 years)
Spain	1988	---	65-70	(school begins 6 years)
Britain	1988	2	35-40	(school begins 5 years)

(Source: Adapted from European Commission Childcare Network, *Childcare in the European Community*, 1985-1990, Women of Europe Supplement no. 31 (Brussels, 1990: 10), cited in Rodger, J.J. (1996: 127) *Family Life & Social Control: A Sociological Perspective*, Basingstoke: Macmillan)

According to One Parent Families Scotland (OPFS, 2001), there is "a common assertion that children brought up in lone parent families are more likely to become delinquent." However, a Family Policy Studies Centre conference held in 1994, found that family structure – that is whether children are brought up by one parent or two – was of far less significance than the parent's ability to provide appropriate supervision (OPFS, 2001).

We have now been presented with quite different causes for some of the current challenges facing families. First, lone parenthood has been attacked as part of the wider debate about contemporary social and moral conduct in society. Second, two-parent families have also been viewed as contributing to anti-social behaviour if they maintain 'workaholic' lifestyles. Furthermore, it has also been claimed that the trend away from shared family meals has contributed to the deterioration of family life in Scotland.

While such factors as lone parenthood, 'distant' parents, and a lack of shared family experiences have been variously discussed in relation to changes (and problems) within family structures, the increase in teenage pregnancy and teenage motherhood has also impacted on Britain's families. Britain is regularly indicated in media reports as being the western European state with the highest numbers of teenage pregnancies, lone-parent families and divorces. Only the United States has a higher number of teenage pregnancies than Britain among developed nations (*The Guardian*, 29 May 2002).

Trigger

1. Why do you think there are such opposing views for the apparent breakdown in family life?
2. What argument do you consider to be most persuasive in terms of delivering reasons for this supposed deterioration?

Teenage pregnancy in Scotland

In Scotland, 9,218 births across the teenage years (ages 13-19) were provisionally recorded in 1998 (Information and Statistics Division (ISD) Scotland, 1999). Table 7.2 (below) paints a vivid statistical portrait of the prevailing 'problem' across Scotland.

As the data in Table 7.2 (below) shows, the highest rates of teenage pregnancies are recorded in Tayside, Ayrshire and Arran, and Fife with 51.2, 49.7 and 48.5 teenage pregnancies, respectively, per 1000 women. The lowest levels were recorded in the Western Isles where 16 pregnancies occurred per 1000 women in the 13-19 years age group. Compared to England and Wales, Scotland had a lower than average conception rate for under-18s and percentage of conceptions leading to abortion (*BBC News*, 5 December 2000). In general, the long-term prospects for teenage mothers and fathers have been found to be disadvantaged compared to parents who had delayed childbearing, with less likelihood than older parents of becoming owner-occupiers and a lower net family income (OPFS, 2001).

Nevertheless, OPFS (2001) reject the myth "that teenage mothers are or have been promiscuous and are having their babies outside steady relationships." In reality, claims the organisation, "75 per cent of teenage mothers register the birth jointly with the baby's father and the great majority of these couples are cohabiting." Additionally, OPFS (2001) refutes the notion that there has been a big increase in births to teenagers in recent years. Figures provided by ISD Scotland (1999) do demonstrate a general pattern of *decrease* between 1989 and 1998, the exceptions being the health board areas of Ayrshire & Arran and Forth Valley.

The high level of teenage pregnancies (at least in relation to other European countries) has been linked, among other factors, to inadequate and belated sex education. As OPFS (2001) reports:

Despite fears that sex education leads to increased early sexual activity, research suggests that young people who are given sex education in school start their sex lives later, take fewer partners and are more responsible about contraception.

This seems to support the sentiments of teenage mothers themselves who "often reported being shocked or surprised to find they were pregnant even if they had not been using contraception" (Policy Studies Institute (PSI) Press Release, 30 October 1998). Certainly, as a challenge to some of the popular mythology that surrounds teenage motherhood, Professor Isobel Allen, who co-authored the report, *Teenage Mothers: Decisions and Outcomes*, argues that:

> Teenage mothers should not be stigmatised and treated as a universal problem. They are not all lone mothers living on benefits in council housing. But our research shows that this does happen to a substantial number of them and there is certainly a need for better education in sex and personal relationships to help dispel romantic views of life as a teenage mother. Young men need to share the responsibility for teenage pregnancy and motherhood.
> (Policy Studies Institute (PSI) Press Release, 30 October 1998)

Thus far, we have looked at the structure of families, discussed some recent changes in family patterns, and concentrated particularly on single parent households and teenage parenthood that have variously been the subject of debate around the decline of family values. Though it may seem that some of the viewpoints have been very negative, it must be remembered that it is often 'negative' issues that are the subject of sociological attention. Inevitably, there will be positive issues around all family structures, including single parenthood, 'workaholic' parents and teenage parenthood, just as there will be negative issues around two-parent families and 'ideal' family units. Parenting pressures, problems of poverty and social exclusion touch many families, with families in Scotland being no exception (see Chapter 8: Poverty).

Nevertheless, the 'ideal' of family life remains very popular, evidenced in part by the increasing number of people who are members of reconstituted families. There are on average 40,000 stepfamilies in Scotland, involving a broad range of children, stepchildren, parents and stepparents (Factfile Scotland, 2002). It is anticipated that by the year 2010 reconstituted or step families are likely to be the largest single form of family unit: "outnumbering so-called normal families" (*The Herald*, 2001). This clearly indicates that the family, however it is constituted, still plays an important role for many people.

Table 7.2 Teenage Pregnancies by Health Board Area of Residence Across Teenage Years 13-19

1998[1] Rates[2]			1998[1] Rates[2]		
Argyll and Clyde	750	(40.8)	Ayrshire and Arran	812	(49.7)
Borders	123	(29.7)	Dumfries and Galloway	241	(41.1)
Fife	737	(48.5)	Forth Valley	540	(44.9)
Grampian	894	(39.4)	Greater Glasgow	1646	(42.3)
Highland	391	(44.4)	Lanarkshire	996	(38.8)
Lothian	1179	(38.9)	Tayside	841	(51.2)
Orkney	18	(20.6)	Shetland	30	(29.4)
Western Isles	20	(16.0)			

(Source: Adapted from ISD Scotland Health Briefing Number 99/04 issued June 1999 'Teenage Pregnancy in Scotland 1989-1998')

1 1998 rates are based on 1997 population statistics

2 Rates per 1000 females

In Scotland, 9,218 births across the teenage years (ages 13-19) were provisionally recorded in 1998 (Information and Statistics Division (ISD) Scotland, 1999).

Trigger

"High numbers of pregnancies are in areas classed as urban and industrial, where there are high levels of unemployment, a higher number of semi-skilled or unskilled workers and more living in terraced or social housing" (*BBC News*, 5 December 2000).

Why do you think socio-economic conditions apparently have such an influence on teenage pregnancy rates?

We shall now consider the different theoretical approaches to the study of the family that have influenced both public policy and public perceptions of the family. We will start by looking at the structural functionalist perspective (See Chapter 2: Sociological Theory and Chapter 3: Sociological Methods).

Functionalist Approaches to the Family

Prior to the 1970s structural functionalism was the dominant sociological tradition in the sociology of the family. The functionalist perspective characterised the family as an institution that performed a number of important tasks, essential to the smooth functioning of society. For example, structural functionalists saw the nuclear family and the sexual division of labour "as performing functions necessary to the survival of society" including "the need for the regulation of sexual behaviour and procreation, for child-care and for the socialisation of children into the values of society" (Elliot, 1986: 10).

In his book, *Social Structure* (1949), the functionalist, George Murdock (1949), claims that the nuclear family is not only a necessity but also a universal social institution.

Another major proponent of structural functionalism was the American sociologist, Talcott Parsons, who argues that the role of the modern nuclear family had become more specialised following industrialisation. Parsons (1977) believes that many of the roles which were undertaken by the family had now been taken over by other institutions in society, for example, he recognises that most families do not make their own clothes or bake their own bread anymore but instead buy in these products ready made. Furthermore, the advent of universal education at the end of the nineteenth century also meant that the family was no longer primarily responsible for educating children and preparing them for their future careers. Some commentators believe that this 'loss of functions' was indicative of the decline of the family. However, Parsons (1977: 50) claims that although specialisation had led to a "decline of certain features which have been traditionally associated with families; [...] whether it represents a 'decline of the family' in a more general sense is another matter; we think not." Rather, Parsons argues that the modern nuclear family had become focused upon two major social functions: primary socialisation of children and "the stabilization of the adult personalities" (Parsons, 1977: 57).

In Parsons' schema, the primary role of the family was the rearing and socialisation of children and he portrayed the family as "factories which produce human personalities" (Parsons, 1977: 57). Parsons believes that through socialisation children learn appropriate behaviours and knowledge, which enable them to fully participate in society. Socialisation also has an important social control function, teaching the child what constitutes acceptable ideas and behaviours (Farmer, 1970).

The second interconnected function highlighted by Parsons is what he calls the 'stabilisation of adult personalities'. This emotional support is more a function of marriage. However, Parsons also argues that parenthood enhances the "emotional balance of the parents themselves" (Parsons, 1977: 60). This function, he believes, was all the more important in contemporary society where there is less contact and reliance on the extended family and kinship networks for emotional support.

These are not, however, the only functions of the family. Other writers have highlighted a number of other functions of the family. For example, William Goode (1964: 5) suggests that the main functions of the family include "reproduction of the young, physical maintenance of family members, social placement of the child, socialization and social control." Mary Farmer (1970) emphasises the importance of the family in determining your class, culture, ethnicity and religion. Farmer (1970: 17) claims that the family is:

> [T]he most essential link between the individual and society [...]. From the family the individual initially receives a socially *ascribed status*, so that membership of a family gives the child a position in the social hierarchy.

More recently, some writers have argued that the family acts as a refuge from the stresses and strains of modern society. Ferdinand Mount (1982: 1) has argued that the family is "a subversive organisation" and that one of the primary functions of the modern family "is to act as a point of resistance against the encroachment of state authority" (Dallos and Sapsford, 1995: 163). Black feminist writers have also argued that the family in ethnic minority communities offer a refuge from a racist society (Abbot and Wallace, 1990).

The structural functionalist perspective on the family and the work of Talcott Parsons has been heavily criticised in recent years for its optimism, sexism and for ignoring the diversity of family forms. Parsons presents an idealised picture of the family in which the man was the breadwinner and head of the household and the woman stayed at home and was primarily responsible for domestic duties subservient to the male demands:

> The adult feminine role has not ceased to be anchored primarily in the internal affairs of the family, as wife, mother and manager of the household, while the role of adult male is primarily anchored in the occupational world, in his job and through it by his status-giving and incoming-earning functions for the family.
>
> (Parsons, 1977: 56)

However, relatively few families conform to this idealised nuclear family pattern. For example, dual income families where both the husband and wife go out to work are now widespread and, as seen in the previous section, there are a growing number of lone parents who act both as breadwinners *and* 'housewives'. Parsons offers us a very particularistic view of the family, which is largely based upon "the white middle-class suburban family" while other family forms "tended to be ignored or dismissed as deviant 'problem families'" (Jackson, 2000: 161).

Box 7.2 The Family as a 'Universal Institution'

Murdock (1949) studied 250 different societies ranging from simple hunter-gatherer to complex industrial societies, claiming that a basic nuclear family structure could be found in all societies and that only this structural form, with its particular sexual division of labour, could efficiently meet the functions of the family as he defined them:

"The family is a social group characterised by common residence, economic co-operations and reproduction. It includes adults of both sexes, at least two of whom maintain a socially approved sexual relationship, and one or more children, own or adopted, of the sexually co-habiting adult" (Murdock, 1949).

Murdock's claim that the nuclear family is universal and that it has common functions does not, however, survive longitudinal and cross-cultural examination:

- *Common residence*: Contemporary families may be separated by business or immigration restrictions. Among the Nayor of Malabor, Mexico, the husband and wife live apart and children live in a kibbutz, in dormitories, separate from all parents.
- *Economic co-operation*: Nayor husbands had no maintenance obligation and all property is owned collectively in the kibbutz. Many contemporary households have female 'breadwinners'.
- *Reproduction*: Any visiting warrior could feasibly father a Nayor child and surrogate and IVF children today are increasingly more common.
- Not all families are characterised by adults of both sexes. West African *matrifocal* families (i.e. mother, grandmother and children) were accepted as a necessary response to poverty. In the contemporary West, many lone-parent families exist.
- Adultery and sexually dysfunctional relationships have meant that not all families include two persons who maintain a socially approved sexual relationship.
- Problems arise over establishing whether children of the sexually cohabiting adults actually originated from the husband. No permanent conjugal arrangement existed in the Ashanti of Ghana; today, reconstituted families are common in Western society.

Trigger

Talcott Parsons believes that the nuclear family is uniquely suited to the demands of modern industrial society.
1. List the major functions of the family.
2. Could the needs fulfilled by the family be met by other institutions in society?

Critical Approaches to the Family

One of the big differences between the earlier and later sociological studies of the family is that writers such as Parsons tended to be uncritical of the family. These writers predominantly portrayed the family positively and argue that the family served a positive function for both the individual and society. However, later theories, particularly contemporary Marxist and feminist, argue that the family itself is a site of oppression and that through the family major inequalities in society are propagated and enforced.

Marxist perspectives

The Marxist critique of the family has been informed by both Karl Marx's and Fredrich Engels' call for the 'abolition of the family' in the *Communist Manifesto* (1848), and by Engels' more in-depth work on *The Origin of the Family, Private Property and the State* (1884). This critique argues that through the institution of the family, property and capitalist ideas are passed to the next generation, which serves to uphold the class structure of society. The family is portrayed as one of the central institutions involved in the reproduction of class inequalities in society and it is argued that through the family, both privilege and poverty is transmitted from generation to generation:

> The family becomes a central unit in the continuity of classes over generations, the maintenance and expansion of class privilege and the establishment of methods of social closure. The family as an institution ensures the continuity of the havenots as well as entrenching the power and privilege of the haves.   (Morgan, 1985: 214)

Seccombe (1974), in an article entitled *The Housewife and Her Labour under Capitalism*, demonstrates three important ways in which the family bolsters capitalism.

First, the family reproduces labour power through producing and rearing the next generation of workers and by making sure that the subsistence needs of the current workforce are met. Women clearly play a central role, here, through their unpaid domestic chores that "create[...] value through creating, and servicing, labour power – i.e. male wage earners and future wage earners" (Gittins, 1993: 112).

Second, the family not only bolsters capitalism through the production of labour power but also through its consumption of goods and services. The family is a basic unit of consumption that buys what capitalism produces. Historically, the family itself was a unit of production with many families engaged in subsistence agriculture. However, following the industrial revolution and the rise of industrial capitalism, it became usual for people to work outside the home and therefore the family became primarily a unit involved in consumption (Berger and Berger, 1983).

Third, the family is also important in transmitting the capitalist ideology to the next generation through its core function of socialising the young into the values and beliefs of society. The family not only teaches young children to accept the capitalist ideology, but as Morgan (1985) argues, also instils in them obedience, conformity and discipline which are essential for any productive workforce. Morgan (1985) also argues that the family is important in two further ways. The first is that the family acts as an important agent of social control. Parents are considered to be responsible for their children's behaviour. This has been underlined by recent debate concerning truancy and parental responsibility – recently in the UK, we have witnessed the imprisonment of a single mother whose two daughters were consistently absent without reason from school (*The Guardian*, 13 May 2002). The second way, Morgan (1985) argues, is that it is through the family that we learn our place in the social system and who we are as individuals. Thus, he suggests that the family is important in giving us our identity.

The Marxist perspective on the family has been criticised by feminists for assuming that sexual inequalities would disappear with the overthrow of capitalism. The emphasis on class struggle and class conflict necessarily meant that inequalities based upon gender were seen as being of secondary importance. For example, Gittins (1993: 54) claims that both Marx and Engels "ignored the importance of patriarchal relations throughout history." However, Engels does recognise the unequal power relationship that exists between men and women in the family and goes as far as to suggest that: "within the family the woman was the proletariat while the man was the bourgeois" (Morgan, 1985: 215). Despite this, Barrett and McIntosh (1991) claim that faced with widespread support for the family amongst the working class, "socialists have long back-pedalled on the critique of the family" (Barrett and McIntosh, 1991: 132).

Feminist perspectives

Feminists generally view the family as one of the primary sites of women's oppression since the family restricts and controls women while at the same time offering men the maximum freedom to participate in the wider cultural, economic and social life of society. Conversely, women were constrained by their biology and their social roles and responsibilities in marriage, which ensured their exclusion from male culture and career paths. Not surprisingly, feminists such as Betty Friedan (1963), in the *Feminine Mystique*, argue that women's liberation would be necessarily predicated upon women's freedom from the family unit. Similarly, Hannah Gavron (1966) in the *Captive Housewife* highlights the isolation and despair felt by many women confined to the home and locked into their role of housewife and mother.

These early feminist writings were the basis upon which a radical critique of the family was built. This critique saw the family as "patriarchy's chief institution" (Millet, 1971: 55) that oppressed women in three major ways: (1) through the sexual division of labour; (2) through the control over women's sexuality and fertility; and (3) in constructing and reproducing gender identities (Elliot, 1986; see also Chapter 5: Gender.)

The first major way in which Elliot (1986) argues that the family oppresses women is through the sexual division of labour, which refers to the way duties and responsibilities are distributed in the family on the basis of gender. The family, and the sexual division of labour within the family, restricts women's ability to fully participate in the labour force and dictates what are perceived to be gender appropriate occupations. Women's domestic chores can be seen as central to their oppression (Barrett and McIntosh, 1991). Ann Oakley (1974), in *The Sociology of Housework*, found that housewives with young children worked on average 77 hours per week, and that this work was both monotonous and repetitive, had a low status and was largely unappreciated both within and out-with the family (Segal, 1995). Furthermore, many housewives did not have the luxury of being able to choose to be a full-time mother and housewife and instead had to juggle both domestic labour and paid work outside the home. While some women have always been forced into the labour market, since the 1950s the proportion of women in the workforce has steadily increased (Jackson, 2000).

Domestic labour also significantly impacts on female employment patterns. Child-rearing and family commitments have led to women working part-time much more than men. Recent figures published by the Equal Opportunities Commission (EOC) (2000) found that 40 per cent of women aged between 16-44 work part-time, while men only make up 17 per cent of part-time workers. The impact that domestic chores and child-care has on women's ability to work was highlighted by Pauline Pinder (1969), who identified three main phases in women's working life: (1) until the birth of their first child the majority of women work full-time; (2) when their children are young they either stop working altogether or work only part-time; and (3) when all the children are in school they return to full-time labour (Oakley, 1975). This hiatus inevitably has an impact on the progression of women's career. While men climb the career ladder women are frequently left at the bottom in the lower paid and less prestigious jobs. Perhaps not surprisingly, research in the United States (US) has found that female executives are considerably less likely to be married than male executives (Hewlett, 1988). Therefore, women, unlike men, are often left with making a choice between having a family and having a career.

The second major way in which Elliot (1986) argues the family oppresses women is through its considerable control over women's sexuality and fertility. Shulamith Firestone (1988), in *The Dialectic of Sex* (originally published in 1970), argues that motherhood constrains women and stops them from achieving their true potential outside the family. Motherhood and women's biology were viewed as feminine shackles that ensured women's dependence upon men. Not surprisingly, the first of Firestone's revolutionary demands was "the freeing of women from the tyranny of reproduction by every means possible, and the diffusion of the child-rearing role to society as a whole, men as well as women" (Firestone, 1988: 193).

The family, marriage, children, and in some of the more radical feminist critiques heterosexuality, became seen as the major obstacle to women's liberation. Many feminists in the late 1960s and early 1970s, therefore, "rejected the whole package – marriage, motherhood and children – as a bad life-choice for any woman" and instead sought to "clone the male competitive model in the market place" (Hewlett, 1988: 151).

The final way in that Elliot (1986) argues that the family oppresses women is through its central role in the construction and structuring of gender identities. Barrett (1980) argues that not only do boys and girls learn gender specific behaviour through socialisation in the family, but that the 'ideology' of the family through the construction of male and female roles constructs our gender identity. It is through the family that we learn what it means to be a boy or a girl and this significantly influences how we believe we should behave and what we expect from life (Dallos and Sapsford, 1995).

Furthermore, the family and the wider kinship network have been central in defining the identity of women and children. A woman is defined as being a daughter and then a wife, whilst "men, although located within the kinship system, have been defined primarily in terms of their place within the occupational system" (Gittins, 1993: 35). Women, therefore, have been defined essentially by their relationship to men and the family whilst men have largely been defined by what they do outside the family. A good example of this is in terms of social class, where it is the occupation of the husband that determines the social class of the family, not the occupation of the wife.

In these three ways, feminist theorists have argued that the institution of the family is central to the control, exploitation and oppression of women. The family is not only a primary site in which sexual inequalities are constructed, but through the family these inequalities are also perpetuated. The family is able to do this since it is seen as both 'natural' and 'desirable'. As Dallos and Sapsford (1995: 156) claim:

> '[T]he family' is an essentially ideological object. It may be seen as a form of domestic organization which is presented as normal and to be desired as working for the interest of all its members, while in fact it creates, maintains, reproduces and justifies a set of labor relations which embody very strong gendered inequalities.

Although both Marxist and feminist critiques of the family see it as being exploitative, playing a central role in the control and oppression of women, they disagree on who benefits. Marxists and, in particular, Marxist-feminists, believe that the family primarily serves capitalism. Many feminists, on the other hand, argue that the family bolsters patriarchy and serves the interests of one primary group in society – white middle class men. Hence, Abbot and Wallace (1992: 140) argue that:

> [T]he family helps to support and sustain patriarchal capitalism, a system that advantages white middle-class men over other groups in society. It serves their interests while disadvantaging and exploiting others.

Feminist perspectives on the family have themselves been heavily criticised. For example, Barrett and McIntosh (1991) note that the anti-family stance of the women's movement came up against considerable opposition from women themselves. In particular, Sylvia Ann Hewlett (1988) argues that feminists, in reacting against the ideal of the 1950s housewife, went too far. Hewlett argues that it was not possible to build a mass movement of women around an anti-motherhood stance since, she argues, that "for the majority of mothers their children constitute the most passionate attachment of their lives" and she goes on to argue that "it is absurd to expect to build a coherent feminist movement, let alone a separatist feminist movement, when you exclude and denigrate the deepest emotion in women's lives" (Hewlett, 1988: 152).

Such views led many feminist writers to reassess their views on the family, and in particular motherhood. Leading the way in such reassessment, Adrienne Rich (1976) argues that women need to take control of their bodies, including their reproductive function. Among many feminists, motherhood became celebrated and was seen by many women as giving them a special insight into the world (Segal, 1995). Margaret Wetherell (1995: 249) also argues that this reassessment led some feminists "to stress the joys of motherhood and mothering as a crucial sphere of power and authority for women."

168

Elliot (1986) also raises a number of other criticisms of the feminist position on the family. She is critical of the tendency in feminists' writings to portray the family as being totally oppressive while at the same time portraying women as "helpless and passive victims" (Elliot, 1986: 130). She also questions whether the abolition of the family would necessarily lead to the positive changes envisioned by feminist theorists. This suggests that they underestimate the role played by the wider economic and political structures in women's oppression. Finally, Elliot (1986) argues that while claiming that there is no single family form, the feminist critique of the family does not seem to recognise this diversity that they claim exists. For example, in the postscript to the second edition of the *Anti-Social Family*, Barrett and McIntosh (1991: 167), in reacting to criticism from black feminist writers, recognise that much of their critique of the family is "specific to the white family in Britain." However, they defend their view that family is an anti-social institution on the basis that even if black and ethnic minority families are oppressive in different ways, they still are oppressive to women. An example of this is the way in which some ethnic minority women are forced into arranged marriages. The Scottish President of the Council of British Pakistanis estimates that up to 10 per cent of Asian women in Scotland have been forced into marriages against their will (*The Sunday Times*, 28 April 2002). Abbott and Wallace (1990: 39) suggest that:

> Rather than the family being a marginalized and privatised domestic prison, in many ethnic households it remains the central area of subsistence and is less likely to consist of an isolated couple and more likely to consist of a supportive network of kin.

Trigger

Both Marxists and feminists believe that the family perpetuates gender inequality in society, however, they disagree on who benefits. Marxists argue that the family bolsters capitalism whilst feminists argue that it is patriarchy that is the main beneficiary.

Which of the arguments do you find to be the most convincing, and why?

The 'Dark Side' of Family Life

Feminists have not just been concerned with the ideology of the family and the impact that this has had on women's lives, they have also focused on physical violence and sexual abuse in the home, or the 'dark side' of family life. For example, during the 1970s, sections of the women's movement began to draw attention to the plight of women in abusive relationships. In order to combat this problem, Women's Aid Federation refuges were opened throughout the UK and local authorities are now obliged to re-house women with children who have experienced domestic violence (Carew-Jones and Watson, 1985; Abbot and Wallace, 1990; Barrett and McIntosh, 1991).

Feminists argue that it is 'the family' that gives men considerable power over women, and which is primarily responsible for domestic violence. A study conducted in Scotland by Dobash and Dobash (1980) concluded that domestic violence is a problem arising "out of the patriarchical family system, a system in which the husband's authority over the wife creates a particular marriage power relationship and a subordinate position for wives and mothers" (cited in Abbot and Wallace, 1990: 177). This problem was exasperated, until recently, by both the police and the legal systems' unwillingness to become involved in cases of domestic abuse (Dunphy, 2000).

For many feminists the physical and sexual abuse of women and children (and the recently recognised phenomenon of 'elder abuse') is symptomatic of the inequality inherent in the traditional nuclear family. Domestic violence undermines the assumption implicit in the ideology of the family that all "fathers and husbands, will protect their families from rapists, abusers, and murderers – that is, from other men" (Gittins, 1993: 170). Every day in Scotland approximately 90 women are victims of domestic abuse, and the figures are rising. In 2000, 36,000 cases were reported, which was 3 per cent more than in 1999, with many being repeat offences (*The Daily Record*, 18 December 2001). For many, then, rather than being a place of safety and a refuge from the stresses and strains of modern living, the family is a place of fear.

It has also been recognised that it is not just women and children who experience domestic abuse, and that there is also a significant number of male victims (Gelles, 1995). The 2000 Scottish Crime Survey found that 3 per cent of men and 6 per cent of women reported either being threatened or physically assaulted by their partner in 1999 (Macpherson, 2002). Although half as many men as women reported experiencing domestic abuse, the findings of the Scottish Crime Survey suggest that men, even more than women, are less likely to report instances of domestic violence. This can be illustrated by the official police statistics, which indicate that of the 26,000 reported incidents of domestic violence in Scotland between April and December 1999, 94 per cent of complainants were women (Macpherson, 2002). This may reflect the relative seriousness of the offences committed against women.

Trigger

It has been recognised that not only can the family promote inequality, but that domestic violence and sexual abuse is more widespread than previously thought.

Considering this, should the Scottish Executive, along with various religious groups, really be promoting the institution of the family?

Conclusion: The Future of the Family?

Numerous questions remain about the continued relevance of the family to modern society, and whether the family can and should survive in its present forms. For some commentators, recent changes in the economic and social organisation of western society, such as more women entering work, albeit largely part-time and/or temporary, have placed considerable strain upon the family. For example, Jeffrey Weeks (1992) has argued that three major trends have led to increased pressure on the institution of the family.

First, there is increasing stress being made upon the family by the changing situation in the labour market and the demands that this has placed upon women. Second, there is a lack of emotional support in the nuclear family resulting from the declining importance of the extended family in everyday life. Third, the family appears to be continuously changing form.

However, throughout history the family has demonstrated its resilience, and it would be foolhardy to suggest that the family is in danger of becoming extinct. Although critics have identified numerous problems associated with the ideology of the family, the inequalities it perpetuates and the abuse and violence that the family can hide, the family remains stubbornly popular. This popularity, in part, stems from the emotional support and security that can be derived from belonging to a cohesive family unit. Even those, like Barrett and McIntosh (1991: 133), who characterise the family as 'antisocial', accept that it remains the primary and socially acceptable way in which the majority of us choose to satisfy real needs such as "affection, security, intimacy, sexual love, parenthood."

While critics of the family believe that we should find better ways of meeting these needs, the family also has many supporters, and has been actively promoted by successive British governments. In the 1980s, influenced by the 'New Right's' economic agenda and the activities of Christian moral crusaders, the family became seen as central to the rolling back of the welfare state and a panacea for almost every serious social problem, including juvenile delinquency, drug abuse and teenage mothers (Abbott and Wallace, 1992; Dunphy, 2000). Pro-family policies were central to the New Right's anti-welfare agenda and many, like the economist Patrick Minford, believe that "the provision of direct social services is [...] something the family should undertake" (Minford, cited in Abbot and Wallace, 1992: 135). During both the Thatcher (1979-1990) and Major (1990-1997) Conservative administrations, the family was expected to increasingly shoulder "the 'caring' work that is involved in the provision of welfare, particularly in relation to the 'dependent' population of children, people who are sick or have disabilities and older people" (Clarke and Lagan, 1993: 65). Typically, the burden of this 'caring work' was placed upon women who continue to be seen as the primary carers in western society (Muncie and Wetherell, 1995).

Following their election victory in 1997, the 'New' Labour government in Britain has also continued to stress the importance of the family. For example, in July 1998, Jack Straw, then home secretary, stated "that strengthening the institution of marriage as a basis for bringing up children was a cornerstone of Labour's family policy" (Dunphy, 2000: 189). In Scotland, despite the repeal of the notorious Section 2A of the Local Government Act 1986, which banned the positive 'promotion' of homosexuality as an alternative way of life by local authorities, the Scottish Executive has also remained a staunch defender of the family. This has been demonstrated by their guidance to the Directors of Education that "Pupils should be encouraged to appreciate the value of stable family life, parental responsibility and family relationships in bringing up children and offering them security, stability and happiness" (Scottish Executive Circular, 2/2001).

Chapter Summary

- Defining the family is problematic as there is no one definitive family form.
- Family structure is constantly evolving. Contemporary forms include the nuclear or conjugal, extended, lone-parent, reconstituted, co-habiting couples, and 'families of choice' – including lesbian and gay partnerships and people who choose to live alone.
- Lone-parent households are overwhelmingly headed by women, with increasing incidence. Lone-parent families are significantly disadvantaged in terms of income and standard of living, housing, education and training and employment.
- There is a high incidence of teenage pregnancies in Scotland compared to other European countries, which may be caused by a variety of socio-economic conditions.
- Despite the growth of alternative family structures, the family as the ideal social institution remains very popular.

- The functionalist perspective examines the functions of the family in relation to wider society and how the family, as a social institution, responds to social change. Murdock's (1949) claim that the nuclear family is universal does not appear to survive longitudinal and cross-cultural examination.

- The Marxist perspective focuses on how the family serves the needs of capitalism by reproducing capitalist relations of production through the maintenance, reproduction and socialisation of the labour force.

- Feminist perspectives view the family as a primary site of women's oppression, restricting their freedom to participate in the wider cultural, economic and social life of society.

- There is a significant 'dark side' to family life characterised by violence and sexual abuse. The situation is Scotland mirrors that found in the UK at large.

- Despite the recent increase in alternative family structures and evidence that contemporary families are under increasing stress, the family remains a major feature of contemporary social life.

- New Labour has continued the tradition of successive British governments since the 1980s of actively promoting the importance of the family and marriage.

Further Reading

Barrett, M. and McIntosh, M. (1991) *The Anti-Social Family*, 2nd Edition, London: Verso

Dunphy, R. (2000) *Sexual Politics: An Introduction*, Edinburgh: Edinburgh University Press

Gittins, (1993) *The Family in Question: Changing Households & Familiar Ideologies*, 2nd Edition, Basingstoke: Macmillan

Middleton, S., Ashworth, K. and Walker, R. (1994) *Family Fortunes: Pressures on Parents and Children in the 1990s*, London: CPAG

Muncie, J., Wetherell, M., Dallos, R., and Cochrane, A. (eds.) (1995) *Understanding the Family*, London: Sage

Taylor, S. (ed.) (2000) *Sociology: Issues and Debates*, Basingstoke: Palgrave

Useful Websites

www.gro-scotland.gov.uk General Register Office for Scotland – provides masses of information on the Scottish population.

www.statistic.gov.uk Statistical Division of the British Government – An extensive collection of statistics on the British population and more specific information on Scotland. This site will be a useful companion to the General Register Office for Scotland site.

www.europa.eu.int/comm/eurostat/ This website for the European Union has a collection of data on the European population. Students should find this useful for comparing the situation in Scotland and the rest of the UK with our European partners.

www.eoc.org.uk Equal Opportunities Commission – contains a large collection of data on gender inequalities that students will find useful for exploring the sexual division of labour.

www.opfs.org.uk One Parent Families Scotland is a charity whose website provides lots of information related to lone parent families including legal advice, reports and statistics. Students will find their fact files particular useful.

www.nch.org.uk National Children's Home Factfile has a broad range of information, such as, statistics on the prevalence of different family forms. It also deals with related issues, like social exclusion, teenage runaways and Lesbian, gay, bisexual and transgender young people.

Bibliography

Abbot, P. and Wallace, C. (1990) *An Introduction to Sociology: Feminist Perspectives*, London: Routledge

Abbot, P. and Wallace, C. (1992) *The Family and The New Right*, London: Pluto Press

Allen, I. (1998) *'Teenage Mothers: Decisions and Outcomes*, London: Policy Studies Institute

Berger, B. and Berger, P.L. (1983) *The War over the Family: Capturing the Middle Ground*, London: Hutchinson

Carew-Jones, M. and Watson, H. (1985) *Making the Break: A Practical, Sympathetic and Encouraging Guide for Women Experiencing Violence in their Lives*, Harmondsworth: Penguin

Chambaz, C. (2001) 'Lone-parent families in Europe: a variety of economic and social circumstances' in *Social Policy and Administration* [abstract], Vol.35 (6), Dec 2001, p. 658-71

Clarke, J. and Langan, M. (1993) 'Restructuring Welfare: The British Welfare Regime in the 1980s' in Cochrane, A. and Clarke, J. (eds.) *Comparing Welfare States: Britain in International Context*, London: Sage/The Open University

Cochrane, S. (1998) *Gender and Families*, Thousand Oaks: Pine Forge Press

Crow, G. and Hardey, M. (1992) 'Diversity and Ambiguity Among Lone-Parent Households in Modern Britain' in Marsh, C. and Arber, S. (eds.) *Families and Households: Divisions and Change.* London: Macmillan

Dallos, R. and Sapsford, R. (1995) 'Patterns of Diversity and Lived Realities' in Muncie, J. *et al* (eds.) *Understanding the Family*, London: Sage

Dobash, R. and Dobash, R. (1980) *Violence Against Wives: A Case Against the Patriarchy*, London: Open Books

Elliot, F. R. (1986) *The family: Change or Continuity?* Basingstoke: Macmillan

Engels, F. (1972) *'The Origin of the Family, Private Property and the* State', London: Lawrence and Wishart

Equal Opportunities Commission (2000) *Women and Men In Britain: The Labour Market*, Manchester: EOC

Farmer, M. (1970) *The Family*, London: Longman

Finch, J. and Mason, J. (1993) *Negotiating Family Responsibilities*, London: Tavistock/Routledge

Firestone, S. (1988) *The Dialectic of Sex: The Case for Feminist Revolution*, London: Women's Press

Friedan, B. (1963) *The Feminine Mystique*, New York, NY: Dell

Gavron, H. (1966) *The Captive Housewife*, London: RKP

Gelles, R. (1995) *Contemporary Families: A Sociological View*, London: Sage

Giddens, A. (2001) *Sociology,* Fourth Edition, Cambridge: Polity Press

Edition, Basingstoke: Macmillan

Goode, W. (1964) *The Family*, Englewood Cliffs, NJ: Prentice-Hall

Halsey, A. H. with Webb, J. (2000) *Twentieth-Century British Social Trends*, Basingstoke: Macmillan

Hewlett, S.A. (1988) *A Lesser Life: The Myth of Women's Liberation*, London: Sphere

Hinds, K. and Park, A. (2000) *Interchange 64 – Parents' Demand for Childcare in Scotland*, Edinburgh: Scottish Executive Education Department

ISD Scotland (1999) 'Teenage Pregnancy in Scotland 1989-1998' *Information & Statistics Division; part of the Common Services Agency for the Scottish Health Service*, Health Briefing number 99/04 – issued June 1999

Jackson, S. (2000) 'Families, Households and Domestic Life' in Taylor, S. (ed.) *Sociology: Issues and Debates*, Basingstoke: Palgrave

Jones, G. (1992) 'Short-term Reciprocity in Parent-Child Economic Exchanges' in Marsh, C. and Arber, S. (eds.) *Families and Households: Divisions and Change*, London: Macmillan

Litwak, E., and Szelenyi, I. (1977) 'Kinship and Other Primary Groups' in Anderson, M. (ed.) *The Sociology of the Family*, Harmondsworth: Penguin.

Macionis, J. and Plummer, K. (2002) *Sociology: a global introduction*, Second Edition, London: Prentice Hall

Macpherson, S. (2002) *Domestic Violence: Findings from the 200 Scottish Crime Survey*, Scottish Executive Research Unit, Edinburgh: Scottish Executive

Marx, K. and Engels, F. (1968) 'The Communist Manifesto' in *Selected Works in One Volume*, London: Lawrence and Wishart

Millett, K. (1970) *Sexual* Politics, London: Doubleday

Moore, S. (1987) *Sociology Alive!* Cheltenham: Stanley Thornes

Morgan, D.H.J. (1985) *The family, Politics & Social Theory*, London: RKP

Mount, F. (1982) *The Subversive Family: An Alternative History of Love and Marriage*, London: Jonathan Cape

Muncie, J. and Sapsford, R. (1995) 'Issues in the Study of the Family' in Muncie, J. *et al* (eds.) *Understanding the Family*, London: Sage

Muncie, J. and Wetherell, M. (1995) 'Family Policy and Political Discourse' in Muncie, J. *et al* (eds.) *Understanding the Family*, London: Sage

Murdock, G. P. (1949) *Social* Structure, Basingstoke: Macmillan

Oakley, A. (1974) *The Sociology of* Housework, Oxford: Marin Robertson

Ostner, I. (2001) 'Cohabitation in Germany – rules, reality and public discourses' in *International Journal of Law, Policy and the Family* [Abstract], Vol.15 (1), Apr 2001, p. 88-101

Parsons, T. (1977) 'The Family in Urban-Industrial America: 1' in Anderson, M. (ed.) *The Sociology of the Family*, Harmondsworth: Penguin

Popay, J., Rimmer, L. and Rossiter, C. (1983) *One Parent Families: Parent, Children and Public Policy*, London: Study Commission on the Family

Rich, A. (1976) *Of Woman Born: motherhood as experience and institution*, London: Virago

Rodger, J.J. (1996) *Family Life & Social Control*, Basingstoke: Macmillan

Scottish Household Survey (1999) *Scotland's People: Results from the 1999/2000 Scottish Household Survey*, Scottish Executive: National Statistics Publication

Scottish Household Survey (2002) *Bulletin 7 – Life Cycles*, Scottish Executive: A Scottish Executive National Statistics Publication

Schmidt, V.H. (1992) 'The Differentiation of Households and Working Time Arrangements in West Germany' in Marsh, C. and Arber, S. (eds.) *Families and Households: Divisions and Change*, Basingstoke: Macmillan

Segal, L. (1995) 'A Feminist Looks at the Family' in Muncie, J. *et al* (eds.) *Understanding the Family*, London: Sage

Scottish Executive (2001) S*ocial Justice Annual Report Scotlan*d, Edinburgh: Scottish Executive

Social Trends (2002) *National Statistics United Kingdom No 32*, London: The Stationery Office

Waaldijk, K. (2001) 'Small Change: How the Road to Same-Sex marriage Got Paved in the Netherlands' in Wintemute, R. and Andenaes, M. (eds.) *Legal Recognition of Same-Sex Partnerships*, Oxford: Hart Publishing

Weeks, J. (1992) 'The Body and Sexuality', in Bocock, R and Thompson, K. (eds.) *Social and Cultural Forms of Modernity*, Cambridge: Polity Press

Weston, K. (1991) *Families We Choose: Lesbians, Gays, Kinship*, New York: Columbia Press

Wetherell, M. (1995) 'The Psychoanalytic Approach to Family Life' J. Muncie, J. *et al* (eds.) *Understanding the Family*, London: Sage

Willmott, P. and Young, M. (1960) *Family and Class in London*, London: Routledge and Keegan Paul

Additional resources include the following media: *BBC News*, *The Evening Times* (Glasgow), *The Guardian*, *The Herald*, *The Record*, *Scotland on Sunday*, *Sunday Times* and *The Daily Telegraph*.

Chapter 8　　Poverty

Gerry Mooney

Introduction

The study of poverty represents one of the most widely contested areas of the contemporary social sciences. Not only is the poverty 'field' plagued by definitional and conceptual disputes, but it also mobilises a variety of competing explanations and theories. Within sociology, poverty also connects with many of the other issues and themes that are explored elsewhere in this Book. With questions of class, gender, ethnicity, the analysis of poverty is also closely linked with matters of health and mortality, with changing patterns of work, with crime and, of course, with questions of culture. Elsewhere, the study of poverty is also crucially linked with political science and policy studies. Since 1997, New Labour has made great play of its goal of reducing poverty, especially child poverty and in the process this has renewed sociological interest in the study of poverty.

In this Chapter we can only refer in passing to some of these links, others are there for you to establish yourself through your studies and as you encounter other chapters in this Book. Importantly, however, what this Chapter is concerned to provide is an introduction to the study of poverty; to alert you to the myriad of competing interpretations that are on offer, and to provide you with the sociological tools through which you can further your own interest in and analysis of poverty. From the outset, however, we need to be alert that the history of the study of poverty is characterised by the use of a terminology that has tended to describe people defined as poor in the most condemning and derogatory of terms. From a concern with the rogues, vagabonds, the residuum, the idle or disreputable poor in the nineteenth century through to the problem families, dysfunctional communities and underclass of the late twentieth and early twenty-first centuries, how we talk about the poor says much about our understanding of the underlying *causes* of poverty. This is an area of sociological investigation that is highly susceptible to moral condemnation and to blaming the poor for their own situation. Poverty is a highly political concept and the study of poverty is a politically charged activity. As you work through this Chapter you should be alert to some of these issues.

As in other fields of sociological inquiry, we start with issues of definition and by attempting to disentangle poverty and inequality.

Distinguishing Poverty and Inequality

If poverty and inequality are seen as inextricably linked, this is a product of their analysis and explanation, *not* because they refer to the same relations and processes. Marxist theorists, for example, will see poverty as a direct result of the social divisions (primarily of class) and the accompanying inequalities of capitalist society (see Chapter 2: Sociological Theory and Chapter 4: Social Class). In this respect they will see poverty and inequality as crucially inter-related. But while it is important to understand the connections between poverty and inequality, it is also important to separate them.

Trigger

Why is it important to distinguish between poverty and inequality?

Like poverty, inequality can be defined in many different ways. One of the most commonly used measures is to compare differences in income and wealth between different sections of the population. Thus, for instance, government studies and reports, together with more academic accounts, tend to examine the contrasting fortunes of the top income groups, with the middle and lowest income groups in different ways. The greater the degree of difference between them, the greater the extent of inequality. Rising levels of inequality, as in the UK and Scotland since the late 1970s, does not *necessarily* mean that there will be an increase in poverty. Rising inequality can be accompanied (though not often) by a general raising up of income standards of all income groups in society, so while the least well off may be falling further and further behind the richest groups, their income might still be rising. Thus, it is possible to have inequality but no poverty. By contrast, it is not possible to have poverty and no inequality.

Defining Poverty

It is important from the start to make one major qualifying point – it is extremely difficult to provide an objective definition and explanation of poverty. The question of poverty (and what, if anything, to 'do about it') goes to the heart of our own world-views, our own political attitudes and to our understanding of society. How we define poverty, that is, how we construct the 'problem' of poverty, will determine what we think should be done about it. For instance, if we see poverty as the consequence of individual failures (such as 'laziness', 'fecklessness' or some other 'weakness') then we may support policies that force poor people into paid employment, cutting benefits in the process. If, on the other hand, we see poverty as an outcome of structural inequalities in society, then we may tend towards policies that promote a far-reaching redistribution of wealth and income in society.

Already it is hoped that you can begin to grasp that this is an area that is full of disagreements and ongoing controversies. These disagreements underpin many of the important questions that are central to this area of study: what is poverty? How do we best measure it? How is poverty to be distinguished from inequality? What are the main causes of poverty? How do we distinguish between poverty and social exclusion? What does the study of policy tell us about the nature of social and welfare policies in a society such as contemporary Scotland?

The 'absolute measure' of poverty
Booth and Rowntree
The study of poverty is hardly a new field of sociological endeavour. It was during the nineteenth century that poverty began to emerge as a distinctive field of sociological investigation. Throughout this period, as John Scott describes (Scott, 1994), poverty was a matter of significant public and political debate. Amidst the rapid industrialisation and urbanisation of Britain, rising concerns were to be voiced about the 'problem of the poor' in the slum areas of the burgeoning cities (see also Mooney, 1998). One of the most notable studies of the urban poor was Charles Booth's massive 17 volume series of books under the umbrella title of *Life and Labour of the People in London*, published in 1902-03. Booth is credited with a number of important innovations in the study of poverty: his is widely regarded as the first serious sociological investigation of poverty involving as it does the systematic house-by-house surveys of the poorer parts of London, mapping in the process the key social characteristics of different parts of the city (see Scott, 1994 for a fuller account of Booth's methodology).

Booth's surveys were prompted in part to refute claims by contemporary Marxist groups in London that almost one-third of the population of London lived in poverty. Unfortunately for him, Booth's study confirmed what he had set out to reject and he estimated that 1.3 million people (one-third of the population) were poor. To allow him to draw such conclusions he established what has since become a somewhat problematic if common way of defining poverty – a 'poverty line'. Booth set his poverty line for a family of two adults and up to three children at 21 shillings (around £1.05) per week. Above this families could avoid poverty, below this line they were effectively poor.

Booth's studies of poverty in London in the late 1880s and 1890s were soon followed by Seebohm Rowntree's investigation of poverty in York, beginning in 1899. Rowntree was a Quaker from a family of confectionery manufacturers. His study involved the collation of evidence from almost 12,000 working class families in York. Published in 1901 as *Poverty: A Study of Town Life*, Rowntree established what has since come to be referred to as an 'absolute measure of poverty'. This measure or definition of poverty is based upon a precise calculation of the minimum income necessary to maintain physiological efficiency. From this, he came up with a list of bare necessities to maintain a subsistence level of existence. In addition to the food requirement for an adult male worker, 80 per cent of a man's ration for a woman and up to 30 per cent for each child depending on age, Rowntree added fuel, light, clothing and replacement of household items. From this he estimated that each family of two adults and three children would require 12s 9d per week for food, 1s 7d for one room and 2s 6d for two rooms and an allowance for heating, lighting etc. This would cost a minimum of 4s 11d per week. On this basis he estimated that a family of two adults and three children would require a minimum income of 21s 8d per week to meet their basic subsistence needs. This became his poverty line. Families with an income below this level were divided into groups: those in 'primary poverty' – families whose income were insufficient to meet basic needs, and those in 'secondary poverty', where income was above the poverty line but 'wasteful' expenditure or the mismanagement of income meant that the household failed to meet basic or minimum standards. On these measures, Rowntree estimated that 9.9 per cent of the people of York lived in primary poverty and a further 18 per cent in secondary poverty (Rowntree, 1901).

From the vantage point of the early twenty-first century the studies of Booth and Rowntree appear almost quaint and given the criticisms that have been made of them, it is easy to dismiss them without reserve. However, we should not underestimate the contribution that both studies made to the study of poverty. While the methods used may be crude by comparison with the methods of investigation that are deployed by sociologists and other researchers today, nonetheless both Booth and Rowntree helped to pioneer large scale population surveys and provided the basis for future generations of research. In other ways there are what we can terms a series of *enduring legacies* from their work: notably the idea of a 'poverty line'.

The idea of a basic minimum standard definition of poverty – an absolute measure – was utilised by William Beveridge in his plans for the post-World War Two welfare state (Beveridge, 1942) and many other governments in Britain and elsewhere have adopted a similar kind of approach. Further, both Booth and Rowntree were very much products of their time in that they shared the prejudices that many middle class and wealthy people had of the poor. They both deployed a language that was in important respects highly condemning of poor people, of their culture and daily lifestyles. Rowntree in particular, however, was one of many who since the Poor Laws of the 1830s, made a distinction between what in simple terms can be termed the 'good' and 'bad' poor. The good poor – or to utilise the language of the nineteenth century, the *respectable poor*, were poor largely as a consequence of factors beyond their control. By contrast, the *disreputable* or *bad poor* were largely to blame for their situation. Rowntree, for instance, saw in alcohol and in other 'vices' many of the factors contributing to what he defined as 'secondary poverty'. This attempt to divide the poor into two component groups has long been a feature of poverty studies and of the wider politics of poverty and, as we shall see below, the idea that the poor have to a considerable measure contributed to their poverty has been a feature of more recent debates about the emergence of an 'underclass' in late twentieth century Britain.

The 'poverty line'

Not surprisingly the absolute measure of poverty has been widely criticised. Despite pretences that an absolute measure represents a scientific or objective definition, it is far from being neutral, reflecting both the biases and attitudes of the researcher and/or of the government of the day. What is the absolute minimum necessary for human survival? Who decides where the poverty line should be set? Should we take into account wider societal expectations? One further limitation of the attempt to establish a minimum poverty line is that there will always be many whose income is marginally above that line yet who are effectively poor. Tony Novak (2001) has also drawn our attention to the limitations of the idea of a poverty line, claiming that this substitutes measurement for a definition of poverty. He writes:

> The use of a poverty line as a way both of defining and measuring poverty has ever since (the late nineteenth century) dominated studies of the problem. In practice the measurement of poverty has become a substitute for its definition. When we say that the poor are those who have less than £x a week (at whatever level the line is drawn), we end up defining poverty by the way we measure it. In the process we lose any independent definition of what poverty actually is (other than just a certain amount of money), and above all we are left with no way of explaining it.
>
> (Novak, 2001: 182)

The one advantage – and even this is subject to dispute – of the absolute measure is that it permits us to debate the extent of poverty in Britain. While the government, either in London or in Edinburgh, has no official poverty line as such, deploying instead figures based on dependence upon and take-up of means-tested benefits, the notion of an absolute line below which people should not be allowed to 'fall' allows for public scrutiny of government policies and approaches to poverty. However, the absolute measure can also distort the true picture of poverty by focusing on the poor as a distinctive group in isolation from a consideration of wider structural factors and social inequalities, such as race, class, gender, etc.

The 'relative measure' of poverty

While the absolute approach enjoyed some degree of popularity among academics and policy-makers during the 1950s and early 1960s, if certainly not among those defined as poor, then this was to be undermined by the so-called 'rediscovery of poverty' in the 1960s. The idea of a rediscovery of poverty is something of a misnomer in that poverty had never gone away in post-1945 Britain, with the introduction of the welfare state. Amidst the conditions of the economic 'boom' of the late 1940s through to the 1960s, it was widely believed that the battle against poverty had finally been won. Such claims were fuelled not only by the emergence of virtually full employment during the 1950s, but also by the development of the welfare state in the post-war period. The idea that the welfare state would look after the most vulnerable sections of the population 'from the cradle to the grave' became an important defining characteristic of the entire post-1945 period. By the early to mid-1960s, however, it was already clear that Britain's economic growth was beginning to slow down and in areas such as west-central Scotland, Dundee, Fife, south Wales, north-east England and in other major northern English cities, the long term decline of staple industries such as coal mining, iron and steel and shipbuilding contributed to rising unemployment and to renewed concerns that the welfare state was failing to meet the needs of the poorest sections of the population.

One of the most notable studies of poverty to emerge at this time was Brian Abel-Smith and Peter Townsend's *The Poor and the Poorest* (1965). Not only did this book serve as a timely reminder that poverty was still a prevalent feature of British society, it also rejected the absolutist measure deployed by William Beveridge in his plans for the post-war welfare state. Instead Abel-Smith and Townsend developed what has become known as the 'relative definition of poverty'. In *The Poor and the Poorest*, they stated:

> Poverty is a relative concept. Saying who is in poverty is to make a relative statement – rather like saying who is short or heavy.
>
> (Abel-Smith and Townsend, 1965: 63)

Arguably, as Brian Lund points out, Abel-Smith and Townsend effectively *re-defined* poverty rather than *rediscovering* it (Lund, 2002: 141). Against what they regarded as the numerous limitations of the absolute measure, the relative approach was concerned to relate poverty to wider social expectations. In other words, the incomes and standards of living of the poorest groups in society have to be defined *relative* to average incomes and lifestyles. As Townsend was to comment some 28 years later:

> People are relatively deprived if they cannot obtain, at all or sufficiently, the conditions of life – that is, the diets, amenities, standards and services – which allow them to play the roles, participate in the relationships and follow the customary behaviour which is expected of them by virtue of their membership of society. If they lack or are denied resources to obtain access to these conditions of life and so fulfil membership of society they may be said to be in poverty. People may be deprived in any or all of the major spheres of life – at work where the means largely determining position in other spheres are earned; at home, in neighbourhood and family; in travel; in a range of social and individual activities outside work and home or neighbourhood in performing a variety of roles in fulfilment of social obligations.
>
> (Townsend, 1993: 36)

In the mid-1960s using a relative definition that took the basic 'national assistance level' (poverty line) plus 40 per cent, Abel-Smith and Townsend found that the percentage of the population living on an income of less than 40 per cent above the national assistance level had increased from 7.8 per cent in 1954 to 14.2 per cent in 1960.

Townsend's Poverty in the United Kingdom *(1979)*

Peter Townsend has done more than anyone else in Britain to develop not only a relative approach to poverty, but to construct a fully sociological definition. From the mid-1960s he has been to the fore in poverty debates, arguing that poverty prevents people from taking part in the activities that are regarded as customary in society. For example, taking one's children on a holiday may be regarded as customary or as a norm to which we should all aspire. In his mammoth study, *Poverty in the United Kingdom* (1979), Townsend argued that poverty was not simply about a lack of money or failure to meet bare necessities, but a failure to become a full participant – a full citizen – in society. Poverty, then, was about more than money; crucially, it was about the lack of things that are widely perceived as necessary in society. From this, he argued that it is possible to be objective about the kinds of things that are widely regarded as necessities, for example, a telephone or television set. In his 1979 study, he developed a 'deprivation index' of some 60 items falling into this category that were then tested in public attitude surveys. Townsend's approach then attempted to combine both household incomes and the deprivation index.

Trigger

What are the advantages and disadvantages of the relative definition of poverty?

One of the main advantages of the approach developed by Townsend is that it helps us to avoid seeing the poor as a distinctive group in isolation from wider inequalities in society. In arguing that we must take account of societal expectations and norms and values, Townsend (along with other sociologists who have advocated this relative approach) highlights that poverty is about more than a lack of income, important that this may be. Has Townsend helped to develop an objective approach as he has claimed? Let us return to the deprivation index.

David Piachaud (1981) has argued that Townsend ignores the huge diversity in lifestyle in modern Britain. Many people who would not be defined as poor may not indulge in the activities deemed necessary by respondents to the deprivation index survey. How many families today sit down for a 'Sunday roast' for example? This was identified as one the 60 items on the deprivation index, but the failure to have a Sunday roast may be more a question of lifestyle than deprivation. It may also be more a question of culture, race, class, gender, whether someone is vegetarian or not, etc. Following criticisms from those such as Piachaud, Townsend and other researchers (Mack and Lansley, 1985; Gordon and Pantazis, 1997; Gordon *et al*, 2000) have attempted to improve on the deprivation index. As this has been updated and reworked though, critics continue to argue that the relative measure *confuses* poverty and inequality. In years to come (if not already!) a mobile phone and home computer may come to be widely perceived as absolute necessities. Would the failure to have these be more a question of inequality and of choice rather than of poverty?

As the debate around the usefulness of the relative measure continues, the attractiveness of the absolute approach – though not for the poor – is all too evident in that it provides a clear-cut measure and definition of poverty. However, both approaches share some similar limitations: the claims to objectivity are more assumed than proven; both are based on often arbitrary and subjective measures and the question of whose interests are paramount when the calculations are made are all too frequently side-stepped.

From the discussion thus far it is evident that poverty is a much-debated issue. Our assessment thus far is that poverty is an essentially contested concept that is open to competing definitions and interpretations. However, it is largely agreed that we need to relate poverty to the standards that are regarded as 'reasonable' in a given society. As the European Commission defines it:

> '[T]he poor' shall be taken to mean persons, families and groups of persons whose incomes (material, cultural and social) are so limited as to exclude them from the minimum acceptable way of life in the Member States in which they live.
> (EEC Council Decision, 1984, quoted in Howard *et al*, 2001: 19)

In attempting to go beyond what an increasing number of sociologists now regard as a rather futile and sterile debate over the respective advantages and disadvantages of the absolute and relative approaches, the economist, Amartya Sen, has argued that both definitions need to be seen as interconnected. They are interconnected in that the core of the *relativist* approach is an *absolutist* measure while the *absolutist* core is also *relativist*, in that it takes account of changing expectations and standards of living (Sen, 1983). We close this Section by quoting from the 1995 United Nations World Summit for Social Development in Copenhagen, that defined poverty in the following broad terms:

> Poverty has various manifestations, including lack of income and productive resources to ensure sustainable livelihoods; hunger and malnutrition; ill-health; limited or lack of access to education and other basic services; increased morbidity and mortality from illness, homelessness and inadequate housing; unsafe environments and social discrimination and exclusion. It is also characterised by lack of participation in decision making and in civil, social and cultural life. It occurs in all countries: as mass poverty in many developing countries, pockets of poverty amid wealth in developed countries, loss of livelihoods as a result of economic recession, sudden poverty as a result of disaster or conflict, the poverty of low-wage workers, and the utter destitution of people who fall outside family support systems, institutions and safety nets.
> (United Nations, 1995)

From Poverty to Social Exclusion

In the previous section we noted that there had been a steady shift towards an understanding of poverty that attempted to relate this to wider societal expectations. In seeing poverty in terms of relative deprivation, as in the work of Peter Townsend and others, there was a recognition that the poor were not isolated from the 'rest of society' and that poverty had to be understood as a structural feature of that society. Arguably, this understanding has been developed further through the notion of 'social exclusion'.

While the idea of social exclusion has risen to prominence in discussions of poverty in Britain since the early 1990s, the concept has a much longer historical pedigree in other European societies and is central to the policy approaches to poverty that have been developed by the European Commission in recent decades. In Britain, the concept began to enter academic and policy making discourses in the late 1980s and early 1990s, but it was not until the General Election success of New Labour in 1997 did it become consolidated as the dominant approach to understanding poverty. We return to consider some aspects of New Labour's approach to social exclusion shortly, but before we proceed any further there are, once more, definitional and conceptual issues that must be explored.

As with Townsend's notion of relative deprivation, social exclusion encompasses a wide range of issues in addition to income. Here, social exclusion is regarded as a more useful notion than poverty because of its *comprehensiveness*. It is concerned with different aspects of social integration and citizenship – economic, social, cultural and political. It is also attractive to many sociologists and policy makers as it is seen as a more *dynamic* notion of poverty, in that it refers to processes whereby different individuals and social groups become marginalised or *excluded*, not on the outcomes in themselves. To be socially excluded, then, encompasses a range of social situations. Some groups may be politically excluded, for instance, or excluded from good health, good education and/or housing.

The attractiveness of the idea of social exclusion is all too apparent here in that there is recognition of issues and inequalities of power and that poverty and social exclusion are part and parcel of the ways in which society is structured. Despite this attractiveness – and it is difficult to underestimate the fashionable status of the notion of social exclusion today – there remain numerous conceptual problems. Social exclusion and poverty are often used as substitutes for each other. However, they are not necessarily referring to the same processes or situations. Poverty tends to be understood as a lack of material resources, for example, low income, poor wages or poor housing. Social exclusion, by contrast, focuses on the relationship between the socially excluded and the rest of society. Members of ethnic minority groups, for instance, may be socially excluded as a consequence of racism and discrimination, but they may not be poor (see Chapter 6: Race and Ethnicity). In other words, it *is* possible to be socially excluded but *not* materially deprived.

In other ways the ideas of social exclusion and poverty also differ. Social exclusion is primarily concerned with the lack of educational and employment opportunities while poverty can relate to those in employment. This is further reflected in the policy differences that the concepts can give rise to. While there are obvious overlaps between anti-poverty and social inclusion strategies, anti-poverty policies have tended to emphasise redistribution of wealth and income in order to attain some equality of incomes, whereas policies aimed at promoting social inclusion are much more driven by a concern to enhance opportunities.

The idea of social exclusion has permeated much of sociological and social scientific discourse in the late 1990s and early twenty-first century, reflecting its rise to prominence in political and policy-making circles. However, the attractiveness of the notion of social exclusion should not blind us to its ideological components and to the political basis of the notion. There are many different definitions and numerous interpretations of the notion of social exclusion. Its obvious flexibility is a key to its attractiveness, but flexibility is also a source of weakness, in that the term may be being used by different sociologists in different ways without an awareness of this variability. There are different political traditions and perspectives underpinning different understandings of social exclusion.

New Labour and social exclusion

As the term, social exclusion, is used in Britain in the late twentieth/early twenty-first by the New Labour government, it is possible to detect a mix of social reformist (or 'old Labour') politics, as well as conservative and liberal ideas. The sociologist, Ruth Levitas (1998), has analysed the numerous different perspectives that can underpin the notion of social exclusion, dividing these into three main discourses:

1) The *redistributionist* discourse
2) The *social integrationist* discourse
3) The *moral underclass* discourse.

The 'redistributionist' discourse emphasises diverse aspects of exclusion including material exclusion, or poverty. This approach argues for far-reaching programmes of redistribution in order to reduce inequalities. By contrast, the 'social intergrationist' discourse focuses primarily on exclusion from the labour market and in turn social inclusion is defined largely in terms of take-up of paid employment. The third discourse, which Levitas terms the 'moral underclass' discourse, tends to focus on the poor/socially excluded as a distinctive sub-group in society; distinctive, that is, in relation to their lifestyles and cultures.

Levitas (1998) notes that it is possible to detect aspects of all three discourses in New Labour's understanding of social exclusion. However, they do not share equal weighting, with the social intergrationist and moral underclass approaches dominant to varying degrees, while the 'Old Labour' concern with redistribution has been almost totally abandoned by New Labour. New Labour's approach to social exclusion/inclusion is worthy of some discussion here (see also Byrne, 1999; Mooney and Johnstone, 2000; Novak, 2001; Social Exclusion Unit, 2001).

The notion of social exclusion is attractive to New Labour for a variety of different, though inter-related, reasons. It promised to widen the poverty debate beyond a concern solely with material inequalities and lack of income or money. That it is multidimensional meant that it would be possible for politicians to focus on different processes whereby different groups of people became excluded, for instance, in relation to education or employment. Social exclusion was also regarded and presented as a new problem requiring modern policies. As Tony Blair expressed it in 1997:

> It is a very modern problem, and one that is more harmful to the individual, more damaging to self-esteem, more corrosive for society as a whole, more likely to be passed down from generation to generation, than material poverty. (Blair, 1997: 4)

We can see here that a sharp distinction is being made between material poverty and social exclusion. In the process, this has helped to marginalize issues of poverty and inequality under New Labour. Blair, and other leading New Labour politicians, have argued that tackling social exclusion is more important than raising the incomes of the poorest groups in society. The ex-cabinet minister, Peter Mandelson, presented this view as follows:

> Let us be crystal clear on this point. The people we are concerned about, those in danger of dropping off the end of the ladder of opportunity and becoming disengaged from society, will not have their long term problems addressed by an extra pound a week on their benefits.   (Mandelson, 1997: 7)

Thus, instead of a return to the redistributive policies that successive governments pursued (to a limited extent, it must be said) in the 1950s and 1960s, with New Labour the emphasis of anti-poverty and social inclusion policy is on the promotion of *opportunities*. Here, as Levitas (1998) among others have noted, the whole thrust of New Labour's approach to social exclusion becomes clear: social inclusion is largely understood to be *inclusion through paid employment*. New Labour inherited from the Conservatives an antipathy to welfare 'dependency', that is, reliance upon state benefits.

In Europe, the dominant understanding of social exclusion is largely derived from the French tradition of sociology with its foundations in the work of Emile Durkheim (see Chapter 2: Sociological Theory). Here, social exclusion is viewed as a consequence of a breakdown in the social order and by the fragmentation of integrating institutions such as the labour market, family and community. Social exclusion, therefore, is seen as a threat to social cohesion. In Britain, however, the dominant approach to social exclusion is much more narrow; it is viewed primarily in terms of exclusion from paid work.

As one might expect there has been considerable debate and ongoing controversy over the usefulness of the notion of social exclusion. The initial attractiveness of the notion has steadily though tentatively given way to some much more critically informed interpretations. Levitas (1998) and Novak (2001), for instance, have argued that the notion of social exclusion implies that we can make a clear distinction between two groups in society – the *included* and the *excluded*. However, neither the included nor the excluded are homogenous groups. It is suggested that the included are a majority against the minority excluded, at times referred to as 'the two thirds, one-third society'. Can we, though, reasonably claim that the *included* share a common social position and a mutuality of interest? What are being neglected here, then, are issues of power and inequality. There is an excluded group in society, but some sociologists writing from a Marxist-inspired perspective see this not as the poor but as a self-reproducing class of the rich (Westergaard, 1995). The major fault line is a class cleavage between the rich and the vast majority of the population, not between the so-called included and the excluded.

The debate over social exclusion/inclusion continues. As with other definitions and approaches to poverty, the use and validity that one sees in the notion is largely shaped by our wider politics and view of the world, its problems and what to do about them. We should not ignore the ways in which the idea of social inclusion has helped to re-focus the poverty debate in Britain away from a traditional if somewhat unhelpful approach that is concerned primarily to define who the poor are and to measure them. Instead, there is much more concern with processes and with the social relations through which certain groups and individuals come to be marginalised within society. At the same time, though, we need to be alert to the problems and limitations of the notion of social exclusion and acknowledge that issues relating to material poverty and inequality have been largely sidelined.

Explaining Poverty

The key task for sociologists is always to explain. And the study of poverty is no exception. Space constraints do not allow us to provide a full and exhaustive account of all the competing theories and interpretations that have been developed. Instead, we focus on some of the predominant ways through which poverty has been analysed and explained: the idea of a 'culture of poverty', the notion of an 'underclass' and

Marxist approaches to poverty. In other Chapters in this Book you will encounter debates from other perspectives, such as feminism (see Chapter 5: Gender), as well as those that focus on racism and discrimination (see Chapter 6: Race and Ethnicity). You may wish to reflect on the ways in which these can help to illuminate different aspects of poverty.

'Cultures of poverty' and the 'cycle of deprivation'

The idea of a 'cycle of deprivation' has been used to explain the persistence and reproduction of poverty and disadvantage across generations. This idea has been around for some considerable time, albeit in different forms and guises. It is possible to identify a number of different interpretations of inter-generational poverty. Here we focus on two of these explanations.

Cultural explanations

We have touched on these already to some extent. These have their origins in the nineteenth century, when the poor were all too frequently divided into two groups – the 'respectable poor', who were poor through no fault of their own; and a 'disreputable/dangerous' poor whose poverty was largely attributed to their lifestyle and habits, in other words to their culture (see Chapter 13: Culture for further discussion on the meaning(s) of culture). Culture in this respect is being used to refer to a system of values, beliefs and norms that are regarded as normal for a particular group of people. With respect to the culture of poverty, what is being argued is that a set of values are being passed from one generation to another that do not allow for the development of attitudes and behaviours that would help people to escape from poverty. The social anthropologist, Oscar Lewis, in his study of poor Puerto Rican communities in the late 1950s and 1960s, provides what is perhaps the best-known account of the culture of poverty (Lewis, 1959; 1961; 1966). For Lewis, the development of a culture of poverty among these communities effectively insulated the poor from the dominant culture in society, resulting in a high degree of alienation and apathy. Their culture revolved around the pursuit of immediate gratification, random violence and uncontrolled sexuality. Street level criminality, 'illegitimacy' and family breakdown were among the most significant features of this culture of poverty. The culture of poverty in the account offered by Lewis, amounts to the emergence of a distinctive deviant subculture that is passed on from generation to generation (see Chapter 11: Crime and Deviance for further explanation of sub-cultures).

The idea of a culture of poverty was to become influential among policy-makers in the United States during the 1960s and early 1970s as a means of explaining the persistence of poverty among African Americans. It was popularised in Britain as a *cycle of deprivation* in the 1970s by the Conservative politician, Keith Joseph, who argued that the persistence of poverty in the context of general economic growth was the consequence of deep lying factors within the structure of the poor family. Such poverty would not be removed by increased welfare payments, he argued, but by a transformation in the attitudes and values of the poor. These ideas have also been developed and further popularised by the American social commentator, Charles Murray, in his account of welfare dependency and a developing underclass in the United States and in Britain, to which we will return shortly.

Citizenship-centred explanations

Foremost here are the arguments advanced by the American political scientist, Lawrence Mead (1986) (see also Jordan, 1996). He argues that the 'cycle of disadvantage' is primarily the result of the failure of government's and policy makers to *enforce* the work (and related) obligations of citizenship. Against the more cultural type explanations offered by Lewis and Murray (above), Mead argues that the poor *do not* have a distinctive subculture of norms and values that set them aside from the rest of society, but lacked the ability to conform to the dominant cultural values in society. Mead argued that the solution was to push the poor towards self-reliance and out of welfare dependency. Paid employment should become a condition of state assistance through social security and other benefits. Through work the poor would become more responsible and would increasingly begin to meet the obligations of citizenship.

This approach has been influential in the United States since President Bill Clinton's Democratic administration in the 1990s. More recently, New Labour in Britain has adapted it through its 'Welfare to Work' programme. Breaking the cycle of disadvantage has become central to New Labour social inclusion programmes and here again the promotion of paid work as a source of personal salvation is all too evident. As Tony Blair commented in 1997, "work must be made to pay if welfare is to be made to work." The notion of a cycle of deprivation lives on, albeit in a different and arguably more sophisticated way than in the 1960s and 1970s.

As might be expected there have been many criticisms of the culture of poverty thesis. Critics argue that the approach ignores the wider structures and inequalities of power that operate to marginalize particular groups in society. It is further claimed that if there is indeed a culture of poverty, this should be seen more as a response to the debilitating and oppressive conditions that make day-to-day survival so precarious, rather than a cause of poverty as such. We can also see in the culture of poverty approach a similar type of 'blame the victim' arguments that you should now be familiar with from reading this Chapter. Opponents of the culture of poverty thesis argue that, in blaming the victim, wider class inequalities are completely ignored.

The 'underclass'

The notion of an underclass shares some common ground with the cultural perspectives discussed above. The influence of neo-liberal and conservative thinking is all too evident as is the focus on a group of people – the so-called underclass – who, it is claimed, represent a distinctive sub-group in society. While again there are different interpretations and definitions of an underclass, we focus here upon the most influential and notable approach that is provided by the American social commentator and sociologist, Charles Murray. While the idea of an underclass has been around for some considerable time in Britain, having being used in the mid-1960s and early 1970s to refer to poor ethnic minority groups in some of Britain's urban areas, it re-emerged in a new and more potent form in the 1990s – thanks largely though not exclusively – to the work of Murray (Murray, 1984; 1990). In the United States, the notion of an underclass had become a byword for the black poor. When visiting Britain in 1999 as a guest of *The Sunday Times* to investigate if an underclass existed in Britain, Murray left readers in no doubt of the 'problems' that the underclass was posing for British society. He writes:

> I arrived in Britain earlier this year [...] a visitor from a plague area, come to see whether the disease is spreading and (my) conclusions were as dramatic as they were predictable: Britain has a growing population of working-aged, healthy people who live in a different world from other Britons, who are raising their children to live in it, and whose values are now contaminating the life of entire neighbourhoods.
>
> (Murray, 1990: 4)

This one short comment by Murray has clear echoes of nineteenth century fears about the residuum or disreputable poor. Here he mobilises images and a language of disease and contagion to refer to the poorest sections of British society. Importantly, for Murray and other right wing sociologists and social commentators, what made the underclass poor was not so much a lack of material resources, but their abnormal and deviant behaviour, culture and values. Indeed, the main argument made by Murray was that the provision of welfare and other social security benefits had contributed to the growth of an underclass in both Britain and the United States as it encouraged laziness and 'worklessness' – a rejection of the work ethic. Such ideas were to become influential on conservative politicians on both sides of the Atlantic, while the echoes of the underclass discourse still resonate among some of New Labour's policy makers.

The idea of an underclass has, not surprisingly, been subject to far-reaching debate and argument (see Byrne, 1999; Jones and Novak, 1999; Morris, 1994; Novak, 2001; Young, 1999). Again we can see some of the enduring legacies of the past in the attempt to argue that the poor are largely to blame (along with state benefits) for their circumstances. However, more importantly, we again can see here the effort to distinguish the poor from the rest of society. The idea of an underclass implies a group that is cut off from 'normal' or 'mainstream' society, typified by a different set of norms and values. In this regard the whole underclass approach represents a middle class normalising discourse. In other words it takes as an assumed and unproblematic norm a middle class outlook on life characterised by law abiding family centred life revolving around paid work. By contrast the criminally predisposed underclass are anti-social.

The underclass and social exclusion

Once more it is important not to underestimate the influence of the underclass thesis. In some respects, while the notion of social exclusion is regarded by many as more attractive, as it less condemning and pejorative than that of the underclass, they can share some common sentiments in the ways in which poor people are constructed and portrayed. Social exclusion, as with the idea of an underclass, can be viewed almost as a form of *self-exclusion* with many of the poor perceived to be lacking the moral responsibilities and obligations that the 'rest of us' have. However, even in its most condemning forms the notion of social exclusion avoids the harsh and anti-poor language of the underclass thesis.

One of the major problems with the underclass approach is that the concept itself is highly ambiguous. There is no objective set of criterion through which it can be established if indeed an underclass does in fact exist and the substitution of forceful argument for any empirical evidence was perhaps one of the most telling limitations of the thesis (MacNicol, 1987; Morris, 1994).

Marxist explanations of poverty

You have already explored some of the main ideas and components of the Marxist approach in Chapter 2: Sociological Theory and Chapter 4: Social Class, in particular. Here we seek to apply some of these ideas to the study of poverty.

Trigger

In what ways would Marxist theorists approach the question of poverty?

As might be expected, the entire thrust of the Marxist approach is to locate the discussion and analysis of poverty within the wider context of class relations and inequalities within capitalist society (see Ferguson, Lavalette and Mooney, 2002; Novak, 1988). In this respect, Marxists make no attempt to isolate the poor from the rest of society, but to see poverty as part of a relationship of inequality, materially and politically. Thus, poverty is related to inequalities of wealth and income: it cannot be understood outside of the relationship to inequalities of wealth. Here, for Marxists, the production and accumulation of wealth is also simultaneously the production and accumulation of poverty, want and misery. From this position Tony Novak (1988) argues that:

It is the economic and social relationships of capitalist society – the division between a minority who own and control the world's wealth and those who have no choice but to work for them – that is at one and the same time both the root cause of poverty and the motor of capitalist growth and development [...]. Poverty thus needs to be understood not just as the end-product of a particular system of distribution – which is how most studies of poverty approach it – but as an essential precondition for the process of production itself. Poverty is not simply about the way that society's resources are distributed, but also about the way these resources are produced.

(Novak, 1995: 70)

In arguing this, the Marxist approach immediately stands out from the other perspectives outlined above that seek to define and measure the poor in isolation from wider society. They also stand apart from the social exclusion approach which, while recognising that social exclusion results from wider social processes, ignores the class based inequalities of capitalist society. Both the social exclusion and Marxist approaches see poverty as a relationship, but they understand and analyse this in very different ways. Through the Marxist approach, poverty is viewed as the product of the normal operations of capitalist society, not an abnormal state of affairs. Its study and analysis, therefore, must be located within those very relations by understanding it as a relationship of inequality between a highly powerful and affluent minority and the mass of ordinary workers.

Poverty and Social Exclusion in Modern Scotland

On its election victory in 1997, New Labour stressed its commitment to tackling poverty after almost two decades of Conservative rule in which poverty was sidelined as at best a marginal issue. The Scottish Parliament reaffirmed these commitments for Scotland in 1999. From the time of the first meeting of the reconvened Parliament in 1999, there have been repeated statements by successive First Minister's that have committed the Parliament to tackling what has been labelled 'the scourge of Scotland'. Donald Dewar, the inaugural First Minister in Scotland (1999-2001), stated in 1998 that many people in Scotland were excluded from full societal participation, such as through unemployment, lack of education and skills, poor housing, poor health, etc. Those who enjoyed a better experience in these aspects of social life had a responsibility to those who did not. True to New Labour's form, though, such discussion was couched in the language of addressing social exclusion. It was only by addressing such problems of social exclusion could an appropriately fair model of society be promoted, Dewar argued.

With the Scottish Parliament's re-establishment, leading Scottish politicians and their representatives made great play about developing "Scottish solutions to Scottish problems," with poverty and social exclusion high on the list of priorities. In this new context of devolved government, Westminster still held many of the keys to anti-poverty policy, particularly social security. However, many of the services that make up the modern welfare state, for example, education, housing, childcare, youth

193

services, health and community care, became the direct responsibility of a Scottish Executive held accountable by the Edinburgh Parliament.

Scotland's poverty 'problems'
There can be little doubt that Scotland bore a disproportionately high burden of Britain's poor in 1997 and faced the biggest challenge when trying to fulfil Labour's promise to make Britain "a more equal society." The poverty facing the new leaders of Scotland on the eve of devolution in 1999 was significant. Twenty-three per cent of households had an income below 60 per cent of the UK median income; 33 per cent of children lived in low income households; 45 per cent of adult employees were on low pay; life expectancy for men was 2.3 years less than for men in the rest of the UK; and the number of households assessed as homeless stood at 32,000 (Brown *et al*, 1999; Kenway *et al*, 2002).

Statistical analysis, based largely on figures from the Households Below Average Income reports, shows that between 1997 and 2001/2002 (Brown *et al*, 2002; Kenway *et al*, 2002):

- There had been no real fall in relative poverty. Around a quarter of individuals still lived in low-income households: 24 per cent below the 60 per cent median threshold. This remains higher than the UK average. There has, however, been a fall in the percentage of households living in 'absolute' low income; therefore, some real rises in real income, but no closing of the gap between the rich and poor
- Child poverty stubbornly remains at around 29/30 per cent of children. The proportion of children living in households with relative low income is about 7 percentage points higher than for the population as a whole and two-fifths of low income households with children are more than £50 a week short of the low income threshold. Current policies have moved children in households from just below the poverty threshold to just above it, but critics note that the more difficult task facing the government is to lift children who are "a long way below the threshold and every child some way above it" (Bradshaw, 2001)
- The proportion and number of children living in households below 50 per cent and 60 per cent of the mean income thresholds in Scotland over the period 1994/1995 to 2001/2002 was higher than under the Conservatives by 30,000 and 40,000, respectively. Thirty-two per cent or 42 per cent of children live in poverty so, defined whereas in 1994/1995 it was 28 per cent and 37 per cent, respectively (Scottish Executive, 2003: Table 3)
- There was a rise in the number of low-income households containing someone who is working. These 'working poor' accounted for around 40 per cent of the low-income, working age households in the period 1998-2001. In addition, in 2001 nearly 210,000 working age households had been without

work for three years or more, the highest number for at least a decade. A high and rising proportion of unemployed people are only able to find short-term work.

Within this overall picture the poverty that faced the new leaders of Scotland there was significant geographical unevenness. Parts of Scotland, for example, experience some of the worst rates of poverty in the UK and Europe.

- Glasgow is home to many of the worst levels of deprivation in the UK, with many areas still trying to cope with atrocious standards of income, health, educational attainment and access to services (Turok, 2003)
- Child poverty rates in four wards in Glasgow were above 80 per cent in 2001. Glasgow accounts for 12 per cent of all children in Scotland, but 20 per cent of children in poverty
- Some of the worst rates of morbidity and mortality in the developed world are found in parts of Scotland (Shaw *et al*, 1999)
- Sixteen of Scotland's most deprived areas are in Glasgow. Glasgow and Dundee have more than half their wards within the worst 10 per cent of wards across Scotland. There are, by contrast, no wards in the top 10 per cent of deprived areas in the thriving economies of Aberdeen, St. Andrews or Edinburgh (Social Disadvantage Research Centre, 2003)
- Geographic inequalities in employment grew between 1997 and 2001, with the Scottish Borders and West Dunbartonshire recording job falls of 10 per cent, and Aberdeenshire and West Lothian recording rises of up to 30 per cent (Kenway *et al*, 2002).

In 2002, following a series of UK wide studies, the New Policy Institute produced its first specific report on poverty in Scotland, *Monitoring Poverty and Social Exclusion in Scotland* (Kenway *et al*, 2002). Considering policy areas that are both reserved and devolved, it measured changes in the picture of poverty in Scotland since devolution across 34 different indicators. The report concluded that of the 34 indicators, seven showed some improvements over the five-year period, six had worsened and fifteen had remained steady. While there had been an improvement in the proportion of the working age population receiving benefit as well as in death rates, income inequality, low pay and the risk of low income all increased. The authors of the Report noted:

> [T]he stubborn refusal of so many of the key measures of poverty and exclusion in Scotland to show any signs of movement.   (Kenway *et al*, 2002: 10)

This, then, is the picture of poverty in Scotland since devolution in 1999.

As elsewhere in Britain, the causes of poverty are varied. In Scotland they encompass a range of issues, such as long-term economic decline, structural inequalities, the expansion of relatively poorly paid jobs in the service and leisure sectors, polarisation within and between different parts of the country, and demographic change. However, government priorities and policies in the economic and social spheres cannot be ignored. They are key factors causing and determining the extent of poverty. Conservative government priorities before 1997 focused on reducing expenditure and state provision and supporting the 'enterprise culture'. Reductions of inflation rather than unemployment were the primary target. These policies increased poverty and inequality. As was pointed out earlier, since 1997 the New Labour government and the devolved Scottish Executive have prioritised tackling poverty and social exclusion. At the same time, they have also sought to promote Scotland as one of the most attractive economies for inward investment. Key to this is the creation of a cheap and flexible labour market. One of the main criticisms made of the government's approach to social exclusion (both in London and Edinburgh) is that in prioritising inclusion through paid employment, it ignores the plight of the growing numbers of the 'working poor'; that is those with a job but who receive what many would interpret as poverty wages or low pay. The implementation of a national minimum wage was in part intended to address this, but it was set at such a low level as to leave millions of workers vulnerable to continuing low pay and to look to forms of state support to supplement their income.

Poverty is unevenly spread across Scotland: it affects different groups of people and different areas in different ways. Poverty is both an urban and rural phenomena, and while the extent of rural poverty should not be ignored, it is the depth and intensity of poverty in many of Scotland's cities and towns that have received most attention from the policy makers. However, poverty is not only uneven geographically. It affects some groups more than others, including lone parents, the low paid, the sick and disabled, many of the elderly and the unemployed, though old age, disability or lone parenthood are not in themselves the cause(s) of poverty. What links the different groups here tends to be their shared class background, compounded by inequalities of gender and ethnicity.

Poverty and social exclusion continue to be major problems facing modern Scotland. While the Scottish Executive has sought to develop new policies to address these, there is still a long road to travel before we can say that these policies have worked.

There are also signs, however, that other policies are contributing to rising levels of poverty.

Conclusion

This Chapter has introduced you to some of the main issues and debates that continue to feature most prominently in the sociology of poverty. It has not provided an exhaustive discussion of the entire poverty spectrum, instead it is hoped that the account offered here has whetted your appetite for more investigation and study in this field. It is important to recognise that debates and controversies surrounding poverty, social exclusion and inequality are on going. Poverty continues to be a prevalent feature of modern Scotland, Britain and of many societies around the world today. As it haunts hundreds of millions of people on a day-to-day basis, sociologists, social policy analysts and policy-makers will continue to develop new ways of understanding and measuring poverty. However, it may be argued that unless poverty is understood and analysed as one side of an unequal relationship with wealth, it will continue as a pervasive feature of modern societies.

Chapter Summary

- Poverty is a highly contested concept open to many competing definitions and interpretations.
- Within the UK much of the study of poverty has been devoted to measuring and quantifying the numbers who are poor, through the use of absolute and/or relative measures of poverty.
- Since the 1990s, there has been a growing recognition that poverty is about much more than the lack of income or material resources, but crucially also about the processes through which certain groups of people and individuals come to be marginalized or excluded from good health, good housing and education and from secure employment.
- Throughout the history of poverty studies in the UK there have been repeated attempts to divide the poor into two main categories: those who are largely responsible for their own situation and those whose poverty is due to factors and circumstances beyond their control.
- There are a variety of different explanations of poverty, ranging from those that focus on the characteristics of the poor themselves, through to more structural perspectives that emphasise wider social divisions and patterns of inequality.
- Poverty continues to be a major feature of contemporary Scottish society. Since devolution in 1999 the Scottish Executive has prioritised anti-poverty policies, but there are signs that some of New Labour's economic policies may be contributing to rising levels of poverty, especially among the working poor.

- Poverty is a global phenomenon affecting hundreds of millions of people in the early twenty-first century. The development of policies that will effectively tackle poverty must also tackle the structural inequalities that are such a prevalent feature of the world today.

Further Reading

Byrne, D. (1999) *Social Exclusion*, Buckingham: Open University Press

Ferguson, I., Lavalette, M. and Mooney, G. (2002) *Rethinking Welfare*, London: Sage

Hughes, G. and Lewis, G. (eds.) (1998) *Unsettling Welfare*, London: Routledge

Jones, C. and Novak, T. (1999) *Poverty, Welfare and the Disciplinary State*, London: Routledge

Levitas, R. (1998) *The Inclusive Society: Social Exclusion and New Labour*, London: Macmillan

Lund, B. (2002) *Understanding State Welfare*, London: Sage

Pantazis, C. and Gordon, D. (eds.) (2000) *Tackling Inequalities*, Bristol: The Policy Press

Percy-Smith, J. (ed.) (2000) *Policy Responses to Social Exclusion*, Buckingham: Open University Press

Seymour, J. (ed.) (2000) *Poverty in Plenty: A Human Development Report for the UK*, London: Earthscan

Shaw, M., Dorling, D., Gordon, D. and Davey Smith, G. (1999) *The Widening Gap: Health Inequalities and Policy in Britain*, Bristol: The Policy Press

Walker, R. (ed.) (1999) *Ending Child Poverty*, Bristol: The Policy Press

Useful Websites

Child Poverty Action Group: www.cpag.org.uk

Child Poverty Action Group Scotland: www.childpoverty.org.uk/cro/scotland.htm

Department of Work and Pensions (DWP): www.dwp/gov.uk

Joseph Rowntree Foundation: www.jrf.org.uk

London School of Economics Centre for the Analysis of Social Exclusion (CASE): www.sticerd.lse.ac.uk/

Low Pay Unit: www.lowpayunit.org.uk/

The Poverty Alliance: www.povertyalliance.org/

Scottish Low Pay Unit: www.scotlpu.org.uk

Scottish Poverty Information Unit: www.spiu.gcal.ac.uk

Social Exclusion Unit: www.socialexclusionunit.gov.uk/

Townsend Centre for International Poverty Research: www.bris.ac.uk/poverty/welcome.htm

Bibliography

Abel-Smith, B. and Townsend, P. (1965) *The Poor and the Poorest*, London: Bell and Son

Blair, T. (1997) Speech by the Prime Minister at Stockwell Park School, Lambeth, Dec. 8

Booth, C. (1902-3) *Life and Labour of the People in London*, 17 volumes, London: Macmillan

Beveridge, W. (1942) *Social Insurance and Allied Services*, Cmd. 6404, London: HMSO

Bradshaw, J. (2001) 'Child Poverty under Labour', in Fimister, G. (ed.) *An end in sight? Tackling child poverty in the UK*, London: Child Poverty Action Group

Brown, U., Scott, J., Mooney, G and Duncan, B. (eds) (2002) *Poverty in Scotland 2002: People, Places and Policies*, London/Glasgow: Child Poverty Action Group/Scottish Poverty Information Unit

Gordon, D. and Pantazis, C. (1997) *Breadline Britain in the 1990s*, Aldershot: Ashgate

Gordon, D., Adelman, L., Ashworth, K. *et al* (2000) *Poverty and Social Exclusion In Britain*, York: Joseph Rowntree Foundation

Hills, J. (1998) *Income and Wealth: The Latest Evidence*, York: Joseph Rowntree Foundation

Howard, M., Garnham, A., Fimister, G. and Veit-Wilson, J. (2001) *Poverty: The Facts*, 4th Edition, London: Child Poverty Action Group

Jordan, B. (1996) *A Theory of Poverty and Social Exclusion*, Cambridge: Polity Press

Kenway, P., Fuller, S., Rahman, M., Street, C. and Palmer, G. (2002) *Monitoring Poverty and Social Exclusion in Scotland*, London: New Policy Institute

Lewis, O. (1959) *Five Families*, New York, NY: Basic Books

Lewis, O. (1961) *The Children of Sanchez*, New York, NY: Random House

Lewis, O. (1966) *La Vida*, New York, NY: Random House

Mack, J. and Lansley, S. (1985) *Poor Britain*, London: Allen and Unwin

MacNicol, J. (1987) 'In Pursuit of the Underclass', *Journal of Social Policy*, 16, 2

Mandelson, P. (1997) *Labour's Next Steps: Tackling Social Exclusion*, London: The Fabian Society

Mead, L. (1986) *Beyond Entitlement*, New York, NY: Free Press

Mooney, G. (1998) ''Remoralizing' the Poor?: Gender, Class and Philanthropy in Victorian Britain', in Lewis, G. (ed.) *Forming Nation, Framing Welfare*, London: Routledge

Mooney, G. and Johnstone, C. (2000) 'Scotland Divided: Poverty, Inequality and the Scottish Parliament', *Critical Social Policy*, 63, pp.155-182

Morris, L. (1994) *Dangerous Classes: The Underclass and Social Citizenship*, London: Routledge

Murray, C. (1984) *Losing Ground*, New York, NY: Basic Books

Murray, C. (1990) *The Emerging British Underclass*, London: Institute of Economic Affairs

Novak, T. (1988) *Poverty and the State*, Milton Keynes: Open University Press

Novak, T. (1995) 'Rethinking Poverty', *Critical Social Policy*, 44/45 pp.58-74

Novak, T. (2001) 'What's in a Name? Poverty, The Underclass and Social Exclusion', in Lavalette, M. and Pratt, A. (eds.) *Social Policy*, Second Edition, London: Sage

Percy-Smith, J. (2000) 'The Contours of Social Exclusion', in Percy-Smith, J. (ed.) *Policy Responses to Social Exclusion*, Buckingham: Open University Press

Piachaud, D. (1981) 'Peter Townsend and the Holy Grail', *New Society*, September 10, pp.419-421

Rowntree, B.S. (1901) *Poverty, A Study of Town Life*, London: Macmillan

Rowntree, B. S. and Lavers, G.R. (1951) *Poverty and the Welfare State*, London: Faber and Faber

Sen, A. (1983) 'Poor, Relatively Speaking', *Oxford Economic Papers*, 35, pp.153-169

Shaw, M., Dorling, D., Gordon, D. and Davey Smith, G. (1999) *The Widening Gap: Health Inequalities and Policy in Britain*, Bristol: The Policy Press

Scott, J. (1994) *Poverty and Wealth*, London: Longman

Scottish Executive (2003) *Households Below Average Income Analysis 2001/02 – Figures for Scotland Using the Range of Low Income Thresholds, 1994/95-2001/02*, Edinburgh: Scottish Executive

Social Disadvantage Research Centre (2003) *Scottish Indices of Deprivation 2003*, Oxford: University of Oxford, Department of Social Policy

Social Exclusion Unit (2001) *Preventing Social Exclusion*, London: Stationery Office

Townsend, P. (1979) *Poverty in the United Kingdom*, Harmondsworth: Penguin

Townsend, P. (1993) *The International Analysis of Poverty*, Hemel Hempstead: Harvester Wheatsheaf

Turok, I. *et al* (2003) *Twin Track Cities: Linking Prosperity and Cohesion in Glasgow and Edinburgh*, Glasgow: University of Glasgow, Department of Urban Studies

United Nations (1995) *Report of the World Summit for Social Development*, Copenhagen, March 6-12

Westergaard, J. (1995) *Who Get's What?* Cambridge: Polity Press

Young, J. (1999) *The Exclusive Society*, London: Sage

Chapter 9   Education

Dave Brown

Introduction: What is Education For?

It may seem obvious what education and schools are for. Most people have had experience of the formal education system, even though they may not always have seen the relevance of what they learned in terms of what they did after they left school. Consequently, in answering such a question they might say that it helps one understand the world. More pragmatically, they might claim that education gives them the knowledge about the things they have to know or the qualifications they require in order to obtain the job of their choosing.

Sociologists often wish to look beyond these 'common sense' approaches and ask questions designed to strip away the surface explanations given for the existence of the institutions that make up our society. In other words, they seek to develop what C. Wright Mills (1959) referred to as *The Sociological Imagination*. These help form important contributions to contemporary debates regarding the nature of education in our society. This Chapter focuses specifically on the issue of 'differential achievement' in education and does not, therefore, seek to provide a comprehensive coverage of all issues raised in the sociology of education.

In Scotland, it is widely assumed that education has held a special place in the hearts of the population, who have long believed that Scottish education has provided for democratic access to the benefits of education regardless of social background. It has been claimed by many that Britain is a 'meritocratic' society; that is, that educational success and occupational status is determined by a combination of ability and effort as opposed to the reproduction of privilege, class position, gender and ethnic background. To what extent is this notion mythical?

This key question will be addressed throughout this chapter, which will begin by looking at how mainstream sociological theories are used in the sociology of education.

Theoretical Perspectives on 'Differential Achievement'
The functionalist perspective

Of all sociological perspectives, the ideas expressed in the functionalist perspective are most likely to coincide with common sense explanations of education. Put simply, for functionalists, the education system plays an important role in enabling children to take their place in the adult world. It does so by equipping them with the knowledge and skills required for jobs in a complex division of labour in industrial society and by supplying them with the norms and values of wider society. It teaches children to 'fit' into the culture of their society.

Durkheim (1858-1917) was an early proponent of what has come to be termed, the functionalist approach on education and its role in society (see Chapter 2: Sociological Theory). As a teacher of teachers, and the first professor of sociology, he was convinced that education played a vital role in preparing children to take up their role(s) in society. To achieve this, education had a duality of purpose that served both society and the individual. First, it was charged with producing in children adherence to that homogeneity of values that binds society together; the 'value consensus'. Second, it had to prepare children for their particular role in society – their 'special milieu' according to Durkheim (1956 [1922]).

However, while Durkheim (1956 [1922]) seems to display concern that education should serve the needs of the individual, for him, the individual had to be subordinate to society, since, left to their own devices, humans would lead lives of untrammelled, individualistic greed. For the individual to be moral, therefore, they must submit to the 'will of society' as manifested in the imposition of 'common sentiments' by the state through the education system. This latter point is illustrated in one of two main themes in his work: *homogeneity* and *diversity*. Education should create homogeneity through teaching "the essential similarities that collective life demands" Durkheim (1956 [1922]: 70), but should also allow for *diversity* in that individuals should be encouraged to find their own *milieu* in the complex division of labour found in industrial societies. Such diversity was the basis of cooperation in society as each recognises interdependence on the talents and abilities of others. Therefore, for Durkheim (1956 [1922]), it is natural, inevitable and, even, desirable that individuals should achieve differently in education.

Like Durkheim, Talcott Parsons (1902-1979) was interested in the socialisation function of the school in engendering a moral commitment to society. He was much more concerned, however, over the school's role in the efficient allocation of human resources to the labour market. For Parsons (1961), an important part of the school's function is to identify and select those individuals that are best suited for the many and diverse roles in modern society. It does this through objectively judged achievement. The most able will obtain the qualifications that will give them access to the most difficult but prestigious occupations, while those who fail will be allocated to the mundane world of unskilled labour.

This 'efficient' honing of talent could not be achieved in the family unit, as parents will always favour their own child. Consequently, the school acts as a 'bridge' between the home and the wider social world. In the home the child is judged by *ascriptive* and *particularistic* values. In simple terms, the child is valued for *who* they are. In contrast to this, the school introduces the child into the wider world where they will be valued for *what* they are. In other words they are judged according to objectively assessed attainment, and 'universalistic' values.

Trigger

In your experience do people who do not do well at school blame themselves or the school system?

Whilst Parsons (1961) claims that education systems in liberal democracies are meritocratic, he recognises the potential for conflict. Educational failures who, consequently, are allocated poorly rewarded, low status, positions, may resent the rewards accrued by the successful. To ensure social harmony, therefore, it is important that the school socialises not only for success, but also for failure. As attainment is objectively judged in a school system to which everyone has equal access, those who lose out in terms of attainment will see that they have been treated fairly and that their lack of success is simply a product of their lack of merit.

Evaluating the functionalist approach
Durkheim (1956 [1922]) assumes that the moral standards taught in schools are self-evident and widely accepted. Bowles and Gintis (1976), however, argue that the values taught in school are those of the upper and middle classes. As such, they are designed to maintain class inequalities in education by presenting them as 'natural' and 'just'.

The assumed neutrality of the state's role in education in contemporary society can also be questioned. It could be argued that educational policy reflects the wider ideological aims of the administration in power at the time. Willis (1977) rejects Durkheim's 'structuralist' assertion that children are 'passive receptors' for what is taught, arguing that children, to a large extent, can shape their *own* destinies in the school system.

Parsons assumes that the United States, at his time of writing, was a meritocratic society. Bowles and Gintis (1976) dispute this claim, arguing that educational success in the US is based on social class origin rather than ability. Doubts also exist over the status of the evidence upon which Parsons bases his argument. In 'The School Class as a Social System' (Parsons, 1961) many statements begin with the expressions "I think" or "It is my impression," which is hardly a recipe for objectivity (see Chapter 2: Sociological Theory and Chapter 3: Sociological Methods for further discussion on *objectivity* and *subjectivity* in sociological research).

The Marxist approach

Bowles and Gintis' (1976) *Schooling in Capitalist America* is a classic Marxist (see Chapter 2: Sociological Theory and Chapter 4: Social Class) study of education that is, arguably, as applicable to modern Scotland as it was in the US at the time of writing. It views schooling in capitalist societies as a 'tool of the state apparatus' that serves the needs of the economic elite. Schools, they argue, do this in two ways.

1) ***The myth of the meritocracy***: They claim that children of the same measured ability levels do not end up in similar positions in the occupational hierarchy. On the contrary, family background and personality traits are more powerful predictors of occupational destination than measured cognitive ability. They account for this in terms of the class based differences in family cultures. Families from different class backgrounds socialise their children in different ways, they argue, and this impacts on the "well being, behaviour and personal consciousness of individual" (Bowles and Gintis, 1976: 143). A major component of this influence is the working world of the parents that tends to be reproduced in the consciousness of their children. In other words, parents prepare their children for working roles similar to their own. The values and norms into which each social class socialises its children, helps to produce a 'correspondence' (see point 2) between the social relations of the family and those of the workplace, and, in so doing, they help to reproduce class structures in capitalist society

2) ***Correspondence Theory***: Whilst it may be obvious why those in privileged positions in society might be content to support an educational system that effectively reproduces such privilege, it may be less clear why those who are denied privileged positions also seem to accept their (lowly) position without much protest. Bowles and Gintis (1976) claim that since force alone cannot guarantee the docility and commitment of the working masses to the capitalist system, the education system has been co-opted to create an 'inner

policeman', which ensures required levels of passivity and submissiveness. The notion of the correspondence principle implies that the experiences of young people in school correspond to the experiences they will have at work. In doing so, it prepares them for working life in the hierarchical structure that is the modern corporation. Bowles and Gintis (1976) refer to a number of correspondence links between schools and work. Principal among these is the relationship between the organisation of schools and work and the apparent fact that the types of personality traits rewarded by schools reflect those desirable in the world of work. Rules and regulations in working class comprehensives emphasise docility and submissiveness to external control, while private sector schools emphasise leadership, motivation and self-control.

Bowles and Gintis (1976: 116) conclude that the myth of meritocracy in education serves to "legitimate an authoritarian, hierarchical, stratified and unequal economic system, and to reconcile individuals to their objective position within the system." In other words, educational attainment in schools mirrors patterns of advantage and disadvantage found in wider (capitalist) society.

Evaluating the Marxist approach
Bowles and Gintis' (1976) work was highly influential in the sociology of education at the time and remains an important point of reference for current debates on meritocracy. There are, however a number of weaknesses in their work.

Willis (1977) (see below and in Chapter 3: Sociological Methods) casts doubts over the school's role in reproducing a docile and compliant workforce. The political ideology that shapes the imperatives of current educational policy is complex and often contradictory. In Scotland, consistent with New Labour policy in England and Wales, a commitment to a programme of social inclusion that includes 'lifelong learning' as well as increasing numbers progressing to higher education may appear to help promote the educational opportunities of children from poorer backgrounds. However, in both national regions higher education student grants have been abolished for all but the very poorest groups and in England and Wales 'top up fees' have been introduced. Moreover the focus of educational provision under Blair lies firmly on how it can serve the needs of industry in the face of global economic competition, resulting in an intensification of 'vocationalism' in the curriculum.

Indeed, as if to confirm the relevance of the correspondence principle today, Bowles and Gintis (2001) have revisited their work. They claim that in the intervening years new evidence substantiates their original findings and that the "Correspondence Principle is [...] by and large [still] correct" (Bowles and Gintis: 2001: 20). This would suggest, therefore, that claims that modern capitalist societies had become more open and meritocratic were unfounded.

Trigger

In what ways might Marxist approaches to education explain the continued existence of educational inequalities?

Interactionist approaches

By the late 1960s/early 1970s, the claim made by Parsons (1961) that schools were devoted to the task of selecting on the basis of ability regardless of social origin, was being challenged by research from an 'interactionist' perspective (see Chapter 2: Sociological Theory).

Rosenthal and Jacobson's (1967) *Pygmalion in the Classroom*, claimed to demonstrate a 'self-fulfilling prophecy' effect regarding student performance (see Chapter 2: Sociological Theory and Chapter 11: Crime and Deviance). Pupils of varying ability were selected at random and presented to their teacher as *expected* to develop intellectually. After a year of the experiment, it was found that the children selected had indeed increased their IQ scores. In Britain, Hargreaves (1967) focused on the practice of *streaming* in a secondary modern school. Streaming is a traditional practice adopted in some schools where children are grouped, and often taught, separately in terms of ability level as defined by test results which, he claimed, led to the development of an anti-school culture among those in the bottom stream who felt rejected by the school and who responded by behaving 'badly' and neglecting their studies. Teachers felt that the negative attitudes displayed by pupils in the low streams reinforced their original assessment of their abilities, thereby illustrating another example of the self-fulfilling prophecy concept.

Some 30 years later Aggleton (1987) came to the same conclusion as Hargreaves (1967), that streaming helps create an anti-school culture. Removing such a practice might mean that:

> The school might not produce so many highly qualified pupils as measured by certificates. However, even on the purely meritocratic principle there would probably be the improvement that there would be fewer anti-school pupils and, therefore, fewer pupils with bad behaviour records, missed assignments and ultimately fewer pupils with very poor qualifications.   (Abraham: 1995, 137)

Resistance theory

Paul Willis' (1977) seminal study, *Learning to Labour*, utilises the structuralism of a neo-Marxist orientation along with the focus on 'human agency' employed by an interactionist approach (see Chapter 2: Sociological Theory). In doing so, he qualifies *two* important aspects of Bowles and Gintis' work (1976). First, whereas

Bowles and Gintis (1976) suggest that schools in capitalist societies exist to provide the industrial system with docile and compliant workers, Willis (1977) looks at a small sample of twelve boys, whom he calls the 'lads', and notes that their noisy and rebellious attitude to school would be seen by prospective employers as anything but ideal preparation for the world of work. Second, Willis (1977) rejected the view of Bowles and Gintis (1976) that working class children are subjected to a propaganda process that renders them the passive and willing tool of the capitalist system. On the contrary he sees the 'lads' as culturally based actors unwittingly aiding the reproduction of the very class divisions that disadvantage them (see Box 9.1).

Box 9.1 Paul Willis (1977) 'Learning to Labour'

The basis of resistance
At the root of the 'lads'' rebellion in school is their ability to see through or 'penetrate' the 'con tricks' perpetrated by schools at the behest of an exploitative economic system. For example, as the 'lads' place a great deal of emphasis on enjoying life, they resent the school's demands on their time and their freedom to choose what they want to do. They are disparaging of those pupils who conform in school – the 'earholes'. Consequently, the disruptions to the class, the avoidance of work, and the importance of having 'a laff' are all ways in which the demands of the school for control over their 'selves' are circumvented.

They also question the usefulness of what the school has to offer them .The teachers make constant reference to the value of qualifications for school children. The 'lads', however, are highly sceptical about these claims, recognising that qualifications do not actually create jobs. Nor do qualifications mean that opportunities for more meaningful work increase as work, in itself, is inherently meaningless other than as a means of making money. Similarly, qualifications are not necessarily the route to social mobility. For the 'lads', such mobility is largely a myth for they reason that not everyone can advance in life. In this system there must be losers as well as winners. On these grounds the 'lads' question the logic of investing a great deal of personal time and energy into working for qualifications that will return, at best, marginal enhancements in their living conditions.

Reproducing the Class System

Willis (1977) maintains that working class children end up seeing the divisive nature of a system that advantages some at the expense of others, as natural. However, he sees the 'lads' themselves as active participants in the process rather than as 'passive dopes' on which society imposes itself. He claims the 'penetrations' of the 'lads' have the potential to form the basis of a class-consciousness that could lead them, and others of a like mind, to come together to form organisations capable of effecting radical social change. They are prevented from doing so because of their belief that education and mental diligence are 'feminine' pursuits. For them, the male wage packet is earned by hard physical labour. However, in allowing this masculinity to distort their vision, 'the lads' lose the potential of seeing through the exploitation of capitalism. Therefore, they inadvertently aid the stability of capitalist relations of production through the reproduction of class inequality and the diversion of challenges away from the system.

Trigger

To what extent does Willis successfully combine Marxist and interactionist approaches to education in the study?

Evaluation of Willis (1977):

There is no doubt that Willis' (1977) work represents a notable attempt to overcome the perceived 'economic determinism' of structuralist Marxism (see Chapter 2: Sociological Theory). His work highlights the unintended consequences of the clash between working class culture and the school. However, social reality may be even more complex than that described by Willis, for resistance is not especially limited to white, working class males and not all working class males rebel against school. In order to further evaluate Willis' (1977) contribution, a number of points can be made:

- Research by Reynold (2001) indicates that high achieving middle class boys in primary schools are also very aware of the perceived 'femininity' of learning and the dangers to their social standing in a hierarchy of masculinities of appearing too studious
- Aggleton (1987) found that the middle class subjects of his research left school early to attend, rather unsuccessfully, the local further education college. As with Willis' lads, school was seen as demanding excessive conformity that would blunt their creativity. However, whereas Willis' 'lads' expected to labour at the lower end of the occupational hierarchy, Aggleton's 'adolescents' expected to be successful and to go onto higher education. Even though they failed at school and college because of poor attendance and a preoccupation with hedonist pursuits, they remained secure in their belief in their own intellectual superiority. In fact, most had obtained jobs in creative arts six years after the study, at a time of high youth unemployment. This may indicate that the way the labour market works in favour of the middle class is more important than attitudes to schooling

- It is not only boys who reject school. McRobbie (1991) found that working class girls often abandoned school for a world of teenage romance that had the effect of reproducing traditional oppressive domestic relations
- One *major criticism* that could be made of Willis (1977) is that he builds his argument on the basis of a small sample of boys from one school. While it may well be the case that many schools have on their rolls equally disaffected youngsters, Brown (1987) found that the majority of ordinary working class children conform to the demands of school and are content with the prospect of employment in, what they perceive to be, respectable working class jobs
- By failing to take into factors such as gender and ethnicity, Willis may in fact be "expressing a more deeply structured oppression at the level of culture" (McFadden, 1995: 296). McFadden (1995) argues that what is needed is not merely a critique of the education system, but ways of teaching that promote challenges to these oppressive structures by the children themselves. However, given that in the recent past in both Scotland and England, a number of reforms directed towards increasing vocationalism in schools have placed limitations on the autonomy of classroom teachers it is difficult to see how this could be accomplished, even if the teachers were so inclined (see also Abraham, 1995: 143-144).

Trigger

In what way would Marx's view of class and revolution be seen as a 'grand narrative'?

Postmodernism, Education and Differential Achievement

Postmodernism and its adherents would object to a functionalist or a Marxist understanding of the role and function of education, for example, which they might term a 'grand narrative'; that is, a universal theory based on notions of human progress, that attempts to explain the world from single perspective, or 'one big idea' (see Chapter 2: Sociological Theory). Education is an obvious target for postmodernists, as they would see it as the main vehicle for the transmittance of the grand narrative of societal improvement.

Usher and Edwards (1994), for example, question a number of commonly held views on the benefits of education. First, they suggest that it cannot be understood as a "transcendental good or something that follows naturally from a recognition of the essential attributes of 'man'" (Usher and Edwards, 1994: 125). They argue that the history of education is littered with the voices of authority figures, be they educationalists or politicians, who claim that they know what education should be. The issues they raise, such as differential achievement, the lowering of standards, or the appropriateness of the content and process of education essentially reflect ideological perspectives and despite all the theorising and policy initiatives, they argue that little has been accomplished. Working class children still fail disproportionately and questions are still asked about standards and content as it becomes clear that so-called 'experts' cannot provide solutions.

Second, Usher and Edwards (1994) challenge what they see as a dangerous trend in education. They claim that despite the presentation of knowledge as a disinterested search for truth, the powerful seek to marginalize and disparage rival interpretations of what constitutes truth. Indeed, they argue that a major purpose of education is to suppress rather than encourage independence of mind. As such, education is used as a substitute for external forms of coercion. In other words, the purpose of what Foucault (1982) calls a 'regime of truth', as espoused at any point in history, is to encourage public acceptance of some kind of standard of behaviour or appearance that they will endeavour to adhere to. In this context, the subject becomes governable without the need for coercion or regulation. This has special relevance for new developments in education that put an emphasis on producing workers who are self-supervising, so that management costs can be reduced (see section below on reforms in education).

The introduction of National Vocational Qualifications (NVQs, or SVQs in Scotland) may fit with this model. As the NVQ/SVQ system is designed for the training for, and testing of, competences that meet the needs of employers, other forms of knowledge that are not directly related to the work place are marginalized. In this way, workers are preserved as 'unreflecting actors' in a system that aims to exploit them.

Evaluation of postmodernist views of education
The post-modern message that there are no universal truths able to inspire human progress may present an overly pessimistic view of the future of the human condition. A number of other evaluative points have, however, been made by critics:

- It could be argued that there is inadvertently a structural element in the work of Usher and Edwards (1994). Their claim that education has a self-regulation function is not dissimilar to classical functionalist and Marxist explanations
- Apple (1995) argues that while post-modern academics focus on avoiding simply replacing one authoritative voice with another, their theorising and research has very little impact on policy making in the real world. In the US, for example, policy making is dominated by the conservative right who tend to view education as a way of providing capitalist society with efficient producers and consumers. Postmodernism fails to offer a challenge to the injustices inherent in that system

- Apple (1995) goes on to argue for the continued use of the concept of social class, because it is that which determines who has the power to define what knowledge is, what goes on in schools, and who goes on to higher education
- Kenway (1995: 131) equates postmodern approaches with those of the 'New Right' in that have both "officially removed the concept of social justice from the educational agenda." (See Chapter 2: Sociological Theory.) Contemporary feminists have also become so preoccupied with the internal theoretical and political difficulties produced by an infatuation with postmodernism and post-structuralism, that they leave the world of educational policy untouched, she states
- There may also be an internal contradiction at the heart of postmodernism, since it denies all other truths except the 'truth' of postmodernism.

Trigger

What are the strengths and weaknesses of the postmodern perspective on education?

Differential Achievement and Social Class

Perhaps the most persistent theme in the sociology of education has been how to account for the differences in educational attainment between middle and working class children. *Three* such models can be identified, those that link social class to:

- Intelligence and learning
- Material conditions
- Parental attitudes.

Intelligence and learning

Explanations which link intelligence, as an innate capacity, to social class tend to be non-sociological and/or from a right-wing perspective. *Three* main arguments are forwarded by these approaches:

1) Intelligence is a fixed, innate, commodity that can be scientifically measured
2) Working class pupils are less intelligent than their middle class counterparts as measured by Intelligence Quotient (IQ) tests, which explain class inequalities in educational attainment
3) Intelligence is genetically inherited, which explains the maintenance and reproduction of class inequalities in educational attainment.

Proponents of this approach include Herrenstein and Murray (1994), who have argued that a racial underclass in the US exhibit 'profligate and feckless lifestyles' as a consequence of their low intelligence (see Chapter 2: Sociological Theory and Chapter 6: Race and Ethnicity). Peter Saunders (1996) argues that natural ability is a more efficient predictor of future educational attainment than any of the following factors:

- The social class of the parents
- The length of time parents spent in education
- Over-crowding in the home and lack of basic amenities
- Parental aspirations for the child and parental interest in the child's education.

Inherited intelligence, then, according to Saunders, is more important determinant of educational attainment than the social and material advantages available to middle class children.

Gould (1995) argues, however, that the idea that intelligence can be reduced to a single score in an IQ test is not, of itself, very intelligent. Nisbet (1995) points to the importance of intervention in improving IQ. He cites, for example, one study that showed that large increases could be made in measured IQ through programmes designed to aid young children deemed at risk. Gardner (1995) notes that, in general, there has been a 15-point rise in IQ in the US since the end of the Second World War, which belies the notion that intelligence is fixed.

Finally Saunders' (1996: 8) work is predicated on the assumption that "employers can be expected to seek out the brightest individuals to fill the most responsible positions." However, according to Goldthorpe (1997), the notion of 'merit' is not something that can be defined so concretely, but involves subjective judgements.

Whilst there is no substantive research into how managers define and use merit, there is evidence from a variety of sources that suggests a "single comprehensive scale of merit does not exist" (Goldthorpe: 1997: 672). Some may select on the basis of education, but others use in-house assessments based on criteria such as dependability, loyalty, commitment, adaptability and capacity for teamwork. Thus, Goldthorpe (1977: 667) argues that:

> Even when employers use educational qualifications as a criterion for entry, this is not necessarily an indication of merit. Senior executives may select new recruits on the basis that the educational experience of the candidate is an expression of background and life style that is similar to their own, even if this is not central to the operational efficiency of the organisation.

Material conditions

This explanation focuses on the impact that material deprivation, such as poor housing and low income, has on working class children. Douglas (1964) found that poor housing conditions had the effect of lowering educational performance. Halsey *et al* (1980) claim that 'family climate' (defined as the values and aspirations of parents) was an important factor in the choice of a school, but material circumstances determined how long children stayed on at school. Those with the poorest material circumstances tend to leave school at the earliest opportunity.

In recent years, there has been considerable controversy concerning the publication of league tables of school achievement as measured by examination results. The main criticism of this development has been that the publication of raw scores does not take into account how well schools might do with pupils who come from disadvantaged backgrounds. Consequently, an interest in how material conditions effect the attainment of children has been revived in the context of establishing methods of calculating how much schools add 'value' to the education of children. Research in Scotland carried out by Smees *et al* (2002), found that while schools can make a difference to attainment:

> [...] The value added analyses showed that pupils eligible for free school meals also made less progress from S2 to S4. In addition, a compositional effect related to the percentage of pupils eligible for free meals was also found. In schools where there were higher proportions of disadvantaged pupils from low-income families, results for all pupils tended to be depressed.   (Smees *et al*, 2002: 20)

Parental attitudes

Douglas (1964), in his classic work, *The Home and the School*, makes the claim that class differences in educational attainment are correlated with parental interest in the schooling of their children and pre-school socialisation. This interest is made manifest by attending school parents meetings and requesting meetings with the teaching staff and head teacher about their child's progress. Middle class parents were seen to the most interested while the working class were deemed to be the least interested. There is, however, one notable problem with Douglas' methodology as he based his judgement of levels of parental interest solely on teacher's perceptions, rather than on discussions with the parents themselves.

Other studies have expressed doubt about the claim that working class parents are somehow less interested in their child's education. Sharpe and Green (1975) argued that parents who had been defined by the teachers in the school they studied as being uninterested in their child's education:

[…] Were very ready to talk about their children's education, very articulate about their reasons for holding the views they had, and had readily available, and for them, adequate criteria for justifying them […].   (Sharpe and Green, 1975: 204)

Lareau (1997) also found that working class parents in the US were just as interested in the education of their children as were their middle class counterparts. They found that the most significant impact on pupil attainment was the extent to which parents possessed the cultural resources that allowed them to achieve what the teachers perceived as proper involvement with their children's education.

Lareau (1997) concludes that although both sets of parents wanted their children to be educationally successful, teachers appraised their interest in education differently. While teachers believed middle class parents were interested, they often felt that working class parents were not. The key element in this appraisal was the differences between the parents in the ways in which they promoted success in education. Whereas middle class parents were involved as partners, their working class counterparts thought it was the schools responsibility to teach their children.

Box 9.2 'Help toddlers and then let students pay their own way'

This is education week. Three government reports in a row are pumping out all the wicked issues. Yesterday it was the 14-19 curriculum and "gold standard A-levels in danger shock!" (Oh yes, and something about vocational education which is not for" children like ours".) Today it's university top-up fees. Tomorrow comes the first league tables attempting the tricky task of assessing how much schools improve their pupils, not just what class of pupils they take in. These three issues take us to the heart of Britain's education dilemmas and, as ever, all three point to the same old elephant on the table – Britain's extreme and dysfunctional level of social inequality.

Today's university funding white paper will cause the usual uproar. The 'well-off' will be vociferously angry at having to pay more, with the Daily Mail as their mouthpiece. (They want it free but still not pay more in tax.) In unholy alliance, the left will be incandescent on behalf of poorer students. It does indeed matter that poorer A-level students reach good universities, but this impacts only marginally on wider social justice. All this harrumphing greatly exaggerates the importance of universities, for by the time pupils have passed A-levels, they have already jumped the life-determining hurdles: most poor children fall before the first fence. Here is the really shocking fact that emerged from an education minister at a Fabian Society seminar this week. Take babies tested for attainment at the age of 22 months: at one end of the scale is a very bright child from a poor home and at the other end is a dim but rich baby.

At just under two years old, the bright child scores 85 points on the scale while the dim one scores only 10. But the two children are already on a steep trajectory in the opposite directions, the poor/bright one travelling fast downwards, the rich/dim moving up as their social backgrounds counteract their inborn abilities. By the time they hit nursery school, at the age of three, they nearly converged - (poor/bright scores only 55 now, while rich/dim has risen up to 45). At the age of six the children's lines cross, and then diverge for ever more as they off into different futures. Anything that happens by the time they reach school is only remedial, seeking to pull up the poor child's scores to where it began. What these figures show is how very little impact education has on poor children, and how every year of privilege goes on raising the score of the dim/rich child.

Results have improved steeply since Labour came to power: where half of all children left primary school illiterate, now only a quarter fail to reach the 11-year-old-standard. But even so, a quarter of children are still unable to read at all well, unlikely to ever catch up. Even worse, one half of all secondary schoolchildren leave school with no qualifications at all. Research estimates that 66% of all the differences in the results at age 16 in GCSEs are due to family income and not to inherent ability. Britain is almost at the bottom of the OECD league for pupils still in education at age 17.

These figures show how virtually all extra money should go to children before they reach school, catching them before the family effect destroys their chances. As it is only 2% of all money spent on children from 0-19 goes on Sure Start and the children's fund. (Sure Start is an excellent programme modelled on the US Head Start scheme, which showed that every $1 spent on two years of intensive teaching and parenting help for children at risk of failure saved $7 latter in life in crime, social security, housing and mental health, while greatly improving school success.) What is needed is a nursery education wrapped together with childcare, drop-in centre s for mothers and babies linked to health visiting and parenting groups, with special support for childminders, struggling families and depressed young mothers as well as IT and job training for parents. The 50% of children leaving school with nothing can be rescued here far more cheaply than later.

(Source: Polly Toynbee, *The Guardian*, 2 January 2003)

Trigger

With reference to the passage in Box 9.2, above, answer the following questions:

1. What evidence is used by the author to argue that the importance of universities is exaggerated?
2. What particular sociological explanation for the educational failure of poor children does the evidence of this article support? Which one does it definitely not support?
3. Describe briefly the benefits of programmes such as 'Head Start' in the US.

Working class Culture

Lareau's (1997) study draws on Bourdieu's (1977) concept of 'cultural capital'. Bourdieu (1977) argues that schooling, language and knowledge are defined and imposed by the middle classes. Whereas working class children find in school a world very different from that experienced in their home and community, the middle class child enters a world in which their values and attitudes correspond with those of teachers. The cultural capital, gained through the socialisation process, allows them to understand the rules, processes and significance of schooling in ways working class children cannot. In this manner, the social reproduction of the dominant class is achieved. The main purpose of schools is not to transmit knowledge, but to define the cultural and language skills of the middle class as superior, and hence more valuable than that of the working class.

Pugsley's (1998) paper on the differences between middle and working class students is a good example of Bourdieu's (1977) theory in action in higher education. As many working class families are first time consumers of higher education, universities are seen as a strange world – "Ivory towers contained within secret gardens" (Pugsley, 1998: 78). For one of their children to be contemplating entry into such an august institution is cause for mixed emotions of pride and concern. Middle class families experience no such confusion. The choice about whether or not to go university is rendered invisible, entwined as it is in the strands of family history. In highly educated families progression to university for siblings becomes a taken for granted assumption.

As working class families lack first hand experience of higher education, they lack the resources to help them find their way through the institutional and administrative maze. They admit to feeling out of their depth, bewildered and even frightened by the mechanical process of applying. Consequently, their sons and daughters have to rely on advice from school and further education colleges. For the middle class family, success is not derived from simply securing a place in higher education. They have the cultural capital to make distinctions between institutions, and the final choice is often made by assessing *value* in relation to *future employment*.

There were also class differences with regard to the geographical selection of a university. Whereas middle class parents encouraged their children to leave home to attend a prestigious institution, working class parents preferred to keep their children close to them. There were also obvious financial constraints on sending their children away. Consequently, many working class students attended local universities regardless of their standing.

Differential Achievement and Gender

With the advent of modern feminism in the late 1960s, feminist sociologists quickly turned attention to the processes in the social and education systems that depressed female achievement (see Chapter 5: Gender). Much of that effort was concentrated on *three* key causes of female under-achievement:

- The socialisation processes experienced by girls that orientated them towards family and children rather than education and work
- The gendered curriculum and the male culture of schools
- Gender – specific subject choice.

By the mid-1990s, however, the situation had changed. The total number of female examination entries had increased the gender gap was closing at GCSE and A level. Indeed girls began, by the late 90s, to outdo boys at GCSE level. Moreover, in Scotland females are out performing boys in both Standard and Higher Grades (Scottish Social Statistics, 2001).

It should be noted, however, that the picture is made complicated by the fact that despite the fact that females' performance in Higher Grades were improving at a quicker rate this did not translate into success in higher education. Despite the fact that in 1995 the ratio of female graduates to men was 52:48 in their favour, fewer women achieved First Class Honours degrees (Riddell, 1999: 861-862).

While the media reaction was to express concern over what they saw as the relative decline of male attainment, academics such as Mitsos and Browne (1998) produced a more balanced approached. They qualify the recent focus on male underachievement by pointing out that males still achieve better grades than females at A level; that males tend to select subjects that *secure access* to more prestigious jobs, and, most importantly, it is males who still occupy the most powerful positions in society.

Nevertheless, Mitsos and Browne (1998) go on to explain male underachievement in terms of *two* main factors. First, boys often adhere to a 'culture of masculinity' that embodies anti-school values that interpret studying and orderly behaviour as feminine traits (see Willis, 1997, above). Second, economic changes such as 'deindustrialisation' have brought about the virtual elimination of many male-dominated occupations and a 'feminisation' of the workplace. Consequently, they claim, some modern males suffer from an 'identity crisis' that contributes to a failure to achieve in schools.

The reasons given for the improvement in the attainment of females include the impact of the feminist movement and other sociologists who drew attention to the limitations placed on females in education and work, as well as changing economic circumstances that encouraged women to seek educational qualifications (see Chapter 2: Sociological Theory and Chapter 5: Gender). Increased occupational opportunities for females may now encourage them to seek to secure higher levels of academic qualifications in order to pursue careers.

The recent concerns over the 'under-achievement of males' may actually be best seen as a perceived threat to male dominance (Weiner, Arnot and David, 1997). They note that a closer analysis of statistics on attainment by gender reveals that while females have improved in terms of examination entries and attainment at GCSE, at A level males and females still choose different subjects and the boys' grades are superior to that of the girls "in nearly all subjects", even in subjects such as English where females are thought to be more able (Weiner, Arnot and David, 1997: 625). They do, however, note that the grade advantage enjoyed by boys is being gradually eroded.

Weiner, Arnot and David (1997) go on to argue that the recent media concern with male disadvantage in education represents a backlash against feminist successes set against a background of changing economic and social processes perceived as disadvantaging men in the labour market (see Chapter 5: Gender). Further concerns exist over the threat to social order posed by unemployed males, unrestrained by the civilising influences of traditional mothers and wives. It is, in fact, a 'moral panic' designed to silence the demands for increased equity for girls and women and thus maintain the hegemony of masculinity that is such a defining characteristic of our society, they argue.

The situation regarding grade advantage in Scotland is similar to that of England, with the exception that relatively few females take Physics (Scottish Social Statistics, 2001). Although males in Scotland have recently lagged behind females, they have improved *overall* performance if measured by attainment in Credit Standard Grades and Highers. Indeed, as Tinklin *et al* (2001) confirm, this is a process that has been going on for some time. They found that:

- Average levels of attainment have increased for both males and females over the past three decades, but the gain in attainment for males has lagged behind that of females
- Girls have been outperforming boys in school examinations since the 1970s
- Social background is a greater predictor of inequality and underachievement than gender.

Consequently, they argue it is too simplistic to speak of a 'gender gap' and more helpful to use the term 'gender jigsaw'. They conclude that some males and females achieve and others do not, and, significantly, that social class has a greater impact on attainment levels than gender.

If some males continue to attain in education it raises the question over how they do so in the context of a masculine disregard for education. Also, questions are raised about how boys manage their relations with girls in the school when faced with challenges to their expected dominance. Research by Reynold (2001) provides a very interesting insight into how boys in primary schools, who are both high and low achievers, manage their masculine identities in these contexts.

She found that two-thirds of the boys (from both middle and working class backgrounds) went to great lengths not to be thought of as studious. To be perceived of in this way risked being labelled a 'swot' or a 'nerd' or a 'geek' and to invite bullying. To avoid such labels the boys recognised that they had to be adventurous and to be good at sports such as football. They also adopted various strategies such as 'mucking around' and 'having a laugh' in class. This was especially true of those who "were described as 'middle class', 'clever' and whose SAT results confirmed above average academic ability" (Reynold, 2001: 374). Boys who adhered to this culture of 'hegemonic' masculinity went to great lengths to denigrate the work and achievements of girls (see Chapter 2: Sociological Theory, for further discussion on hegemony). Thus:

> Being academically orientated for a boy is often devalued and denigrated because of its equation with 'femininity'. Despite the positionings associated with academic success, however, there was still a strong need to assert their academic superiority over girls which [...] often took the form of depicting their 'achievements' as failures', belittling their serious commitment to schoolwork and mocking their contributions in whole class discussions.   (Reynold, 2001: 375)

Why do girls choose different subjects from boys?
While it may be the case that females have improved in overall academic performance, subject choice still remains gendered. The situation in higher education reflects that at secondary school level. Females out number males in Arts and Humanities and males out number females in Maths and Natural Sciences. At

Standard Grade in Scotland, males are more likely to choose physics, computer studies, physical education and craft design, whereas females are more likely to take biology and office and information studies. Exceptions include Maths, English and French, which prove to be equally popular with both sexes. At Higher Grade, 1 in 10 girls take physics compared to 1 in 4 boys. Computing studies are popular with males but do not figure in the top 10 choices for females. Languages other than French suffer a similar fate for boys' choices (Scottish Social Statistics, 2001).

Colley (1998) has reviewed the available literature on subject choice and concluded that it is by and large a reflection of gender stereotypes acquired during socialisation and reinforced by contemporary beliefs about the roles of males and females in the world of work. Special programmes to counteract these trends have encouraged females into science and technology, but no equivalent programmes exist to encourage males into studying languages other than French. Such a move may be seen by some as progressive, but others, such as Abraham (1995) and Reynold (2001), show that school is a hostile environment for girls who often select subjects avoided by boys as a survival mechanism (Ridell, 1999: 862).

The single sex school
Colley (1998) also looked at the evidence regarding the alleged benefits for females studying in single sex schools. She came to the cautious conclusion that females do tend to do better in science subjects in such schools. Others, such as Harker (2000), disagree. He concludes from his research in New Zealand that any apparent difference in attainment level derives from the fact that single sex schools tend to select pupils on the basis of ability. Harker (2000) does not advocate single sex schools as a proper policy option, but asserts that the present dominant masculine model of education elevates science based subjects over others. Females may be moving into subjects once dominated by males, but there has been no reciprocal movement of boys into female dominated subjects. Only then could there be a truly coeducational school system.

Trigger

Make a list of the subjects you did not take in secondary school. Are there any on the list that you did not take because you felt that it was not appropriate for someone of your gender to do so?

Differential Achievement and Ethnicity
Concern exists over the fact that children from ethnic minority backgrounds in Britain do not do as well as their white counterparts in education (see Chapter 6:

Race and Ethncity). This is especially true of children of Afro-Caribbean and Bangladeshi ethnic origin. Sociological explanations for differential attainment of minority groups have tended to concentrate on (1) factors in the school and (2) factors in the home in the search for causes.

Statistics relating to attainment

Research from the PSI Fourth National Survey of Ethnic Minorities (Nazroo, 1997) focused on the second and present generations and gives cause for some hope as well as concern. While it is the case some minority groups have progressed in terms of educational attainment, others still lag behind.

With regards to male subjects, Chinese, African Asians and Indians were proportionately more likely to achieve to degree level than whites. By contrast, the least well qualified are those from Caribbean, Pakistani and Bangladeshi backgrounds. Caribbean men tend to seek vocational qualifications. For women there was a similar pattern, with the exception that those of Caribbean origin who did better than whites at A level/below degree level, generally were not as well qualified as men from of similar backgrounds. Second-generation minorities did much better in terms of qualifications than those who came to Britain as migrants. However, again there is cause for concern as Pakistanis and Bangladeshis still lagged behind other minority ethnic groups. Finally, with regards to post-compulsory education, it would appear that minority groups stay on longer in full time education than their white counterparts and are over represented in higher education. For example, twice as many Indians (aged 18 to 27) as whites proceed to university as a proportion of their total population. Black students are also over represented, but only among students aged 21 and over.

Factors in the school

Mason (2000) acknowledges the fact that significant progress has been made by minority groups relative to whites, but warns that it is important not to over look the evidence of continuing disadvantage. He argues that schools must bear the main responsibility for the continuing problems faced by minorities. He cites the work of Smith and Tomlinson (1989), which indicates that ethnic minority pupils are subject to systematic disadvantage due to racism, rather than being the arbitrary victims of poor schools.

To back up his claim, Mason (2000) relies on the ethnographic studies of Wright (1992) and Mac an Ghaill (1992), that show that ethnic minority children are the subjects of stereotyping by teachers. For example, Afro-Caribbean boys were seen as being good at sports, but troublesome, while Asian girls were labelled as submissive. These labels had a significant impact on the level of examinations for which pupils would be entered. From the minorities' point of view, they felt held back by a curriculum that was seen as being white 'ethnocentric'. This reinforced the feelings of being an outsider, someone who was 'different'. There were also concerns about the racial violence and harassment experienced by ethnic minority children. Children were left demoralised and discouraged while the schools tended to be in denial or blame the home life or culture of minority groups.

Given all these problems Mason (2000) makes the point that the progress made by minority children is all the more remarkable. It is testament to the high levels of commitment, motivation and resilience of the individuals and their communities who succeed in the face of discouragement and racism. Further, schools that produce good results do so by actively countering racism and racial disadvantage in their organisation and curriculum. Such schools go beyond bland notions of celebrating diversity in multi-cultural education and seek to implement specifically anti racist policies.

For Mason, then, difficulties minority ethnic groups face in education lie primarily within the boundaries of the school.

Factors in the home
Pilkington (1999) agrees that Afro-Caribbean boys are treated differently and pejoratively in schools. He argues, however, that such treatment does not derive from preconceived stereotypes held by teachers of what minority boys are like. Black youngsters are more likely to be punished for bad behaviour simply because they indulge in it more than other groups. The source of the bad behaviour is the boys' adherence to subcultural values, developed as a reaction to their perception that they have poor post-school prospects due to racist attitudes in wider society (see Chapter 13: Culture and Chapter 11: Crime and Deviance, for further discussion on subcultures).

Pilkington (1999) suggests that any explanation of the differential treatment of young blacks must recognise the 'vicious cycle of amplification' at play. The existence of racist attitudes in wider society has the affect of encouraging 'bad' behaviour in school while such behaviour is interpreted by teachers as threatening and, more significantly, typical of young black students. This results in teachers being 'heavy handed' on young blacks, which, in turn, exacerbates the indiscipline that they exhibit.

Finally, whilst the findings of Nazroo (1997) seem to indicate relative educational progress by minority ethnic groups as a whole, racism does seem to play an important part in determining attainment levels if only in the minds of some individuals or groups. However, minority ethnic groups cannot be viewed as a homogeneous mass. Some groups perform better than others and some individuals within groups are able to perform independently of ethnic origin.

Trigger

Can you think of factors other than those discussed above (i.e. class, gender, ethnicity) that might impact on an individual's achievement levels?

Educational Reforms

Politicians have always seen education as a powerful tool for controlling or changing populations. In the aftermath of the Second World War, education was seen as the vehicle of the new open society in which equality of opportunity was to be the lynch pin. To this end, the 1944 Education Act introduced 'comprehensivisation' – free and compulsory secondary education for all. Intelligent children could be objectively identified by examinations and IQ tests and promoted through the social hierarchy by the grammar and senior secondary schools systems. Through the provision of secondary education for all, financial barriers were to be removed from entry into grammar schools. The 1944 Act failed inasmuch as it did not greatly increase the number of children from manual-worker backgrounds attaining the educational qualifications necessary for 'social mobility' (see Chapter 4: Social Class). As a consequence it was felt by many that the system of selection was socially divisive and wasteful of talent.

Among those concerned was Harold Wilson's Labour government that came to power in 1964. Almost immediately, it invited education authorities to draw up plans for comprehensive schemes, and by 1978 the majority of state secondary schools were organised along comprehensive lines in which selection was eliminated. In this setting, it was argued, children would learn in an integrated and unified culture, which would eradicate social class divisions, lead to greater social cohesion and halt the wastage of working class talent. The school leaving age was raised from 15 to 16 to help accomplish this. Practices such as streaming or setting, popular in many comprehensive schools also became seen as socially divisive and was, in some cases at least, replaced by mixed ability teaching.

However, some sociological research claims to show that comprehensives have failed to achieve their aims. For example, Ford (1974) argued that the continued use of streaming in some schools led to social divisions being maintained, while in England, Heath (1987) found that whereas standards of attainment for working class children had improved, so had those of middle class children. Consequently, the gap in attainment continued to persist. In Scotland, comprehensivisation seemed to be more successful. As such, McPherson and Williams (1987) found that:

- The average attainment for all groups had increased in the period 1976 to 1984
- There was still a large degree of class difference
- However, attainment levels had been rising faster among working class children.

It may not be surprising that the experience of comprehensivisation may have been manifest differently north of the border, as Scotland retains a different schooling system compared to England and Wales.

The New Right and the marketisation of education

By the end of the 1970s, there was a rising demand for reform among educationalists, employers and politicians. Even before the election of the Conservatives in 1979, James Callaghan, the then Labour prime minister, had initiated the 'great debate' that focused on the perception that the education system was failing the needs of industry and an economy facing increased global competition. After 1979, the intensity of debate and pace of reform increased. The incoming Thatcher-led Conservative government was influenced by what has come to be known as the New Right critique of state provided education (see Chapter 2: Sociological Theory).

This perspective argued that increased economic 'globalisation' had meant that Britain now had to develop a workforce able to compete with the economies of countries such as South Korea, which was characterised by an educated work force, low wages and minimal welfare provision. Creating efficiencies in an education service that consumes a large part of the welfare budget would cut costs for British industry and allow it to compete more effectively.

The Conservatives believed that schools must serve the needs of the economy and the individual. To achieve these ends there had to be a weakening of state monopoly through the introduction of markets into the education system. This operates by freeing schools from local authority control, making them compete with each other by arranging a system where funding follows the pupil and by allowing parents to choose which school their children should attend by providing information on the performance of schools. Publicly announced figures of pupil achievement in terms of GCSEs and A levels provided the standard for secondary schools, while the introduction of testing did the same for primary schools. Schools are, therefore, forced to become responsive to the needs of their 'stakeholders', in that they supply an education that raises standards and equips their children with qualifications needed for competition in the work place. Those who are able to do so will prosper, while those who do not (or cannot) will wither away. The Conservatives also claimed that marketisation of schools would increase social equality as working class parents would not be limited to sending their children to the local comprehensive school. The 1988 Education Act put this thinking into action.

In Scotland, both parents and teachers resisted these ideas. Only two schools opted out, relatively few parents chose to send their children to schools out with their locality, and testing in primary schools was eventually only accepted when it was agreed that the outcomes were only to be used to assess pupil performance.

Alongside these developments, there was an increased emphasis on vocationalism and training in education. This was reflected by the introduction of NVQs/SVQs into further and higher education, and the entrepreneurial values of the new City Technology Colleges (CTCs). It also pervaded schools, with the introduction of TVEI (the Technical, Vocational Education Initiative). Universities also increased the number of courses focusing specifically on the jobs market, and the New Labour government in England is proposing (at the time of writing) a two-year vocational degree that will be designed by employers and the universities.

In short, then, these reforms were designed primarily to:

- Enhance economic efficiency by focusing on standards and vocationalism
- Increase opportunity for all by providing information that would allow parents to choose schools for their children.

New Labour and Education

While New Labour have continued many of the educational reforms introduced by previous Conservative administrations, their emphasis has been on creating an education system focussed on the production of a highly skilled, flexible workforce trained to produce customised goods in a quickly changing market place. These workers would form the core of a 'magnet economy' by attracting high levels of inward investment. This would help solve problems of unemployment, as those without skills would be encouraged to retrain to increase opportunities for inclusion in a rapidly changing workforce. A further benefit would be derived from a general reduction of inequality in society.

Consequently, New Labour's educational reforms were designed to improve standards and reduce inequality of opportunity. Policies introduced in England and Wales to achieve the former were:

- The reduction of class sizes in primary schools
- Timetabled slots for literacy and numeracy
- Targets for achievement

- Direct intervention in failing schools, including the management of schools by private companies, and the introduction of City Academies often designed to replace failing inner city schools.

In order to achieve the goal of equality of opportunity, a number of policies were introduced under the rubric of 'social inclusion' (see Chapter 8: Poverty). In England and Wales, measures included 'Sure Start' to help children from deprived areas, and Education Action Zones (EAZs) where Private/Public Partnerships sought to attract finance to improve schools in areas of deprivation.

Since the advent of the Scottish Parliament, policies to promote social inclusion in Scotland have included Community schools, whose integrated services of education, social and medical services are designed to find a way for schools to help strengthen communities; the abolition of up-front higher education fees; and additional Access financial support for students from low income families.

One of the interesting aspects of New Labour polices, is that these reforms for social justice exist alongside the continuance of the Conservative initiatives on marketisation. As such, policies should be judged on how well they have achieved their stated objectives. It would be useful, therefore, to consider the evidence available.

The economic argument

Munn (2000) examined the debate whether schools can be directly related to productivity and economic growth. While she concluded that there is an indirect and uncertain relation, she argued that schools are more than "a production factory for the economy" (Munn, 2000: 121). Moreover, she claims that rather than schools enhancing the economy, economic policies out with the control of the school can depress the attainment of children. Glasgow, more than most other urban areas in Scotland, has suffered from the loss of manufacturing jobs and as a consequence harbours a disproportionate number of areas of deprivation. The city's schools may wish to promote the policies of lifelong learning, flexibility and up-skilling, but they have to do so in the context of the reality of high levels of unemployment. As Munn (2000: 122) suggests:

> [...] Glasgow schools must have a tough job convincing their pupils of the intrinsic worth of qualifications - their value in the labour market.

The raising of standards

In Scotland, the general opposition to Conservative reforms discussed above were based on an assumption that standards were already satisfactory. This complacency was shattered by the realisation that Scottish children's performance trailed other nations, including England, in Maths and Science (OECD reports, cited in Denholm and Macleod, 2002: 122). The reaction of the incoming Labour administration of 1997, was to make standards its priority and schools were set targets for upping achievement levels.

The egalitarian argument

The Scottish educational system has historically made claim to being socially inclusive. Paterson (2000) points to evidence that may suggest that comprehensive schooling has reduced inequalities in terms of social class, gender, religion and ethnicity. Moreover, he claims that further education colleges in Scotland carry out more higher education functions than their counterparts in the rest of Britain and attract a high degree of students from working class backgrounds who are thereby provided with an alternative route into universities. Additionally, marketisation in Scotland has not widened social divisions in the same way it seems to have done in England. As referred to above, only two Scottish schools opted out of local authority control, one of which has opted back in, and there has been considerably less interest shown in placing requests that allow parents to select their child's school (David, 1993: 127).

It would, however, be a misconception to assume that Scotland is a meritocratic country. The Howie Report noted that in 1992 over a half of all fifth year pupils left school with one or no Highers. In 2001, only 31 per cent of all Scotland's pupils in sixth year attained 3 Highers. This latter figure hides an alarming social class gap as 52 per cent young adults from the affluent suburbs of East Renfrewshire achieving that level compared to only 19 per cent in Glasgow (all figures cited in Denholm and Macleod, 2002: 122). Similarly, David (1993: 125-7) reports research that has found that although the impact of placing requests on Scottish schools was modest, what there was had the effect of increasing social segregation.

This situation is replicated in higher education. Osbourne (1999) notes that Scotland does not do as well as other UK regions in attracting young people from disadvantaged backgrounds into universities. Furthermore, there is no clear evidence to support Paterson's (2000) assertion above that further education colleges provide a pathway into higher education for young people from disadvantaged backgrounds.

Private education can be seen as another source of social division. Munn (2000) argues that as access to independent schools is determined largely by the ability to pay, they are the very antithesis of social inclusion. They may represent only 7 per cent of the UKs school population (4 per cent in Scotland, but 20 per cent in Edinburgh), but their ex-pupils are over represented in Oxford and Cambridge universities and have a disproportionate influence in the upper echelons of society. She is not impressed by the common arguments that are used to defend them and wonders why the Scottish Executive does not attempt to address this issue.

Trigger

The three common arguments used to defend private education examined by Munn were:

- They preserve the highest standards against which state schools can be measured.
- In a free society parents should be able to choose to pay.
- It is politically too difficult to do anything about them. And anyway their intake represents only 4 per cent of the Scottish school population.

Make an argument against *all three* points.

Canning (1999) argued that recent trends in Scottish education and training have led to a polarisation of the work force. The emphasis on expanding the number of graduates is matched by government policies to certificate low skilled and unemployed workers, at the expense of traditional high quality intermediate qualifications. Education, therefore, reinforces labour market inequalities by failing to bridge the gap between the highly educated and low skilled undereducated. Increasing the number of graduates has not increased the number of jobs that graduates can do, but has rather allowed employers to employ qualified people to do jobs previously done by non graduates.

Like Brown and Lauder (1997), Canning argues that the marketisation of education allows the middle classes to extend and tighten their grip on the better-paid jobs by investing in the 'cultural capital' of their young. Unfortunately, this can only be achieved at some cost to a growing underclass that becomes socially and economically excluded.

Conclusion

The above may well be just one example of the contradictions contained in the UK-wide educational policies of New Labour, which seem to be trying to maintain the support of their newly won middle class voters and enhance economic competitiveness. At the same time, however, they are remaining true to their traditional values of social justice. The government's reaction to the recent row concerning Bristol University's apparent rejection of highly qualified candidates from the private sector, in favour of applicants from the state system, is perhaps typical of the muddles such policies bring. Despite the fact that it is stated government policy to create an access regulator in England and Wales whose job it will be to ensure that universities achieve targets for the inclusion of students from state schools, in the face of accusations from the right-wing press of lowering standards for the sake of the dubious ends of egalitarianism, Prime Minister Blair told the Commons that places should be "gained on merit, not on class background" (cited in Toynbee, 2003).

Brown and Lauder (1997) are emphatic about the real impact the reforms will have on social justice in England and Wales. According to them, the reality is that social justice cannot be achieved through educational reforms designed to react to the demands of a global labour market. The middle and upper classes may still have preferential access to elite institutions, as there is little in New Labour's reforms designed to promote social justice that cannot be neutralised by the effects of marketisation. By maintaining the shibboleths of the New Right of parental choice and diversity in a market context, New Labour appears to have abandoned its quest for a truly meritocratic society. They may have also failed to solve the problem of achieving social solidarity in a system that increasingly pits one against the other.

In Scotland, however, it has been argued by Paterson (2000) that:

> Devolution has allowed us *not* to do what David Blunkett and Estelle Morris [when respective education secretaries] have done down south. There will be no specialist schools, probably no private money in school management, and there will be a much less aggressive regime towards teachers, and of testing and target setting.
>
> (Cited in Denholm and Macleod, 2002: 123)

Will, then, Scotland's more conservative path in the post devolution era achieve the desired ends of social justice and economic growth? According to Canning (1999), this will not be achieved without reforming the education and training system to provide high quality, work based vocational training at intermediate level that will bridge the gap between higher education and the certification of the unskilled.

Chapter Summary

- The classical sociological theories still have a role to play in aiding our understanding of differential achievement in the UK today. In particular, the increasing emphasis on vocationalism revives interest in the correspondence principle as developed by Bowles and Gintis (1976).
- A central purpose of a liberal, social democratic sociology of education has been to explain differential achievement in terms of class, gender and ethnicity, in a search to enhance policymaking directed at social justice. To a large extent this process has been sidelined by the usurpation of the education agenda by 'New Right' policies of marketisation.
- Nevertheless, the interest in explaining why working class children achieve less than their middleclass counterparts continues in the sociology of education.

- The intelligence debate has been re-ignited as a part of the New Right's search for economic efficiency by justifying the denial of access to educational goods to those deemed unable to benefit through lack of intelligence. The central premises of this 'new IQ movement' have been thoroughly tested not least by Goldthorpe (1997) who questions the link between intelligence, merit and occupational destination.

- With regards to gender, the challenge has been to explain the advance of female achievement and the social reaction to it. It is important to note the attainment of boys has not declined, but has failed to increase at the same rate as their female counterparts. Research has shown that regardless of class background many, but not all, young males have an ambivalent attitude to education.

- The explanation of female attainment is located in the social and economic changes of post war Britain. However, true equity has been elusive. There is a problem with subject choice and men still dominate the world of work. Moreover, Weiner, Arnot and David (1997) draw our attention to the growing male backlash to the challenge faced by masculine hegemony of female attainment.

- The debate in the sociology of education with regard to ethnicity has centred on the location of the problems faced by mainly boys of Afro Caribbean, Pakistani and Bangladeshi origin. A solution to the dilemma has been suggested by Pilkington (1999) who argues that the racist attitudes found in wider society, creates negative attitudes in the boys to which the school reacts by pejorative labelling, thereby setting up a vicious cycle of disadvantage.

- The problem of explanation is exacerbated by evidence that indicates that some minority ethnic groups do well in education and that second and third generations have improved attainment levels compared to previous generations.

- Educational reforms of the late 20th century have been driven by economic globalisation and the needs of a rapidly changing labour market. New Labour, while wishing to appear true to their roots of social justice, has attempted to combine social inclusion with policies of marketisation. There are important differences between Scotland and the rest of the UK in this context.

Further Reading

Bryce, T.G.K. and Humes, W.M. (eds.) (1999) *Scottish Education*, Edinburgh: Edinburgh University Press

Halsey, A.H., Lauder, H., Brown, P., and Wells, A. (eds.) (1997) *Education, Culture, Economy, Society*, Oxford: Open University Press

Heaton, T. and Lawson, T. (1996) *Education and Training*, Basingstoke: Palgrave

Useful Websites

On classical studies of underachievement: http://www.arasite.org/3studs.html
The Office for Standards in Education (England and Wales): http://www.ofsted.gov.uk/
The Scottish Qualifications Authority: http://www.sqa.org.uk/

Bibliography

Abraham, J. (1995) *Divide and School: Gender and Class Dynamics in Comprehensive Education*, London: Falmer Press

Aggleton, P. (1987) *Rebels without a Cause? Middle Class youth and the transition from school to work*, London: Falmer Press

Apple, M.W. (1997) 'What Postmodernists Forget: Cultural Capital and Official Knowledge', in Halsey, et al (eds.) *Education, Culture, Economy, Society*, Oxford: Oxford University Press

Ball, S.J, Bowe, R, and Gerwitz, S. (1994) 'Market forces and parental choice', in Tomlinson, S. (ed.) *Education reform and its Consequences*, London: IPPR/Rivers Oram Press

Bernstein, B. (1971) 'Education cannot compensate for society', in Cosin, B.R. *et al*, *School and Society: A sociological reader*, London: Routledge and Kegan Paul/OUP

Bourdieu, P. (1977) *Outline of a Theory of Practice*, Cambridge: Cambridge University Press

Brown, P. (1987) *Schooling Ordinary Kids: inequality, unemployment and the new vocationalism*, London: Tavistock

Bowles, S. and Gintis, H. (1976) *Schooling in Capitalist America: Educational Reform and the Contradictions of Economic Life*, London: Routledge and Kegan Paul

Bowles, S. and Gintis, H. (2001) *Schooling in Capitalist America Revisited* (accessed at:

Brown, P. and Lauder, M. (1997) 'Education, globalisation and economic development', in Halsey, A.H. *et al* (eds.) *Education, Culture, Economy, Society*, Oxford: Oxford University Press

Canning, R. (1999) 'Post-16 Education in Scotland: credentialism and inequality', in *Journal of Vocational Education and Training*, Vol.51, No.2

Colley, A. (1998) 'Gender and subject choice in secondary education', in Radford, J. (ed.) *Gender and Choice in education and Occupation*, London: Routledge

Cosin, B.R. *et al* (1971) *School and Society: A sociological reader*, London: Routledge and Kegan Paul/OUP

David, M.E. (1993) *Parents, Gender and Educational Reform*, Cambridge: Polity Press

Denholm, J.W. and Macleod, D. (2002) 'Educating the Scots: The Renewal of the Democratic Intellect', in Hassan, G. and Warhurst, C. (eds.) *Anatomy of the New Scotland: Power, Influence and Change*, Edinburgh: Mainstream

Durkheim, E. (1956 [1922]) *Education and Society*, New York, NY: Free Press

Durkheim, E. (1961) *Moral Education*, Glencoe, IL: Free Press

Eysenck, H. (1971) *Race, Intelligence and Education*, London: Temple Smith

Ford, J. (1974) 'Ability and opportunity in a comprehensive school' in Eggleston, J. (ed.) *Contemporary Research in the Sociology of Education*, London: Methuen

Foucault, M. (1982) 'The Subject and Power' in Dreyfus, H. and Rabinow, P. (eds.) (1982) *Michel Foucault: Beyond Structuralism and Hermeneutics*, Brighton: Harvester Press

Fraser, S. (1997) 'Introduction to *Bell Curve Wars*' in Halsey, A.H. *et al* (eds.) *Education, Culture, Economy, Society*, Oxford: Oxford University Press

Furlong, V. (1976) 'Interaction sets in the classroom' in Hammersly, M. and Woods, P. (eds.) *The Processes of Schooling*, London: Routledge and Kegan Paul

Goldthorpe, J. H. (1997) 'Problems of Meritocracy' in Halsey, A.H. *et al* (eds.) *Education, Culture, Economy, Society*, Oxford: Oxford University Press

Gorard, S and Fitz, J. (1998) 'The more things change … the missing impact of marketisation?' *British Journal of Sociology of Education*, 19, pp.365-376

Gorard, S. and Taylor, C. (2002) 'Market Forces and Standards in Education: a preliminary consideration', in *British Journal of Sociology*, Vol.23, No.1, pp.5-18

Hargreaves, D.H. (1967) *Social Relations in a Secondary School*, London: Routledge and Kegan Paul

Harker, R. (2000) 'Achievement, Gender and the Single Sex/Coed debate' in *British Journal of Sociology of Education*, Vol.21, No.2, pp.202-218

Hartley, D. (1999) 'Education and the Scottish Economy' in Bryce, T.G.K and Humes, W.M. (eds.) *Scottish Education*, Edinburgh: Edinburgh University Press

Hassan, G. and Warhurst, C. (eds.) (2002) *Anatomy of the New Scotland: Power, Influence and Change*, Edinburgh: Mainstream

Heath, A. (1987) 'Class in classrooms', in *New Society*, 17 July 1987

Herrnstein, R. and Murray, C.A. (1994) *The Bell Curve: Intelligence and the Class Structure*, New York, NY: Free Press

Kamin, L. (1977) *The Science and Politics of IQ*, Harmondsworth: Penguin

Kenway, J. (1995) 'Having a Postmodernist Turn or Postmodernist Angst: A disorder Experienced by an Author Who is Not Yet Dead or Even Close to it' in Halsey, A.H. *et al* (eds.) *Education, Culture, Economy, Society* Halsey, Oxford: Oxford University Press

Keddie, N. (1971) 'Classroom Knowledge' in Young, M.F.D. (ed.) *Knowledge and Control: New directions for the sociology of education*, Basinsgstoke: Collier- Macmillan

McFadden, M.G. (1995) 'Resistance to Schooling and Educational Outcomes: questions of structure and agency' in *British Journal of Sociology of Education*, Vol.16, No.3

McPherson, A. and Williams, J.D. (1997) 'Equalisation and Improvement: Some effects of Comprehensive Reorganisation in Scotland', in Halsey, A.H. *et al* (eds.) *Education, Culture, Economy, Society*, Oxford: Oxford University Press

Mason, D. (2000) *Race and Ethnicity in Modern Britain*, Second Edition, Oxford: Oxford University Press

McRobbie, A. (1991) *Feminism and Youth Culture: from 'Jackie' to 'Just Seventeen'*, Basingstoke: Macmillan

Mills, C. Wright (1959) *The Sociological Imagination*, New York, NY: Oxford University Press

Mitsos, E. and Browne, K. (1998) 'Gender differences in education: the underachievement of boys', in *Sociology Review*, September

Mortimore, P. (1997) 'Can Effective Schools Compensate for Society?' in Halsey, A.H. *et al* (eds.) *Education, Culture, Economy, Society*, Oxford: Oxford University Press

Munn, P. (2000) 'Can Schools make Scotland a More Inclusive Society?' in *Scottish Affairs*, No.33, Autumn

Murray, C. (1994), *Underclass: The Crisis Deepens*, London: IEA Health and Welfare Unit

Nazroo, J. (1997) *The Health of Britain's ethnic minorities: Fourth national Survey of Ethnic minorities*, Fourth National Survey Text, Report No.835, London: PSI

Noden, P. (2000) 'Rediscovering the Impact of Marketisation: dimensions of social segregation in England's secondary schools, 1994-1999', in *British Journal of Sociology of Education*, Vol. 21, No.3, pp.371-385

Osbourne, R.D. (1999) 'Wider Access in Scotland?' in *Scottish Affairs*, No.26, Winter

Parsons, T. (1961) 'The School Class as a social System: Some of its Functions in American society', in Halsey, A.H. *et al* (eds.) *Education, Economy, Society*, New York, NY: Free Press

Paterson, L. (2000) 'Social Inclusion and the Scottish Parliament', in *Scottish Affairs*, No.30, pp.68-77

Pilkington, A. (1999) 'Racism in Schools and Ethnic differentials in Educational Achievement: a brief comment on a recent debate', in *British Journal of Sociology of Education*, Vol.20, No.3, pp.405- 411

Radford, J. (ed.) (1998) *Gender and Choice in education and Occupation*, London: Routledge

Reynold, E. (2001) 'Learning the 'Hard Way': boys, hegemonic masculinity and the negotiation of learner identities in the primary school', in *British Journal of Sociology of Education*, Vol.22, No.3, pp.369-385

Reynolds, D. (1987) 'School Effectiveness and Truancy', in Reid, K. (ed.) *Combating School Absenteeism*, London: Hodder and Stoughton

Riddell, S. (1999) 'Gender and Scottish Education', in Bryce, T.G.K. and Humes, W.M. (eds.), *Scottish Education*, Edinburgh: Edinburgh University Press

Saunders, P. (1996) 'A British bell curve? Class, intelligence and meritocracy in contemporary Britain', in *Sociology Review*, November 1996

Scottish Social Statistics (2001) *Education and Training: Attainment* (accessed at: http://www.scotland.gov.uk/stats/sss/docs/sss00-01.asp)

Smees, R, Sammons, P, Thomas, S. and Mortimore, P. (2002) 'Examining the effect of pupil background on primary and secondary pupils' attainment: Key findings from the improving school effectiveness project', in *Scottish Educational Review*, Vol.34, No.1

Tinklin, T, Croxford, L, Duklin, A. and Frame (2001) *Gender and Pupil Performance* (accessed at: www.scotland.gov.uk/library3/education/ic70-01.asp)

Tomlinson, S. (ed.) (1994) *Education reform and its Consequences*, London: IPPR/Rivers Oram Press

Toynbee, P. (2003) 'The middle class will take the lot if Blair lets them', *The Guardian*, 5 March

Usher, R and Edwards, R. (1995) *Post Modernism and Education*, London: Routledge

Weiner, G., Arnot, M. David, M. (1997) 'Is the Future Female? Female Success, Male Disadvantage, and Changing Gender Patterns in Education', in Halsey, A.H. *et al* (eds.) *Education, Culture, Economy, Society*, Oxford: Oxford University Press

Werthman, C. (1971) 'Delinquents in Schools', in Cosin, B.R., Dale, I.R., Esland, G.M. and Swift, A.F. *School and Society*, London: Routledge and Kegan Paul

Willis, P. (1977) *Learning to Labour: how working class lads get working class jobs*, Farnborough: Saxon House

Chapter 10 Work and its Organisation

Neil Etherington, John Lewis and Tony Sweeney

Introduction

The nature of work and its organisation fills a central place in the understanding of sociology, primarily due to the importance of work to individual and collective identity in society. When making an assessment of the nature of work and its organisation, one of the key problems that the sociologist encounters is trying to establish a single definition. This is due to the *subjective* nature of work. This chapter will reflect on why definitions of work are so complex.

Having established notions of complexity around the topic, we will then go on to examine the classical theorists, each of whom try to determine the importance of work in society and inform contemporary understanding of the topic. Emile Durkheim (1947 [1893]), the 'founding father' of functionalist thought, is optimistic about industrial society's ability to self-stabilise. Any dysfunctions, such as 'anomie' (i.e. normlessness), are assumed to be temporary conditions. Karl Marx (1976 [1867]), a 'conflict theorist', felt that the alienating effects of work under capitalism were inevitable, but *would* lead to social change. Max Weber (1947 [1922]; 1958 [1930]), however, a social action theorist, believed that certain attitudes and forms of 'rationality' were required for capitalism and its organisation to be successful (see Chapter 2: Sociological Theory and Chapter 3: Social Class).

The central role of Marxist analysis can be found in the seminal work of Braverman (1974), who picked up notions of the 'degradation' and 'deskilling' of work through 'labour process theory' (see below). Significantly, in the face of what now appears to be a more flexible workplace and workforce, labour process theory has still proved a useful tool for explaining new trends in the workplace, due its 'structural' appreciation of what it sees as the inherently divergent interests between 'capital and labour' (see Chapter 2: Sociological Theory). Thus, students are encouraged to examine issues of 'alienation' and 'control' as central characteristics of work and its organisation.

This chapter will discuss, by way of illustrative examples, the changing nature of work in UK and Scottish society, and how it has shifted from a mature 'Fordist' model – with a system of full employment and marked by 'a job for life' stability in 'a golden age' of capitalism – to what has increasingly been seen as the development of 'flexibilisation', where greater and greater demands are being made on workers in the form of the *flexible* workplace, the *flexible* contract and *flexible* wages. All of this *flexibility* takes place in a more diverse and uncertain world, where the forces of global capitalism mean that work and its organisation is subject to continual change. For some commentators, such as Marx and contemporary Marxists, however, the end result remains a work relationship based upon exploitation of the worker.

Nevertheless, despite such flux and the debates about whether work takes place in an extended bureaucratic or a 'post-bureaucratic' environment, whether work is now multi-skilled or multi-tasked, examples of significant inequality are evident when the sociologist examines *how* work actually takes place. With this in mind, students are encouraged to reflect on the UK and Scottish labour markets, which illustrate that the shift from manufacturing to service sector industries brings with it new forms of work, although old patterns of 'Taylorist' (see below) work design are still evident in call centre work (see also Chapter 5: Gender). Perhaps, then, nothing new is happening in the workplace – only the extension of old and familiar work patterns and practices.

This chapter is concerned with providing an introduction to work and its organisation and is, therefore, not exhaustive. You should consider links with other chapters (a number of which are indicted for you) in search of an understanding, but also reflect on how changes in the workplace will influence your own experiences of work both now and in the future.

The Problem of Defining Work
The first task is to unravel the complex nature of work because:

> Work tends to be an activity that transforms nature and is usually undertaken in social situations, but exactly what counts as work is dependent on the specific social circumstances under which such activities are undertaken and, critically, how these circumstances and activities are interpreted by those involved.   (Grint, 1998: 6)

The importance of work can be demonstrated by identifying how work affects people and structures much of the cycle of people's lives right through to retirement. Work is, therefore, a critical contributor to our "self concept and personal identity" (Keyser *et al*, 1988: 4). Dickinson and Elmer (1992) note that the instruments and agents of economic socialisation, such as language, family, mass media, peer groups and school are linked to cognitive skills; and it is our relationship to these that helps us begin to understand the nature of the exchange relationship in work. Thus:

> Qualities that typify the dominant character structure in an employment culture are already strongly established before individuals actually enter employment relations.
> (Dickinson and Elmer, 1992: 38)

Notions of our *compulsion* to work due to necessity, contrasts with our individual 'realms of freedom', or pursuit of leisure interests (Ronco and Peattie, 1988).

However, distinctions between work and non-work are less clear because of their – at times – 'seamless' nature. In other words, we cannot always draw clear distinctions as to what we consider work and what we consider leisure.

A conventional model of work as meaning paid employment tends to be too simplistic. Therefore, defining work is by no means straightforward. However, work assumes certain characteristics of societal value, with the result that both housework and unemployment, for example, which are conducted without value in a conventional sense, are not considered to the category, 'work'. Indeed, for Pahl (1988: 749):

> [I]t is at the end of the 20th Century we have to make a conscious effort to unlearn the model of work as a male dominated activity.

Coventional models of work, therefore, tend to be 'patriarchal', merely serving to remind us of the gendered division of work in society (see Chapter 5: Gender). Willmott and Young (1960, cited in Pahl, 1988: 749) found that women, in overwhelming numbers, regarded domestic 'roles' such as cleaning, washing clothes and washing up, as work. Large swathes of (predominantly male) public opinion, and even some sociology, perhaps, do not! Hence, we must consider the nature of any 'embedded' (socialised) meanings of work within the range of social relations, in order to fully understand the experience of work.

Being an economic agent (or, in other words, in paid employment) brings with it certain aspirations and divisions, which are not fixed but, instead, change over time, both for the individual and society. Such aspirations differ between the employer and employed, and the employed and unemployed. Nevertheless, the idea of working for a wage is considered by some writers (Dickinson and Elmer, 1992) to be a relatively recent innovation in society. A working wage is synonymous with the growth of industrialisation, as it was with the onset of this that the selling of labour for a wage came to be accepted as a form of 'economic rationalisation'. Certainly, looking back through the history of work ethics enables us to trace the rise of economic rationalisation, as such rationalisation, or 'ordering of work', is not necessarily a natural state.

In Ancient Greece, we find notions of work discredited; particularly, that associated with physical labour was viewed as a loathsome activity mainly done by slaves (Keyser, 1988). Certain concepts of Christianity see work as being a *punishment* for 'original sin', with labour being a route to redemption. Later, Calvinists proposed that work, rather than prayer, could elevate the soul. Such is where notions of a 'Protestant work ethic' come from. It was in this period that work came to be seen as a crucial social activity and is transformed from a *necessary chore* to a *moral duty*. According to

Max Weber (1958 [1930]), in *The Protestant Ethic and the Spirit of Capitalism*, this was a watershed in the expansion of capitalism.

In pre-industrial society, 'time and task' in work activity had been inseparable. Now, notions of timed (paid) labour are present, as the evolution of organisational life becomes more complex. With the onset of industrial society, the beginnings of the divorce between work and leisure become evident. Work as an unavoidable necessity embraces notions of self-esteem, which enables workers to kindle intrinsic work motivations, even under poor working conditions. The 'work ethic' hence becomes a major value in human existence, with idleness (being without work) seen as a deviation from social norms (see Chapter 11: Crime and Deviance for further discussion of deviance).

The Victorian period witnessed a proliferation of writing linked to notions of the work ethic. Thomas Carlyle (cited in Wilmer, 1985: 25) was one of the earlier writers to insist that human beings have a right to work:

> Mans moral nature was expressed through work, therefore governments who propagated laissez faire policies were doing people an injustice – a crime against nature.

Significantly, work in the Victorian period appears to be infested with the "sinews of class" (Grint, 1998: 18), as it acquires a moral substance and hierarchy. To *work* came to mean to *be* working class, *not* to mean being part of the aristocracy. However, for the working class, work constituted a cruel necessity in order to assure survival. In other words, if people did not work, they would not get paid, and if they did not get paid, they had no means of paying rent, buying food, etc. Comparative analysis of work experience in the last years of the twentieth century shows that the growth of multi- and trans-national corporations (MNCs/TNCs) has affected the geographical nature of work, which can now be seen as a truly global phenomenon. Such development has witnessed a proliferation of work in many ways, as developing countries experience forms of industrialisation alongside a growth in service sector provision, such as call centres relocating from the UK and the United States to India, where the workforce is cheaper. However, global inequity is evident, as for many, work is about assuring *survival* and not personal *satisfaction*.

Contemporary Western orientations to work seem to suggest that monetary reward acts to compensate workers from alienating work experiences. The crux of the question could be whether, 'what you do', necessarily becomes 'who you are'. The societal construction becomes part of the 'common sense' view, whereby the meaning of work for the individual in modern society perhaps focuses on *having a job* rather than the *nature of the particular activities* associated with the status of paid employment.

Work, then, is a fluid yet complex concept requiring careful analysis by the sociologist. Its definition is elusive and a simple contrast with leisure or domestic activities does little to explain it. It is with this in mind that we must consider a number of factors:

- The social setting and cultural *mores* of work
- The interpretation of work for its participants
- Historical and geographical/spatial contexts of work
- The institutions that order/control work activities.

By making such an analysis it is possible to understand and see the role work plays in reproducing wider social structures.

Trigger

1. What makes attempts at defining work a complex problem?
2. Consider what factors might differentiate work, non-work and leisure?

Classical Interpretations on Work: Anomie, Alienation and Rational Commitment

The rapid social, economic and political transformation of Western societies in the movement from a rural (agrarian) to urban (industrial) setting from about 1750 on, is synonymous with the emergence of sociology as a discipline in the nineteenth century. This becomes evident in the emphasis placed on work in the accounts of the 'founding fathers' of the sociology of work. For Marx, the move to an industrial/capitalist society from a rural/feudal one brought with it inherent exploitation and conflict (see Chapter 2: Sociological Theory and Chapter 4: Social Class). Durkheim (1947 [1893]) used terms such as 'integration' and 'consensus structuralism' to analyse the 'new', 'modern' society. Weber, however, adopted a 'social action' approach, incorporating the notions of 'rational commitment' and 'attitude to work'.

Durkheim and the promise of industrial society

The contribution of Emile Durkheim (1858-1917) in relation to work is brought into perspective through his book, *The Division of Labour in Society* (1947 [1893]). Here, he wrestles with issues of 'social solidarity' and integration in a period of dramatic social and economic upheaval. It is from this work that we are presented with the concept of 'anomie' or 'normlessness', whereby industrial society produced rapid social change that had the effect of disrupting the norms that governed social behaviour. Despite reservations, Durkheim viewed the increasing division of labour and the move from agrarian to urbanised society as having many advantages that outweighed the disadvantages.

In forming his thesis, Durkheim critiqued the writings of a number of his contemporaries (also seen as the 'founding fathers' of sociology). Auguste Comte (1798-1857), he claimed, exaggerated the amount of consensus in society and overplayed the need for state regulation, whereas he questioned Herbert Spencer's (1820-1903) obsession with economic self-interest (cited in Lukes, 1992).

Durkheim recognised the problems at the beginning of twentieth century society and noted that a disintegration of morality in pursuit of selfish individualism could result in anomie, which was evident in industrial or economic crises. Nevertheless, Durkheim believed that collective solidarity and morality were fundamental for individual freedom to prosper, and the conditions of 'egoism' (self interest) leading to anomie were only temporary as society came to terms with social change. There would eventually be a combining of individualism and social solidarity as a consequence of an increasing division of labour, whereby mutual dependence would be encouraged.

There was a sharp distinction between pre-industrial and industrial society, marked in the former by "common ideas and sentiments" (Lukes, 1992: 139). This related to a common experience that undermined and restricted the individual and, in industrial society, also restricted the new social institutions that required a change in the nature of morality. Durkheim agreed with Tonnies (cited in Lukes, 1992) that the historical transition was characterised by uniformity and 'mechanical solidarity' ('*Gemeinschaft*'/pre-industrial). The industrial mode of life was marked by greater individualism as a consequence of the increasing division of labour, a process referred to as 'organic solidarity' ('*Gesellschaft*') by Durkheim.

Durkheim believed that the spreading of norms of behaviour would result in a 'mechanical' society being replaced by an 'organic' society, which would, then, lead to a disappearance of anomie. It was the new conditions of industrial life that needed time for adjustment, as well as time for the development of new organisations, whereby equilibrium would eventually be restored and *meaningful work* would then be a feature of society. Despite being cautiously optimistic about change, Durkheim did stress that it was necessary for administrative councils/corporations attached to, but distinct from, the state to regulate the conditions under which labour worked. These occupational associations, acting as *regulatory* bodies between trade unions and employers, would also act as a *mediating* force between individuals and the state. It was this institutionalised apparatus of dispute resolution in the workplace that would assist in reversing the temporary condition of anomie.

Durkheim also thought that the forced division of labour occurred when unjustifiable inequalities were present. This was mainly due to personal inheritance, of which he advocated abolition. Although Durkheim was not an egalitarian, he was supportive of the notion of a meritocratic society (see Chapter 9: Education), and envisaged this as desirable under normal conditions. This was, in part, due to the fact that Durkheim thought individual egotism posed a great threat to society, and only through social regulation would resolutions be found to control these egotistical desires, such as greed. In this society, workers would be meaningfully employed and better co-ordinated in a labour market characterised by an increasing division of labour. This would also be central to the promotion of social solidarity and increasing the skills of workers.

Evaluation of Durkheim:

- Whilst notions of anomie helped pinpoint the apparent 'ills' of capitalism, such as unregulated competition, class conflict and meaningless work, it characterised them as "abnormal" (Lukes, 1992: 174). In so doing, Durkheim fails to explain the root causes of these 'ills'
- The notion that the increasing division of labour would result in higher levels of skill has been overturned in the twentieth century. Georges Friedmann (cited in Lukes, 1992: 178) has noted that the development of 'Taylorist' work methods (see below) and other forms of mass production are incompatible with notions of 'organic solidarity'. Where such work practices have been introduced, they have led to a 'degradation' of the individual and the work situation
- Few empirical grounds exist to suggest that Durkheim's ideal state of normality (harmony and consensus) is represented in industry. Durkheim sees problems in industrial society as being 'temporary' and 'correctable', provided that adequate institutional adjustments are met
- Durkheim's essentially 'structural' approach leaves little scope for individual agency.

Trigger

Consider whether anomie is evident in the rapidly changing society of the late twentieth/early twenty-first century?

Marx and alienation in a capitalist society

Karl Marx (1818-1883) (see Chapter 2: Sociological Theory) believed that the organisation of society around the bases of material existence and the material needs of human beings, is essential in understanding social change. It is through Marx's theory of 'historical materialism' that he is able to explain how work is a *primary* human activity. Social change occurs over time. People enter into relationship's to produce goods to meet human need, and such relationships tend to change as the history of production unfolds.

Significantly, for Marx, it is *not* industrial society that is problematic, *but* capitalism itself. In the capitalist mode of production, work (or production) is a means of exploitation, which prevents workers from realising their 'true potential'. The utilisation of human labour as a means of satisfying human need, has achieved a vast array of accomplishments throughout history, with the rapid pace of technological development from the beginning of Britain's Industrial Revolution at the end of the 18th century to today providing a clear demonstration of this. Under a capitalist system, however, human need is subordinated to the profit motives of individual capitalists. It is through this process that any 'intrinsic' value in work 'for the good of society' is lost, as workers become 'alienated'.

A true understanding of the economic division of labour, based on notions of exploitation and conflict, is found in Marx's (1976 [1867]) *Capital*. In *Capital*, Marx points out that there exists a two-class system that operates under the capitalist 'relations of production'. First, there are those who are able to expropriate the 'means of production' (the factories, raw materials, etc.) and become 'buyers' (employers) of labour in order to accumulate wealth. These Marx calls the bourgeoisie or ruling class (i.e. the employers). Second, there are those who sell their 'labour power' in return for wages. It is these whom Marx calls the industrial 'proletariat', or working class.

Integral to the process of the accumulation of capital (wealth) is the linking of *constant capital* (the means of production – factories, raw materials, etc.) and *variable capital* (labour power – the cost of which goes up as well as down, as wage-earners among us may understand) to the process of *valorisation*; that is, the creation of 'surplus value' – in common parlance, profit (Marx, 1976 [1867])!

Profit, or surplus value, is obtained by paying the workers *less* than the value of their labour. It is within this valorisation process that exploitation occurs. According to Marx, this process 'shackles' the proletariat to a life of exploitation and subordination under capitalism. Under such a binding exploitative relationship, we can see the inequalities and antagonisms of working life in a capitalist economic system. Because capital is accumulated through such exploitation, conflict becomes an unavoidable part of this relationship. Each side strives to make gains at the expense of the other: the bourgeoisie to increase their surplus value; the proletariat to enhance their financial remuneration and the quality of their working life (see Chapter 2: Sociological Theory and Chapter 4: Social Class).

For Marx, work provides the most important and vital means for people to fulfil their basic needs. Through the process of work, workers can – theoretically – experience a deep satisfaction. Nevertheless, the origin of alienation was found in a capitalist economic system, where *all of the products of labour* (goods and the workers who produce them) become 'commodities', because the workers *do not* own the goods they produce, and they have to 'sell' their 'labour power' in order to make ends meet. Alienation, therefore, increases as workers become 'removed' from the act of production (i.e. the products they make with their labour are taken from them and sold for profit), from others in society (i.e. they have to *go to* work, and *work* when they get there) and, ultimately, from their individual self (i.e. unhappiness).

As science continues to develop and apply new technology to the production process, and hence, work, Marx argues that labour processes under capitalism intensify. Examples of this could be the speeding-up of a conveyor belt in a car-manufacturing plant, or automatic speed dials being used in a call centre. In both circumstances, workers find that their 'free time' between each task is eradicated, and with it their opportunity to communicate with their fellow workers. This, according to Marx, is part and parcel of the process of alienation. This process, introduced with the advent of industrialisation, has continued unabated throughout the 20th century and into the new Millennium.

According to Marx, the 'seeds' for the downfall of capitalism are always present, since the workers employed in the capitalist system are the people who are 'immiserated' (made miserable) by their work and wider conditions of life. Capitalism is also difficult to control, in that the profit motive is central to its operation and continued survival. Workers are, therefore, bound together in a relationship that is conflict-ridden – capitalists will strive to increase their profits, thus alienating their workers further, whilst workers will try every means at their disposal to improve their conditions of work. It is these very alienated workers who, according to Marx, have the potential to develop class-consciousness, and rise up and overthrow capitalism. In other words, the proletariat has revolutionary potential.

Whilst we have not, in the West (or anywhere), witnessed the advent of a proletarian revolution, Marx's predictions of an intensification of work under capitalism do not necessarily mean that his theory is invalid. On the contrary, Chapter 4: Social Class discusses what is perceived in sociology and more broadly, to be a renewed enthusiasm for his explanation of the processes of capitalism, if not his theory of the revolutionary overthrow of the state.

Evaluation of Marx:

1) Marxists have been criticised for elevating the importance of work above all other social activities. It is work, they argue, which produces the fundamental bases of alienation. As (paid) work under capitalism is seen by Marxists as being synonymous with experiences of alienation, they often ignore other social relationships that might prove 'alienating', such as race and gender

2) One reason why worker alienation might persist in capitalist society could lie in the socialisation process, whereby individuals (of the working class in particular) come to see differences (in the distribution of resources, for example) as inevitable, logical and perhaps even desirable. As such, they do not perceive conflicts of interest or that there might be possible alternatives to worker alienation. For Marxists, then, this is a clear demonstration of false class-consciousness

3) The historical process of social and economic development necessitates a constant revaluation of Marxist principles as conditions change. As Thompson (1989: 58) notes, "Marx failed to reconcile adequately his analysis of the transformation of work and the form and content of workers struggles."

Comparing Marx and Durkheim on work

There is an irony when comparing Marx and Durkheim, since both view work in from a structural perspective (i.e. omitting the role of agency), both see work as a central social activity, and both are optimistic about the potential for positive social change, albeit for different reasons. Marx, however, envisages the breakdown of society under capitalism as the result of class conflict, whilst Durkheim sees integration and social solidarity as essential for consensus and, consequently, the maintenance of social order and the smooth functioning of society. Whilst Durkheim sees anomie as a temporary condition due to the periodic failure of existing rule-making bodies that govern social relations, Marx sees alienation as endemic and inherently associated with the capitalist labour process. Meaninglessness, as a feature of work in industrial capitalist societies, was, for Marx, unavoidable, but, for Durkheim, was merely a temporary feature.

Marx was *not* against industrialisation as such, but rather, its manifestation under capitalism. Durkheim, however, could envisage solutions to the problems of industrial society, but failed to tackle the fundamental roots of inequality. Durkheim espoused a social democratic position whereby equality of opportunity was central to a meritocratic society; although he never went as far as advocating the abolition of private property and did *not* see revolution as likely, or even desirable. However, Marx was *against* capitalism and the ownership of private property and advocated its overthrow by revolutionary means.

Weber and the commitment to rational economic activity

Max Weber's (1864-1920) understanding of the commitment to work of individuals is grounded in the relationship between the economy and society, together with what work *means* to the individual. There is an emphasis on the reciprocal interaction between the economy and a whole set of social factors, which provide a focus for Weber's analysis of work. In his examination of society, Weber relies on the extrapolation of 'ideal types' from historical processes and on the 'social action' method of understanding ('*verstehen*') in order to comprehend society (see Chapter 2: Sociological Theory).

Weber's attention is primarily focused on the origins of capitalism and the conditions that underpinned its development. It is in this process that rational thinking and action become fundamental to the progress of capitalism. However, Weber felt that this rational economic activity, which was a dynamic feature of capitalism, had its genesis in, and was underpinned by, various institutional and political, conditions (Dimitrovna, 1994).

Work and the Protestant ethic

It is through Weber's (1958 [1930]) focus on the importance of religion in shaping social change, that the sociologist is able to ascertain the focus for the link between the values and beliefs of ascetic Protestantism and the incentive for 'rational economic actions. Work became a 'moral duty' in the context of the Calvinist doctrine of *predestination*. This is because it constituted part of the search to quell some of the anxiety over whether a person would attain salvation. This search for salvation meant that hard work, as part of a frugal lifestyle, was considered virtuous and dutiful. With this attitude came a commitment that facilitated the organisation and the reinvestment of money gained through work. Such attitudes and actions provided the foundations for capitalism to prosper, as work became the means by which individuals could demonstrate their 'Godliness'. Grint (1998) notes that this new attitude to work, through the rise of Calvinism, was a cultural change associated with the rise of capitalism itself.

Weber did, however, come to have a fairly pessimistic view of the outcome of this relationship between Protestantism and capitalism. He was aware of the problem attached to the simple application of such a spiritualistic emphasis on societal development. This was, he was aware, a mono-causal understanding of culture and history. As such, Weber was seen to be *qualifying* his theory (Dimitrovna, 1994) and this was exacerbated by his feelings that the original Protestant work ethic was called into question due to the decline of religious faith, which was replaced by the excessive nature of individualism and self-satisfaction that capitalism seemed to herald in. Thus, Weber is aware of the 'replacement' of religion by technical and economic conditions, which serve to support capitalism more effectively, as machines come to determine 'the lot' of people. Weber felt that it was no longer a case of rational capitalism needing Protestantism to provide the appropriate conditions for capitalism to prosper. Instead, such ideal conditions were being instituted by scientific progress. Weber is pessimistic about the outcome, because he sees society as being *trapped* by the progress of capitalism (in what he refers to as an 'iron-cage') in the context of rational, technical and bureaucratic organisations, where the individual will eventually become 'dehumanized' (i.e just another 'cog in the wheel').

Rationalisation and bureaucracy

Weber recognised that contemporary society was grounded in rationality, which serves the interests of capitalists and enhances capitalisms' social control. Rationalisation would manifest itself in capitalism, through the development of legal codes and the advancement of rational bureaucracy. The pre-cursor to this was the replacement of affective and traditional forms of action with a rational form, which was 'rule-bound', thereby challenging the more emotional and Divine interpretations of society. Whilst Weber identified bureaucracies as constructions that pre-dated capitalism, it was the rational basis on which they would come to be founded that differentiated their form from earlier times.

The elements of a rational bureaucracy were composed of forms of 'legitimate authority, whereby:

- There was a 'code' of impersonal formal rules
- It was based on a hierarchy
- There existed a career structure
- There was *non*-ownership of office
- There were expert skills and knowledge.

These features of organisations were to be fundamental in the organisation of work, particularly concerning whether bureaucracy is still the most efficient form of organisation. This will feature in our discussion later in this Chapter.

Evaluation of Weber:

1. Rational capitalism is *not* confined to Protestant nations and it is not clear in his argument why *material success* and diligence should be the route to salvation and good grace

2. There is also the problem of a dependency on non-ascetic consumers to underpin the wheels of capitalism. Therefore, as Sennett notes, "[Weber] omit[s] any consideration of consumption as a driving force in capitalism" (Sennett, 1998: 105)

3. It is possible to suggest that the causal link between capitalism and Calvinism centred on association rather than causation

4. Weber's emphasis on the rational approach and formalised bureaucracy as being the most efficient forms of work organisation, fails to take into account the *informal* structures of organisations. He also fails to acknowledge forces that can work to destabilise an organisation, such as economic fluctuations, trade unionism, corruption and greed, etc.

5. Weber challenges the structural approach of both Marx and Durkheim, in favour of an interpretative understanding, or *verstehen*. However, when he writes about bureaucracy it is, contradictorily, very much in the context of structural forces impinging on the individual; in essence, a 'cause and effect' analysis more akin to the structuralist approach.

Comparing Marx and Weber on work

- There is a tendency to regard the works of Marx and Weber as alternatives and, even, as oppositionist. Nevertheless, both perspectives examine the existence of conflict, although the structural approach of Marx and his 'materialist dialectic' is in contrast to the social action of Weber and his reliance on understanding (*verstehen*), together with the use of 'ideal types' from history. Marx stressed the *objective conditions* for the development of capitalism with an emphasis on class conflict. Alternatively, Weber examined the *origins of capitalism* by explaining the role of culture and religious values to its development

- Both Weber and Marx concur that control in industrial society is borne from economic need and both recognise the importance of property ownership

- Whilst Marx is always searching for the revolutionary potential of the worker as the result of class conflict, Weber counters this by noting that the revolutionary nature of society is curbed because of *fragmentation* (i.e. lack of common interest) in the class system

- Weber stresses that stratification is more complex than the bi-polar (two-class) system of Marx. Whilst Weber acknowledges class as being synonymous with a persons economic or market position (whether employee or employer), he also notes other factors like 'status' (prestige) and 'party' (social or political associations) as having a cross-cutting affect on revolutionary solidarity (see Chapter 4: Social Class)

- Weber emphasises the means of administration in his understanding of the development of rational bureaucracy and the organisation of work

However, Marx believes that the ownership of the means of production (or lack thereof) was the key to explaining alienation and class conflict

- There appears to be an irony in the fact that Marx is optimistic about social change occurring through the dynamic of revolution, whereas Weber is pessimistic about society as, for him, rationalisation led eventually to workers being trapped in the 'iron-cage' of bureaucracy. The commitment to work that is espoused by Weber is threatened and he notes the dangers of his own form of alienation, as workers become mechanical and 'de-humanised' under a 'seamless web' of bureaucratic regimes.

Trigger

"[I]f the work ethic doesn't exist how do we explain the almost compulsive work behaviour of some" (Grint, 1998)? Discuss.

Labour Process Theory
Braverman and the 'degradation of work'
Contemporary interest in the labour process was effectively established through Harry Braverman's (1974) seminal work, *Labour and Monopoly Capital: The Degradation of Work in the Twentieth Century*, and provided the catalyst for numerous debates on the nature of the work process. Braverman (1974) recast the exploitative nature of the capitalist labour process along the same route as Marx, concentrating on the 'deskilling' and 'degradation' of work. Such a path clearly supports Braverman's, like Marx's, prognosis that labour will become increasingly 'proletarianised' (i.e. the working class will develop class-consciousness) and the class structure 'homogenised' (i.e. classes converging) during the evolution of capitalist working relationships (Marx and Engels, 1968: 35-46; see also Chapter 2: Sociological Theory and Chapter 4: Social Class).

The *core values* of labour process theory are, as Thompson (1989) notes:

- The employer-employee relationship is built on material exploitation through the expropriation of 'surplus value' (profit)
- 'The logic of accumulation' and the levels of competition mean the labour process in capitalism needs to be constantly revolutionised (Thompson, 1989)
- The control imperative is shaped by the aforementioned
- The social relations between capital and labour are based on structured antagonism, even if this is not visible in the form of conflict (Thompson, 1989).

Braverman versus 'Taylorism'

Braverman (1974) builds a critique of the capitalist labour process by focusing on the ideas of Frederick Winslow Taylor (1980 [1911]), as promoted in his book, *The Principles of Scientific Management*. Such ideas were based on a management *science* replacing 'rule of thumb' working practice. This *scientific management* would become more systematic by ameliorating the personal idiosyncrasies that distinguished workers as individuals (Beninger, 1986). Taylor (1980 [1911]) labelled his ideas 'scientific management', because he felt that their quantitative empirical basis would result in a more rationalised form of control in the workplace. Taylor's (1980 [1911]) diagnosis of industry can be reduced to the fairly simple theme of inefficiency on the part of *both* workers *and* management. Taylor's technical prescriptions for change form a distinct package:

1. Recommendations for organisational structure and a 'routinization' of work (or rational bureaucratisation – slimmed-down work practices, such as one person, one repetitive task)
2. The measurement of work and design of tasks. For example, Taylor's study of the Bethlehem Steel Company, where he discovered the optimum load for shovelling pig iron and a 'systematised' workforce
3. The motivation of workers to grasp routine operations linked to economic reward.

Taylor (1980 [1911]) felt that an ideal "authentic industrial partnership" (Rose, 1975: 34-37) between management and worker would be created, and that acceptance would follow because it was "scientific-impartial universal, law like in both the scientific and juridical senses" (Rose, 1975: 34-37). Therefore, workers would lessen their resistance, because *all* would benefit from an increase in material rewards and the disappearance of irrationality from the system.

For Braverman (1974), however, scientific management was about shifting control in favour of capitalist owners in an attempt to effect the real subordination of labour. This would, therefore, bring about increased surplus value:

> It starts, despite occasional protestations to the contrary, not from the human point of view but from the capitalist point of view [...]. It investigates not labour in general, but the adaptation of labour to the needs of capital. It enters the workplace as the representative of science, but as the representation of management masquerading in the trappings of science.
>
> (Braverman, 1974: 86)

Braverman (1974) goes on to say that Taylor's system was:

Simply a means for management to achieve control of the actual mode of performance of every labour activity, from the simplest to the most complicated.

(Braverman, 1974: 90)

Taylor's (1980 [1911]) application of scientific management principles to the production process, in essence, led to a de-skilling and fragmentation of work tasks. He separated the 'constructs of execution' (*the doing*) from the 'conception' (*the thinking*). In plain terms, he created the division of manual and mental work. This process necessitated the adoption of a hierarchy to oversee the rationalisation of work, leading to what has pejoratively been termed, 'bureaucratisation'. Management, for Braverman (1974), becomes the *vessel* for the knowledge, whilst skill, which has been wrested by management from the workforce through rationalisation, becomes the 'conception' function of the collective labour process.

The deskilling process would increasingly become a feature of work and would affect the establishment of white-collar (office) work as "privileged position" (Braverman, 1974: 407). Deskilling and degradation would occur through reduced autonomy in the design and planning of work and the institutionalising of meaningless fragmented tasks. This would result in a weakened market position for workers (as their previously 'skilled' tasks become simplified or rationalised) and the move to modern Taylorist forms of control.

Critical comments on Braverman:

1. Braverman's (1974) notion that scientific management was widespread and constituted the only form of control appears to fall into the trap of assuming there is a single best way of organising capital in practice. Deskilling becomes only one of a number of possible consequences of managerial control over the workforce. Also, empirical evidence to support the widespread adoption of scientific management appears inadequate

2. Thompson (1989) also points out that for management to have a monopoly of conception "runs against a parallel requirement for some level of creative participation of shop-floor workers to keep production going" (Thompson, 1989: 133). It is following on from this that Braverman tends to ignore the *subjective* experiences of workers and how, through individual and collective agency, a variety of forms of resistance feature in the labour process

3. Braverman (1974) approaches the notion of 'skill' as an unproblematic category, which in essence ignores its social and historical context. To fully understand skill as a category, it is important to examine its development through empirical means. Some would suggest that new skills have been a feature of twentieth century life, as a result of a process of '*up*skilling' rather

248

than *de*skilling taking place as a result of the introduction of information technologies.

Strategies of control or consent?

Thompson and McHugh (2002) point out that because of a general confusion between Taylorism as a system of managerial control and management control in general, questions on the role of managerial strategy have periodically been revitalised.

There have been numerous criticisms of Marx and his contemporary, Braverman, including from some who come from *within* the labour process tradition. Andrew Friedman (1977) questions the 'determinism' of Marx's view. He argues that capitalists and their agents can select from a range of control mechanisms, but this must be seen within the context of other factors, such as the strength of the workforce (in terms of its size and trade union activity) and various external market pressures (such as troughs in economic activity and rising unemployment). Friedman (1977) identifies that there are *other* direct control strategies that are similar to Taylorism. Additionally, he also addresses the example of 'responsible autonomy', whereby workers are given responsibility with varying degrees of company/production decision-making. An example of the latter might be the Swedish car manufacturer, Volvo, which experimented with a more 'corporatist' decision-making model, where a whole range of production processes, including car design, were taken by both the management and the unions (see Chapter 3: Research Methods, for a further discussion on this).

Richard Edwards (1979) provides an historical account of the emergence of successive managerial strategies of control. In *Contested Terrain*, he maps out *three* forms of control: *simple* (observed/direct), *technical* (inscribed and epitomised by the assembly line) and *bureaucratic* (rules and procedures). Edwards (1979) uses a framework that illustrates how changes within the workplace reflect socio-economic conditions. Therefore, managerial strategies take into account workforce reaction and resistance to company policy.

Nevertheless, both Friedman (1977) and Edwards (1979) have been criticised for using categories that are too narrow, which has the effect of creating a restrictive framework of analysis. The strategies of control need to be able to be discussed in combined forms if their rigidity is to be overcome. Management styles are, therefore, developed to accommodate changing circumstances, allowing for flexibility in management style, where necessary.

This management control debate has itself been subject to the criticism that management will always try to find models of control to solve problems, and that control theorists have a tendency to construct *all-embracing* management control models (Thompson and McHugh, 2002). The explanations of managerial strategies of control, such as that favoured by Braverman (1974), for example, are often questioned on the grounds that workers may be perfectly capable of controlling themselves through the generation of *consent* (Thompson, 1989: 153). This is central to the analysis of Michael Burawoy in *Manufacturing Consent* (1979), and later in *The Politics of Production* (1985).

Whereas both Marx and Braverman (1974) had envisaged *no* role for consensual employer-employee relations, Burawoy (1979; 1985) argues that workers are coaxed into believing that they enjoy rights and benefits in their workplace and that they should, therefore, 'play the game'. Further, Burawoy (1979; 1985) argues that managers *do not* control workers too closely and workers believing they do results in them contributing to their own exploitation. Grievance procedures and collective bargaining imbue workers with the idea that they have achieved 'industrial citizenship' and serve useful functions in the production of workplace consent. However, critics of Burawoy (1979; 1985) would point out that workers are not so easily persuaded but, instead, have no option but to follow management decisions.

Trigger

Having examined 'labour process theory' do you think it is about *control* or *consent*? Why?

A Changing Context and New Methods of Work?
From Taylorism to 'Fordism'

The period of Western industrialisation witnessed a great movement of people from the countryside to the ever-burgeoning towns and cities. The experience of work during this period became increasingly characterised by the introduction of technology. With the introduction, then, of Taylor and his scientific management, the emphasis on work/production practices moved to a standardised Taylorist control. Whilst Taylorism oversaw the decline of highly-skilled craft production in favour of broken-down or rationalised work tasks, 'Fordism' applied an even more formidable dynamic to Taylorism. This saw the introduction of the assembly line, at the beginning of the twentieth century, as process by which not only could work tasks be rationalised, but also mass-produced.

Henry Ford's 'flow-line production' (the assembly line), used to produce the Model-T Ford car, was unveiled in 1914 in the United States. Workers at Ford's Michigan-based car plant operated under an extreme division of labour, with work-rate controlled by a moving assembly line. The large volume of production necessitated a "just in case" philosophy (Ritzer, 2000: 31), whereby parts are stored, often in large warehouses, "just in case" in case they are needed for the production line and in the expectation of mass consumer demand. Fordism saw the introduction of more skilled planners and managers and placed a heavy emphasis on the application of Taylorist management principles, including its preoccupation with job design and bureaucracy (see Weber, above). Whilst Taylor used 'piece-rates' (payment per good produced), Fordism orchestrated the manipulation of a complicated assembly line to simplify work and gain a tighter control over the worker. In spite of this, passive acceptance of the system was less straightforward, and due to worker-resistance and two world wars, it was some time before Fordism consolidated.

The maturity of Fordism was a feature of post-World War II society. The period from the early 1950s to the mid-1970s generally came to be considered by economic historians as a "golden age of capitalism" (Dawson, 2000: 85). The system of mass production and mass consumption was underpinned by 'Keynesian' economics, which presented a solution to the ills of unemployment that were symptomatic of the world depression of the 1930s. These economic principles worked by raising government expenditure, which would have the effect of increasing demand for goods and, consequently, of raising employment levels. The economic system was essentially social democratic in nature, stressing notions of equality of opportunity, social justice and a comprehensive welfare system.

Fordism appeared to solve many of the problems, both social and economic, that had been prominent features of the earlier 1920s and 1930s with peoples spending power increasing in the post-war period. This helped create huge production surpluses. Indeed, for some theorists, such as Priore and Sabel (1984), the maturity of Fordism was about a 'regime of accumulation' that was more than just a method of production. More importantly, they argue, it was about incorporating Taylorism and bureaucratic structures into the workplace.

Alternatives to Fordism/Taylorism

Despite the apparent success of 'Keynesian' economics, the 1970s witnessed the beginning of a series of transformations, stemming from increases in international competition, technological changes and diversified markets. Rising unemployment and inflation and, perhaps, a deliberate strategy brought about by the emergence of New Right politics (see Chapter 2: Sociological Theory and Chapter 4: Social Class), eventually meant that governments moved away from Keynesian economic management towards monetarist policies. These policies particularly stressed a cutting-down of government spending. At this time, manufacturing experienced a huge decline in employment in what was a period of increasing de-industrialisation and a movement towards service industries.

Debates about the effectiveness of Fordism as a system has resulted in a whole series of ideas associated with the notions of a 'post-Fordist' organisation and society and the scholar is faced with a confusing array of terms and ideas under this umbrella which also include postmodernism (see Chapter 2: Sociological Theory). Terms are often interchangeable in usage and signify the fragmented nature and diversity of events.

Theorists advocating 'flexible accumulation' propose a model that views the transition from the stricter Fordist 'regime of accumulation' to a more flexible mode of accumulation. Those following the 'regulation school' of thought (Aglietta 1979; Lipietz 1986) referred to this new mode of accumulation as 'neo-Fordist'. Others, such as Priore and Sabel (1984), see more radical trends in place with a transformation in production and consumption through the onset of 'flexible specialisation'. This approach envisages that the Taylorist/Fordist model no longer has credence due to its inflexibility and has, therefore, ceased to exist. The solution arises, they argue, in the application of sophisticated technology and customised 'batch production', with its shorter product runs and lesser organisational lead-in time. Changes to the Weberian bureaucratic model, with its emphasis on hierarchical control of organisations, were being replaced in favour of worker flexibility, *multi-*skilling, greater team-working and reduction in job demarcation.

Notions of flexibility are evident in the service industries through the use of the term 'flexible firm' (Atkinson, 1985, cited in Thompson and McHugh, 2002: 145). This model assumes the existence of *core* and *periphery* workers and is based on the notion of 'functional flexibility'. The core worker is assumed to be multi-skilled and have more favourable conditions of employment. The peripheral worker, however, is likely to be employed in a casual, unskilled capacity, with fewer rights and less remuneration. Also, 'numerical flexibility' is achieved through establishing a bank of workers who are part-time, on temporary contracts or subcontracted. Work is also 'outsourced' in the flexible firm as services such as cleaning, security and hospitality activities, not considered part of the core business activity, are contracted out. These sub-contractors then take over the work process, often employing the same people who had previously done the job, to do *more of the same job*, in *less time* and usually for *lower wages*. This practice also allows for the removal or reduction of these tasks at short notice and without redundancy (which becomes far more likely) payment. One problem with this model is that flexible practices have the underlying assumption of being explicit management orientations or occur as a consequence of more general structural change in the economy.

A model of production that would give the appearance of a movement away from Taylorist/Weberian bureaucracy in favour of 'flatter' company structures is the so-called 'Japanization' of production. This model presents a series of working practices that emphasise flexibility in the context of *teamwork* and 'quality circles', whereby workers collaborate to solve problems occurring within work processes. Conti and Warner (1993) liken working methods in Japan to scientific management and as complementary to today's innovations of 'total quality management' (TQM) and 'just-in-time' (JIT). They suggest that whilst some see JIT as the *reversal* of Taylorism and Fordism, others claim that it is not an alternative, but rather a *complementary* system aiding the process of the rationalisation of work. Another view is that "the Japanese out-Taylor us all" (Conti and Warner, 1993: 35). Despite workers being encouraged to acquire technical skill, which appears to contradict classical Taylorism, Conti and Warner (1993) suggest that the legacy of scientific management is present both directly and indirectly within the Japanese production system, albeit in a moderated form.

Others suggest that new production systems that appear to devolve greater responsibility to the worker, do not lead to greater autonomy, but "rather a set of tasks which are closely monitored and strictly controlled" (Thompson, 1993: 20). Thompson (1993) suggests that perhaps multi-*skilling* is being confused with multi-*tasking* and a greater subordination to corporate culture and norms. There has been a major intensification of labour as new technology eliminates the traditional informal processes of 'slack time'. An example of this might be the New Labour government' suggestion that all teachers should be provided with a laptop computer to 'help' their workload. What this does in reality, however, is ensures that the teacher, whether at home or travelling on public transport to or from work, is permanently in possession of a resource that will allow him or her to 'stay ahead'. In reality, of course, teaching, like many professional work practices, is an occupation that persistently demands that one 'stays ahead'.

Another such example of how technology might eliminate the informal processes of 'slack time' is the introduction of the mobile phone. Again, travel to and from work, evenings, weekends and holiday periods can all be consumed to greater or lesser degrees by work-related calls. By way of resisting this culture of work intensification, the left-wing former Labour MP and one-time cabinet minister, Tony Benn, made a humorous yet serious, response to the Blair government's policy of all Labour MPs being continually 'on-message' (by carrying a mobile phone or bleeper). Benn suggested that whilst politics was a potentially noble line of work carrying with it very long hours, that did not extend to his 'managers' having the right to electronically tag him. He was after all, he pointed out, not a criminal.

Also, the increased use of management information systems (MIS) are seen as being instrumental in increasing productive output, as intermediate managers of universities and colleges could no doubt tell you.

Of course, some of the above examples of changing workplace practices, most notably the use of the laptop computer and mobile phone, from what might be deemed a 'postmodern' perspective, have seen the traditional boundaries of the office or classroom or other workplace increasingly eroded.

Trigger

1. Which of the 'upskilling' or 'deskilling' models of the labour process do you find most convincing, and why?
2. Have you, in any work experiences that you might have had, found that you have been 'deskilled' or 'upskilled'?

Bureaucratic or Post-Bureaucratic Organisation of Work?

The debates about the organisation of work spark a multitude of questions. With an increasing globalisation (see Chapter 2: Sociological Theory) of the economy, and hence work, the following question possibly has a particular resonance:

- *With the introduction of the 'flexible firm' and 'flexible specialisation' as central features of a post-Fordist society, are we seeing the end of bureaucracy as a form of organisation and distinctive feature of modernity?*

'McDonaldization'

The American sociologist, George Ritzer (2000), in *The McDonaldization of Society*, depicts a situation characterised by an 'amplification' of the processes of bureaucratisation and rationalisation. This amplification (or more widespread use) has its roots in the work of Weber, Taylor and Ford. This process, called 'McDonaldization', is considered inevitable in industrial societies and encompasses areas of life outside the traditional large-scale organisation. This is defined as:

> The process by which the principles of the fast food restaurant are coming to dominate more and more sectors of American society as well as of the rest of the world.
> (Ritzer, 2000: 1)

Ritzer (2000) uses the McDonalds fast food chain to portray "a quantum leap in the process of rationalisation [of work practices]" (Ritzer, 2000: 39), illustrating some of the harmful effects of this extension of bureaucracy to other areas of life and how such methods of organisation have influenced (and been imitated) by other businesses.

McDonalds employs various classic Weberian bureaucratic principles, such as a clear division of labour with jobs broken down into small basic steps, underpinned by uniform rules based on the assumption that this makes the process of serving food efficient and effective. The compelling attraction for other sectors imitating McDonalds lies in the model's economic success, with high profits and lower labour costs.

Ritzer (2000) identifies *four* aspects on which this rationalisation process is founded:

- First, is that increased 'efficiency' is linked to achieving optimum output by the most effective means possible. The Weberian model of *substantive* rationality (whereby rational means, based on particular rational values, are adopted to achieve goals) is contrasted with *instrumental* rationality (the optimum means of achieving these goals by streamlining and simplifying processes). Ritzer (2000) suggests that the consumer or customer is now central to organisational objectives and the creation of surplus value. This occurs through the customer carrying out unpaid labour tasks for the company. In McDonald's *restaurants*, for example, customers 'wait on' their order rather than get 'waited on' in the traditional sense of a restaurant. They then take their meal to their table themselves and eat it. They also sit in an environment that is brightly lit and generally not designed for comfort. This means that the experience of eating becomes very functional, with them leaving once they have finished their meal (and cleared up after themselves!). This means that McDonald's, like many other fast-food chains, are able to increase their profit margins by utilising the customer as unpaid labour. This means that they do not require a large workforce. For those who are in McDonald's employment, they do not get the opportunity to build up traditional catering industry skills, like waiting tables, etc. Thus, for Ritzer (2002: 144), these customers are "not paid less than the value they produce, they are paid nothing at all." Customers, then, are involved in an increasing number of tasks previously undertaken by an organisation's employees, other examples of which include supermarkets and automatic teller machines (ATMs/cashpoints)
- Second, Ritzer (2000) refers to 'calculability', whereby everything becomes reduced to numbers. Obtaining resources in large amounts and sizes means reduced costs. *Quality* is often a secondary consideration. Examples of this could include further and higher education teaching, where quality is considered in *quantifiable* terms, such as the amount of publications produced, pass rates and league tables, all of which tend to overtake any focus on the *quality* of teaching provision
- Third, and linked to the above in a reciprocal relationship, is the practice of making tasks, products and workers similar – this increases the level of

255

'predictability' (Ritzer, 2000). Examples of this uniform approach are evident in shops like Ikea, which adopts the "Disney look" (Ritzer, 2000: 93), where employees all look and act alike. Notions of standardisation can also be applied to other products of consumption and areas of life such as cars, music and foods

- Fourth, Ritzer (2000) argues that increased 'control' underpins the aforementioned processes and is implemented with the maximum substitution of non-human labour in a military-style robotic operation. Hence, labour processes are increasingly deskilled as a means of counteracting economic inefficiency.

Ritzer (2000) argues that through McDonaldization, the Weberian/Fordist model is continuously being extended to many other areas of social life in a universal model of rationality. Therefore, just as Weber was increasingly pessimistic about the de-humanising and irrational effects of bureaucracy, so, too, is Ritzer (2000) about the impact on society of McDonaldization. From increased queues at cash points, to an increase in traffic travelling to/from the rising number of fast food restaurants, to the impact on health of higher levels of fast-food consumption, Ritzer (2000) notes that vast profits are made, but raises questions about whom they are made for. The ramifications of an extension of such bureaucratic rationality would, in essence, replicate Weber's argument that tedium in his 'iron-cage' undermined skill and creativity, whilst increasing a standardisation and routinization of social life.

This assumption of an increased standardisation of social life is countered by other sociologists, such as Clegg (1990; 1992), who feel that bureaucracy has been displaced by other identifiable styles. Clegg (1990; 1992) emphasises the way cultures can influence the development of organisations, and uses examples from the Far East to suggest that factors evident in the success of Japanese corporations rely on cultural explanations. This is underpinned by ideas such as postmodernism, which stress *diversity* and *fluidity* rather than *uniformity* and *rigidity*. Therefore, the principles associated with Weberian bureaucracy are no longer applicable to the individualised desires of consumers. There is a certain tone in Clegg's (1990; 1992) work that suggests, as with other aforementioned writers, that Japanese models of production spell the foundations for *organisations of the future*.

The common element in all debates, whether in favour of continuity or supporting discontinuity, is that organisations operate in a manner that generally best suits the needs of capitalism and the profit motive. Therefore, depending on circumstances, it is possible to see models of organisation that do not necessarily strictly conform to either bureaucratic rational principles or the more diverse postmodern picture (see Chapter 2: Sociological Theory, for further discussion on postmodernism).

> **Trigger**
>
> Consider the merits of Ritzer's (2000) theory? How might his theory be used to explain life in other workplaces in Scotland?

Insecurity in a Changing Labour Market?

There are various models of change that have featured extensively in contemporary debates on work. The UK, throughout the 1950s to the early 1970s, seen as a society of stability, security and continuity, characterised by full employment and notions of a 'job for life', moved very rapidly throughout the late 1970s and beyond to a society based on diversity and uncertainty, characterised by unemployment, instability and insecurity.

'McJobs' for Britain and Scotland?

The period of change in the 1980s and 1990s under successive Conservative administrations, was further consolidated by New Labour government policies based on the assumption of the demise of the manufacturing sector and the rise of service industries. UK manufacturing fell from 28 per cent of employment in 1900 to 14 per cent in 2000, whilst agriculture fell from 11 per cent to two per cent in the same period. Although other figures illustrate that the decline in agriculture has not been as profound in Scotland (6.5 per cent) in recent years as the rest of the UK (averaging 20.2 per cent) (Lindsay, 2003). The change in the UKs industrial composition, along with the rise in service sector jobs, has meant a shift in industry to what has been characterised by some as a 'post industrial' society. In such an 'information' society, white collar jobs have become the norm (Bell, 1973).

In Scotland, there were 2,391,000 employees according to official figures, in autumn 2001. This represents approximately 8.7 per cent of the total UK workforce, with 23 per cent of these being part-time workers. Of this total, 77 per cent of the Scottish workforce were employed in service sector jobs, where there was a growth of 161,000 employees since 1994 (Miller, Scottish Further Education Unit, 2002). Certainly, Ritzer (2002) is dubious about claims alluding to the post-industrial society, as deskilled jobs have proliferated due to the spread of what have been referred to as 'McJobs' (employment offering little creativity or satisfaction) that have come about as part of the process of McDonaldization.

The 30:30:40 society

The effect of sweeping changes in society has been to create a labour market where divisions are becoming more profound; none more so than that between the employed and unemployed. These social divisions are equated to what has been called a "thirty, thirty, forty society" (Hutton, 1996: 105).

The first 30 per cent are described as the "disadvantaged" (Hutton 1996: 10) and considered likely to lead an uncertain existence. This group includes those out of work, others who do not receive unemployment benefit, unemployed women and women whose partners are economically inactive, as well as those on government schemes.

The second 30 per cent consist of the "marginalized and insecure" (Hutton 1996: 106). These are defined by their relationship to the labour market, whereby jobs are "insecure, poorly protected and carry few benefits" (Hutton, 1996: 106). It includes those in full-time work with insecure tenure, and those on less than average wages and whose position has been weakened by the decline of collective bargaining, employment law and the trade unions. Trade union membership reached its peak in the late 1970s and represented 50 per cent of those in employment, but by 2000 it was down to under 29 per cent, the lowest in 60 years (Lindsay, 2003). Those in part-time work (some 5 million, of which 80 per cent are women, with two-thirds on low pay) and in casual, temporary work, also figure predominantly in this group. Exceptions may be those people who are from dual income households working part-time, some of whom who have held their jobs for more than five years and so will perhaps not feel as insecure.

The last category are the "privileged" (Hutton 1996: 108), standing at about 40 per cent, who have seen their market power increase since 1979. This group are those who are full-time with secure tenure, but also part-timers that have held a job for five years or more. This section of the workforce is generally covered by significant trade union membership. Divisions between the rich and poor are evident as many in full-time work are on low wages, but remain relatively privileged due to secure income.

It becomes apparent from Hutton's analysis of the labour market that the 'job for life' has gone. Dawson (2000: 97-98) notes that increased competition and flexibility means inefficient producers face collapse, whilst those seeking work are also inefficient if they are not prepared to lower their demands and take lower, more 'flexible', wages. The flexible labour market orders people more dynamically, suiting those workers with particular skills at certain times. The contest between workers means some prosper whilst other workers face uncertain futures, with the polarisation of advantaged and disadvantaged becoming ever more acute. The impact of a shifting labour market, for Thompson and McHugh (2002: 346), has meant stable career development is "in effect a misnomer for many in modern occupations." Callaghan and Thompson (2001), in their study of the call centre,

Telebank, illustrate the employment experience as being characterised by routine work, modest pay and flat promotion structures.

Alienation and Control Revisited – Call Centres

A theme throughout this chapter has been that control is a feature of working life resulting in particular states of mind in workers. This is so, because this chapter has discussed sociological debates that focus on how different types of work affect levels of alienation. Blauner's (1964) classic study of several industries (motor vehicle industry, textiles, chemical production and printing) suggests that the highest levels of alienation were evident in car workers involved in assembly line work. This was due to them having a lack of control, little relief from monotony, lacking personal satisfaction and in general being detached from the final product. Blauner's (1964) prognosis was that alienation was a result of the technology employed, which stands in contrast to that of Marx, who considered capitalism to be the underlying and inevitable cause of alienation. Generally, debates about control and alienation have been reinvigorated with the rise of service work. The explanation by Ritzer (2002) of McJobs resulting in high levels of resentment, job dissatisfaction, alienation, absenteeism and turnover (300 per cent in the US fast food industry) provides us with a clearer understanding of this type of work.

The call centre is also envisaged as a new form of assembly line "in the head" (Taylor and Bain, 1999), increasingly forming the key point of contact between service users and providers, with the integration of telephone and computer technologies. For some sociologists, this development represents "a new strategy by capital to create controlled and cost efficient environments that can restructure and expand the provision of services to the customer" (Callaghan and Thompson, 2001: 2). In line with this, Taylor and Bain (1999: 115) explain call centres as "new developments in the Taylorisation of white collar work."

The call centre is defined as:

> A dedicated operation in which computer-utilising employees receive inbound – or make outbound – telephone calls, with those calls processed by an automatic call distribution (ACD) system, or perhaps by a predictive dialling system.
>
> (Taylor and Bain, 1999: 102)

Although Taylor and Bain (1999) later point out that further technological developments mean more elaborate definitions are perhaps necessary, nevertheless "the call centre remains defined fundamentally by the integration of telephone and computer technologies" (2002: 134). Call centres are differentiated on whether calls are predominantly inbound or outbound and also by the complexity and variability of the product, together with the level of knowledge required in dealing with customers (Callaghan and Thompson, 2001). The development of call centres encompasses a number of different industries in the public, private and voluntary sectors, including business and financial services, leisure and transport, retail and telecommunications, among others. In line with this, the call centre is regarded as a significant step in the evolution of white-collar work (Bain *et al*, 2002: 173).

Throughout the UK, estimates on call centre employment vary from approximately 300,000 in the sector (Fraser, 2003), towards a more recent figure from the Sector Skills Council's (2003) 'Contact Centre Survey' of 867,000 in UK call and contact centre employment (IDS, 2003: Report 884). Difficulties do occur in providing an accurate estimate of numbers employed in the sector, due to a lack of workable definitions as to what represents a contact centre worker. Despite this, figures in most estimates are significant, with Scotland home to approximately 220 call centres employing around 46,000 staff in 2000. This compares to 119 centres with 16,000 employees in 1997 (Taylor and Bain, 2001). In the Glasgow area alone, there were more than 96 call centres in 2000 (Taylor and Bain, 2001). The 'Central Belt', from Greenock in the west to Edinburgh in the east – including Fife, accounts for 84.3 per cent of all call centre employment in Scotland (Taylor and Bain, 2001). It is clear, then, that call centre jobs across Scotland – the pattern is similar in the rest of the UK – are generally concentrated in areas that were blighted by the loss of manufacturing jobs in the 1980s and 1990s.

The development of the call centre has led to a significant sociological interest in the field. Certainly, Thompson and McHugh (2002) take note of the fact that call centre development has led to the institution of theories that focus on surveillance, although whether this constitutes the necessity for the development of new theories is questionable. Hence, the 'electronic sweatshop' theories derived from the thinking of Michel Foucault (1926-1984), that imply total control and power in the hands of management are called into question by the more traditional labour process approach, which stresses a continuity in patterns of control and resistance (Callaghan and Thompson, 2001) (see Box 10.1, below).

The Income Data Services sixth annual survey of pay and conditions in call centres (incorporating 133 organisations, operating over 300 call centres and employing 106,000 staff) across all regions of the UK (IDS, 2002: Report 864), provides a further insight into the development of call centre work. The survey indicated that call centres were having difficulty recruiting and retaining staff, with around five in ten organisations reporting problems (up from four in ten in 2001). Staff turnover also rose across all organisations at 24.5 per cent (up from 22 per cent in 2001) with turnover being highest in the West Midlands, the South-east and London, and lowest in the North-west and Scotland. Salaries also varied widely between regions and sectors, with Wales being the lowest paid region (eigth per cent lower than the UK average) and the South-east the highest (eigth per cent higher). Salaries reflected the nature of roles and responsibilities, with the average starting salary being £12,400 and half of all salaries ranging from £10,400 to £13,700. The lowest salaries in call centres were found in the leisure and transport sectors with the higher salaries in the public sector. Significantly, however, *The New Earnings Survey* (2002) recorded the average annual earnings of *all* workers as being £24,603. This, then, puts the labour market position of many call centre workers into a worrying perspective (IDS, 2002: Report 869).

Indeed the conditions in call centres prompted Unison Scotland, a major call centre union, to draw up a 'charter' to raise standards in what have been described as the 'modern day sweat shops'. The initiative, 'Raising the Standard', called for fair pay and conditions, a work/life balance, better job design, opportunity to join a trade union, training and development and good health and safety, in an effort to develop best practice in the industry (*Unison News*, 10 June 2003).

Trigger

Consider how such conditions as indicated in Box 10.1 (below) impact on staff turnover in call centres.

1. How can this scenario be related to notions of *alienation* or an extension of *bureaucratic rationality* and *McJobs*?
2. Is this really a continuing application of *Taylorist* methods?

Box 10.1 Call Centres in Scotland

The qualitative study of Telebank, by Callaghan and Thompson (2001), mainly using semi-structured interviews with customer service representatives (CSRs) and managers, focuses on the Scottish call centre operation of banks. The study concentrates on the contested nature of the labour process and in doing so seeks to extend the notion of control by employing the model used by Richard Edwards (1979) to explain structural control (see above).

Callaghan and Thompson (2001) feel that call centres mainly use a system of technical control with management directing the pace and substance of work tasks, through the use of automated call distribution systems (ACD). Nevertheless, Callaghan and Thompson (2001) attempt to overcome some of the problems with Edwards' (1979) model not being able to demonstrate how types of control can be configured together.

261

They do this by dispensing with the 'linear nature' (Thompson and McHugh, 2003) of his original model to explain how bureaucratic control is enforced as management define skills, tasks and dictate behaviour and performance in the workplace. The notion that management has total control is questioned, as CSRs are not necessarily passive and in fact actively engage with each element of control. In so doing, they can attempt to resist control - "workers can identify 'blind spots' in the system and use them to influence the pace at which they work" (Callaghan and Thompson 2001: 12).

Other studies (Taylor *et al*, 2002) have also critiqued the notion of the simplistic surveillance model associated with earlier attempts to explain call centre work. The study by Taylor *et al* (2002) of two call centres involved intensive observation of work processes. The first call centre, 'M' was an established financial services company and the second, 'T', a multi-business outsourced centre and both were located in Glasgow. The study concentrated on the nature of diversity in call centre work organisation between straightforward calls, with tight time scales and scripted approaches, to a more complex customer interaction, stressing more flexibility and relaxed call times. The findings revealed that whilst there were distinctions between the types of work undertaken in terms of the characteristics of quantity and quality, there were limits to this heterogeneity. Taylor *et al* (2002) suggests that it is difficult to treat all call centre work as a hybrid of routinization. Nevertheless, it is evident that "due to cost minimisation it is likely that there will be 'a further growth of routinization and intensification" (Taylor *et al*, 2002: 148) with a minority of workers perhaps experiencing conditions with higher levels of discretion and creativity.

The contradictory nature of call centre recruitment policies is summed up by Callaghan and Thompson (2001), after them having spent two years studying a Scottish call centre. Management expressed a wish to recruit 'good communicators', though in reality uniformity and targets seemed to dominate the quality of service to customers.

"Dealing with 120 calls a day, many from impatient and sometimes hostile customers, staff had to manage their emotions, ooze tolerance and understanding, and deliver a uniform standard of customer service. The result, unsurprisingly, was high levels of frustration on the part of staff who had been selected for their outgoing personalities, but who then found themselves unable to use them."
(Quote source: Gaber, I., 'Crossed lines', *The Guardian*, 14 November 2001 (accessed at: http://education.guardian.co.uk/higher/)

Recent analysis of call centres perhaps suggests that trends are moving towards the transferral of work abroad, prompting some commentators to suggest that employment in call centres in Scotland is facing a crisis (Fraser, 2003). The study by Mitial (cited in Fraser, 2003), based on interviews with 400 businesses operating call centres, forecasts employment in call centres dropping from 300,000 as it stands in 2003 to 220,000 by 2005 (see Chapter 3: Sociological Methods, for further discussion on interviews as a research method). Employment in Scottish call centres is expected to slump 23 per cent, from 50,000 to 38,500, over between 2003 and 2005 (Fraser, 2003). This trend has been compounded by other media stories of British call centres, such as those operated by BT, announcing that it will transfer 2200 call centre jobs – 1200 of which are Glasgow based – to India. Tesco, too, announced that it was transferring 350 posts, including some based in Dundee, to an IT support centre in India (Henderson, 2003).

Whilst the migration of jobs from the UK to India is likely to be a feature of the call centre industry, this needs to be put into context. Some suggest that this drop off will be in the 'basic transaction' business, with more complex transaction business expanding in the UK. This view ostensibly propagates the notion that the low-skill, high volume call centre jobs will tend to disappear in the face of growing competition from lower cost operations in India. Thus, call centre jobs in Britain will be of higher quality and be better paid (IDS, 2003: Report 881).

The Income Data Services (2002) survey on pay and conditions in call centres had average starting salaries of customer service advisers in Britain ranging from £8,208 to £24,119 with maximum rates being between £9,325 to £33,000 (IDS, 2002: Report 864). Given sector and regional variations, perhaps this is an indicator of the difference between *quantity* low-level skill and *quality* work.

Nevertheless, the findings of Taylor *et al* (2002), above, do suggest that routinization is likely to feature for the majority of call centre workers. This is perhaps compounded by Bain *et al's* (2002) extensive research into four call centres in central Scotland, where they claim that "target setting lies at the heart of management strategy" (Bain *et al*, 2002: 183), and is dependent on product, customer base and competitive pressures (see Box 10.2).

Box 10.2 Call Centres in India

Media headlines have illustrated a growing trend towards relocating call centres abroad and sparked controversy about the future of the industry in Scotland and the wider UK.

The Communication Workers Union approximated that "workers in India were paid about 70p an hour, or £3000 a year" (Simpson, 2003), a fraction of wages in Britain.

There are, however, suggested problems with foreign relocation:

- Economic incentives may appear as one consideration in transferring work abroad, although other factors appear to be relevant, illustrating a more complex picture.
- Customers wanting a local service and expecting familiarity with 'cultural' matters. Encouraging Indian workers to speak with localised British accents could have a negative affect on both the perceptions of customers, company image and the workers themselves.
- The notion of a 24-hour service in India is perhaps hindered by infrastructure problems associated with power supply, extreme weather conditions, time differences and transport to and from work.
- Due to the nature of business and the complexity of calls, some sectors, i.e. banking and finance, are not suited to exporting certain kinds of work.
- Indian employers may want to climb up the 'quality' chain, i.e. become involved in more sophisticated quality work rather than a level of work associated with 'back office' accounts activities or low level work that is difficult to automate. However, the logistics of setting up more sophisticated operations may prove too costly for employers who are restrained by legislation, concerned about image and the problem of losing calls.

Trigger

1. Having examined Box 10.2, and from your reading thus far, discuss why the exporting of call centre work to India may be an attractive though not straightforward issue for the companies concerned?
2. Why should the *attrition rates* of workers in India or Scotland be any different, given the strictly controlled Taylorist design and methods of work?

Conclusion

New technology tends to imply changing working conditions, which for some (Braverman, 1974) is seen as a process of *de*skilling rather than *up*skilling. According to Keyser *et al* (1988: 39):

> It is clear new technology is influencing the work of a significant proportion of many nations' labour forces.

However, it is unclear how these changes will influence the *meaning* of work as experienced and perceived by those who do work (not only in paid employment). A challenge in the future could be that people must develop conceptions of work when work itself is changing.

This chapter has attempted to investigate the central meaning of work and concludes that work is a social construction. With new divisions and spatial redistributions of labour will come new forms of polarisation, which may indeed transform our notions of work and *non*-work. To work hard at something worth doing is affected both by the nature of our culture and notions of 'time' and 'space'. Therefore, to try and understand what is meant by working hard at something worth doing it is necessary to go beneath the taken for granted assumptions about work and work rules. What we might find is a culture that services the needs of capitalism, and which is subject to the structural controls of the capitalist workplace.

The emphasis on fulfilment and self-image attained through work will no doubt change, depending on the various contexts within which the meaning of work is being constructed. However, work and its organisation invariably serves the needs of a capitalist society.

The following quote by the American Republican statesman and one time president, Theodore Roosevelt, could be taken as a fundamental feature of any discussion of work:

> Far and away the best prize that life offers is the chance to work hard at work worth doing. (Address at the State Fair, Syracuse, New York Labour Day, 7 September 1903 in Jay 1996)

He did, however, like so many other politicians, journalists, social scientists and social commentators, exclude any reference to some key structural factors – class, gender and race.

Chapter Summary

- Work is considered to be a complex concept, meaning that reaching an objective definition is difficult. The social setting and circumstances of work; interpretation of participants; historical and geographical contexts of work; cultural mores and the institutions that order work activities, are all important in any analysis.
- The classical theorists all note the importance of work in society. Durkheim ('anomie'), Marx ('alienation') and Weber ('rationalization').
- Contemporary labour process theory (Braverman, 1974) concentrated on the degradation and deskilling of work due to the application of scientific management principles, although there is an assumption that Taylorism is the only effective way of controlling labour.

- Further theories on managerial strategies of control developed models and frameworks to explain control (Friedman; Edwards), whilst others stressed consent (Burawoy) in the labour process.
- The debate about a movement from Fordist (mass production, mass consumption) to a post-Fordist system, with more customized products and flexible production, is far from clear. Associated work methods (Japanization) are critiqued as different forms of control.
- Evidence exists that society is witnessing an extension of bureaucratic rationality along he lines of Weberian/Fordist/Taylorist lines (Ritzer) with Fordist and post-Fordist structures coexisting.
- Sweeping changes in the labour market has meant an end to the 'job for life' producing instead flexible work, wages and contracts. A polarised workforce between the advantaged and disadvantaged now exists in what Hutton (1996) describes as a '30:30:40 society'.
- Call centres have brought with them new forms of work but also familiar patterns of Taylorist work design.

Further Reading

Grint, K. (1998) *The Sociology of Work*, Second Edition, Cambridge: Polity Press
Noon, M. and Blyton, P. (2002) *The Realities of Work*, Second Edition, Basingstoke: Palgrave
Thompson, P. and McHugh, D. (2002) *Work Organisations*, Third Edition, Basingstoke: Palgrave

Useful Websites

Income Data Services at: www.incomesdata.co.uk for current updates on pay and work patterns in the UK economy
Labour Research at: www.lrd.org.uk provides news and information for trade unionists
National Statistics at www.statistics.gov.uk for current reports on the labour market including statistical trends
The Guardian at: http://education.guardian.co.uk as a general source of information on the UK labour market
The Herald at: http://www.herald as a general source of information on the Scottish and UK labour markets.

Bibliography

Aglietta, M. (1979) *A Theory of Capitalist Regulation*, London: Verso
Bain, P. and Taylor, P. (2001) *Call Centres in Scotland in 2000*, Glasgow: Rowan Tree Press
Bain, P., Watson, W., Mulvey, G. and Gall, G. (2002) 'Taylorism, targets and the pursuit of quantity and quality by call centre management', *New Technology, Work and Employment*, 17:3
Blauner, R. (1964) *Alienation and Freedom*, Chicago, IL: University of Chicago Press
Braverman, H. (1974) *Labor and Monopoly Capitalism: The Degradation of Work in the Twentieth Century*, New York, NY: Monthly Review Press
Burawoy, M. (1979) *Manufacturing Consent*, Chicago, IL: University of Chicago Press
Burawoy, M. (1985) *The Politics of Production*, London: Verso

Callaghan, G. and Thompson, P. (2001) *Edwards Revisited: Technical Control and Worker Agency in Call Centres*, Open Discussion Papers in Economics, Number 25, Milton Keynes: Open University

Clegg, S.R. (1990) *Modern Organisations*, London: Sage

Clegg, S.R. (1992) 'Modern and postmodern organisations', *Sociology Review*, Vol.1, No.4

Conti, R.F. and Warner, M. (1993) 'Taylorism, New Technology and Just-in-Time Systems in Japanese Manufacturing', *New Technology, Work and Employment*, Vol.8, No.1

Dawson, G. (2000) 'Work: from certainty to flexibility?' in Hughes, G. and Fergusson, R. (eds.) *Ordering lives: family, work and welfare* (DD100: An Introduction to the Social Sciences: Understanding Social Change), London: Routledge/Open University

Dimitrovna, D. (1994) 'Work, Commitment, and Alienation', in Smelser, N. J., *Sociology*, Oxford: Blackwell

Durkheim, E. (1947 [1893]) *The Division of Labour in Society*, New York, NY: Free Press

Edwards, R. (1979) *Contested Terrain: the transformation of the workplace in the twentieth century*, London: Heinemann

Fraser, I. (2003) 'SE slams call centre slump predictions', *The Sunday Herald*, 9 February (accessed at: http://www.sundayherald.com/print31188)

Friedman, A. (1977) *Industry and Labour, Class Struggle at Work and Monopoly Capitalism*, Basingstoke: Macmillan

Gaber, I. (2001) 'Crossed lines', *The Guardian*, 14 November (accessed at: http://education.guardian.co.uk/higher/socialsciences/story/0,9846,593241,00.html)

Goldblatt, D. (2000) 'Living in the after-life: knowledge and social change', in Goldblatt, D. (ed.) *Knowledge and the social sciences: Theory, method, practice* (DD100: An Introduction to the Social Sciences: Understanding Social Change), London: Routledge/Open University

Grint, K. (1998) *The Sociology of Work*, 2nd Edition, Cambridge: Polity Press

Liepitz, A. (1987) *Miracles and Mirages: The Crisis of Global Fordism*, London: Verso

Hartley, J.F. and Stephenson, G.M. (eds.) (1992) *Employment Relations: The Psychology of Influence and Control at Work*, Oxford: Blackwell

Henderson, D. (2003) ' Tesco transfers 350 jobs to India', *The Herald*, 18 July

Hutton, W. (1996) *The State We're In*, London: Vintage

Income Data Services (2002) 'Pay and conditions in call centres', Report 864, September, pp. 9-19, London: Income Data Services

Income Data Services (2002) *New Earnings Survey*, Report 869, November, pp.2-3, London: Income Data Services

Income Data Services (2003) *The labour market*, Report 878, April, pp.16-20, London: Income Data Services

Income Data Services (2003) *Viewpoint*, Report 881, May, p.2, London: Income Data Services

Income Data Services (2003) *Call Centre Workforce*, Report 884, July, pp. 14-15, London: Income Data Services

Jay, A. (ed.) (1996) *The Oxford Dictionary of Political Quotations*, Oxford: Oxford University Press

Keyser, V., Quale, B., Wilpert B, and Ruiz Quintanilla, S.A. (eds.) (1988) *The Meaning of Work and Technological Options*, New York, NY: Wiley

Lindsay, C. (2003) 'A century of labour market change: 1900 to 2000', *Labour Market Trends*, March

Kumar, K. (1995) *From Post-Industrial to Post-Modern Society*, Oxford: Blackwell

Lukes, S. (1992) *Emile Durkheim: His Life and Work*, London: Penguin

Marx, K. (1976 [1867]) *Capital*, Volume 1, Harmondsworth: Penguin

Marx, K. and Engels, F. (1968) *Selected Works*, London: Lawrence and Wishart

Miller, M. (2002) *The Scottish Labour Market*, Briefing and Information Services Briefing Paper, September, Stirling: Scottish Further Education Unit

Mackintosh, M. and Mooney, G. (2000) 'Identity, inequality and social class', in Woodward,K. (ed.) *Questioning Identity: gender class, nation* (DD100: An Introduction to the Social Sciences: Understanding Social Change), London: Routledge/Open University

267

Pahl, R.E. (ed.) (1988) *On Work*, Oxford: Blackwell

Priore, M.J. and Sabel, C.F. (1984) *The Second Industrial Divide: Possibilities for Prosperity*, New York, NY: Basic Books

Ronco, W. and Peattie, L. (1988) 'Making Work: A Perspective from Social Science', in Pahl, R.E. (ed.) *On Work*, Oxford: Blackwell

Ritzer, G. (2000) *The McDonaldization of Society*, New Century Edition, Thousand Oaks, CA: Pine Forge Press

Ritzer, G. (2002) *McDonaldization: The Reader*, Thousand Oaks, **CA**: Pine Forge Press

Rose, M. (1975) *Industrial Behaviour*, Harmondsworth: Penguin

Sayers, S. (1988) 'The Need to Work: a Perspective from Philosophy', in Pahl, R.E. (ed.) *On Work*, Oxford: Blackwell

Sennett, R. (1999) *The Corrosion of Character*, New York, NY: Norton

Simpson, C. (2003) 'Protest over plan to take BT jobs to India', *The Herald*, 17 July

Smelser, N. J., *Sociology*, Oxford: Blackwell

Taylor, F. (1980 [1911]) 'Scientific Management', in Pugh D.S. (ed.) *Organisation Theory: Selected Readings*, Fourth Edition, Harmondsworth: Penguin

Taylor, S. (1998) 'Emotional Labour and the New Workplace', in Thompson, P. and Warhurst, C. (eds.) *Workplaces of the Future*, London: Macmillan

Taylor, P. and Bain, P. (1999) '"An Assembly Line in the Head": Work Enterprise Relations in the Call Centre', *Industrial Relations Journal*, 30 (2): pp.101-17

Taylor, P., Hyman, J., Mulvey, G. and Bain, P. (2002) 'Work organization, control and the experience of work in call centres', *Work Employment and Society*, Volume 16, Number 1, March: pp.133-150

Thinning, W. (2003) '100,000 call centre jobs could be lost as industry relocates to India', *The Herald*, 19 July

Thompson, P. (1989) *The Nature of Work*, 2nd Edition, Basinsgstoke: Macmillan

Thompson, P. (1993) 'The labour process: changing theory, changing practice', *Sociology Review*, Vol.3, No.2

Thompson, P. and McHugh, D. (2002) *Work Organisations: A Critical Introduction*, 3rd edition, London: Macmillan

Thompson, P. and Warhurst, C. (eds.) (1998) *Workplaces of the Future*, Basingstoke: Macmillan

Unison News (2002) 'Scots call-centre staff stressed and in pain', 10 June (accessed at: http://www.unison.org.uk/news/news_view.asp?did=193)

Weber, M (1958 [1930]) *The Protestant Ethic and the Spirit of Capitalism*, New York, NY: Charles Scribner's

Weber, M. (1947 [1922]) *The Theory of Economic and Social Organisations*, New York, NY: Free Press

Wilmer, C. (1985) *Introduction: Unto This Last and Other Writings*, Ruskin John, Harmondsworth: Penguin

Chapter 11 Crime and Deviance

Hazel Croall

Introduction

Crime is a major feature of everyday life – we unconsciously take precautions against it by locking doors and avoiding places where we might be attacked. It is also a popular subject of literature, TV drama, film and newspapers. Apparent rises in crime rates are headline news and politicians compete to be 'tough on crime'. Sociologists are interested in many aspects of crime and deviance. How are they defined and socially constructed? How can the extent of crime be measured? How can it be explained? Are offenders 'mad, bad or sad'? How is crime related to social inequalities and social exclusion? How can it be reduced? How should offenders be punished? This chapter will explore many of these issues.

Defining Crime and Deviance

The word *deviance* immediately suggests a departure from the 'normal' and it has been defined as "banned or controlled behaviour [which is] likely to attract punishment or disapproval" (Downes and Rock, 1995: 28-9). This directs attention to rules surrounding behaviour and how they are enforced. Rules may be informal, where, for example, groups of friends ridicule or exclude the person who does not fit in, or where parents punish a child who has misbehaved. More formal rules and punishments are found in social institutions, such as schools, colleges or workplaces and in respect of the criminal law that involves formal agencies of control, such as the police. Defining deviance depends very much on the social context of behaviour, as the same behaviour can be *deviant* in some situations but *normal* in others. Talking loudly or fooling around is considered normal in, for example, a school playground, but would be disruptive in a classroom. Definitions of what is deviant also change over time and vary between cultures. In a new environment, for example, we need to establish the informal rules, expectations and likely sanctions for breaking them. While deviance is often associated with 'bad' behaviour, extremely good behaviour can also be deviant – the person who complies with every rule or the student who hands in all work on time, can also be subject to disapproval. Thus, to the sociologist Howard Becker (1963: 8-9):

> Social groups create deviance by making the rules whose infraction constitutes deviance and by applying those rules to particular people and labelling them as outsiders. From this point of view, deviance is not a quality of the act the person commits, but rather a consequence of the application by others of rules and sanctions to an 'offender'. The deviant is one to whom that label has successfully been applied; deviant behaviour is behaviour that people so label.

Crime, on the other hand, implies more formal legal rules and the simplest way of defining crime is as behaviour that breaks the criminal law. Like deviance, however, crime is 'socially constructed', and definitions change, too, over time. Examples of this include homosexuality and abortion, which were previously against the criminal law but are now, in some circumstances, 'legal'. Other offences depend on situational interpretations – what, for example, is 'disorderly' behaviour? When does 'borrowing' something become 'theft'? When does 'conning' or misleading someone become fraud? Cultural norms may also differ from legal definitions. Words like 'theft' or 'crime' indicate strong disapproval, whereas other words like 'perks', 'fiddles', 'cons' or 'scams' indicate milder disapproval – yet they describe similar behaviour which is technically criminal (Mars, 1982). Criminal law is enacted by Parliament and thus the definition of crime involves political processes and interest, or campaign groups have attempted to 'legalise' or 'decriminalise' cannabis or to toughen up laws in relation to paedophiles. The use of drugs, discussed in Box 11.1, provides an interesting illustration of the problematic boundaries between crime, deviance and normality.

Box 11.1 Drug Use - Shifting Conceptions Of Deviance, Crime And Normality

The boundaries between legal and illegal, normal and deviant drug use have shifted throughout history although drug use is now felt to be so common among young people that it has been 'normalised'. A report from 'The Scottish Crime Survey' provides some information about drug misuse in Scotland (Fraser, 2002). A sample of 2,886 people were asked about their use of cannabis, stimulants and hallucinogens, such as Amphetamines, Ecstasy and LSD, opiates such as Cocaine, Crack cocaine, Heroin and Methadone and drugs such as Temazepam, Valluim, Poppers and Anabolic steroids. Some of its main findings were that:

- Drug misuse is relatively uncommon and short lived. One in five of all age groups reported taking an illicit substance during their lifetime, whereas only one in 15 had done so in the last year.
- Use of illicit substances was more common in younger age groups.
- For those aged 16-29, one in six had taken drugs in the last year (8 per cent men and 6 per cent women), and one in eight in the last month.
- Young people who went out in the evenings more used drugs more.
- Cannabis is the most commonly used illegal substance with one third of those aged 16-24 reporting having used cannabis at some time – 12 per cent in the last month.
- The use of heroin and crack cocaine was extremely rare – only 1 per cent of the sample reported ever using them.
- Compared with previous surveys it concludes that drug misuse may have fallen, which was particularly marked with cannabis.

Trigger

Consider the following questions:

1. Under what circumstances is drug taking 'normal' or 'abnormal'? Provide some examples from your own experience.
2. Does this vary between different groups? If so, in what ways does it?

Explaining Crime and Deviance

Attempts to explain crime have involved looking at the characteristics of individual offenders, at cultures and subcultures and at the social structure. Popularly, criminals can be depicted as 'evil', psychopathic, or simply 'crazy', implying that individual characteristics are to blame. Other explanations look to 'nurture' rather than 'nature' and focus on the family or the social environment of offenders. Cultures can be seen as 'deviant' or permissive, while others blame social inequality or social exclusion – drawing attention to the structural roots of crime. This section will outline the main sociological theories after looking briefly at biological and psychological approaches.

Individual theories – are criminals 'different'?

Individual-based theories focus on the characteristics of individual offenders and generally attempt to compare convicted offenders to members of the general population in order to 'spot the difference' (Coleman and Norris, 2000).

Biological factors

In the late nineteenth century the Italian criminologist. Cesare Lombroso (1897), measured the physical characteristics of prisoners, claiming that a 'criminal type' was characterised by 'physical stigmata' such as large hands, feet or tattoos – he did not however compare prisoners to the general population, thus his findings had little validity. Later attempts to link physique and crime included that of Sheldon (1949), who related aggression to 'athletic' body types and criminality to height and weight. Others explored the relationship between genetics and crime, starting with studies of identical twins reared apart to establish the effects of 'nature' or 'nurture' – many, however, were inconclusive. Later work looked at the possibility of a criminal 'gene', based on studies at the Carstairs institution for mentally disturbed offenders, which found that some offenders possessed an additional 'Y' chromosome (Williams, 1994). This was also, however, found in the general population. The search for biological factors continues with recent research having investigated the effects of heart rate, blood pressure, blood sugar levels and the relationship between crime and brain disorders, such as epilepsy or head injuries (Coleman and Norris, 2000).

Psychological factors

Psychologists have explored the relationships between features such as personality traits, mental illness, psychoticism and social learning and crime. Eysenck (1977) related a tendency to crime to extraversion and neuroticism, but this was not substantiated in later research. Crime has also been attributed to a psychopathic personality, associated with an inability to form loving relationships, a lack of responsibility for one's actions or a failure to feel or admit guilt and aggressiveness. Despite the popularity of this notion, there is little evidence that these features are exclusively found amongst those in prison (Williams, 1994). It is also popularly assumed that mental illness is related to some forms of crime. While some offenders do suffer from mental illnesses, such as depression or schizophrenia, not all do, nor are all those suffering from mental illness likely to be criminal.

Individual theories – the sociological critique

While many of these approaches are useful their validity as general explanations is limited as they do not clearly distinguish offenders from non-offenders. While some individual criminals may have biological or psychiatric disorders, these cannot account for 'crime' in general. It is also possible that some offenders, particularly those whose crimes are more serious and difficult to comprehend, are more readily labelled as 'abnormal'. Sociologists, as will be indicated below, have identified a number of problems with individual approaches.

Trigger

1. If crime is socially constructed, how can it be biologically or psychologically determined?
2. Is a comparison of criminals with the 'normal' population a valid methodology?
3. What is the effect of culture and structure?

Sociological Theories on Crime and Deviance

Sociological theories focus on the cultural and structural aspects of crime. Early approaches were dominated by a functionalist approach in which crime was seen as 'social pathology', although Durkheim advanced the argument, outlined in Box 11.2 (below), that crime is a normal and 'healthy' part of a society.

Box 11.2 Is Crime Functional?

Durkheim (1964, [1895]) established statistically that crime was a feature of all societies. It was, therefore, a social 'fact', and could be regarded as 'normal'. Indeed, he argued, deviance and morality are inseparable and it is difficult to imagine a society without deviance. Thus:

"Imagine a community of saints in an exemplary and perfect monastery. In it crime as such will be unknown, but faults that appear venial to the ordinary person will arouse the same scandal as does normal crime in ordinary consciences. If therefore that community has the power to judge and punish, it will term such acts criminal and deal with them as such."

As it is normal, crime is functional and it clarifies and heightens 'moral sentiments' and the 'collective conscience' of a community:

"[C]rime brings together upright consciences and concentrates them. We have only to notice what happens, particularly in a small town, when some moral scandal has been committed. They stop each other on the street, they visit each other, they seek to come together to talk of the event and wax indignant in common [...] there emerges a unique temper [...] that is the public temper."

By identifying 'deviance' normality becomes clearer and society unites in condemnation of the deviant. A healthy level of crime is, therefore, functional although too little crime might indicate stagnation and too much may be destructive.

Durkheim also developed the concept of *anomie*, an absence of norms, which could arise from social change during which norms which have previously guided behaviour become irrelevant. Rapid economic growth and the decline of traditional, rural societies led, he argued, to people developing 'boundless aspirations', but they lacked the moral regulation previously provided by families, communities or religion. This could lead to suicide or crime. This notion was taken up in the 1930s by Robert Merton (1938), writing in the US, who linked crime to a 'structural strain' produced by the conflict between the cultural goals of society, which stressed economic success and consumerism and the legitimate means for achieving these goals, which stressed education and employment. Not everyone could achieve the goals legitimately, particularly those from lower class backgrounds, who faced 'blocked opportunities'. While most people aim for the goals and conform (*conformists*), others adopt deviant adaptations. Thus, *innovators* achieve the goals by using 'innovative', often criminal, means, while *retreatists* reject *both* the goals and the means by 'dropping out', turning possibly to alternative lifestyles or drug-taking. *Ritualists* continue to conform, although they may have abandoned all hope of achieving the goals, and *rebels* reject both the goals and the means, and try to substitute an alternative order, attempts which might involve for example, terrorism.

Merton's (1938) model provides a very useful starting point for exploring the relationship between social inequality, social change and crime (Downes and Rock, 1998). Nonetheless, it has several important limitations. Like all functionalist theory it is based on the assumption that there is widespread consensus over the goals. Furthermore, not all societies have a formal ideology of equal opportunity, therefore, not all would expect to achieve. He also assumed, in common with theories of the time, that crime was more common in the lower classes.

Subcultural theories

Merton's (1938) model did not suggest how people would take up these different adaptations and others pointed out that crime is often committed in groups, within subcultures in which it is seen as normal. This is particularly the case with youth crime and 'subcultural theory' focused on these deviant or delinquent subcultures (see Chapter 13: Culture). Some writers in this tradition, such as Cloward and Ohlin (1960), followed Merton's strain model, seeing subcultures as a 'collective solution' to these problems. They identified *three* main forms of delinquent subculture:

- *Conflict*: based around violence
- *Criminal*: based on criminal activities such as theft
- *Retreatist*: based on a drop out or alternative life style.

Young people, they argued, were exposed to the subcultures of their locality, which also provided a structure of illegitimate opportunities. Subcultures provide a set of values and the knowledge and skills required to participate in crime. Stolen goods need to be disposed of and an existing criminal economy with a range of outlets is a prerequisite for converting stolen property into money. A drug-taking subculture requires the existence of a drugs market. Other areas have a historical and cultural tradition of violent gangs that form the basis of a conflict subculture.

A different account is provided by Albert Cohen (1955) in his work on delinquent boys. To him, much delinquency was negative and violent rather than goal-directed. Indeed, subcultures could be seen as oppositional to society's goals and norms. These emerged out of young people's feelings of frustration at failing to live up to a 'middle class measuring rod', an ideal standard of living portrayed in the mass media, films, advertising and reflected in schools and formal institutions. This failure produced a 'reaction' against the ideal model and subcultures expressed this rejection.

These early subcultural theories were extremely influential, but raised many questions. Were youth as committed to these subcultures as the theory suggested? Were they applicable to Britain with its different culture? Matza (1964), for example, argued that they accounted for too much delinquency as many youth simply 'drift' in and out of crime. In a study in London, Downes (1966) argued that many young boys were 'dissociated' from mainstream values having failed at school and being bored by dead end jobs. At a time of growing youth consumer culture, theirs was a 'leisure problem', and the 'delinquent solution' represented a search for fun and kicks of which crime was a small part. In Glasgow, a city for long associated with conflict style gangs, a study in the 1960s by James Patrick (1973) suggested that while there were hardcore members of delinquent gangs, many followers were less committed (see Chapter 3: Sociological Methods, for a further discussion on Patrick's study). Since the 1960s, there have been many further examples of youth subcultures, often seen as deviant or linked to crime. Mods and rockers, hippies, football hooligans, punks and skinheads are some examples, and more recently there have been concerns about drug subcultures, 'raves', 'lager louts', biker boys and girl gangs (See Chapter 13: Culture). Newer versions of subcultural theory emerged to account for some of this.

In Britain, a Marxist version of subcultural theory was developed by Stuart Hall and his colleagues (Hall *et al*, 1976; 1978). Looking at subcultures such as mods and skinheads, they argued that each generation of young people face a unique set of problems in the context of social and economic change. Many lower class young men are brought up to aspire not to middle class goals but to the goals of their parent's lower class culture – aiming to be, for example, dockers, miners or factory workers. These goals became unachievable with the decline of traditional industries. Youth could not become 'men' according to their parent culture, but developed a 'style' which expressed a cultural resistance to implications of failure. The style of skinheads for example, with their aggressively working class dress and hostility to immigrants could be interpreted as attempting to re-instate tough white male working class values. Subcultural theories, therefore, interpret youth subcultures as a means of finding cultural 'space' in response to blocked opportunities in periods of social change. While this is a valuable approach, they also present a number of problems:

- To some subcultural theories, delinquency or youth crime can be seen as a form of unconscious rebellion – is this view justified?
- Does it provide a romaniticised view of cultures that may support extreme violence or racism?
- Do they exaggerate a commitment to crime and deviance?
- Do they rely too much on interpreting the 'symbols' of youth culture?

Most early theories assumed that crime was a sign of pathology and they also assumed, following statistics based on convicted offenders, that most crime took place amongst the lower classes. Later theories questioned these assumptions and focused more on the relationship between crime and social control. Interactionists focused on the processes through which deviants were 'labelled' and Marxists on how the criminal law defined crime by criminalising primarily lower class activities.

Labelling perspectives

Labelling approaches followed the work of interactionists such as Howard Becker (1963), quoted earlier. Labelling, to interactionists, is a crucial stage in a process of 'becoming deviant'. Lemert (1951), for example, distinguishes between:

- *Primary deviance*: the initial act which has not been 'labelled'
- *Secondary deviance*: actions that take place after a label has been applied.

Labelling someone as deviant can lead to them reacting by becoming involved in further deviance, and a deviant 'identity' can be formed as a result of a process of *action* and *reaction*. In the classroom, for example, pupils labelled as 'troublesome' might respond by becoming more troublesome and they may form a group in which making trouble becomes a key part of the group identity. This leads to even stronger reaction and eventually exclusion. This is an example of what interactionists describe as a 'deviancy amplification' process that is associated with a 'self-fulfilling prophecy' in which the reaction to deviance produces more deviance (see Chapter 2: Sociological Theory). Being arrested by the police or convicted in court can set a person apart from others and they may suffer from the stigma of being labelled as criminal. They may find it more difficult to get a job or be accepted in their previous groups. They might then seek the company of other 'deviants' and become 'outsiders'.

Labelling perspectives have been enormously influential and they suggest that a 'softly-softly' approach, based on minimal intervention and re-integrating the deviant, may be more useful than creating a hostile reaction. Research in the labelling tradition moved away from a focus on the pathological features of individual offenders to the interactions between the police and suspect groups. Stan Cohen's (1972) classic work on 'moral panics' and 'deviancy amplification' looked at how press, police and public reaction to the Mods and Rockers – who were prominent in English seaside towns during the 1960s – contributed to an increase in their activity. Nonetheless, a number of questions can be asked about the labelling approach:

- Is it too deterministic?

- The deviancy amplification spiral suggests an almost inevitable process – can it be resisted?
- Can it explain primary deviance?
- The focus is primarily on secondary deviance rather than on explaining how the deviance occurs.
- Interactionists focused on the offender's view – Becker talks, for example, of the 'view from below'. To what extent is this too sympathetic to the deviant, while neglecting victims?
- Does it neglect structural factors?
- By focusing on the process of 'becoming' deviant, labelling perspectives were criticised for neglecting the 'structural' basis of labelling. Labels are often applied by those with power – professionals such as doctors, teachers, social workers or the police.

Conflict and Marxist perspectives

This latter point was taken up by what came to be called 'new', 'critical' or 'radical' criminology based on conflict and Marxist perspectives (see Chapter 2: Sociological Theory). To them, existing theories had taken for granted that definitions of crime and deviance emerged out of consensus, thus crime was seen as a 'pathology'. To conflict theorists, however, law, including the criminal law, is created following political negotiations and conflict, and to Marxist theories, it reflected the interests of the most powerful groups and the ruling class. More lower class people were convicted not because the lower classes committed more crime, but because the law was more likely to criminalise lower class behaviour which was seen as threat to the ruling class, whereas the crimes of the powerful, or white collar crime, were often not seen as crime and dealt with more leniently (see Box 11.3).

Box 11.3 White Collar Crime

White collar crime was defined by Edwin Sutherland (1960) as "crime committed by persons of high social status and respectability in the course of their occupations." Its existence is often taken to challenge a focus on 'lower class crime' and to indicate class bias in relation to criminal law and its enforcement. It includes: fraud and theft; corporate crime in which employees, owners or managers of organisations fail to comply with laws and regulations to protect the public or the environment, i.e. health and safety; the environment; consumer protection.

In 1997, 21 elderly people died in Wishaw, Lanarkshire, from E.coli 157. The butcher, whose business was the source of the contamination, was found to have had a lax attitude to regulations and was subsequently convicted (Croall, 2001).

White collar crime, therefore, has enormous costs but is not widely regarded as part of the 'crime problem'. Such crimes may be relatively 'invisible'. They take place in private as opposed to on the 'street', victims are often not aware of being victimised and many offences are not reported to the police.

- Offences often involve the abuse of complex financial, technical or legal knowledge making them difficult to detect and prosecute.
- Many offences are not socially constructed as 'crime' in the same way as violence or theft.
- Many offences are dealt with by specialist agencies who prefer to deal with them 'out of court'.

This can produce a situation in which wealthier and more powerful offenders escape the full force of the criminal law. Many argue that the sentences for white collar offenders are more lenient in that offenders more often receive fines and are less often sent to prison. The butcher involved in the Ecoli case, for example, was fined £2,500, which attracted much criticism (Croall and Ross, 2002). White collar crime is, therefore, often seen as an example of class bias in criminalisation and law enforcement.

The approaches outlined in Box 11.3 focus on control agencies and the state, arguing that criminal law and enforcement is used to control the lower classes during periods of crisis. Stuart Hall and his colleagues (1978) looked at the rise of the *moral panic* surrounding mugging, popularly linked with black youth. They illustrate how the police, the media and politicians, by quoting each other, 'orchestrated' consensus by linking mugging with black youth and a 'crisis' in English cities, which become a focus for re-iterating values of 'Englishness' that were said to be under threat. The police, they argue, will more actively police areas perceived to be 'high crime' areas such as peripheral estates or those containing large numbers of black or other minority ethnic groups. These groups may, therefore, be subject to a *criminalisation process*, which is defined as "the application of the criminal label to an identifiable social category" (Scraton and Chadwick, 1991: 172). Specific groups, such as black youth, become associated with crime and thereby subject to heavier policing. Recent examples of criminalisation might be seen in the way in which asylum seekers are often described as 'bogus' and perceived to be in need of control and detention, or where Muslims are suspected of being linked to terrorists after the events of 11 September 2000. Critical criminology, therefore, asks some very searching questions about the uses of the criminal law and how some groups are criminalised. At the same time, however, a number of questions can be asked over how easy it would be to identify 'ruling class' interest or involvement in law and its enforcement and how these approaches could be tested empirically.

Feminist perspectives

Feminists were also critical of earlier approaches (see Chapter 5: Gender). Men are convicted of crime more often than women, and many approaches focused on men and boys without raising the issue of gender; in other words, they were 'gender blind'. Feminist approaches have focused on some major questions in relation to women's experiences of crime and the relationship between gender and crime (Heidensohn, 2002; Gelsthorpe, 2002; Walklate, 2000).

1) ***Do women really commit crime less often than men?*** Some argued that women's lower rates of conviction were due to 'chivalry' on the part of the police who might fail to suspect a woman or not proceed with the case. Little evidence was found to support this and most now agree that women are involved less in crime

2) ***Why do women commit crime?*** Early criminological approaches tended to explain female crime in sexist and pathological terms. Prostitutes were depicted as sexually motivated, shoplifters were seen as 'kleptomaniacs' and delinquent girls as oversexualised. Feminists, such as Pat Carlen (1985; 1988), however, argued that women can commit crimes for very much the same reasons as men – prostitution was often economically motivated and much women's crime may be related to poverty

3) ***What happens to female offenders?*** There are far fewer women in prison than men and the 'chivalry' hypothesis also applied to courts – assuming that women were less likely to receive severe sanctions. This could, however, be accounted for by findings that women's crimes tended to be less serious than men's and that they tended more often to be first offenders. Some feminist research further suggested that where women failed to live up to ideals of femininity by, for example, being single parents or not defined as 'good women', they could be seen as 'doubly deviant' – being condemned for their offence and for being 'bad women' – which could lead to harsher punishment (Carlen and Worrall, 1987).

Women as victims

A major thrust of feminist criminology was to draw attention to the considerable victimisation of women in the home, hitherto not seen as a major 'criminal' issue. Feminists were also critical of how incidents of domestic violence were dealt with by the police as they often failed to arrest offenders. Furthermore, rape victims were not taken seriously and deterred from reporting rapes because they felt they would not be believed and in court, and possibly be treated as if it were they who were on trial. Feminist campaigns have successfully led to the reform of the law on rape and many policy changes in dealing with domestic and sexual violence.

Is crime related to masculinity?

Some explained women's lower involvement in crime by arguing that crime was not 'natural' for women, although others drew attention to the greater social control and surveillance exercised over women/girls. Women would often be 'at home' or have constant care reponisbilities for young children, which would restict their movement, somewhat. Some feminists, however, asked a different question – why do boys and men commit more crime? This points to a potential relationship between masculinity and crime – to what extent is 'being a man' in some cultures associated with crime? Crime could also be linked to a 'crisis' in masculinity as in some areas in contemporary society it may be more difficult to 'prove' masculinity through employment. Bee Campbell (1993), for example, linked 'car culture' and 'car crime', such as joyriding, to aggressive masculinity.

Feminist approaches ask some very important questions about the gendered nature of crime, including women's victimisation. While attributing crime to 'masculinity' may be too general, as by no means all men commit crime, it does provide a useful direction for further exploration.

Crime as 'rational choice'

Other criticisms centred around the failure of earlier approaches to predict rising crime rates or provide solutions to crime. Pathological approaches, by assuming a 'problem' seemed to promise a 'cure', yet had failed to produce either clear explanations or solutions. Sociological approaches, such as anomie, by linking crime to social inequality, suggested that a reduction in poverty and inequality would reduce crime. Increasing, affluence and the growth of the welfare state were, however, accompanied by rising crime levels. This led to a re-examination of theories and, for governments, ways of thinking about how crime could be reduced. This led to a focus on the immediate situations in which crime occurred which, it was felt, provided opportunities to commit crime. Offenders, it was argued, make a 'rational choice' to commit crime and weigh up the benefits of the crime against the chances of being caught and punished (Clarke and Mayhew, 1980). The situation in which a crime is committed is, therefore, important – customers will be less likely to shoplift if there is a CCTV camera or a member of staff to observe the theft (see Box 11.7, below, for further discussion of the use of CCTV as ameasure to control crime). Burglars interviewed by Bennet (1989) revealed that they preferred detached houses to those in a terrace as there was less chance of being seen, and security systems, dogs and neighbours also put them off. The overall appearance of a house or the kind of car outside it suggested likely rewards. This approach suggests ways in which these situations can be altered to reduce crime and led to the growth of crime prevention strategies (see the section, Controlling Crime: Punishment and Crime Prevention, below). It is nonetheless limited as an explanation for crime (Croall, 1998; Downes and Rock, 1998).

```
Trigger

1. Is everyone a potential criminal who would commit crime if the opportunity
   presented itself?
2. Why do you think some do not avail themselves of the opportunity to commit crime?
3. Think of reasons why you do not commit crime.
```

Control theories

An interesting approach is provided by control theories who, rather than asking why people commit crime, ask why most people do not? This draws attention to controls over behaviour. Most people probably do not commit crime because they think it is wrong or because they are afraid of the consequences, particularly how their family or friends would react and what impact this could have on their identity. This indicates a commitment to conventional morality and lifestyle. Following studies of delinquent youth, Hirschi (1969) argues that the following factors are related to lower rates of delinquency:

- *Attachment* to conventional values and caring about what others think
- *Commitment* to a conventional life style by achieving status and material goods legitimately
- *Involvement* in conventional activities, such as employment and leisure
- *Belief* in conventional morality.

How people are controlled is, therefore, a crucial factor affecting whether or not they commit crime, and this also draws attention to features such as parental supervision. These theories have been very influential although, like rational choice theories, they tend to neglect the social patterning of crime (Downes and Rock, 1998).

Left realism

The link between crime and social inequality, which to many was neglected in rational choice and control theories, is central to another contemporary approach described as 'left realism', developed by Young and his colleagues (Lea and Young, 1993; Young, 1997). They criticised earlier approaches for only looking at one aspect of what they see as a 'square of crime'. Individual approaches focus on offenders but neglect the social processes through which crime is defined and offenders are 'labelled'. Labelling and critical approaches, on the other hand, neglect the 'reality' of crime and its harmful impact on victims. Explaining any form of crime must, therefore, take account of the relationships between offenders, victims, agencies of control and the general public who witness and define crime and affect how it is controlled. The 'reality' of crime can be explored by looking at victims' experiences, at the relationship between offenders and victims and at how the law and control agencies target their attention on the activities of different groups. Not all crimes, they argue, can be explained in the same way as different relationships are implied by the study of, for example, white collar crime, violence or property crime. Social inequality is, however, a crucial feature of these relationships and they relate crime to *relative deprivation* (see Box 11.4) and social exclusion (see Chapter 8: Poverty).

Box 11.4 Left Realism

Left realists reject the notion that crime is related to absolute deprivation (for example, levels of poverty, low income) because:

- Crime has increased during periods of rising affluence.
- Research has failed to establish a clear relationship between poverty, unemployment and crime.
- During periods of extreme poverty, for example the economic depression of the 1930's, crime did not rise.
- Crime is found among all social groups – the wealthy as well as the poor.

Many groups react to perceived injustices by taking political action – but this is less open to those who are marginal or excluded. It is amongst these groups (for example, the unemployed or minority ethnic youth who may feel deprived in comparison to white youth) that relative deprivation is more likely to lead to crime. One of the strengths of this approach is that it can potentially explain the crimes of all social classes – white collar offenders may commit crime also because of relative deprivation (a failure to be promoted for example).

(Source: Lea, J. and Young, J. (1993) *What is to be done about Law and Order?*, Second edition, London: Pluto Press)

Crime in Contemporary Society

Statistics about crime can be readily obtained on the Internet (see the list of Websites at the end of this Chapter). These are generally based on police records of how many crimes they record, statistics about convictions and on victim surveys. Before looking at some of these figures, it is important to consider how they are compiled, as an incident goes through a series of stages before being officially 'counted' as a crime, and many potential crimes are not 'counted'. In order for a 'crime' to be reported it must first be:

- *Observed by a member of the public, a victim or the police*: some crimes are more visible than others – crimes that take place in private, in the home or workplace, for example, are less visible, whereas crimes taking place on the street are more visible. Some crimes, such as the sale or use of illegal drugs, have no direct victim and apprehending offenders depends on action by the police
- *Defined as 'crime'*: Many 'incidents' such as a fight or rowdy behaviour may not be defined as 'criminal' and as seen above, subcultural definitions of crime vary. This will affect the extent to which they are likely to be reported
- *Considered important enough to be reported to the police*: some incidents may be seen as too trivial to report or it might be assumed that the police will take no action. Victims may fear reprisals or be embarrassed to report them – as might be the case, for example, with domestic violence or workplace crime, where companies may fear bad publicity if they reveal the extent of workplace theft
- *Recorded by the police*: the police do not record all reports. In some cases it may be decided that 'no crime' has taken place – something assumed stolen may have been lost or complainants may decide that they do not wish the case to be taken further.

After being recorded by the police, the following processes take place before an 'offender' is convicted:

- *The crime must be 'cleared up' and an offender identified*: 'Clear up' rates vary – for some crimes, such as assaults, the offender may be known to the victim. In others, such as housebreaking, the police must identify the offender
- *The police or Prosecutor must decide what action to take*: Not all offenders are taken to court. For example, in Scotland, most children under 16 are referred to Children's Hearings (see Box 11.6 later in this Chapter) or the Procurator Fiscal may administer warnings or fines without taking a case to court.

Official statistics based on police reports are not, therefore, an accurate measure of crime and there is a large 'hidden figure'. Rises or falls in crime rates can, therefore, reflect police activities rather than indicate any change in the 'real' rate of crime. The bulletin on Recorded Crime in Scotland (2001) notes, for example, that a rise in vandalism in 2001 can be explained by 'improved recording by Strathclyde Police of minor vandalism'. Similarly, the increase in recorded cases for possession of drugs is attributed to 'targeted police campaigns against drugs'. Table 11.1 (below) provides some details of recorded crime, while other figures indicate the 'process of attrition' as a result of which out of a total of 423,172 crimes recorded by the police in 2000, of which 45 per cent were 'cleared up', only 49,248 were proceeded against in court (Scottish Executive Statistical Bulletin, 2000).

Table 11.1 Crimes recorded by the Police in Scotland, 2001

Non sexual crimes of violence	23,751
Serious assault	7,296
Handling an offensive weapon	8,671
Robbery	4,228
Other	3,556
Crimes of indecency	5,987
Rape and attempted rape	753
Indecent Assault	1,154
Lewd and indecent behaviour	2,365
Other	1,715
Crimes of Dishonesty	239,892
Housebreaking	44,868
Theft by opening a lockfast place	8,470
Theft from a motor vehicle	31,279
Theft of a motor vehicle	23,208
Shoplifting	31,575
Other Theft	74,722
Fraud	17,410
Other	8,360
Fire- raising, vandalism, etc.	94,924
Fire-raising	2,774
Vandalism, etc.	92,150
Other Crimes	56,539
Crimes against public justice	20,250
Drugs	36,175
Other	114
Total crimes	**421,903**

(Adapted from *Recorded crime in Scotland, 2001* (Scottish Executive Statistical Bulletin CrJ/2002/1) Published April 2002. Details available: www.scotland.gov.uk/stats)

The limitations of these kind of figures indicated in Table 11.1 led Governments, who wanted to know more about the extent of crime, to introduce crime and *victim surveys* that ask samples of the population about their experiences of victimisation (Coleman and Moynihan, 1996). The British Crime Survey (BCS), which began in

1982, covers crime in England and Wales and now takes place annually. Scottish Crime surveys (SCS) were introduced in 1993. These surveys provide a wealth of information about victims' experiences of crime and people's fears and worries about crime and give a more accurate picture of amounts and trends in crime than police records. They show higher levels than police records as many victims do not report crime to the police. In 1996, for example, the SCS estimated that the amount of vandalism, housebreaking, theft of cars and bicycles, assault and robbery was around 2.7 times higher than police figures (Smith and Young, 1999). Like police records, victim surveys miss out some crimes, though most are limited to crimes with individual victims and, therefore, exclude crimes against businesses (such as shoplifting) and white collar crime. Reasons why crimes may go unreported:

- Victims may be embarrassed to report some incidents to surveys
- Victims may exaggerate incidents or not be able to remember accurately when they took place
- Surveys are restricted to households with relatively permanent addresses and may miss out some age groups – some for example do not include anyone under 16.

Some of these limitations have been overcome by specially focused surveys, on, for example, crimes against businesses and domestic violence or taking specific samples of minority ethnic groups or young people. Despite their limitations, they provide invaluable information. Taking together official statistics and victim surveys, what kinds of information do we have about crime?

Is crime increasing?
Recorded crime rose steadily in Britain and many other Western countries throughout the twentieth century (Maguire, 2002) although this growth has declined in recent years. To what extent, however, do these figures reflect a 'real' rise in crime? People may have become more likely to report crime, particularly property crime, as victims wish to claim on insurance. Analysing crime trends in Scotland from 1950-1995, Smith and Young (1999) conclude that:

- Violent crimes and sexual assaults rose until 1993, after which increases tailed off
- Recorded thefts rose consistently until 1971, rose sharply until 1991, but fell from 1991-1995
- Housebreaking increased more slowly than theft and dropped after 1991
- There is evidence of a drop in recorded crime from around 1992
- Part of the rises can be accounted for by increasing reporting, which levelled from around 1995.

These trends are broadly similar to other European countries and increases over the last century can be partly explained by the vast increase in opportunities – the growth of consumerism, for example, has increased the amount of desirable consumer goods and the increased use of motor cars created new offences such as joyriding, stealing of and from cars, and driving offences such as reckless or drunken driving and driving without a licence (Croall, 1998).

How Do Countries Compare?

It is difficult to compare crime rates across different countries as recording and classification systems are different, although some comparisons can be made if similar questions are asked in victim surveys. Scotland is often compared with England and Wales, with some indications of a greater propensity to report crime in Scotland, but a slightly lower rate of some crimes (Smith and Young, 1999). The International Crime Victims Survey confirms this (Barclay and Tavares, 2002). In 1999, 26 per cent of respondents had been a victim once or more in England and Wales, compared with 23 per cent in Scotland and 15 per cent in Northern Ireland. There were more similarities between England and Wales and Scotland in relation to robbery, assaults and sexual assaults, whereas Scotland had a much lower rate of theft from a car and housebreaking.

Who is Convicted of Crime?

In common with most countries, rates of conviction are much higher for younger age groups, peaking for both sexes at 18 (194 male and 24 female per 1,000 head of population in Scotland) (Scottish Executive Bulletin, 2000) and are considerably higher for males than females. Men and women have a different pattern of convictions with women making up proportionately more offenders in relation to crimes of indecency, which include prostitution, and shoplifting – although their rates for this remain lower than men (Burman, 1999). Interpreting these figures involves looking at the factors, listed above, which affect reporting and conviction rates.

In relation to age, for example, the following questions must be asked:

- Are young people's crimes more visible? Young people spend more time in the streets, which attracts attention from the public and the police. Crimes taking place in private such as domestic violence or white collar crime are more likely to be committed by older persons
- Are young people more likely to be apprehended by the police? The police may target youth crime and be drawn to areas associated with youth disorder
- Do young people have different criminal opportunities? Young people have fewer opportunities to commit crimes in employment which have a lower chance of being detected.

While young people may be convicted more often, this can therefore reflect the kinds of crimes they commit and the kinds of activities which attract the attention of the public and the police (see Box 11.5).

Trigger

Read the case study extract in Box 11.5, below:

1. Are the activities of boys more likely to attract the attention of the police and public?
2. Do boys spend more time on the streets? Might girls attract less suspicion?

Box 11.5: Young People – Offending And Victimisation

Case study: Anderson *et al* (1994) *Cautionary Tales: Young people, crime and policing in Edinburgh*, Aldershot: Avebury

While much attention centres on the problem of 'youth crime', offending may be a transitory phase for young people and their victimisation is often ignored. A study by Anderson and his colleagues of 11-15 year olds in Edinburgh explored young people's experiences of crime in the context of their everyday lives, as victims, witnesses and perpetrators.

Violence among gangs, or 'casuals', was seen as a major problem by the press and the Police, whereas to the young people it was a relatively everyday occurrence. Fights, while exciting, appeared to involve little actual violence. The authors comment that, "while it is important to recognise the real damage that can be done both by and to young people by crime, it is equally important to remember that crime can be fun for the young."

To the authors, the study reveals the different ways in which young people experience crime. Much petty crime, found in most areas (seven out of ten reported having committed a crime at least once although this often involved no more than rowdiness on the street, with more serious offences in peripheral estates and amongst boys) can be an extension of play and learning, whereas for others, particularly those in poorer areas who were more likely to be involved in serious offending, it can be related to economic inequality and social divisions.

Girls and Violence

Overall, girls *do* appear less likely to commit the same kind of crimes as boys. There have been recurrent press stories about 'girl gangs', a rise in violence amongst girls and depictions of 'girl thugs'. How accurate, though, are these images? A study carried out by researchers from Glasgow University (Batchelor, 2001; 2002) looked at the experiences of and attitudes towards violence of a group of over 800 girls aged between 13 and 16 in Scotland, drawn from a broad range of backgrounds. Some of its main findings were that:

- Girls' ideas of 'what counts' as violence was broader than physical violence and included verbal abuse, name calling (being called a 'ned' or 'fat cow'), threats, taunts or ridicule. Ninety one per cent of the sample had experience of this, which was seen as 'normal' and 'routine'. They did not consider 'fights' with brothers or sisters as 'violence'
- Most girls (over 98 per cent) had witnessed violence, usually a local fight, 41 per cent had been victims, but only 30 per cent admitted to having hurt someone by hitting, punching or kicking them
- Violence among girls was strongly related to 'falling out' with friends, which could involve verbal abuse and intimidation. Friendship groups were particularly significant to girls
- A very small number, 10 per cent, reported being routinely violent – having committed seven or more different types of violent acts (deliberately pushing, kicking, spitting at, cutting or hitting someone) with only five per cent defining themselves as violent
- The small group of 'violent girls' were generally older, but were not exclusively from deprived, inner city environments. They reported a high tolerance of violence, and also higher levels of self-harming, verbal abuse and violent victimisation. They were more likely to hang around on the street and more likely to stay out without their parents' knowledge. They also reported other 'delinquent' behaviour such as alcohol or drug use. These girls expressed pride in their 'hard' reputation and were routinely involved in fights. Violence was related to a need to 'stick up for yourself', often related to friends and family and a strong sense of defending their territory
- None of the girls were members of girl gangs.

The study, while finding much routine verbal abuse and fear of sexual assault, found no evidence of a huge rise in physical violence or of the existence of girl gangs. Girls, they found, were not quick to use physical violence and adopted strategies to avoid it.

Trigger

1. Discuss, in a group, the term 'violence'.
2. Do you think that girls' and boys' attitudes to, and experiences of, violence are different?
3. To what extent is violence socially constructed?

Crime in Cities and Towns

Crime statistics and victim surveys also reveal higher rates of victimisation in cities compared to rural areas, although there have been concerns about rising crime in rural areas. Such concerns are often attributed to young people, a rise in drug misuse and to 'outsiders' or 'away day' criminals from urban areas. In a study of rural crime trends carried out for the Scottish Office Central Research Unit, Anderson (1999) explored rural crime using crime statistics, survey data and interviews with residents and police officers in four rural areas (see Chapter 3: Sociological Methods, for further discussion on each of these, and other, research methods).

The main findings indicated that rates of personal and property crime were lower in rural areas, such that "for every one rural crime, there are four in urban locations" (Anderson, 1999: 5). The types of crime found were broadly similar. Crimes of dishonesty predominated with only around one in 20 incidents involving violent or sexual crimes. Specifically, 'rural' types of crime were found. Poaching carried out by both 'one for the pot' offenders and 'professional' poaching for commercial gain and farm crime including fly tipping, vandalism and theft of equipment such as tools or chain saws, with sporadic instances of livestock theft, for example, sheep rustling. Crimes against wildlife included thefts of birds and eggs and persecution of birds of prey. These are difficult to quantify as there is no human victim and it often takes place in remote areas such as game-shooting estates.

Compared with urban areas, rural police officers feel that they have a closer relationship with the community and may know potential troublemakers and criminals. They may be more likely to act as mediators, often negotiating an apology and compensation. The nature of policing may be changing as police are less likely to live in the community and communities are becoming larger. Increases in rural crime rates may, therefore, reflect a more formalised approach to criminal justice in such a setting in the future.

Controlling Crime: Punishment and Crime Prevention

Strategies and policies aimed at controlling and reducing crime are related to theories of crime. If crime is a result of individual pathologies or social problems, then policies should aim to rehabilitate offenders or be directed at social welfare. A focus on the rational choice of offenders suggests, on the other hand, policies that increase chances of detection or the severity of punishment or that reduce the opportunities to commit crime. There is, therefore, a tension between policies that stress a punitive orientation and those which focus on the welfare of individual offenders (McAra, 1999).

Forms of punishment have changed with the growth of modernity. In earlier times, punishments were harsh and often involved physically harming offenders. Capital punishment was widely used and executions were public occasions. Prisons developed as places for punishment and during the nineteenth century also came to be seen as places where offenders could be rehabilitated – thus, the focus shifted from physical punishment to attempting to reform offenders. During the twentieth century, social work with offenders increased as did the idea of community sentences, such as community service or probation. This was particularly the case for young offenders, as it was believed that young people could be saved from a life of crime, and most jurisdictions have separate arrangements for young offenders such as Juvenile courts and special institutions for young offenders where they can receive training and education.

Despite their popularity, rehabilitative methods failed to demonstrate that they prevented further offending nor did they have any impact on rising crime rates. The latter decades of the twentieth century saw the growth of 'populist punitiveness' (Bottoms, 1994), which led to higher rates of imprisonment, although this was accompanied by efforts to divert less serious offenders from prison. There was also a greater emphasis on policies directed not at offenders but at preventing crime by increasing security measures along with the increased use of CCTV (see Box 11.7, later in this Chapter). Crime and its control are now major political issues and governments must balance the costs of penal systems against the need for public protection, welfare interests and the need to be seen to be doing something about crime (Garland, 1996; McAra, 1999).

Box 11.6 Children's Hearings

This unique Scottish system was introduced in 1971 as a result of the 1964 Kilbrandon Report, produced as a response to the way children's delinquency was being dealt with by the criminal justice system. The Report suggested that children involved in delinquent behaviour were in need of care, protection and help, as such behaviour was only one aspect of the life experimnce of child offenders. This heralded in a system of court-based hearings to decide on appropraite justice and punishment, taking into account the best interests of the child concerned.

Most child offenders under 16 in Scotland are referred to a Reporter who decides whether to send them to a Children's Hearing. Generally, the minority who commit more serious offences are prosecuted, but children seen to be in need of care or protection (e.g. where parental control is absent or impossible, where truancy is severe, or where they have been subject to or in danger of, physical and/or sexual abuse or neglect) are also referred to hearings.

Scotland has 32 Children's Panels, comprising members from a range of backgrounds. Each panel consists of three members, of which at least one must be male and one female. In an informal seeting – involving the family - the main task of the Hearings is to decide what measures are best for the child; they are *not* courts! A report from a social worker is normally produced and, where necessary, medical or psychiatric reports are also referred to. Panels do not have the power to set fines, but the vast majority of child offenders receive some form of social work supervision, with a small number being sent to secure accommodation.

The Children's Hearings demonstrate an example of the welfare approach predominant in Scotland. However, this is not to suggest that protection of the public is ignored (McAra, 1999). As a result of heightened concern over child protection and persistent offending, the Children (Scotland) Act 1995 enabled courts to place the principle of public protection above that of the child, in circumstances where the child presented a significant risk to the public. More recent proposals for electronic tagging indicate a more punitive element into the system (Asquith and Docherty, 1999).

(Source: Adapted from: *Background to the Children's Hearings System* available at www.childrens-hearings.co.uk)

Why punish?

Modern states are distinguished by the power to impose public, as opposed to private punishment. As this may involve the deprivation of liberty, the state must justify punishment, and a number of theories or philosophies of punishment affect how offenders are sentenced.

- *Retribution*: The notion that criminals deserve punishment in proportion to the harm they have done is one of the oldest justifications for punishment – in biblical terms described as 'an eye for an eye'. More contemporary retributive approaches talk of 'just deserts'. Retributive ideals limit the amount of punishment as it should not exceed the harm done
- *Deterrence*: Another long standing justification for punishment is that it should deter either the offender or the general public from committing a crime through fear of the punishment. Prison sentences should be long and

fines high enough to exceed any possible benefit of the crime. Strongly deterrent sentences may exceed what seems to be fair under retributive reasoning

- *Incapacitation*: Offenders can be prevented from committing further offences by incapacitating them in some way. This is reflected in a number of sentences – it justifies very long periods of imprisonment along with contemporary strategies such as electronic 'tagging'. Drivers can be disqualified and other offenders subjected to curfews. Like deterrence this justifies sentences that may seem disproportionate to the harm done

- *Rehabilitation*: Welfare approaches are based on the argument that offenders need 'treatment' rather than punishment. While often seen as 'soft' on offenders, rehabilitative principles could be used to justify longer and more interventionist sentences on the grounds that offenders needed time for 'treatment' to work

- *Denunciation*: Punishment is also used to express public disapproval of crime. Punishment, like justice, should, therefore, be seen to be done. The role of media is important in relation to denunciation although, like some other theories, it may justify longer sentences

- *Restitution/restorative justice*: A final principle affecting sentences, although not punishment, is the idea that offenders should make good the harm they have done, either to the community or directly to victims. This may also make them more aware of the damage they have inflicted. Restorative justice has become very popular with the growth of 'conferencing' sessions between offenders and victims.

Sentencing policies reflect a combination of these approaches and those passing sentence must weigh up the relative merits of different options considering the offence, the offender, the victim and the interests of public protection.

What Happens to Offenders? The Main Sentencing Options

Sentences are often depicted as a 'tariff' ranging in severity from a fine to a community sentence and, for the most serious offenders, a custodial sentence. *Criminal Proceedings in Scottish Courts* (Scottish Executive, 2001) provides an overview of sentences and also indicates that 'fines' are the most common sentence – used for 65 per cent of convictions in 2000. Other offenders receive community or custodial sentences.

Community sentences

Community sentences consist mainly of Probation and Community Service Orders. Of the 12,400 persons in Scotland given a community sentence in 2000, 7,400 were given a Probation Order, 1,400 of these with a requirement that the offender perform unpaid work and 4,700 were given a community service order (Scottish Executive Statistical Bulletin CrJ/2001/7, 2001).

Probation orders

Probation orders originated with young offenders being placed 'on probation' under the supervision of a volunteer, often from the Church. Their use grew throughout the twentieth century and Probation Officers became qualified social workers, with Criminal Justice social work being a specialised area. As is the case in other countries, there is often a tension between the welfare orientation of social work and the requirements of criminal justice (McIvor and Williams, 1999). Probation orders, which can be for between 6 months and 3 years can be used for any offences except serious offences like murder which require a custodial sentence. Officers prepare a social inquiry report to see if the offender is suitable for probation, to which the offender must agree. If offenders do not comply with the order or re-offend, they can be taken back to court and sentenced for the original offence.

What happens on probation?

On receiving an order the offender will normally have monthly meetings with a case worker. Meetings will focus on an action plan which addresses the offenders' behaviour, relationships, practical problems such as employment, accommodation, finances and drugs and/or alcohol problems. Some orders may also impose requirements such as residence in a specified place; medical or psychological treatment; attendance at programmes dealing with anger management; victim awareness; undertaking unpaid work and payment of compensation to victims (McIvor and Williams, 1999). Offenders do receive considerable help with employment and housing problems although a continued use of drugs, a lack or interest or continuing personal and practical problems may lead to a poor response. In one study, nearly three quarters of probationers were considered to be less likely to re offend at the end of their order than at the start (McIvor and Barry, 1996).

Community service orders

Community service orders, first introduced in Scotland in 1977, involve offenders aged 16 and over who are convicted of an offence punishable by imprisonment, being ordered to complete between 80 and 3,000 hours of unpaid work. They were introduced in the face of overcrowding in prisons and a pessimism about rehabilitation within prisons as it was felt that prison could be damaging and could disrupt family relationships. Community service orders combine several different aims – they deprive an offender of liberty and involve work in the community – which can be seen as retributive, deterrent and restitutive and it is also argued that offenders may be rehabilitated. Their use has rapidly expanded, although there were doubts about whether the courts were really using them as alternatives to prison. During the 1990s the punitive elements of community service came to be stressed more specifically, with a greater emphasis on physically demanding work and an increase in the number of hours.

Custodial sentences

Custodial sentences consist of Young Offenders Institutions (YOI) and Prisons. Their use has increased in many jurisdictions, including in Scotland, where there was an increase throughout the 1990s, although this peaked in 1997 and the average daily population in Scottish prisons in 2000 totalled 5,869. Offenders receive custodial sentences for the most serious offences including robbery, sexual and serious assaults and housebreaking. The average length of custodial sentences in Scotland was 217 days in 2000 with over half of all sentences being for three months or less.

The use of prison is justified on many grounds. The deprivation of liberty is retributive and deterrent principles affected　their design. Prisons should, it was argued, be hard and unpleasant places that people would not want to be sent to. They protect the public by containing those offenders seen as most dangerous, and prisons can also be places for rehabilitation. The special unit at HMP Barlinnie in Glasgow saw the rehabilitation of several seriously violent offenders, including Jimmy Boyle, who wrote his story in *A Sense of Freedom* and became a sculptor and writer. Prisons must also prioritise order and security – riots and disturbances have occurred in prisons in Scotland and England and Wales. These many functions are reflected in the aims of the Scottish Prison Service, which are stated as:

- Keeping in custody those committed by the courts
- Maintaining good order in each prison
- Caring for prisoners with humanity
- Providing prisoners with opportunities to exercise personal responsibility and to prepare for release.

Do Prisons Work?

The popularity of prison sentences may not be justified by their success. To the extent that escapes are rare, they do keep many offenders out of circulation. However, short sentences may limit the amount of public protection. Their effect on crime rates may also be limited as so few offenders receive custodial sentences and rehabilitative efforts are also constrained by short sentences and the nature of prisons themselves – buildings are old and not suited to rehabilitative activities. Prisoners can also lose touch with their families and be less able to cope on release than they were before, leading to many offenders re-offending. Prison is also expensive when compared with non custodial sentences. Taking these considerations into account, McManus (1999: 238) argues that "without clear benefits to match these costs, it is difficult to make a case for the present level of use in Scotland."

Crime Prevention

Sentencing offenders is not the only means of dealing with crime and, indeed, because so few offenders are caught or punished, the criminal justice system may play less of a role in reducing crime than is often thought. Attention has, therefore, increasingly turned to how crime can best be prevented and a host of schemes – including the Safer Cities initiatives and Neighbourhood Watch – were set up along with strategies, such as the increased use of burglar alarms, the use of concierges in council estates, and the spread of Close Circuit Television (CCTV) (see Box 11.7, below). Crime prevention can be described as:

- ***Primary***: *a*iming at the situations in which crime is committed, at the offence rather than offender. This may, for example, involve 'target hardening' through the installation of security devices or 'target removal'
- ***Secondary***: focusing more on dealing with offenders, including early intervention schemes to prevent further offending
- ***Tertiary***: dealing with offenders through the sentences outlined above.

Box 11.7 provides some details about the use of CCTV, often seen as a deterrent to crime, but the effectiveness of which is difficult to evaluate.

Box 11.7 Close Circuit Television (CCTV)

The use of close circuit television (CCTV) has expanded enormously and it has been seen as having a major impact on crime prevention, but questions arise over whether it works. A range of factors must be taken into account from displacement of crime; policing of areas; type of environment and fluctuations in crime rates, when assessing the effectivenss of CCTV (Coleman and Norris, 2000).

The success or otherwise of a scheme can also be seen in relation to the different goals of installing cameras. Are they aimed at preventing crime, increasing detection or more generally at making people feel more secure and attracting investment and people into an area?

Even when all these factors are taken into account, research has been inconclusive, leading Coleman and Norris (2000: 168) to conclude that the 'criminological evidence is far from straightforward: the effects are neither universal or consistent", or, as Ditton and Short (1999: 217) argue "open-street CCTV can 'work in limited ways' [....] in different ways in different situations."

Trigger

1. Using the information in Box 11.7, as well your own knowledge, what do you think are the advantages and disadvantages of using CCTV?
2. If CCTV pushes crime out of one area, where, if anywhere, does that crime go?

Conclusion

Like CCTV, the effectiveness of other crime prevention schemes is difficult to assess, as the crime rate without the scheme cannot be known. On the other hand, they may make people feel safer. A major problem arises in terms of crime *displacement*, which may occur if offenders are deterred from committing crime in one area only to commit it in another. Technological interventions have, however, made some kinds of crime more difficult – a combination of improved security and CCTV has, for example, virtually seen the end of the traditional bank robbery with the skilled safe breaker – but robbers may now choose softer targets, such as small shops or garages (Matthews, 2001). Increased security may have other, more hidden implications. CCTV, for example, could lead to the exclusion of suspicious persons from high streets, shopping malls or leisure events and too many bolts or bars may lead to an unpleasant environment. The resort to security measures can also exacerbate social divisions as the more affluent increasingly secure their homes against the assumed lawlessness of the 'dangerous' classes. To some critics, crime prevention, while valuable, does not sufficiently take account of the wider structural roots of crime.

Chapter Summary

- Deviance is a term that refers to acts considered wrong or innapropriate depending on culture, social context, time or place.
- Crime can be more simply defined as breaking the criminal law, but also varies depending on changes in the law over time and between cultures, as shifting conceptions of drug use illustrate.
- Individual explanations of crime tend to see the criminal as different in terms of biological or psychological factors.
- Sociological explanations of crime focus on crime as a social construction focusing on cultural and structural aspects.
- Classical functionalist approaches, such as those taken by Durkheim and Merton, argue that crime can be functional, 'healthy' and 'normal' in society.

- Cloward and Ohlin (1960) identified *three* main forms of delinquent subculture – *conflict*: based around violence; *criminal*: based on criminal activities such as theft; *retreatist*: based on a drop out or alternative life style.
- Subcultural theories interpret youth subcultures as a means of finding cultural 'space' in response to blocked opportunities in periods of social change.
- Labelling theorists, such as Edwin Lemert (1951), distinguish between 'primary deviance': the initial act that has not been 'labelled', and 'secondary deviance': actions that take place after a label has been applied.
- Becker (1963) argues that labelling someone as deviant can lead to them reacting with further deviance and a deviant 'identity' can be formed as a result of a process of action and reaction leading to a 'deviancy amplification' process; this process is associated with a 'self-fulfilling prophecy' in which the reaction to deviance produces more deviance.
- Conflict theorists, particularly Marxists, claim that in capitalist society, attention is focused on the crimes of the working class. The law, including the criminal law, is created following political negotiations and conflict, and to Marxist theories, it reflects the interests of the most powerful groups and the ruling class.
- White collar crime has increasingly become a focus in studies of crime and has been defined by Edwin Sutherland (1949: 9) as "crime committed by persons of high social status and respectability in the course of their occupations."
- Feminist perspectives have raised the issue that early studies of crime were 'gender blind'. Most agree that women commit less crime than men. Feminist approaches ask some very important questions about the gendered nature of crime including women's victimisation.
- 'Rational choice' theories advocate removing opportunities for crime and harsher penalties based on the assumption that offenders make a 'rational choice' to commit crime and weigh up the benefits of the crime against the chances of being caught and punished (Clarke and Mayhew, 1980).
- 'Control theories' claim that how people are controlled in society is a crucial factor affecting whether or not they commit crime, which also draws attention to features such as parental supervision. These theories have been very influential although like rational choice theories, they tend to neglect the social patterning of crime (Downes and Rock, 1998).
- 'Left Realist' approaches link crime and inequality using notions of absolute and relative deprivation. They assert that explaining any form of crime must take account of the relationships between offenders, victims, agencies of control and the general public who witness and define crime and affect how it is controlled.
- Official statistics based on police reports are socially constructed and are not, therefore, an accurate measure of crime.

- There also exists a large 'hidden figure'. Rises or falls in crime rates can, therefore, reflect police activities rather than indicate any change in the 'real' rate of crime. Despite their limitations, however, official staistics *do* provide invaluable information.

- In terms of punishment and crime prevention, there exists a tension between policies that stress a punitive orientation and those that focus on the welfare of individual offenders (McAra, 1999).

- Modern states are distinguished by the power to impose public, as opposed to private punishment. As this may involve the deprivation of liberty, the state must justify punishment, and a number of theories or philosophies of punishment affect how offenders are sentenced. Justifications for punishment include: 'Retribution', 'Deterrence', 'Incapacitation', 'Rehabilitation', 'Denunciation' and 'Restitution'.

- A number of non-custodial sentencing options exist for Scottish courts including: community sentences, probation orders and community service.

- The debate over whether prison works reveals a number of problems with prison as an adequate form of punishment.

- CCTV as a crime prevention strategy has a number of strengths and weaknesses.

Further Reading

Aggleton, P. (1991) *Deviance*, London: Routledge

Burke, R. H. (2001) *An Introduction to Criminological Theory*, Devon: Willan Publishing

Carrabine, E., Cox, P., Lee, M. and South, N. (eds.) (2002) *Crime in Modern Britain*, Oxford: Oxford University Press

Downes, D. and Rock, P. (1998) *Understanding Deviance: A Guide to the Sociology of Crime and Rule Breaking*, Revised Second Edition, Oxford: Clarendon Press

Duff, P. and Hutton, N. (eds.) (1999) *Criminal Justice in Scotland*, Hampshire: Ashgate

Heidensohn, F. (1989) *Crime and Society*, Basingstoke: Macmillan

Lawson, T. and Heaton, T. (1999) *Crime and Deviance*, Basingstoke: Macmillan

Maguire, M., Morgan, M. and Reiner, R. (eds.) (2002) *The Oxford Handbook of Criminology*, Third Edition, Oxford: Clarendon Press

Moore, S. (1996) *Investigating Crime and Deviance*, Second Edition, London: Collins Educational

Muncie, J. and Mclaughlin, E. (eds.) (1996) *The Problem of Crime*, London: Sage

Muncie, J., Mclaughlin, E. and Langan, M. (eds.) (1996) *Criminological Perspectives: A Reader*, London: Sage

Soothill, K., Peelo, M. and Taylor, C. (eds.) (2002) *Making Sense of Criminology*, Cambridge: Polity Press

Walklate, S. (1998) *Understanding Criminology: Current Theoretical Debates*, Buckingham: Open University Press

Useful Websites

Statistics and research publications about crime from the Scottish Executive can be obtained from: www.scotland.gov.uk/cru/; www.scotland.gov.uk/stats/; for England and Wales see: www.homeoffice.gov.uk/rds/index.htm; www.homeoffice.gov.uk/rds/index.htm

There are many websites with good links including the site for the Centre for Criminal Justice Studies which also publishes the periodical *Criminal Justice Matters*: www.kcl.ac.uk/depsta/rel/ccjs/

On the Scottish Police see: www.strathclyde.police.uk/; www.grampian.police.uk/;
www.lbp.police.uk/ (Lothian and Borders); www.tayside.police.uk/
Scottish Prisons: www.sps.gov.uk; Prisons in England and Wales: www.hmprisonservice.gov.uk
On Scotland's Children's Hearings: www.childrens-hearings.co.uk
Scottish courts and prosecution: www.procuratorfiscal.gov.uk/; http://www.scotcourts.gov.uk/
Victim support: http://natiasso03.uuhost.uk.uu.net/; www.sacro.org.uk/ (SACRO is a national voluntary
organisation working in Scotland to make communities safer and also deals with offenders).

Bibliography

Anderson, S. (1999) 'A Study of crime in Rural Scotland', *Rural Affairs and Natural Heritage Research Findings*, No. 10, Edinburgh: The Scottish Office Central Research Unit

Anderson, S. (1999) 'Crime Statistics and the 'Problem of Crime' in Scotland', in Duff, P. and Hutton, N. (eds.) *Criminal Justice in Scotland*, Hampshire: Ashgate

Anderson, S., Kinsey, R., Loader, I. and Smith, C. (1994) *Cautionary Tales: Young people, crime and policing in Edinburgh*, Aldershot: Avebury

Asquith, S. and Docherty, M. (1999) 'Preventing Offending by Children and Young People in Scotland', in Duff, P. and Hutton, N. (eds.) *Criminal Justice in Scotland*, Hampshire: Ashgate

Batchelor, S., Burman, M. and Brown, J. (2001) 'Discussing Violence: Let's Hear it From the Girls' *Probation Journal*, Vol. 48 (2), June 2001

Batchelor, S. (2002) 'The Myth of Girl Gangs' in Jewkes, Y. and Letherby, G. (eds.) *Criminology: a Reader*, London: Sage

Barclay and Tavares International comparisons of criminal justice statistics (2000) *Home Office Statistical Bulletin* 1207/02, London: Home Office

Becker, H. (1963) *Outsiders: Studies in the Study of Deviance*, New York, NY: Free Press

Bennett, T. (1989) 'Burglars' Choice of Targets', in Evans, D. and Herbert, D. (eds.) *The Geography of Crime*, London: Routledge

Bottoms, A. (1994) 'The Philosophy and Politics of Punishment and Sentencing', in Clarkson, C. and Morgan, R. (eds.) *The Politics of Sentencing Reform*, Oxford: Oxford University Press

Burman, M. (1999) 'Women and the Scottish Criminal Justice System', in Duff, P. and Hutton, N. (eds.) *Criminal Justice in Scotland*, Hampshire: Ashgate

Campbell, B. (1993) *Goliath: Britain's dangerous places*, London: Virago

Carlen, P. (1985) *Criminal Women*, Cambridge: Polity Press

Carlen, P. (1988) *Women, Crime and Poverty*, Milton Keynes: Open University Press

Carlen, P. and Worrall, A. (eds.) (1987) *Gender, Crime and Justice*, Milton Keynes: Open University Press

Clarke, R. and Mayhew, P. (1980) *Designing Out Crime*, London: HMSO

Clarkson, C. and Morgan, R. (eds.) *The Politics of Sentencing Reform*, Oxford: Oxford University Press

Cloward, R. and Ohlin, L. (1960) *Delinquency and Opportunity*, New York, NY: Free Press

Cohen, A.K. (1955) *Delinquent Boys*, New York, NY: Free Press

Cohen, S. (1972) *Folk Devils and Moral Panics*, Oxford: Martin Robertson

Cohen, S. (1985) *Visions of Social Control*, Cambridge: Polity Press

Coleman, C. and Moynihan, J. (1996) *Understanding Crime Data: Haunted by the Dark Figure*, Buckingham: Open University Press

Coleman, C. and Norris, C. (2000) *Introducing Criminology*, Devon: Willan Publishing

Croall, H. (1998) *Crime and Society in Britain*, London: Longman

Croall, H. (2001) *Understanding White Collar Crime*, Buckingham: Open University Press

Croall, H. and Ross, J. (2002) 'Sentencing the Corporate Offender', in Hutton, N. and Tata, C. (eds.) *Sentencing and Society*, Hampshire: Ashgate

Davies, P. Francis, P. and Jupp, V. (eds.) (1999) *Invisible Crimes*, Basingstoke: MacMillan

Ditton, J. and Short, E. (1999) 'Yes, it works – no, it doesn't: comparing the effects of open-street CCTV in two adjacent town centres', *Crime Prevention Studies,* 10, pp.201-223

Downes, D. (1966) *The Delinquent Solution: A study in Subcultural Theory*, London: Routledge

Downes, D. and Rock, P. (1995) *Understanding Deviance: A Guide to the Sociology of Crime and Rule Breaking,* Second Edition, Oxford: Clarendon Press

Durkheim, E. (1996 [1964/1895]) 'The Rules of Sociological Method', [Extract] 'The Normal and the Pathological', New York, NY: Free Press (reprinted in Muncie, J. *et al* (1996) *Criminological Perspectives: A Reader*, London: Sage)

Evans, D. and Herbert, D. (eds.) *The Geography of Crime*, London: Routledge

Eysenck, H. (1977) *Crime and Personality*, London: Routledge and Kegan Paul

Fraser, F. (2002) *Drug Misuse in Scotland: Findings from the 2000 Scottish crime Survey*, Edinburgh: Scottish Executive Central Research Unit

Garland, D. (1996) 'The Limits of the Sovereign State: Strategies of Crime Control in Contemporary Society', *British Journal of Criminology*, Vol.36, pp.455-471

Gelsthorpe, L. (2002) 'Feminism and Criminology', in Maguire, M., Morgan, R. and Reiner, R. (eds.) *The Oxford Handbook of Criminology*, Third Edition, Oxford: Clarendon Press

Hall, S. and Jefferson, T. (eds.) (1976) *Resistance Through Ritual,*. London: Hutchinson

Hall, S., Critcher, C., Jefferson, T., Clarke, J. and Roberts, B. (1978) *Policing the Crisis: Mugging, the State and Law and Order*, Basingstoke: Macmillan

Heidensohn, F. (2002) 'Gender and crime', in Maguire, M. Morgan, R. and Reiner, R., (eds.) *The Oxford Handbook of Criminology*, Third Edition, Oxford: Clarendon Press

Hirschi, T. (1969) *Causes of Delinquency*, Los Angeles, CA: University of California Press

Hutton, N. and Tata, C. (eds.) *Sentencing and Society*, Hampshire: Ashgate

Jewkes, Y. and Letherby, G. (eds.) *Criminology: a Reader*, London: Sage

Lea, J. and Young, J. (1993) *What is to be done about Law and Order?* Second Edition, London: Pluto Press

Lemert, E. (1951) *Social Pathology*, New York, NY: McGraw Hill

Lombroso, Cesare (1897) *L'Uomo Delinquente*, Fifth Edition, Torino: Bocca

McAra, L. (1999) 'The Politics of Penality: An Overview of the Development of Penal Policy in Scotland', in Duff, P. and Hutton, N. (eds.) *Criminal Justice in Scotland*, Hampshire: Ashgate

McIvor, G. and Barry, (1996) *The Process and Outcomes of Probation Supervision* (Research report to the Scottish Office Home Department), Stirling: University of Stirling, Social Work Research Centre

McIvor, G. and Williams, B. (1999) 'Community-based Disposals', in Duff, P. and Hutton, N. (eds.) *Criminal Justice in Scotland*, Hampshire: Ashgate

McManus, J. (1999) 'Imprisonment and Other Custodial Sentences', in Duff, P. and Hutton, N. (eds.) (1999) *Criminal Justice in Scotland*, Hampshire: Ashgate

Maguire, M. (2002) 'Crime Statistics: The 'data explosion and its Implications'', in Maguire, M. *et al* (eds.) *The Oxford Handbook of Criminology*, Third Edition, Oxford: Clarendon Press

Mars, G. (1982) *Cheats at Work, an Anthropology of Workplace Crime*, London: George Allen and Unwin

Matthews, R. (2001) *Armed Robbery*, Devon: Willan Publishing

Matza, D. (1964) *Delinquency and Drift*, New York, NY: Wiley

Merton, R.K. (1938) 'Social Structure and anomie', *American Sociological Review,* Vol.3, pp.672-82

Patrick, J. (1973) *A Glasgow Gang Observed*, London: Eyre Methuen

Scottish Executive (2001) 'Criminal Proceedings in Scottish Courts in 2000', *Scottish Executive Statistical Bulletin CrJ2001/7: 2001* (accessed at: www.scotland.gov.uk/stats)

Scottish Executive (2002) 'Recorded Crime in Scotland 2001', *Scottish Executive Bulletin CrJ/2002/1*, April (accessed at: www.scotland.gov.uk/stats)

Scraton, P. and Chadwick, K. (1991) 'The theoretical and political priorities of critical criminology', in Stenson, K, and Cowell, D. (eds.) *The Politics of Crime Control*, London: Sage

Sheldon, W. (1949) *Varieties of Delinquent Youth*, New York and London: Harper

Smith, D. J. and Young, P. (1999) 'Crime Trends in Scotland since 1950', in Duff, P. and Hutton, N. (eds.) *Criminal Justice in Scotland*, Hampshire: Ashgate

South, N. (2002) 'Drugs, Alcohol and Crime', in Maguire, M. *et al* (eds.) *The Oxford Handbook of Criminology*, Third Edition, Oxford: Clarendon Press

Stenson, K, and Cowell, D. (eds.) (1991) *The Politics of Crime Control*, London: Sage

Sutherland, E.H. (1960) *White Collar* Crime, New York, NY: Holt, Reinhart and Winston

Taylor, I., Walton, P. and Young, J. (1973) *The New Criminology*, London: Routledge and Kegan Paul

Tombs, S. (1999) 'Health and Safety Crimes: (In)visibility and the Problems of Knowing', in Davies, P. Francis, P. and Jupp, V. (eds.) *Invisible Crimes*, Basingstoke: MacMillan

Walklate, S. (2000) *Gender, Crime and Criminal Justice*, Devon: Willan Publishing

Williams, K. (1994) *Textbook on Criminology*, Second Edition, London: Blackstone

Young, J. (1997) 'Left Realist Criminology: Radical in its Analysis, Realist in its Policy', in Maguire, M. *et al* (eds.) *The Oxford Handbook of Criminology*, Second Edition, Oxford: Clarendon Press

Chapter 12 Health

Maria Feeney and Neil G. McPherson

Introduction

Defining the concepts of 'health and 'illness' has long been a strongly contested area in Western society. While a variety of approaches exist, a clear thread running through most definitions is the dominance of the 'biomedical model' in setting the agenda for the explanation and understanding of health and illness. The lay perception of biomedicine and the medical profession is that they simply operate to rid individuals of ill health and disease. However, it has been argued that the power of medicine extends far beyond this focus and that the role of medicine, and the medical profession in general, has developed as one of social control. This chapter will outline the key underpinnings and criticisms of the biomedical model before identifying and discussing key sociological approaches which, in different ways, define medicine as an 'institution of social control'. It will then examine health inequalities that are evident in the contemporary United Kingdom, placing a specific focus on the Scottish context.

Trigger

Read the following two quotes before considering the three questions below.

"Health is a state of complete physical, mental and social well-being and not merely the absence of disease or infirmity." (World Health Organisation, 1948)

"In examining the state of health of a population [...] there are different meanings of 'health' which have different implications for action to improve [it]. On one hand 'health' can be conceived as the outcome of freeing man from disease or disorder, as identified throughout the history of medicine. On the other hand, it can be conceived as man's vigorous, creative and even joyous involvement in environment and community, of which presence or absence of disease is only a part." (Townsend and Davidson, 1988: 41-2)

1. What do the concepts of health, illness and medicine mean to you in your everyday life, and what do you think defines you as 'healthy' or 'ill'?
2. How would you define the difference between 'mild' illness and 'severe' illness?

Historical Development of the Sociology of Health, Illness and Medicine

In the UK, medical sociology emerged from the interwar (1918-1939) debates surrounding medicine and concerns about social patterns of health and illness (Figlio, 1987). In its early period, medical sociology was largely driven by the ideas and values of medicine. However, further sociological approaches have developed that stand apart from the influences of medicine, and exist as an 'alternative social approach' in evaluating the role of the medical profession. The medical sociology of the early period has been overtaken by the sociology of health and illness, which is more critical in its analysis of the role of medicine. The tensions created between the two strands have focused sociology's debate with biomedicine. They have set the agenda for the production of a social model of health and illness, and for the critique of the role of contemporary medicine (Annandale, 1998).

Whereas medical sociology took the biomedical model of health and illness as its starting point, competing sociological analyses of medicine have addressed the social and cultural aspects of health and illness, and questioned the 'common sense' understanding of biomedicine, i.e. as an institution that tackles illness and disease through the discovery and application of 'scientific knowledge'. Before addressing these approaches, it is important to understand the key principals of the biomedical model of health and illness.

The Biomedical Model of Health and Illness
The biomedical model

For over 150 years, biomedicine, with its focus on scientific method, has been the dominant model for the medical profession's approach to health, illness and disease (Jones, 1994). The biomedical approach focuses specifically on the biological aspects of health, illness and disease. Its central concepts can be summarised as follows:

- Medicine is scientific, objective and value free
- Health and illness are explained in biological and scientific terms
- Medical practitioners focus on anatomy and physiology, with little regard to social circumstances
- Health is viewed in mechanical terms. When every part of the body functions 'properly' the other parts to do likewise (a smoothly integrated and functioning biological system)
- Illness and disease are viewed as deviations from 'normal' bodily function
- Illness and disease are caused by malfunction of the body due to, e.g. bacteria, a virus, or a 'faulty' gene

- All illnesses are identifiable and can be specifically classified and diagnosed, leaving little room for disagreement between medical professionals
- Only qualified medical practitioners can diagnose and prescribe treatment of illness and disease. 'Lay people' are not qualified to carry out these tasks
- Illness and disease can be treated by medical intervention, e.g. through the use of drugs, or surgery on the 'malfunctioning' part of the body.

Not all medical practitioners take the above model as a 'given', and some do look at the social circumstances of the individual before making any diagnosis. However, although alternative health models, e.g. osteopathy and acupuncture, are mounting challenges, the biomedical model is the "dominant paradigm in modern western health care" (Gillespie and Gerhardt, 1995: 81).

Having outlined the main characteristics of the biomedical model, key criticisms of this model can now be identified.

Criticisms of the biomedical model:

- It places a focus on cure rather than prevention
- It does not take into account the environmental influences on health and illness
- Biomedicine is rigidly defined and not reactive to social change and new health concerns
- The extent to which biomedicine has led to the decline of infectious disease is questionable. It can be argued that improvements in living conditions have had a greater impact, e.g. improved sanitation (McKeown, 1979)
- Illich (1976) has argued that society has become dependent on biomedicine to the detriment of the individual's autonomy, and that medicine can actually create illness
- Biomedicine exists as an institution of social control
- Marxists have argued that medicine is economically driven, benefiting capitalism and the capitalist class while having a negative effect on the work force
- Feminists have argued that biomedicine is a male-dominated field, which has led to the *medicalisation* of women's health. As a result, women are often viewed as 'passive subjects', rather than 'active agents', by the dominant male definition and evaluation of women's health.

While these criticisms of the biomedical model are valid, its continuing dominance in Western society has enabled medicine to develop as an institution of social control. It has been argued that the power of the medical profession has developed as a direct result of its knowledge and legitimacy in the definition, diagnoses and cure of illness and disease (Jones, 1994).

Trigger

To what extent do health services that you have direct experience of (e.g. visiting the dentist) fit with the biomedical model described above?

Medicine as an Institution of Social Control

This section will look at six key theoretical perspectives that, in different ways, attempt to explain the power of the medical profession and the social control function of medicine in contemporary society.

Medicine: knowledge, power and social control

The medical profession is commonly regarded as being the 'font of all knowledge', with regards to defining and dealing with all forms of health, illness and disease. From where, and how, did they get such power?

The emergence of the biomedical model, highlighted above, and its particular way of viewing the body and of understanding health, illness and disease was only one of a variety of reasons. Others included the setting up of hospitals and clinics where curative medicine was practiced, where medical training could take place, and where medical skills and knowledge could be developed. The power of the medical profession was consolidated by the 1858 Medical Registration Act, which gave the 'medical elite' total control over medical education (Jones, 1994). As a result, it was only those individuals who undertook the accepted training and passed the appropriate exams who could be registered as 'qualified practitioners'. Through these factors the medical profession was able to extend and develop its power base (Jones, 1994). It is due to the extensive influence of this power base, and the social acceptance of the role of medicine, that the medical profession has come to be regarded by many sociologists as an institution of social control. For example, Hart (1985: 96) states that:

> Medicine is a social ideology underwritten by the 'neutrality' of science which quite literally defines our understanding, i.e. our social ideas, about what health and illness are like. The occupation of doctor therefore is not just a job or a means of income, it is an important social status with power over people and their behaviour. It is in this sense that we may speak of medicine as an institution of social control.

It should be stated at this point, that the control function of medicine is not regarded as negative by all sociologists. For functionalists, such as Parsons (1951), medicine provides a necessary control function in society that maintains social order. This section will first examine the functionalist approach to medicine before addressing alternative theories, which do not regard its role in such a positive light.

The functionalist approach
Parsons' concept of the 'sick role'
In order to counteract the scientific approach to health, which the biomedical model takes, the functionalist theorist, Talcott Parsons, highlighted the social dimension of medicine through his discussion of the 'sick role'. Parsons (1951) regarded medicine as an institution that contributed to the social cohesion of society through its regulatory approach to health. In *The Social System* (Parsons, 1951), he stated that illness should be viewed as a form of deviant behaviour that poses a threat to the smooth running of society and should, therefore, be regulated by the medical profession. He saw doctors as legitimate agents of the state, arguing that their power was developed through professional training and strict codes of conduct, which ensured that they worked towards the benefit of society, making certain that patients were treated appropriately. For Parsons, the role for medicine ultimately lay in the curing of the sick, thereby allowing them to return to their position as an integral, and functional, part of society. He regarded biomedicine as an agency of social cohesion, which worked for the benefit of all, operating as an institution that not only treated the sick, but also legitimised sickness and allowed the individual to adopt the 'sick role'. Thus:

> [B]y virtue of being an authority on what illness really is, medicine creates the social possibilities of 'acting sick' [...] its monopoly includes the right to create illness as an *official social role*.
> (authors' emphasis, Freidson, 1970, quoted in Hart 1985: 96)

From this functionalist perspective, Parsons identified the sick role as a means of demonstrating how biomedicine penetrates social aspects of human experience. He argued that medical practitioners' contact with patients allowed biomedicine to project and channel its influence throughout society. For Parsons, the sick role was, in effect, a contract between doctor and patient where illness could be sanctioned, and where both parties were required to operate within a framework of rights and obligations. A summary of these rights and obligations can be seen below.

'Sick role' – patient
Rights:
- Afforded the right to withdraw from certain everyday responsibilities, e.g. paid employment and/or household tasks

- The right to care and attention because she or he cannot simply will themselves into getting well enough to 'function' as a normal member of society.

Obligations:

- Must go to doctor and adhere to medical instructions in a co-operative manner
- Must do everything possible to get well.

Professional role – doctor
Rights:

- Afforded the right to physically examine the patient, even if this involves intimate examination of areas of their physical, psychological and emotional life
- Allowed a high level of autonomy in professional practice and medical decisions
- Can adopt an authoritative role with regards to their relationship with the patient.

Obligations:

- Must use all of her/his medical skills and knowledge to enable the sick person to be returned to full health as soon as possible
- Must always act in the best interest of not only the patient, but also of the whole community/society
- Should never act out of self-interest, whether this is, for example, financial gain or career development
- Must adhere to the accepted rules and regulations of professional practice.

(adapted from Seale, 2001: 153-4)

However, it has been argued that functionalist theory, with its belief in social cohesion and consensus, is inadequate in explaining the existence of conflict in society. This in turn has led to the questioning and criticism of Parsons' concept of the sick role (Hardey, 1998). Some of the criticism that has been levelled against Parsons can be highlighted.

Criticisms of Parsons' concept of the sick role:

- In the twentieth century, chronic illness (over 6 months) is becoming much more prevalent than acute (short term) illness. As a result, Parsons' notion of rights and responsibilities of *both* patient *and* doctor may be irrelevant, since the patient may not be able to be returned to full health and perform her or his normal tasks
- Parsons' concept of illness as deviance, and the sick role's construction of passive and obedient patients, masks the reality of the 'social control' function of medicine
- Not all people feel that there is a 'sick role'. Some refuse to see themselves as 'sick', e.g. 'disabled' individuals who want to carry on a 'normal' life, and who do not wish to be stigmatised by their disability.

Medicine is not morally neutral, and the patient may be stigmatised and further disadvantaged by adopting the sick role. For example, some illnesses that lead to the adoption of the sick role are viewed as self-inflicted, e.g. HIV/AIDS, lung cancer and alcoholism, thus the rights that go with it may not be afforded to the individual.

Nevertheless, while the functionalist approach has been strongly criticised, it has located the study of health, illness and medicine within the wider sphere of social theory. Parsons' concept of the sick role examined health, illness and medicine from outside the institution of biomedicine, thereby creating a starting point for further sociological debate and analysis (Hardey, 1998). This has led to the development of theories which define the institution of medicine as socially, politically and morally intrusive, and which question its perceived neutrality. The key theoretical approaches, which regard medicine in this way, will now be discussed.

Trigger

To what extent does Parsons' concept of the sick role adequately explain any period of sickness that you have had in your own life?

The 'medicalisation thesis'

It has been argued that medicine invades all aspects of life, effectively acting as an agency of social control (Zola, 1972) that can be detrimental to individuals' health (Illich, 1976). From this perspective, medicine's increasingly pervasive role has led to society becoming 'medicalised', resulting in a dependence on the medical profession and an expansion of medicine's control over everyday life.

One of the earliest critics of the *medicalisation* of society was the social theorist and activist Irving Zola. Writing in the 1960s and 1970s, Zola was critical of what he regarded as the 'intrusion' of medicine into many aspects of social life. For Zola (1972), medicine was developing as a major institution of social control, taking over from the traditional institutions that had previously filled this role, i.e. religion and law. Zola (1972: 487) argued that it was becoming:

> [T]he new repository of truth, the place where absolute and often final judgments are made by supposedly morally neutral and objective experts. And these judgments are made, not in the name of virtue or legitimacy, but in the name of health. [This] insidious and often undramatic phenomenon accomplished by 'medicalizing' much of daily living by making medicine and the labels 'healthy' and 'ill' *relevant* to an ever increasing part of human existence.

Put simply, what Zola is arguing is that the institution of medicine is systematically 'medicalising' parts of people's lives that have historically been accepted as 'natural' events, e.g. pregnancy, childbirth, and ageing. He regards medicine's claim to be scientific and neutral as false, highlighting the role of medicine in the prescription of acceptable moral conduct in relation to health, e.g. sexual health and identifying its role as an agency of social control. He states that Western society has created a reliance on the 'expert', a position which medicine has duly exploited (Zola, 1972).

Writing in the same vein, the theologian and philosopher, Ivan Illich (1976), also questions the role of the medical profession, developing a critique of what he regards as the destructive nature of medicine and medicalisation. In his seminal text, *Limits to Medicine: medical nemesis* (Illich, 1976), he outlines the concept of *iatrogenesis*, which basically means 'medical caused illness', and identifies the way in which *iatrogenic* medicine impacts upon society. For Illich, individuals have become, or are at least rapidly becoming, dehumanised, in so far as they turn to the medical profession to 'cure' all their 'problems', including factors associated with everyday living and dying. He states that:

> Medicine undermines health not only through direct aggression against individuals but also through the impact of its social organization on the total milieu [...][Social iatrogenesis] obtains when medical bureaucracy creates ill-health by increasing stress, by multiplying disabling dependence, by generating new painful needs, by lowering the levels of tolerance for discomfort or pain, by reducing the leeway that people are wont to concede to an individual when he suffers, and by abolishing the right to self care.   (Illich, 1976: 49)

For Illich (1976), the process of iatrogenesis can be identified on three specific levels, clinical, social and cultural.

Clinical iatrogenesis

This is the direct result of harmful or negligent medical intervention inflicted by doctors. Examples can range from adverse side effects of prescribed medication, which can lead to the patient having to take further medication to alleviate these side effects, worse still to death brought about by medical intervention, e.g. death caused by allergic reaction to anaesthesia.

Social iatrogenesis

Included here is the medicalisation of everyday 'natural' events, where human conditions are defined within a medical framework, e.g. ageing, anxiety, pregnancy and childbirth. While these conditions were once regarded as part of the natural processes of the individual's life, Western medicine has subsumed and redefined them within the context of biomedicine.

Cultural iatrogenesis

This is not just about the medicalisation of everyday life but, more insidiously, about health professionals destroying the potential for people to deal with their 'human' weaknesses, vulnerability and uniqueness in a personal and autonomous way. For Illich (1976), the medical profession has created a reliance on drugs and medical intervention, which has lead to the inability of individuals to address absence of well being in a more natural way.

Criticisms of the medicalisation thesis:

- Illich and Zola reduce the role of the individual to one of a passive subject of medicalisation. Often the patient can be involved in extensive dialogue with the medical practitioner before medical intervention takes place
- The medicalisation thesis does not account for the health benefits made possible by medical intervention, such as treatment of diabetes and kidney malfunction, where those suffering from the disease can live a 'normal' life as a direct result of receiving medical treatment, but who may die without it
- While surgery may increase levels of illness in the short term, this may be preferable to the patient than having to deal with the long-term effects of illness or disease, e.g. the removal of diseased appendix or operable cancerous tumours
- This thesis does not recognise the autonomy exercised by some individuals in resisting the processes of medicalisation, e.g. the use of alternative therapies
- No credit is given to the preventative work of the medical profession and its influence in the field of health promotion and public health.

The Marxist approach

Marxist approaches to the debate surrounding health, illness and the institution of medicine are located within a wider critique of capitalist society. Here, the structures, processes and actions of the medical profession are examined in relation to their role within the economic and ideological systems of capitalist production. The key thrust of Marxist perspectives on health, which can be clearly identified in the work of the neo-Marxist doctor, Vicente Navvaro (1976, 1978), is that the structures of the medical profession reflect the requirements of the capitalist class. Navarro (1978) regards the medical profession as an institution that serves the interests of capital, and contributes to the smooth running of capitalist society. While certain similarities between Parsons and Navarro can be drawn at this point, it must be noted that where Parsons holds a positive view of the function of the medical profession, Navarro regards it as an agent of the state, replicating the class structure of capitalism and working to benefit the interests of the capitalist class. For Navarro (1978), the social control function of medicine in capitalist societies is, first and foremost, an ideological one; one of the key roles of medicine is to cover-up the fact that issues of health and illness are basically political and collective, *not* individual as the state would have us believe.

Furthermore, for Marxists, the medical profession serves to benefit capitalism through the process of consumption, since medicine, as a major consumer of medical products, drives the market for drugs and medical equipment (Henshaw and Howells, 1999). This consumption can be regarded as primarily working in the interests of capitalism and not for the individual or society as a whole.

The Marxist-feminist, Lesley Doyal (1995), supports Navarro's argument, when she outlines the dynamics of the medical profession's treatment of depression and anxiety in women in the 1970s. During this period, which she describes as the 'tranquilliser epidemic', Doyal (1995) argues that the medical profession over-prescribed medication, such as librium and valium, to women suffering from depression and stress, while failing to consider or address the root causes of patients' anxieties. She states that not only did the medical profession use its authority to 'label' women suffering from depression and stress as 'neurotic', but also created, through the prescription of drugs that allowed their patients to carry out their 'normal' day to day tasks, an increasing demand for the products of the pharmaceutical industry (Doyal, 1995; see also Chapter 11: Crime and Deviance, for further discussion of 'labelling'). In this way, depression and stress in women became 'medicalised', the medical profession extended its 'knowledge' base and authority through its treatment of these patients, and the pharmaceutical companies maintained turnover and profits.

Marxists also argue that medicine tries to make acceptable the *dis*-welfares brought about by a capitalist system focused on making profits at any cost, including that of human lives. This argument can be supported with regard to the following examples:

- The Dalkoi Shield inter-uterine device (IUD), commonly known as the 'coil', was corporately 'dumped' in the US after at least 17 women had died from using it. However, although it was removed from the US market it was not removed from oversees markets where it was still sold for a number of years, even though the potentially life threatening consequences of using the device were already known
- The Thalidomide drug, widely used in the UK during the 1960s to 'treat' pregnant women with morning sickness, was withdrawn due to children of mothers who used it often being born with severe physical disabilities. However this drug was still sold in developing countries for many years after it was banned in the UK.

(adapted from Henshaw and Howells, 1999: 26-7)

For Marxists, the medical profession's focus on curing illness and disease allows individuals to be 'patched up' and returned to work as soon as possible. From this perspective, the only real way to improve health is not through biomedicine, but through addressing the inequalities brought about or caused by the capitalist system.

Criticisms of the Marxist approach:

- It ignores the role of the individual in maintaining good health not all illnesses and ill health are a direct result of the capitalist mode of production
- Countries that have commonly been regarded as 'socialist' (i.e. countries with planned economies built on the key tenets of Marxist ideology) *do not* appear to have a better health record than capitalist countries. In fact, *mortality* and *morbidity* rates have fallen more quickly in countries that have "retained the market as a means of organising economic production" (Hart, 1985: 38)
- Doctors and other health professionals can use their power and status to influence and alter governmental policy, i.e. to positively influence state provision for health care
- Hart (1985) suggests that rather than support capitalism, the medical profession has reduced productivity by increasing the amount of employee 'sick time' it certifies.

Trigger

Having read the section on the Marxist approach to medicine, consider the following questions:

1. When you visit the doctor and are prescribed medication, is it for your benefit alone? Who else might benefit?
2. Is there a financial element to this prescription? Is there profit to be made from ill health?

The symbolic interactionist approach

This theoretical approach is very different to the three approaches already discussed. *Symbolic interactionism* (often referred to as *interactionism*) examines the small scale interaction of people, looking at how the individual affects society as opposed to, for example, structural theories like functionalism or Marxism that tend to focus on how society affects the individual (see Chapter 2: Sociological Theory). In the sociological analysis of health and illness, the value of the interactionist approach lies in its focus on the micro level interactions between individuals (Annandale, 1998; Purdy and Banks, 2001b). For interactionists studying health and illness, it is not the presence of biological abnormality in the individual that is significant, but how it is "perceived, explained and responded to within society" (Jones, 1994: 68), since this has a major influence on the lives of the 'ill'.

This section will focus on *labelling theory*, which developed from interactionism and is most often associated with the works of Howard Becker (1963) and Edwin Lemert (1972), and the concept of *stigma*, which is associated with the work of Irving Goffman (1968). Through the examination of the works of Becker, Lemert and Goffman, the interactionist approach to the social context of health, illness and medicine can be illustrated and the role of medicine as an institution of social control identified.

Labelling theory was first used by Becker and Lemert in the study of crime and deviance (see Chapter 11: Crime and Deviance). They were mainly concerned with how individuals became labelled as deviant and, when labelled, what affect this had on their 'self-concept'. Sociologists studying how illness has come to be viewed by many as a deviant state have taken up the ideas of Becker and Lemert. This can be seen in the work of interactionists whose main concern is how ill and/or disabled people cope with society. As Downes (1999) notes, it is in this context that Lemert's distinction between 'primary' and 'secondary' deviance is important. Primary deviance occurs when a person is labelled, e.g. as being ill or disabled, with

313

secondary deviance occurring when the individual makes changes to her/his lifestyle as a result of the labelling (Taylor, 1999b). It is when an individual is labelled as being in a state of secondary deviation that problems often arise, both for the individual and her/his family and friends.

Interactionists point out that being labelled can have a negative effect on an individual's self-concept, i.e. the way in which she or he may view her or himself. Furthermore, if a label is strong enough it can eventually become the individual's 'master status'. Eventually, the label can bring about a *self-fulfilling prophecy*, i.e. where the individual acts in a manner she or he thinks appropriate to the labelled condition.

As Goffman (1968), another key interactionist, shows, illness and disability often lead to the individual becoming stigmatised. For Goffman, the term stigma is usually used to refer to an attribute that is 'deeply discrediting'. Thus, a stigmatised individual is faced with a situation where she or he has to consider how to 'manage their spoiled identity':

> By definition [...] we [normals] believe the person with a stigma is not quite human. On this assumption we exercise varieties of discrimination, through which we effectively, if often unthinkingly, reduce his life chances. We construct a stigma theory, an ideology to explain his inferiority and account for the danger he represents, sometimes rationalizing an animosity based on other differences [...]. We use specific stigma terms such as cripple, bastard, moron in our daily discourse as a source of metaphor and imagery, typically without giving thought to the original meaning. We tend to impute a wide range of imperfections on the basis of the original one [...]. (Goffman, 1968: 15-6)

Goffman (1968) used the terms 'passing' and 'covering' to explain ways in which those who are not 'normal' try to hide their stigmatising condition. For Goffman, passing can be described quite simply as a means by which the stigmatised attempt to appear 'normal' in social situations. For example, a woman who has had a mastectomy (breast removal) due to breast cancer may have breast implants after surgery. The concept of covering, as the term suggests, is a way in which those with a stigmatising illness conceal their 'problem'. For example, a person who is hard of hearing may lip read, or someone with diabetes may not tell friends. Goffman (1968) warns that the process of passing and covering can cause some people to suffer from anxiety. He argues that the fear of being discovered may well cause the individual further problems.

Goffman (1968) also points out that there are certain individuals who are able to offer help and support to those whom society has stigmatised. He termed such

314

people the 'own' and the 'wise'. The own are those who can empathise because they share the same stigmatising condition or, e.g. attend self-help groups. The wise are 'normal', but their position in life, e.g. doctor, nurse, carer, social worker enables them to be sympathetic and generally more accepting. Goffman (1968) argues that with the wise, individuals with a stigmatising condition can 'be themselves' without feeling anxiety or shame. Furthermore, and on a more positive note, commentators such as Robinson (1988) state that labelling of some illnesses can actually bring great relief to the sufferer, because it legitimises their complaints and validates the 'truth' of their symptoms, e.g. when slowly progressing illnesses such as multiple sclerosis and Parkinson's disease are eventually medically diagnosed (Taylor, 1999b).

While the interactionist approach to the study of health and illness places its focus on the individual rather than the institution of medicine as a whole, the importance of medicine and the medical profession can be seen to lie in the process of labelling. For interactionists, ill health is regarded as "the culturally variable product of deviancy labelling" (Gerhardt, 1989, cited in Jones, 1994: 68), and in contemporary society it is the medical profession that has the power to define and label illness. Through the attachment or removal of specific labels, and the potential for medical intervention, the medical profession regulates what it is to be normal or deviant, healthy or ill, and in doing so can produce/remove stigma. Medicine can apply itself in the processes of what Goffman termed passing and covering, and help the 'patient' to appear 'normal'. For interactionists, it is this role in the definition, labelling and treatment of illness that constructs medicine as an institution of social control.

Criticisms of labelling theory and notions of stigma:

- They do not take any real account of the variety of structural factors that can affect health
- They are often considered as being over deterministic, i.e. they do not really regard the fact that individuals do have choices (although for some these are severely limited – however, Becker did accept that, although extremely difficult at times, labels could be rejected).

Medicine as 'surveillance'

The concept of medicine as a form of 'surveillance' can be seen to emerge in the work of social theorist, Michel Foucault. For Foucault (1971; 1973), medicine controls by creating ideas of what it is to be 'normal', and through the individuals' inclusion in the processes of medical surveillance, i.e. via the processes of self-surveillance.

Foucault (1971) argues that the way in which the medical profession and the layperson view the mind and the body is not the only way in which they have been viewed. For example, in the 17th century those who would now be described as 'mad' or 'mentally ill' were not labelled as such, nor were they separated from the general public, even if their behaviour was what modern medicine would describe as 'a threat to themselves and others'. At this time religious authority was the main administrator of treatment for the sick, and they made little distinction between physical and mental illness (Foucault, 1971). However, through the processes of professionalisation, i.e. training and exam taking, the medical profession grew in size, expanded its activities and replaced religious authorities as the provider of medical treatment.

As the medical profession grew in size and stature so to did its power. Medicine came to be accepted as a progressive approach to the definition and categorisation of illness and disease. Taboos regarding the investigation of the inner workings of dead bodies, previously denied by religious proclamation, were weakened and removed, allowing new approaches to the investigation and discussions on the biological make-up of the human body The body was now opened up to clinical investigation and through its extensive study the concepts of biological normality and 'abnormality' emerged (Jones, 1994). The focus of the medical profession lay first on the classification of the abnormal, i.e. illness and disease, before developing from there to the medical intervention of the surgeon in the removal or repair of the malfunctioning body part.

Foucault (1973) identifies this process of the 're-conceptualisation' of the body as an integral part in the development of what he termed the 'medical gaze'. This approach of investigation, comparison and classification of the body not only allowed the categorisation of the individual, but was also a process that could be extended to society as a whole. Individuals and populations could be investigated, categorised and defined as normal or abnormal. Foucault (1973) argues, that through the 'gaze', the medical profession could survey populations identifying and defining the normal and abnormal through the production of biological data, which in turn could produce a clear legitimacy for medical action and intervention. Through this process the medical profession developed as an institution of social control, characterising and classifying illness and disease, extending and expanding its right to investigate and monitor deviations in health in the individual and the wider population.

From a Foucauldian perspective, the power of the medical profession is generally not coercive power (although it can be at times) but disciplinary (Lupton, 1997). Through the processes of surveillance the medical profession constructs its 'patient', and 'persuades' them to 'understand, regulate and examine' their bodies through comparison with the 'norm', and to think and act in ways that medicine identifies as appropriate (Lupton, 1997). The individual becomes a subject of the medical gaze through the self-surveillance and self-regulation of their health and health practices. In this way, medical discourse controls and regulates health and illness in society through the processes of surveillance, and the construction of the concepts of normal health and health behaviour.

The key Foucauldian concept of *discourse* is of fundamental importance. For Foucault (1972), discourses are ways of speaking about particular subjects or issues. These discourses are not fixed, but are consistently changing as dominant ideas come and go. The emerging medical discourse that replaced religious discourse as the dominant way of 'seeing' the body, not only shaped the language used in discussing the body, but changed the way in which it was constructed, represented and controlled.

Criticisms of medicine as surveillance:

- The language and structure of Foucault's work is often difficult to understand and can appear contradictory in places
- Foucault's concentration on discourse suggests that all power/knowledge comes from the ability to dominate language
- At times it appears that Foucault is arguing that the power the medical profession has over individuals forces them into a passive and compliant role (however, Foucault argues throughout his work that power/knowledge also produce individual and group resistance).

Foucault's work can be seen to have been influential in recent feminist theory, and has been used to explain the way in which women are oppressed by men in society (Sawicki, 1991; McNay, 1992; Lupton, 1995). However, feminists have also recognised that the scope of Foucault's work is limited by the fact that it focuses on the 'masculine subject' to the detriment of the feminine (Jones, 1994).

The feminist approach
The male domination of medicine, and the way in which the medical profession has shaped and defined women's health and health issues, are the key focuses of feminist theorists. While a variety of feminist approaches to women's relationship with biomedicine exist, such as, liberal, Marxist, radical, etc., a common focus lies in the belief that other sociological perspectives do little more than pay lip service to women's experiences (see Chapter 5: Gender).

Historically, women played a central part in the processes of healing and curing. They were taken seriously as lay healers and were solely responsible for delivering children. However, as Doyal (1995), amongst others, points out, as 'male', 'scientifically' founded medicine grew in importance, women were excluded from the practices of medicine other than childbirth. This role was also diminished when high rates of maternal death were blamed on midwives, and reduced further in the late eighteenth century when, amongst other things, the development of childbirth 'tools' by men (e.g. forceps which women were not allowed to use) led to the male obstetrician taking over the role (Annandale, 1998). Women within the medical profession came to be viewed as little more than doctors' 'helpers' in a male-dominated medical practice and midwives came under the supervision of male doctors (Henshaw and Howells, 1999).

Feminists have also been severely critical of medicine in its intervention in the 'natural events' of a woman's life, for example pregnancy, childbirth and the menopause. It has been argued that these processes have been medicalised, thus marginalising women and placing men in control of women's reproductive capacity (Oakley, 1980; Doyal, 1995). These events have been identified as posing a 'risk' to women's health, thereby allowing and justifying the intervention of medicine, leading to the removal of the ability of women to have a natural and 'fulfilling' birth (Oakley, 1980). This argument is supported by Doyal (1995), who states that the medical profession treats pregnancy primarily as a 'pathological' condition and childbirth as 'doctors' work'.

Feminists argue that through the processes outlined above, the institution of biomedicine helps to support and maintain the systems of patriarchy, which oppress women and benefit men. Medicine is seen as an agency of social control where ideas of male superiority dominate and where male oppression of women is legitimised by the male production of 'expert' knowledge. However, there are various criticisms that can be levelled at this approach.

Criticisms of feminist approaches:

- It could be argued that many women have benefited from the medicalisation of women's health, for example, through preventative screening for cervical and breast cancer
- Medical processes such as *in vitro* fertilisation have allowed those who have had 'problems' conceiving, but want to have children, to do so
- The number of female doctors is increasing. Although nowhere near a parity with men, women are slowly extending their influence within the medical profession.

This expansion of women's influence is also evident in the professionalisation of nursing and midwifery – predominately female occupations – that has, amongst other things, benefited women's career chances.

Having discussed the concepts of health and illness through a critical examination of differing theoretical perspectives, which identify medicine as an institution of social control, the second half of this chapter will address factually based aspects of health inequalities. Health inequalities can be seen to be worsening in the UK in general, and in Scotland in particular. This section will examine the health inequalities evident in contemporary society and discuss what can be done to address the problem. It will also identify the implications that the attempt to address these inequalities has for the individual, and society as a whole.

Health Inequalities

> Inequality in health is the worst inequality of all. There is no more serious inequality than knowing that you'll die sooner because you're badly off.
> (Dobson and Department of Health, 1997)

At first glance, it would appear that the health of the individual is a personal and unique experience. However, a closer look at ill health and disease in the UK points to the existence of clear patterns of illness. These patterns are structured and suggest an unequal 'sharing' of good health in contemporary society. Social scientists have studied these patterns of inequality in depth, linking them with levels of poverty, deprivation and social exclusion, thus making a direct connection between levels of health and social class (Townsend and Davidson, 1988; Whitehead, 1988; Shaw, Dorling, Gordon and Davey Smith, 1999). The first section of this chapter addressed theoretical perspectives relating to health, illness and the role of medicine. This section will evaluate health inequalities in relation to social class through the examination of patterns of health and illness in contemporary UK society, placing a particular emphasis on Scotland.

Health inequalities and social class
It should be understood that social class scales based on occupation (see Chapter 4: Social Class) are an abstract concept. They have clear limitations in terms of their ability to define and classify the extensive range of different jobs and employment circumstances that exist in contemporary society. However, due to their comparative ease of measurement and application, occupational scales have been widely used in the study of socio-economic inequality in the UK. With regard to health and health inequalities, this can be seen in the use of the Registrar General's Classification as a tool of analysis in the 'Black Report', published in 1980, which is regarded as the first major contemporary study to link inequalities in health directly to social class:

Inequality is difficult to measure and trends and inequalities in the distribution of income and wealth, for example, cannot yet be related to indicators of health, except indirectly. Partly for those reasons of convenience, therefore, occupational status or class (which is correlated closely with various other measures of inequality) is used as the principal indicator of social inequality in this report.

　　　　　　　　　　　　　　　　　　　　　　　　(Townsend and Davidson, 1988: 42)

The 'Black Report' (1980)

In 1977, David Ennals, the then Secretary for State for Social Services, joined health professionals in expressing concern at life expectancy differences, highlighting the fact that in 1971, the adult male death rate for unskilled male workers was twice that of professional workers (Jones, 1994). Increased governmental attention to differences in life expectancy, allied to growing concern amongst health professionals, led to the setting up of a working group to examine the link between class and health. The group, 'The Working Group on Inequalities in Health', was set up under the guidance of Sir Douglas Black, and undertook an extensive investigation of the relationship between class and health. The working group's report presented compelling evidence of a link between social class and health. Using the Registrar General's Classification, it showed that different social classes had very different experiences of health, and that those in a lower social class were much more likely to be effected by all major diseases (see Chapter 4: Social Class, for the Registrar General's classification system). The report, commonly known as the 'Black Report' found, for example, that:

- For men of economically active age there was a greater inequality of mortality between occupational classes I and V, both in 1970-72 and 1959-63 than in 1949-53
- For economically active men the mortality rates of occupational class III and combined classes IV and V for age groups over 35 either deteriorated or showed little or no improvement between 1959-63 and 1970-72. Relative to the mortality rates of occupational classes I and II they worsened
- For women aged 15-64 the standardised mortality ratios of combined classes IV and V deteriorated. For married and single women in class IV (the most numerous class) they deteriorated at all ages
- Although deaths per thousand live births in England and Wales have diminished among all classes, the relative excess in combined classes IV and V over I and II increased between 1959-63 and 1970-72
- During a period of less than a decade, maternal mortality fell by more than a third. Although that of class I fell less sharply than other classes inequality between the more numerous class II and classes IV and V remained about the same

- Among children between 1 and 4 years of age, there has been a small reduction in the class differential (especially for girls), for children aged 5 to 9 little or no change, but for children aged 10 to 14 an increase in the differential. For boys aged 1-14, mortality ratios for classes IV and V in 1970-72 were *both* higher than for classes I and II for twenty-three of thirty-eight causes of death, compared with only one cause (asthma) where the ratios were lower. For girls the corresponding figures were twenty-two and nought respectively. There is evidence that as rates of child death from a specific condition decline to very low levels class gradients do disappear. The gradual elimination of death from rheumatic heart disease over the post war period provides evidence of this.

> (Townsend and Davidson, 1988: 66-67)

The 'Black Report' focused on mortality rates due to ease of measurement and the problematic nature of defining and classifying morbidity and ill health. It identified a clear and direct link between social class and health inequalities. It also stated that health varied from region to region across the UK, with the South of England experiencing the lowest mortality rates:

> [U]sing [mortality rates] as an indicator of health, the healthiest part of the UK appears to be the southern belt below a line drawn across the country from the Wash to the Bristol Channel.   (Townsend and Davidson, 1988: 49-50)

This regional variation in health was further examined by *The Health Divide* (Whitehead, 1988), which is discussed below. Having highlighted the direct links between social class and health inequalities, the Black Report went on to outline four possible explanations for this relationship, before recommending a programme for the reduction of these inequalities.

Explaining health inequalities
The 'Black Report' offered four 'explanations' for the relationship identified between social class and health inequalities, the artefact explanation, the social selection explanation, the cultural/behavioural explanation and the material/structural explanation. These are briefly outlined below:

1) **Artefact:** This explanation states that the health inequalities identified by the Black Report are merely a product of the research methods used. Class and health are regarded as 'artificial variables', therefore, any research results obtained lack validity (Townsend and Davidson, 1988). From this perspective, this method of measuring social class artificially inflates the size and importance of health differences between classes (Whitehead, 1988), with the dynamic nature of class composition rendering comparison

invalid (Jones, 1994). However, the artefact explanation is commonly regarded as simplistic and unconvincing due to the fact that a variety of research into social inequality points to a consistent relationship between social class and health (Senior and Viveash, 1997). The usefulness of artefact explanations can be seen to lie in the encouragement of researchers to exercise caution with regards to the measurement tools and methods used in their work

2) **Social Selection:** This explanation is loosely based on the Darwinian view of the 'survival of the fittest'. It suggests that people with poor health will naturally 'drift' into the lower classes with healthy individuals climbing the social and occupational ladder. There are few supporters of this explanation and the 'Black Report' states that there is little evidence of a correlation between health status and social drift (Townsend and Davidson, 1998). However, while this explanation can be criticised for accepting, as a given, that improvement in health will lead directly to a higher socio-economic status, it can be argued that there is still some 'truth' in this claim (Moore and Porter, 1998)

3) **Cultural/behavioural:** The basic premise of this explanation is that inequalities in health are caused by negative cultural attitudes, lifestyles and values. It focuses on the individual and identifies their responsibility in influencing their own health (Townsend and Davidson, 1988). An example of this explanation is the suggestion that the 'unhealthy' diet of the 'poor' is not due to lack of income, but to the incorrect choice of foods, lack of exercise and higher rates of smoking and alcohol consumption (Senior and Viveash, 1997). As a result, good health cannot be maintained, eventually resulting in illness. This view has been described as a form of 'victim blaming', whereby individuals are regarded as being responsible for their own health (Senior and Viveash, 1997). Factors such as low income, bad housing and lack of amenities are regarded as having no bearing on the individual's health. However, Blaxter (1990), amongst others, argues that lifestyle is not simply a matter of individual choice, but is shaped by the social environment in which people live. Therefore, access to positive health choices are restricted and individuals must make the most of the resources they have available to them. In this respect, it could be argued that restrictive social circumstances force 'poorer' members of society to make 'reasoned' choices regarding lifestyle, which may be seen as having a detrimental effect on the individual's overall health

4) **Material/structural:** The material/structural explanations suggests that health inequalities exist as a result of differences in material circumstances, which are largely out with the control of the individual (Townsend and Davidson, 1988). This view is supported by the authors of the Black Report,

as well as others, who regard the explanation as central to any discussion of health inequalities (Whitehead, 1988, 1992; Blackburn, 1991). It is argued that there is a direct correlation between poor health and levels of material and structural deprivation in areas of, e.g., income, housing, employment/unemployment and local environment (Senior and Viveash, 1997). Those living in poverty are seen as unable to influence their social position to any great degree and are, therefore, severely restricted in their ability to improve their health. This has led to the call for increased governmental intervention to counteract material and social inequality, and the implementation of social policies that support disadvantaged members of society (Townsend and Davidson, 1988). However, this is a strongly contested political issue with the focus of social support and levels of social provision heavily influenced by governmental ideology (see Chapter 8: Poverty).

Recommendations of the 'Black Report'

In its summary, the 'Black Report' identified material deprivation as the key link between social class and health inequalities. It outlined 37 recommendations to tackle these inequalities, focussing on three key areas – 1) information and research; 2) improved planning of health and personal services (emphasizing prevention, primary care and community health); 3) increased benefits to improve material conditions of the poor, especially children and the disabled (Gillespie and Prior, 1995). By implementing these recommendations, it argued that issues of relative material deprivation could be addressed, which would benefit the health of poorer members of society and, therefore, society as a whole.

Following the submission of the 'Black Report' to the newly elected Conservative government in 1980, its findings and recommendations were largely ignored. The government refused to 'endorse' the main recommendations of the report, questioning the cost of their implementation, and the potential benefits and efficiency of such measures (Gillespie and Prior, 1995). However, while the political will to act on the Black Report was not evident at the time of its publishing, concerns regarding inequalities in health persisted, with the result that studies into health in UK society increased (Gillespie and Prior, 1995).

The Health Divide *(1986)*

In 1986, a study was commissioned by the Health Education Council to update and re-evaluate the findings of the 'Black Report'. This study, entitled *The Health Divide*, supported the findings of much of the research undertaken in the 1980s, including those of the 'Black Report'. *The Health Divide* reaffirmed the existence of class inequalities in relation to health, and pointed towards a widening of the gap in health between the more and less affluent members of society (Whitehead, 1988). While there was a general overall improvement in terms of mortality rates, the report stated that this was not reflected evenly across the class spectrum. Furthermore, it argued that rising levels of chronic ill health were more evident among manual classes than non-manual, providing further evidence of growing health inequalities (Whitehead, 1988).

In addition, the report highlighted the fact that, apart from social class, health inequalities were evident in other direct measures of affluence and poverty, such as housing tenure and employment status (working/non-working), as well as being influenced by ethnic origin, gender, marital status and geographical location, all of which had a direct effect on the health of the individual (Whitehead, 1988; see also Chapter 4: Social Class and Chapter 8: Poverty).

Regional variations in health

The Health Divide investigated 'north/south' variations in health, first outlined in the 'Black Report' (Townsend and Davidson, 1988), which identified the *south of England* as the healthiest area in the UK and the *north* (north of England, Scotland and Wales) as having the poorest health (Whitehead, 1988). It supported the view that a general north/south gradient existed, highlighting research that suggested 'striking regional disparities in health' within Britain (see Table 1). However, it also stated that there was clear evidence of inequalities *between* communities living side by side in the same region, stating that there were distinct differences in the level of health inequalities between occupational class groups across the country, especially in the north where the gap was at its widest (Whitehead, 1988). Whitehead (1988) argued that areas that had higher levels of material and social deprivation exhibited much poorer health and that these areas were concentrated in the north, thereby exaggerating the overall profile of the region.

Table 12.1 Mortality of Men and Women in Different Regions of Britain (1979-80 plus 1982-83) – Direct Age-standardized Death Date Per 1,000

Region	men 20-64	single women 20-59	married women 20-59
Britain	5.57	1.43	2.23
England & Wales	5.43	1.41	2.17
Scotland	6.92	1.62	2.89
Wales	5.86	1.43	2.34

(Source: adapted from Townsend *et al* (1986), derived from OPCS (1986), cited by Whitehead, (1988), in Townsend, Davidson and Whitehead (1988) *Inequalities in Health: The Black Report and the Health Divide*, Harmondsworth: Penguin, p.246)

Conclusions of the 'Black Report' and The Health Divide
Both the 'Black Report' and *The Health Divide* identify a direct link between health and socio-economic status in the UK. While neither report denies that cultural/behavioural explanations can be used to some degree to explain health inequalities, they argue that such factors cannot account for all inequalities in health. Rather:

> [The evidence] suggest[s] that the differences in lifestyle between social groups account for some, but not all, of the observed health gap. Indeed in some cases *most* of the difference in health is not explained by these factors.
>
> (Whitehead, 1988: 296)

Both studies conclude that governmental policies aimed at the individual would be of little use, arguing that any attempt to combat the health inequalities evident in the contemporary UK should focus on wide-ranging social change to address poverty and deprivation by, for example, improving living and working conditions (Whitehead, 1988). However, just as the recommendations of the 'Black Report' were largely ignored, the publication of *The Health Divide* did little to convince the Conservative governments of Margaret Thatcher and John Major that the way to tackle health inequalities lay in the reduction of material deprivation. Instead, the government focused responsibility for health, and the prevention of ill health, on the individual (Gillespie and Prior, 1995).

Trigger

How might the following sociological perspectives explain continuing inequalities in health:

(i) Functionalism; (ii) Marxism; (iii) Symbolic interactionism; (iv) Feminism?

Health promotion – the focus on prevention
In 1992, the government outlined the first national strategy to improve public health through a focus on individuals' lifestyle behaviours, and in doing so took a major step towards justifying governmental influence in day-to-day personal health issues (Adams and Cunning, 2002).

In the government White Paper, *The Health of the Nation* (Department of Health, 1992), targets were set out for preventing ill health and improving levels of morbidity and mortality through the promotion of good health behaviours. It played down the link between material/structural factors and ill health, placing its focus for action on the individual and their cultural/behavioural choices. The paper, which outlined health policy for England, emphasised the need for individuals to improve their lifestyles by paying attention to their 'voluntary behaviours' relating to, for example, diet, smoking, alcohol consumption and exercise (Annandale, 1998). In this way, a *moral* aspect was added to the improvement of health that promoted individual responsibility, while downplaying the influence of wider social and economic factors. Crawford (1977, 1986) has argued that this cultural/behavioural approach to health and illness has led to 'victim blaming', where poor health and illness is attributed to the individual through their actions or inactions relating to personal health. This policy of health promotion and individual responsibility can also be seen in subsequent government publications (Department of Health, 1995, 1998, 1999a, 1999b), and was further supported by the government commissioned report on the future of the National Health Service (NHS), *Securing the Future of Health* (Wanless, 2002).

Trigger

1. Should the fact that an individual largely ignores medical and governmental advice relating to health effect the treatment that is offered on the National Health Service (NHS)?
2. Should non-smokers, non-drinkers and non-drug users be offered priority treatment by the NHS?

In Scotland, responsibility for the promotion of health lies with the Health Education Board for Scotland (HEBS)[1], a branch of the National Health Service. The aim of the Health Education Board is to improve the overall health of the nation and to reduce levels of health inequalities through the promotion and encouragement of good health practices at both the individual and structural level.

> A core goal for HEBS is to support and enable individuals, professionals, communities and organisations to take action throughout Scottish life to improve health with a particular focus on reducing inequalities in health.   (HEBS, 2001)

---

[1] From 1 April 2003, HEBS was amalgamated with the Public Health Institute for Scotland (PHIS), whose role it is to gather information and compile datasets relating to determinants of health and health outcomes in Scotland. The merger will result in the creation of a new health-promoting organisation called 'NHS Health Scotland'.

The Health Education Board (2001) states that individuals require 'supportive environments' if they are to fulfil their full health potential. Therefore, in order to address the inequalities in health evident in Scotland, the promotion of individual responsibility for health must take place within a material/structural framework that addresses the wider issues of social and economic inequality.

Health, Illness and Inequality: the Scottish Context

In 1998, the Labour-led UK government published a Green Paper entitled *Working Together for a Healthier Scotland* (Scottish Office, 1998). The paper outlined a dual approach to improve health in Scotland by first tackling material/structural inequalities and, second, through the promotion of healthier personal behaviours. It stated that in order to improve the health of the nation, poverty, unemployment and poor housing must be tackled in conjunction with the promotion of individual responsibility and proactive behaviour in looking after personal health interests (Scottish Office, 1998). The paper also pointed out that the socio-economic gradient, which could be identified in levels of ill health was also evident in levels of health behaviours, which could be directly linked to poor health.

In this way, lifestyle 'choices', such as smoking, poor diet, lack of physical activity and alcohol and drug misuse, were explicitly linked to socio-economic circumstances, while at the same time being identified, to some extent, as the responsibility of the individual. The Green Paper went on to state that while individuals must make a 'personal investment' in lifestyle choices and be encouraged to take up healthier behaviours, the governmental strategy for tackling illness and ill health must place its focus primarily on addressing their structural underpinnings:

> *Simply addressing disease and lifestyle cannot deliver what is needed.* The first part of a cohesive strategy for a healthier, more equitable, Scotland must be to counter the life circumstances which can give rise to poor health, and foster those which generate good health. Strong foundations must be put in place. These include a job, a home, a good education and an attractive environment [...]. Lifestyle topics are the second level, calling for strong and supportive health education, underpinned by appropriate policies including regulation.
>
> (Scottish Office, 1998: 33)

Around the same time, the *Independent Inquiry into Inequalities in Health Report* (*The Acheson Report)* (Department of Health, 1998) was set up to look at health inequalities in England. Reflecting the findings of the Scottish Green Paper, the report outlined a clear agenda for tackling illness and poor health through the reduction of health inequalities.

Trigger

Thinking back to the explanations for health inequalities given in the 'Black Report', which explanation(s) do you think is/are underpinning the focus of the Green Paper *Working Together for a Healthier Scotland* (Scottish Office, 1998)?

The Widening Gap (1999)

Following *Working Together for a Healthier Scotland* and the 'Acheson Report', a study by the Townsend Centre for International Poverty Research was published, which drew even more attention to the health inequalities in the UK (see Chapter 4: Social Class and Chapter 8: Poverty). In the report *The Widening Gap* (Shaw *et al*, 1999), it was argued that not only were health inequalities still evident in Britain at the end of the 20th century but, moreover, the gap in health between the poorer and better off members of society was growing. Furthermore, following from *The Health Divide*, the report highlighted the inequalities evident between groups living in particular geographical locations (based on parliamentary constituencies), identifying a clear discrepancy between standards of health in the *north* and the *south* of Britain (Shaw *et al*, 1999). Working from standardised mortality rates (a statistical measure which allows groups with different age and sex distributions to be compared – see Shaw *et al*, 1999: xxi), the study compared the million people with the 'best health' with the million people with the 'worst health', according to local government constituency (Shaw *et al.*, 1999). The report showed that Glasgow topped the table of poor health with six of the city's constituencies included in the top fifteen of Britain's 'worst health' areas – Anniesland, Springburn, Maryhill, Shettleston, Pollok, and Baillieston, with Glasgow Govan, Greenock and Inverclyde and Glasgow Kelvin accounting for another 3 places in the 'worst' 15 (Shaw *et al*, 1999). Shettleston was shown to have a death rate 2.3 times the national average and it was calculated that if the people in Shettleston had experienced the same mortality rates as areas showing the lowest rates of mortality, that 71 % of deaths under 65 would not have occurred (Shaw *et al*, 1999).

The report stated that geographical location and socio-economic indicators such as income, wealth, education, and occupation were closely related and had a direct effect on individuals' health status. It also argued that increasing inequalities in health are the product of a 'clustering' of disadvantages relating to "opportunity, material circumstances and behaviours related to health," a "polarisation of life chances" (Shaw *et al*, 1999: 65). As with the *Working Together for a Healthier Scotland* Green Paper, *The Widening Gap* stated that behaviour contrary to good health, e.g. smoking and poor diet, are 'strongly influenced' by the individual's social circumstances, and that the way to tackle health inequalities was to address wider social disadvantage and inequality, "[policies aimed at reducing inequalities] must be aimed at the fundamental causes of inequality, rather than solely at some of the intermediary processes in this chain" (Shaw *et al*, 1999: 106). It argued that inequalities in health should be addressed through the alleviation of poverty, which should be undertaken through a redistribution of wealth and resources:

> Poverty can be reduced by raising the standards of living of poor people through increasing their incomes 'in cash' or 'in kind'. The costs would be borne by the rich and would reduce inequalities overall – simultaneously reducing inequalities in health.   (Shaw *et al*, 1999: 169)

The relative 'poor' health position of Scotland was further highlighted by the Office of National Statistics report *United Kingdom Health Statistics* (Office of National Statistics, 2001), which compared and contrasted the 'health care systems and health outcomes' of Scotland, England, Wales and Northern Ireland. Some key findings of the report were:

- Scotland has the highest mortality rate in the UK (both male and female) although infant death rates (under one year old) are slightly lower than rest of the UK
- In 1999, Scotland had the highest death rates for all ages from ischaemic heart disease, lung cancer, all neoplasms (tumours/abnormal growths) taken together, stroke, suicide, alcohol, drugs and infectious diseases
- Scotland has the lowest life expectancy in the UK – 72.4 for males and 77.9 for females
- The biggest difference between life expectancy for men and women is in Scotland, at 5.5 years, though this has fallen from 6.4 years in 1971. Figures for Scotland are not much different from those for the other regions in the UK
- The proportion of people with diagnosed HIV who contracted it from injecting drugs is much higher in Scotland than in the rest of the United Kingdom, 34 per cent compared with 7 percent in the United Kingdom as a whole
- The overall incidences of malignant cancers are higher in Scotland than the rest of UK.

(adapted from Office of National Statistics, 2001: Chapter 2)

Edinburgh and Glasgow (1999)

The 'Widening Gap' report coincided with the publication of a comparative study entitled, *Edinburgh and Glasgow: contrasts in competitiveness and cohesion*

(Bailey, Turok, and Docherty, 1999), which highlighted the health discrepancies between and within the city regions of Glasgow (Greater Glasgow district) and Edinburgh (Lothian district). The study showed that the national geographical health inequalities identified by The Widening Gap were evident when comparing Glasgow and Edinburgh. While both cities had areas of affluence and deprivation, Glasgow was seen to have a greater percentage of deprived areas and higher than average levels of mortality and morbidity (Bailey *et al*, 1999). The report also highlighted the relationship between economic inactivity and ill health, suggesting a link between the decline of work in Glasgow over the previous decade and increasing levels of mental illness (Bailey *et al*, 1999).

Following on from previous reports, the authors of the *Edinburgh and Glasgow* study argued that the way forward in combating these geographical health inequalities was to address social and economic deprivation in 'poorer' areas at a structural level, while highlighting the importance of tackling behaviour related health issues such as smoking, poor diet and lack of exercise at the level of the individual. However, reflecting the findings of *The Widening Gap*, it stated that 'victim blaming' should be avoided, as behavioural aspects of lifestyle were rooted in surrounding economic and social conditions (Bailey *et al*, 1999).

Scotland's Health: The International Context

Although the evidence shows that health inequalities have been increasing between the poorer and more affluent members of Scottish society, there has been an overall general trend towards improvements in health (Scottish Executive, 2002). However, the *Working Together for a Healthier Scotland* Green Paper stated that Scotland's record in the 'international health league' was 'unenviable', arguing that the progress evident in Scotland's health was 'modest' when compared to other Western European nations (Scottish Office, 1998). This view was supported by the *Health in Scotland 2001* report, published by the Scottish Executive (2002), which stated that while health in Scotland has, in general, improved, a gap between Scotland and other comparable countries remains. Therefore:

> Scotland's health is crucially important. However, it lags behind other Western European countries and many areas of the rest of the UK. Scotland has the potential to be a much healthier nation. It has been held back by deprivation and inequality on a substantial scale as was highlighted in last year's report, *Health in Scotland 2000*. Improvements in health have been achieved but have yet to be shared equally by all members of society. Scotland is keeping track with health improvements in the rest of the UK and Western Europe, but to date remains persistently behind.   (Scottish Executive, 2002: 7)

The report stated that while the improvement of levels of life expectancy in Scotland were improving at "neither the worst or the best rate," if Scotland was to catch up with comparable European countries, "additional health gains" must be made and life expectancy increased at a "faster rate" (Scottish Executive, 2002: 7).

What can be done?

In the *Health in Scotland 2001* report the Chief Medical Officer, Dr E.M. Armstrong, highlighted the key findings of the report and outlined a strategy to promote better health within Scotland. He stated that the report provided a backdrop against which an 'essential programme of investment in Scotland's future health and well-being' could be planned to provide for the 'future of Scotland's health'. Dr Armstrong spoke of the 'double burden' of ill health facing the population of Scotland –the growing levels of chronic disease and the re-emergence of infectious disease – and argued that the way to address these problems lay in the promotion of a healthier lifestyle, improved monitoring of health and more 'successful' management of healthcare. He stated that health services must work in partnership with local authorities and other departments of the Scottish Executive, in tackling the 'causes' of poor health with individuals, communities and the voluntary and public services all accepting their role in the advancement of positive health. The focus of this commitment was identified as lying in the tackling of specific causes of ill health such as "poverty and social exclusion, tobacco, drugs, excessive use of alcohol, poor diet, obesity and lack of exercise" (Scottish Executive, 2002: 5).

The report set out a *threefold* policy for improving health and tackling health inequalities, which included:

1. *Influencing lifestyles* to promote healthy behaviour and minimise lifestyles that cause ill health
2. *Focusing on priority health topics* – including action on coronary heart disease, cancer and mental health, especially in the younger and older age groups
3. *Improving life circumstances* to influence the wider determinants of health.
                                                      (Scottish Executive, 2002: 12)

It identified strategies for addressing the specific areas in which poor health behaviour was seen as detrimental to health, outlining how these strategies should be implemented and setting specific targets in each area. It made the link between structural and behavioural factors affecting health, arguing that through increased knowledge of good health behaviour the individual could actively enhance their lifestyle within a framework of governmental improvement of life circumstances. The report stated that, in this way, the health of the poorest members of society could be improved to the extent that the gap in health between the most and least deprived could be actively closed, benefiting the overall health of Scotland (Scottish Executive, 2002).

It remains to be seen whether the strategies suggested in the *Health in Scotland 2001* report have the effect of reducing the health inequalities in Scotland and the health gap between Scotland and the rest of Western Europe. However, as it stands, Scotland's health in relation to comparable countries is of great cause for concern, and it would appear that the first step in addressing this problem lies in tackling the inequalities in health that are evident at a national level. While poverty and deprivation continue to adversely affect less affluent individuals' health, both at a material/structural and cultural/behavioural level, and while the gap in health between the 'poorer' and 'better off' members of Scottish society continues to widen, there would appear to be little chance of catching up with the rest of Western Europe in the 'international health league'.

Conclusion

After reading this Chapter you should be able to think more deeply about all aspects of health, illness and the role of medicine in contemporary society. Each time you, or someone you know, go to the doctor, attend hospital or take some form of medicine, think back to the social aspects of health and illness discussed in this Chapter. Develop your *sociological imagination* by identifying a picture of the institution of medicine that extends beyond the biomedical understanding of health and illness, and addresses its social role.

Chapter Summary

- The sociology of health and illness developed as an alternative approach to the evaluation of medicine and the medical profession.
- 'Biomedicine' is the dominant model for health and illness in Western society.
- The role of biomedicine has been questioned by sociologists, who have argued that medicine exists as an institution of social control.
- Six theoretical approaches to health were examined – 'functionalist', 'medicalisation thesis', 'Marxist', 'symbolic interactionist', 'surveillance' and 'feminist'.
- The functionalist approach regarded the control function of medicine as positive, whereas the other approaches view it negatively.
- The second section of the chapter focused on the health inequalities evident in contemporary UK society.

- These health inequalities were identified in relation to the 'Black Report' and *The Health Divide*.
- The 'Black Report' offered four possible explanations for the existence of health inequalities – artefact, social selection, cultural/behavioural and material/structural.
- While health in the UK is improving in general, the gap between the richest and poorest members of society is widening.
- Regional variations in health were identified, highlighting particular issues within the Scottish context.
- The role of health promotion was examined in relation to contemporary approaches to improving individuals' health chances.
- It has been suggested that in order to improve overall health in Scotland and reduce health inequalities, action must be taken at both the individual and societal level.
- It was shown that just as material/structural factors influence health chances, cultural/behavioural aspects of health behaviour are also underpinned by social circumstances.
- The *Health in Scotland 2001* report stated that the government must work in conjunction with the individual, in the promotion and management of everyday health and healthcare.

Further Reading

Adams, L., Amos, M. and Munro, J. (eds.) (2002) *Promoting Health: Politics and Practice*, London: Sage

Davey, B., Gray, A. and Seale, C. (eds.) (1996) *Health and Disease: A Reader*, 2nd Edition, Buckingham: Open University Press

Hardey, M. (1998) *The Social Context of Health*, Buckingham: Open University Press

Jones, L.J. (1994) *The Social Context of Health and Health Work*, Basingstoke: Macmillan

Senior, M. and Viveash, B. (1997) *Health and Illness*, Basingstoke: Macmillan

Townsend, P., Davidson, N. and Whitehead, M. (eds.) *Inequalities in Health: The Black Report and the Health Divide*, Harmondsworth: Penguin

Useful Websites

BBC News: Health: news.bbc.co.uk/1/hi/health/default.stm
British Sociology Association – Medical Sociology Study Group: www.britsoc.org.uk/about/medsoc.htm
Department of Health: www.doh.gov.uk/index.html
HEBS/PHIS: www.hebs.scot.nhs.uk/; www.phis.org.uk/
(NHS Scotland) Scotland's Health on the Web: www.show.scot.nhs.uk./
(NHS Scotland) Information and Statistics Division: www.show.scot.nhs.uk./isd/
Social Science Information Gateway – Sociology of Medicine:
www.sosig.ac.uk/roads/subject-listing/World-cat/socmed.html
World Health Organization – Regional Office for Europe:
www.who.dk/eprise/main/WHO/Home/TopPage

Bibliography

Adams, L. and Cunning, F. (2002) 'Promoting Social and Community Development in Sheffield: A reflection of ten years work', in Adams, L. Amos, M and Munro, J. (eds.) *Promoting Health: Politics and Practice*, London: Sage

Annandale, E. (1998) *The Sociology of Health and Medicine*, Cambridge: Polity Press

Bailey, N., Turok, I. and Docherty, I. (1999) *Edinburgh and Glasgow: contrasts in competitiveness and cohesion*, Glasgow: University of Glasgow, Department of Urban Studies

BBC (1999) 'North-South health divide 'widening', http://news.bbc.co.uk/1/hi/health/545517.stm

BBC (2000) 'The health gap – Britain and Europe', http://news.bbc.co.uk/1/hi/health/608905.stm

Becker, H. (1963) *Outsiders: Studies in the Sociology of Deviance*, Basingstoke: Macmillan

Birchenall, M. and Birchenall, P. (eds.) (1998) *Sociology as Applied to Nursing and Healthcare*, London: Bailliere Tindall

Blackburn, C. (1991) *Poverty and Health: Working with Families*, Milton Keynes: OU Press

Blaxter, M. (1990) *Health and Lifestyles*, London: Tavistock

Bunton, R., Nettleton, S. and Burrows, R. (eds.) (1995) *The Sociology of Health Promotion: Critical Analyses of Consumption, Lifestyle and Risk*, London: Routledge

Bury, M. and Anderson, R. (eds.) (1988) *Living With Chronic Illness: The experience of patients and their families*, London: Unwin Hyman

Conrad, P. and Kern, R. (eds.) (1986) *The Sociology of Health and Illness: Critical Perspectives*, New York, NY: St. Martin's Press

Crawford, R. (1977) 'You are Dangerous to Your Health: the Ideology and Politics of Victim Blaming', *International Journal of Health Services*, 7: pp. 663-80

Crawford, R. (1986) 'Individual Responsibility and Health Politics' in Conrad, P. and Kern, R. (eds.) *The Sociology of Health and Illness: Critical Perspectives*, New York, NY: St. Martin's Press

Crompton, R. (1993) *Class and Stratification*, Cambridge: Polity Press

Daykin, N. and Naidoo, J. (1995) 'Feminist critiques of health promotion' in Bunton, R., Nettleton, S. and Burrows, R. (eds.) *The Sociology of Health Promotion: Critical Analyses of Consumption, Lifestyle and Risk*, London: Routledge

Dobson, F. and Department of Health (1997) 'Government takes action to reduce health inequalities', Press Release in response to the Joseph Rowntree Foundation's publication *Death in Britain*, www.newsrelease-archive.net/coi/depts/GDH/coi1581d.ok

Department of Health (1992) *Health of the Nation*, London: Department of Health

Department of Health (1995) *Fit for the Future: Second Progress Report on the Health of the Nation*, London: Department of Health

Department of Health (1998) *Independent Inquiry into Inequalities in Health Report* (The Acheson Report), www.archive.official-documents.co.uk/document/doh/ih/ih.htm

Department of Health (1999a) *Our Healthier Nation: A Contract for Health*, London: HMSO

Department of Health (1999b) *Saving Lives: Our Healthier Nation*, London: Department of Health

Downes, D. (1999) 'Crime and Deviance', in Taylor, S. (ed.) (1999a) *Sociology: Issues and Debate*, Basingstoke: Macmillan

Doyal, L. (1995) *What Makes Women Sick: Gender and the Political Economy of Health*, Basingstoke: Macmillan

Edgell, S. (1993) *Class*, London: Routledge

Figlio, K. (1987) 'The lost subject of medical sociology', in Scambler, G. (ed.) *Sociological Theory and Medical Sociology*, London: Tavistock

Foucault, M. (1971) *Madness and Civilisation: An Archaeology of Medical Perception*, London: Tavistock

Foucault, M. (1972) *Archaeology of Knowledge*, London: Tavistock

Foucault, M. (1973) *Birth of the Clinic*, London: Tavistock

334

Gillespie, R. and Gerhardt, C. (1995) 'Social dimensions of sickness and disability', in Moon, G. and Gillespie, P. (eds.) *Society and Health*, London: Routledge

Gillespie, R. and Prior, R. (1995) 'Health inequalities', in Moon, G. and Gillespie, P. (eds.) *Society and Health*, London: Routledge

Goffman, E. (1968) *Stigma: notes on the management of spoiled identity*, Harmondsworth: Penguin

Hart, N. (1985) *The Sociology of Health and Medicine*, Ormskirk: Causeway Press

Health Education Board for Scotland (HEBS) (2001) 'Health Education Board for Scotland: An overview', www.hebs.scot.nhs.uk/info/about/whofulltext.cfm?CA=whohebs&TxtTCode=166

Henshaw, R. and Howells, B. (1999) *Health*, London: Hodder and Stoughton

Illich, I. (1976) *Limits to Medicine: medical nemesis*, Basingstoke: Macmillan

Lemert, E. (1972) *Human Deviance, Social Problems, and Social Control*, Englewood Cliffs, NJ: Prentice-Hall

Lupton, D. (1995) *The Imperative of Health: Public Health and the Regulated Body*, London: Sage

Lupton, D. (1997) 'Foucault and the Medicalisation Critique', in Petersen, A. and Bunton, R. (eds.) *Foucault: Health and Medicine*, London: Routledge

McKeown, T. (1979) *The Role of Medicine: Dream, Mirage or Nemesis?* Oxford: Blackwell

McNay, L. (1992) *Foucault and Feminism*, Cambridge: Polity Press

Moon, G. and Gillespie, P. (eds.) (1995) *Society and Health*, London: Routledge

Moore, R. and Porter, S. (1998) "Poverty in Health Care", in Birchenall, M. and Birchenall, P. (eds.) *Sociology as Applied to Nursing and Healthcare*, London: Bailliere Tindall

Navarro, V. (1976) *Medicine Under Capitalism*, New York, NY: Prodist

Navarro, V. (1978) *Class Struggle, the State and Medicine: An Historical and Contemporary Analysis of the Medical Sector in Great Britain*, London: Martin Robertson

Oakley, A. (1980) *Women Confined*, London: Martin Robertson

Office of National Statistics (ONS) (2002) *The National Statistics Socio-economic Classification*, www.statistics.gov.uk/methods_quality/ns_sec/default.asp

Office of National Statistics (ONS) (2001) *United Kingdom Health Statistics*, www.statistics.gov.uk/statbase/Product.asp?vlnk=6637&More=N

Parsons, T. (1951) *The Social System*, New York, NY: Free Press

Petersen, A. and Bunton, R. (eds.) (1997) *Foucault: Health and Medicine*, London: Routledge

Purdy, M. and Banks, D. (eds.) (2001a) *The sociology and politics of health*, London: Routledge

Purdy, M. and Banks, D. (2001b) 'Introduction', in Purdy, M. and Banks, D. (eds.) *The sociology and politics of health*, London: Routledge

Robinson, W. (1988) 'Reconstructing Lives: negotiating the meaning of multiple sclerosis', in Bury, M. and Anderson, R. (eds.) *Living With Chronic Illness: The experience of patients and their families*, London: Unwin Hyman

Rowntree, S. (1901) *Poverty: A Study of Town Life*, Basingstoke: Macmillan.

Russell, H. (2002) 'Regeneration and Health', in Adams, L., Amos, M. and Munro, J. (eds.) *Promoting Health: Politics and Practice*, London: Sage

Sawicki, J. (1991) *Disciplining Foucault: Feminism, Power and the Body*, New York, NY: Routledge

Scambler, G. (ed.) (1987) *Sociological Theory and Medical Sociology*, London: Tavistock

Scambler, G. (ed.) (1991) *Sociology as Applied to Medicine*, 3rd Edition, London: Bailliere Tindall

Scottish Executive (SE) (2002) *Health in Scotland 2001*, Edinburgh: The Stationery Office

Scottish Office (SO) (1998) *Working Together for a Healthier Scotland: A Consultation Document*, Edinburgh: The Stationery Office

Seale, C., Pattison, S. and Davey, B (eds.) (2001) *Medical Knowledge, Doubt and Certainty*, Buckingham: Open University Press

Seale, C. (2001) 'Medicalisation and Surveillance' in Seale, C., Pattison, S. and Davey, B. (eds.) *Medical Knowledge, Doubt and Certainty*, Buckingham: Open University Press

Shaw, M., Dorling, D., Gordon, D. and Davey Smith, G. (1999) *The Widening Gap: Health inequalities and policy in Britain*, Bristol: Policy Press

335

Taylor, S. (ed.) (1999a) *Sociology: Issues and Debates*, Basingstoke: Macmillan

Taylor, S. (1999b) 'Health, Illness and Medicine' in Taylor, S. (ed.) *Sociology: Issues and Debates*, Basingstoke: Macmillan

Townsend, P, and Davidson, N. (1988) 'The Black Report' in Townsend, P., Davidson, N. and Whitehead, M. (eds.) *Inequalities in Health: The Black Report and the Health Divide*, Harmondsworth: Penguin

Townsend, P., Phillimore, P. and Beattie, A. (1986) *Inequalities in Health in the Northern Region: an Interim Report*, Bristol: Northern Regional Health Authority/Bristol University

Wanless, D. (2002) *Securing our Future Health: taking a long-term view*, London: Treasury

Whitehead, M. (1988) 'The Health Divide', in Townsend, P., Davidson, N. and Whitehead, M. (eds.) *Inequalities in Health: The Black Report and the Health Divide*, Harmondsworth: Penguin

Whitehead, M. (1992) 'The concepts and principles of equity and health', *International Journal of Health Services* 22, 3, pp. 429-45

World Health Organisation (WHO) (1948) *Preamble to the Constitution of the World Health Organization as adopted by the International Health Conference*, New York, NY: Official Records of the World Health Organization, No.2, p.100

Zola, I. (1972) 'Medicine as an Agent of Social Control', *The Sociological Review*, 20, 4, pp. 487-504

Chapter 13 Culture

Alex Law

Introduction

The term, culture, is commonly used in everyday life in a variety of ways. To some, culture means manners, etiquette and other such characteristics associated with being 'cultured'. Others see knowledge and appreciation of certain 'arts', such as the opera, ballet or classical music, compared to a rock concert or rave, as 'cultured'. What can be found in each of these 'common sense' definitions of culture, then, is that the term embodies codes of 'proper' conduct and what is considered *appropriate* and praiseworthy behaviour.

At the outset and of importance to your understanding, it must be made clear that this chapter does not intend to visit all the particular theoretical dimensions of culture, but to provide you with a more critical approach to the topic. With this in mind you are encouraged to compare ideas that will have been presented to you earlier in this Book with those that are illustrated here. In so doing, you should be making direct links with other chapters.

This Chapter will consider some issues associated with defining culture and examine these in an historical context that demonstrates a separation of culture between and within social classes (see Chapter 4: Social Class).

The challenge of this chapter is for you to identify how notions of culture are central to your everyday lives. Your way of life is structured through material and cultural practices, which helps us make sense of society, although ideas about an ever increasing population/cultural diversity perhaps serves to challenge how we understand the concept of culture. The common sense definitions of culture, as mentioned above, are not the only ones in currency, and thus we will turn to more 'scientific' definitions of the term.

This Chapter will explore the relationship between dominant and subordinate cultures by looking at debates about 'popular culture'. The rise of popular culture in the modern period will be described, before looking at some debates about elite cultures and 'mass culture'. This will lead us into a discussion about different kinds of youth cultures, or sub-cultures as they are known. Finally, we will briefly consider the impact of technology and globalisation on culture and the shaping of cultural tastes by social class.

Defining Culture
Non-sociological definitions

'Sociobiology' is a branch of the academic discipline of biology that seeks to apply the scientific principles of biology and genetics to explaining human behaviour. For example, the sociobiologists, Tiger and Fox (1972), adopt the stance taken by the evolutionist, Charles Darwin (1809-1882), which is that all human behaviour can be explained through biological make up.

Variations in culture and changes over time can be directly related to the biological needs of a community or group; that is, biological need *determines* culture. The zoologist of television documentary fame, Desmond Morris, commonly argues that while culture is essentially socially constructed, the human need to construct cultural codes has genetic roots. Humans, like other animals, have a genetic drive to preserve the life of the group and do so by establishing systems of shared meaning.

Psychoanalytic theory in psychology also ground definitions of culture in notions of biological need. Sigmund Freud (1961 [1923]) suggests that human behaviour is based on a constant interplay between naturally occurring biological needs and learned cultural norms and values. Freud refers to three main psychic structures in the human mind that control behaviour – the *id*, which pursues the fulfilment of biological drives, the *ego*, which is the reflective, rational element and the *superego,* through which we learn the cultural rules that govern behaviour. When cultural rules conflict with natural desires, for example, the associated suppression of natural instincts results in the development of 'psychic disturbances' such as 'neuroses' and 'perversions', according to Freud (1961 [1923]).

Non-sociological definitions of culture, then, argue that the shared meanings, customs and traditions that humans develop can be directly traced to biological roots.

Sociological definitions

Sociological definitions, by contrast, focus on the social origins and aspects of culture. In other words culture, as represented by shared meanings, language and the use of symbols, codes of conduct, religious practices, customs and traditions, norms and values, have *social* rather than *biological* roots. Cultural rules vary over time and place, which necessitates analyses of social context and the 'social forces' that pattern and maintain human life and lifestyle. Cultural rules often differ between and within groups and rely on members of a community, group, or nation sharing sets of unspoken assumptions, as Box 13.1, below, illustrates.

Box 13.1 Rab C. Nesbitt and Scottish Culture

Consider the following scene taken from a script for the popular television comedy, *Rab C. Nesbitt*. What cultural assumptions do we need to share in order to get the joke, here?

Scene 4. The Nesbitts' living room.
Nesbitt enters with a bag.

JAMSIE: Awhaw! Here Rab! Where's my tacos Rab?

DODIE: Got my pakora?

ANDRA: Where's the *mignons morceaux*?

NESBITT: Never mind all that foreign junk food crap! (*Chucking the bag down.*) Yeez can have some good traditional Scottish junk food and like it!

DODIE: What's he got?

ANDRA: Paris buns.

NESBITT: I was reared on Paris buns! Half of Govan was reared on Paris buns! Yi canny afford a dinner? Pamp them full of thae things! Yi know the trouble with youse people, yeez've lost yir national identity!

JAMSIE: I don't like your drift pal. I resent the implication that I don't love Scotland!

DODIE: Aye, I love Scotland better than any of yeez. (*Bearing his bare arm to show 'Bonnie Scotland' tattoo*). Look, beat that!

ANDRA: (*Exposing bare belly showing 'Scotland for ever' tattoo.*) ... Beat that!

JAMSIE: (*Lowering trousers to reveal an arse cheek with an 'I love Scotland' tattoo.*) Beat that!

(Source: Pattison, I. (1992) *More Rab C. Nesbitt Scripts*, London: BBC Books, pp. 43-4)

First, we would need to know that tacos, pakora and *mignon morceaux* are particular kinds of food that are not generally seen as native to Scotland. Then we would need to know what a 'Paris bun' is and that it is considered *native* to Scotland, despite being named after the capital city of France. To more fully get the joke, some idea is also needed that Govan is a well-known, even notorious part of Glasgow. The imagery of Govan depends on a cultural stereotype of the 'Glesga keelie' or 'weegie' (short for Glaswegian), a small-minded, parochial know-all that sees Glasgow (or Govan) as the centre of the known universe. As far as Rab C. Nesbitt is concerned, a diet of Paris buns is one thing that counts towards an 'authentic' Scottish national identity. The other three male characters go to great lengths to display their own patriotism, which has been called into question by their preference for 'foreign junk food'. Tattoos on various bodily parts are displayed as 'badges of national identity' expressing their undying love for Scotland.

Perhaps the key cultural assumption that we need to share to get the joke is that we almost instinctively belong to a certain nation, in this case Scotland. We can use cultural clues such as symbols, food and speech, to mark out what counts as a 'true' Scot from a non-Scot. The characters use of language, the Glasgow dialect, is recognisably Scottish. Words are used like 'canny' (cannot), 'pamp' (pump), 'thae' (those), 'youse' (you, plural), 'yeez've' (you have, plural), 'yir' (your). The Glaswegian accent is part of a living language, but has been viewed in some quarters as a mark of cultural inferiority and ignorance compared to 'literary Scots', a language *invented* by writers and poets. Despite the fact that *nowhere* is literary Scots the spoken language of a community, it is seen to be particularly lyrical and expressive, a mark of cultural distinction. We will look more closely at cultural distinction near the end of this chapter.

Trigger

1. Is the character, Rab C. Nesbitt, a typical product of Scottish culture?
2. How did you come about your answer?

Many in Scotland, therefore, see the kind of images represented by characters like Rab C. Nesbitt as negative and backward looking. One point could be that the 'Rab C. Nesbitt dilemma' *limits* how Scotland and Glasgow are represented culturally, bound up with outdated and unappealing visions of Scottish life. One vision might appear in pictures or on screen posing in vaguely fashionable casual clothes while Nesbitt dresses in string vest, worn-out unfashionable formal suit and a head bandage. A comparison with Nesbitt could be Stuart Cosgrove, well known in Scotland as a 'football fan/pundit' from his radio show, *Off the Ball*, with presenter Tam Cowan. Nevertheless, there are some similarities in that both wish to come across as 'punters'.

Yet Cosgrove, unlike Nesbitt, is also part of a 'cultural elite' in Scotland. He is Channel 4 Head of Programmes for Nations and Regions, a Board Member of Scottish Enterprise and other influential bodies. He is a Doctor of Philosophy, a former college lecturer and has been honoured for his contribution to cultural life by universities such as John Moores in Liverpool, Stirling and Abertay Dundee. *Dr* Cosgrove has what the 'post-Marxist' sociologist, Pierre Bourdieu (1984), called 'cultural capital', in that his cultural knowledge has been recognised and rewarded by the 'dominant' (or elite) culture. Cosgrove, however, does not use his cultural capital to simply reproduce the dominant culture. He is also well versed in popular culture and is the author of a fascinating study of the 'Zoot Suit riots', which occurred in the United States in the summer of 1943.

Cosgrove (1991) tells the story of how urban blacks and hispanic youth – called *pachucos* – were attacked by mobs in Los Angeles and other major US cities, ostensibly because their exaggerated use of clothing material offended wartime rationing of fabrics. Yet the riots were about more than clothing. It was what they stood for *symbolically* that lay behind the attacks. Zoot suits were viewed as 'un-American', un-manly, non-white and associated with gangs, crime and disorder. As Cosgrove (1991: 9) points out:

> Thus the polarisation between servicemen and *pachucos* was immediately visible: the chino shirt and battledress were evidently uniforms of patriotism, whereas wearing a zoot suit was a deliberate and public way of flouting the regulation of rationing.

It would not be unusual for both Rab C. Nesbitt and the *pachuco* to be pictured being accosted by police officers, reflecting the use, historically, of the law to control cultures of the poor and marginalized (see Chapter 4: Social Class, Chapter 6: Race and Ethnicity and Chapter 8: Poverty).

The Rise of Popular Culture

As the 1943 Zoot Suit riots demonstrate, it is useful to place the rise of popular culture in some historical context. As British society entered the modern period around the eighteenth century, culture was transformed in a number of ways, principally by the authorities regulating what the majority of people did and by the gradual commercialisation of cultural activities. Until then, popular recreations were based on the seasonal rhythms of agricultural society and the Christian calendar. Feasts, village football, fairs, parish wakes, and 'blood-sports' were locally organised, participatory and small-scale events. Such pursuits did not add-up to a separate 'folk culture' of the common people. They were patronised by local landowners and aristocrats, who saw in such pastimes a harmless way to maintain 'social order' (see Chapter 4: Social Class), although were contested when such traditions came under threat.

Frequently, popular recreations became the defiant occasion for drunkenness, sexual permissiveness and, sometimes, political rebellion against the enclosure of common land, bread prices or new limits imposed on popular recreations. Such cultures threatened to escape the control of the authorities, undermine the traditional deference of the poor and disrupt regular work patterns being introduced by the new capitalist economy.

The cultures of the upper and lower classes began to separate and diverge by the late eighteenth century. Plebeian (lower class) blood sports, such as bear-baiting and cock-fighting, were seen as a barbaric and uncivilised affront to the new rational, enlightened capitalist morality. Most of these practices were banned by the 1840s.

This had a social class bias, with the 'field sports' of 'gentlemen', hunting and shooting 'wildlife', exempted from such approbation.

Village football, like the communal 'ba' games of the Border towns, also came under increasing attack. Football was never fully embraced by the gentry and was regularly banned between the fourteenth and sixteenth century because it diverted young men away from training in the more useful skills of archery. By the mid-Victorian period, football came under the control of the middle classes with the setting up of the (English) Football Association in 1863 and the Scottish Football Association in 1873. Public school (private; in Scotland the term 'public' school is generally used to refer to state schools) values of amateur status, fair play and gentlemanly conduct influenced football in its early days with middle class 'missionaries' using football to instil class conciliation. This had a tendency to diminish what were distinct working class traditions of informal football games. Urban, industrial districts acquired local teams that began to draw a mass support. In central Scotland, the formation of increasingly professional football teams proliferated throughout the 1870s and 1880s, with Glasgow's 'Old Firm', Celtic (established 1888) and Rangers (established 1873), being an obvious example. Prior to this, Queens Park (established 1867), Kilmarnock (established 1869) and Stranraer (established 1870) were generally of an amateur nature.

Trigger

Consider the extent to which the rising costs of attending a football match in the Scottish Premier League might be alienating football's traditional working class fan base.

By the nineteenth century, culture was being transformed by urban and factory life. The old rural, seasonal traditions no longer made sense in the new setting where life was governed by the mechanical time of the clock. Geographically, the poor lived in filthy, over-crowded tenement buildings separated physically and socially from the factory owner who lived a secluded, private existence on the other side of the town, usually in the West End of the city/town, in tree-lined affluence. In matters of morality, organised religion attempted to compensate for the absence of the middle classes in poor districts. The working class began to develop their own radical culture and robust customs, with the public house becoming a focus for much working class life. In Scotland, excessive and aggressive drunkenness was associated with 'manly' values and as the century progressed, women and the 'respectable' skilled working classes left the pub to less sober male labourers.

A further development was that there was no one, single, culture that bound the working class together, let alone participate in the benefits of middle class culture.

The working class was split by gender, religion and skill. Women were denied access to 'public' culture, and were thus banned from pubs, sports and male-only clubs. As the Irish arrived in great numbers in Scotland, they often encountered sectarian hostility to their nationality, low social status and religion as Catholics living in a predominantly Protestant Scotland (see Chapter 6: Race and Ethnicity). The setting-up of Celtic Football Club was one obvious response to this, as was their disproportionate contribution to radical politics. There was also a separation between 'respectable' skilled workers who increasingly separated themselves socially, economically and culturally from the 'rough culture' of less skilled, poorer paid workers (see Chpter 10: Work and its Organisation, for a discussion of how work can lead to 'alienation').

Trigger

Compare the following definitions of 'rough' and 'respectable' culture given in *The Oxford Companion to Scottish History* (Lynch, 2001: 522, 531).

'Rough culture'
The term is used in a number of different things:

1. To describe aspects of popular, pre-industrial lifestyles under challenge from the more capitalist-oriented cultures that were being created in the 18th and early 19th centuries.
2. To describe those aspects of popular culture which were generally contrasted with the 'improving', rational recreation of the 19th century.
3. To describe a popular culture which rejected the notion of, and the usually middle class control implied in, 'respectability'.

'Respectable culture'
This might be defined as:

- The value system that was used by members of the Scottish working class to differentiate themselves from those who were deemed 'unrespectable' or 'rough'.
- Conforming to accepted forms of behaviour that revolved around sobriety; temperance; hard work; religiosity; self-improvement.
- Thus, members of the respectable working class sought to create a stable social environment for themselves and their families.

Write a couple of paragraphs first noting the major contrasts between these types of explanation and then give some consideration to the kinds of behaviour attached to 'rough' culture. Do you think these kinds of cultural associations are still prevalent in society today?

Notice how 'rough culture' tends to provide a direct and negative contrast to the values associated with 'respectable' culture. The definition of respectable culture talks about values and behaviour and a 'stable social environment', while that of rough culture mentions 'lifestyles', recreation and 'middle class control'. The latter definition lacks a sense that working class 'self-improvement' was a survival strategy often closed-off to the majority of labourers by the precariousness of paid employment and very low wages. Middle class benefactors decided what was 'rough' and what was 'respectable' culture and are deeply interested, as the first definition states, in social, moral and political control and stability.

As the examples of football and the pub show, culture became increasingly commercialised, available as a commodity to be bought in the marketplace, a trend that accelerated into the twentieth century. Variety theatres like the Empire, Coliseum, and Alhambra provided Glasgow with commercially viable, modern entertainment palaces, though Glasgow audiences acquired a reputation among performers for being 'hard to please'. Cinema also took off in dramatic fashion after the first proper 'picture house', the Electric Theatre, opened in Glasgow at the beginning of the twentieth century. However, it was Glasgow's dance halls that caused the greatest 'moral panic' (see Chapter 11: Crime and Deviance), sustained by the original 'slasher' novel, Alexander McArthur and H. Kingsley Long's (1935) *No Mean City*. The cinema, dance and music halls to the football stadium all represented to some extent the institutionalisation of 'rough' culture.

The influence of the kind of culture that appeared before the First World War (1914-1918) survived through to the 1950s. As summarised by the Marxist historian, Eric Hobsbawm (1984: 184-5):

> The working-class culture which became dominant in the 1880s reflected both the new and fully industrialised economy, the growing size of the working class as a potential market, and the striking improvement in average real wages during the period of rapidly falling living costs (c.1873-96). From about 1890 on it also increasingly reflected a growing class consciousness and the changed – and greatly increased – role of the state in national life [...]. It may be argued that the old culture probably reached its peak between 1945 and 1951, for this was the period when trade union membership (as a percentage of the labour force), the electoral strength of the Labour Party (both in absolute terms *and* as a percentage of the total electorate), attendance at football matches and cinemas, and perhaps also the mass circulation newspaper appealing specifically to a proletarian audience, were at their maximum.

Hobsbawm (1984: 184-5) goes on to qualify what he means by 'culture' in this context:

> The term 'culture' is here used in the wider sense familiarized by social anthropologists, for 'culture' in the narrower middle class sense (i.e. literature and the

arts considered as a self-contained phenomenon) were part only of the lives of a section of the working class, generally (but not exclusively) the politically conscious and active and that part of the younger generation which completed a secondary education.

Hobsbawm's (1984) point about different class-based meanings of 'culture' highlights some of the main shifts that affected cultural forms and institutions over the past couple of centuries. New forms of control emerged – state and commercial – that attempted to reach across class-based cultural divisions and prevent social disintegration. If we take on board Hobsbawm's Marxist approach, we would see that an abiding worry for the upper classes appears to have been the potential for culture to become a forum for disorder and rebellion. The upper classes would channel this behaviour, first, by regulation and licence into more rational pursuits (e.g. licensing hours in pubs; education); and, second, by commercial methods into less dangerous pursuits (e.g. regulations and professionalisation of football). What exactly, though, were the frames of reference that made culture such a hotly debated and politically charged issue?

What is Culture?

'Culture' is often thought to mean the opposite of work. As activities that occur outside of paid employment and anything requiring physical effort, culture seems to be more about leisure or pleasurable experiences. However, culture originally meant the agri*cultural* working of the land in the ploughing and cultivation of a field. Culture in this sense is *contrasted* to nature. This is how the Marxist, Leon Trotsky (1926: 83) defined 'culture':

> Culture is everything that has been created, built, learned, conquered by man in the course of his entire history, in distinction from what nature has given, including the natural history of man himself.

Here, culture is viewed as the result of hard mental and physical effort won by human societies (rather than 'men' only) in their struggle for existence with nature. Human societies are thus only able to reproduce themselves based on the accumulated achievements of culture.

Culture is passed on to future generations in *two* ways:

1. Culture takes a physical form in the shape of ***material culture*** deposited in technology, buildings, monuments, artefacts, etc.
2. Second, culture takes a practical and intellectual form – ***cultural practices*** consisting of methods, techniques, habits, etc. – that work on and modify the pre-existing 'material culture'.

Material culture and culture practices are deeply inter-related and mutually shape each other; there can be no cultural objects without cultural activities and neither can there be cultural activities without cultural objects. Once we understand that culture is not just something pre-given, but needs to be produced in the first place and reproduced subsequently on a regular basis, then even great works of art and literature can be seen as products of human labour, albeit of a highly specialised kind. This allows sociology to understand what might seem to be simply the 'genius' of artists like Robert Burns or Pablo Picasso as produced in specific social and cultural contexts. It also raises the thorny question of definition. Attempting to define what is meant by a 'concept' is central to sociology, even if a single agreed definition proves elusive in the end. This also applies to 'culture'. If culture is conceived both as 'lived practices' and 'material objects', then it seems to cover an infinite range of phenomena. Culture can be 'high' or 'low', working or middle class, youth or middle-aged, etc. *Popular* culture seems to suggest something that is broadly based, up-to-the-minute, and commercially produced. Many years ago, Stuart Hall (1982: 8-9) defined popular culture in the following 'class' terms:

> When we come to speak about *popular* culture, we are referring to the lived practices, the common sense and practical ideologies which become identified with the popular classes: the great majorities, the 'common people', of society – those classes marginal to or excluded from the disposition of wealth, property and authority in society. For me, culture always bears an important reference to class relations: as in 'popular classes'. This is because, since class is a fundamental principle in the structuring of society, culture is certain to be significantly shaped by class.

Hall's (1982) idea of 'popular classes' might seem a bit vague. He uses the concept to resist the idea that culture and social class directly correspond to each other in a fixed way. This makes the idea of a separate 'working class culture' difficult to support since society and culture are dominated, above all, by much more powerful classes who shape, control and own the means of cultural production, such as media, retailing, music venues and educational institutions. Further, Hall (1982:9) argues that:

> What defines the 'popular classes', for me, is the fact that they are the classes and the strata which stand in a *subordinate* relation to the other fundamental classes in society. What defines 'popular culture', for me, is the fact that it is the subordinate culture, the one most articulated to the position of the dominated classes in society. It is the *relation* of popular culture to the dominant culture, and the *position* of the popular classes in relation to dominant class positions in society, which matter, for my purposes.

Culture as lived practices and material products always involves unequal relations of power. These relations and positions are rarely stable, however, and, as we have seen, the terms under which 'subordinate cultures' operate have been fought over throughout the modern period.

Trigger

Reflect on Hall's distinction between 'popular classes' and 'popular culture'. Can you re-present his argument in your own words?

Elite culture, mass culture and culture as a way of life

For the purposes of this text, we will now consider three main definitions of culture:

1) Elite culture or 'the best that has been thought and said'
2) Mass culture
3) Culture as a 'whole way of life'.

1) *Elite culture or 'the best that has been thought and said'*

For a long time 'culture' was a label that could only be applied to what were considered the 'highest' forms of cultural production: the 'finest' literature, poetry, classical music, architecture, and painting. Nineteenth century liberal thinkers, like Matthew Arnold (1960 [1869]), wanted to do away with class divisions and the unruly 'inferior classes' by making universally available 'the best that has been thought and said in the world'. *Culture* was needed to prevent society from collapsing into the 'anarchy of the masses', who rioted in London's Hyde Park in 1866. This 'elitist' sense of culture as the preservation of the highest values, assumed that only a tiny, self-selecting, 'intellectual aristocracy' knew what counted as culture. Such an attitude continued well into the twentieth century, though without support for raising the general level of culture among the masses through education (see Chapter 9: Education).

Before 1945, intellectuals like those around the Bloomsbury Group of authors, such as Virginia Woolf, E.M. Forster and Clive Bell, along with Lord Annan, the poet T. S. Elliot, and F.R. Leavis, gathered around the magazine *Scrutiny*. They constituted themselves as an enlightened 'minority culture', embattled by new forms of material culture like the suburbs and tinned food and cultural practices like mass newspaper readerships (Carey, 1992).

The right-wing American sociologist, Charles Murray (2001), in a speech to the Centre for Immigration Studies in Melbourne, Australia, claimed that elite groups throughout the Western world, whose cultural code 'is supposed to set the standard for the society' were experiencing the 'sickness of proletarianisation' (see Chapter 4: Social Class). Elite groups were rejecting traditional 'gentlemanly' (*sic*) codes of

347

conduct such as 'bravery, loyalty, truth and not taking advantage of women' in favour of 'the standards of the underclass'. Murray (2001: 2) stated:

> [C]all it thug code: take what you want, respond violently to anyone who antagonises you, gloat when you win, despise courtesy as weakness, treat women as receptacles, take pride in cheating, deceiving, or exploiting successfully [...]. The hitherto inarticulate values of underclass males are now made articulate with the collaboration of some of America's best creative and merchandising talent.

2) *Mass culture*

The academic study of everyday culture really began in Britain in the 1950s with the emergence of what became known as Cultural Studies. This is not to deny that the cultures practiced by 'ordinary' people had not been seriously discussed and debated before the 1950s. Even in the 1930s and 1940s the elitist tradition did not go completely unchallenged. Studies were carried out into the everyday experiences and behaviour of ordinary people from the late 1930s to the early 1950s by the social research group, Mass Observation. One famous Mass Observation (1943: xv) study was *The Pub and the People*, which described in fine detail:

> [H]ow the pub works in *human* terms of everyday and every night life, among the hundreds of thousands of people who find it one of their principal life interests.

As Mass Observation (1943: xv) continued to argue:

> The real issues of sociology can only be faced if the sociologist is prepared to plunge deeply under the surface of British life and become acquainted with the mass of people who left school before they were 15.

Perhaps the most astute commentator in this remit was George Orwell (1957: 29), who both criticised the all "too Olympian" political and social detachment of self-appointed cultural groups and greatly expanded what could be studied as culturally significant. Orwell analysed the English pub, comic postcards, boys' comic papers and popular fiction, amongst other social and cultural shifts taking place in the 1930s and 1940s. All this added up to a unique, private sense of English culture. Orwell (1957: 66) suggested that:

> We are a nation of flower-lovers, but also a nation of stamp-collectors, amateur carpenters, coupon-snippers, darts-players, crossword puzzle fans. All the culture that is most truly native centres round things which even when they are communal are not official – the pub, the football match, the back garden, the fireside and the 'nice cup of tea'.

He was highly sensitive to cultural change and argued that by the 1940s cultural distinctions between the classes were breaking down as a modern 'indeterminate strata' emerged, *neither* fully working class *nor* middle class, including technicians, higher paid skilled workers, radio experts, film producers, journalists and industrial chemists (see Chapter 4: Social Class and Chapter 10: Work and its Organisation). Additionally:

> There are wide gradations of income, but it is the same kind of life that is being lived at different levels, in labour-saving flats or council houses, along the concrete roads and in the naked democracy of the swimming pools. It is a rather restless, cultureless life, centring around tinned food, *Picture Post*, the radio and the internal combustion engine.   (Orwell, 1941: 542)

Even Orwell is guilty here of adopting a disparaging tone about the banal 'cultureless life' of consumer-driven 'naked democracy'. This disdain for the new, manufactured culture was shared by a group of critical thinkers called the 'Frankfurt School'. They set up the Institute for Social Research in Frankfurt, Germany in 1923, but moved to the United States in 1933 as the Nazis seized power. The main cultural theorists of the Frankfurt School were Theodor Adorno (1903-1969), Max Horkheimer (1895-1973) and Herbert Marcuse (1898-1979). Adorno (1991) argued that the growing use of rational administrative, scientific and technological knowledge in all spheres of social life turns individuals into an homogeneous 'mass'. Mass society is itself dominated by a powerful *culture industry* that uses rational principles to manipulate 'consumers' to efficiently accept standardised, interchangeable cultural products, like the popular song, astrology or Hollywood movies. The functions of the culture industry are, for Adorno (1991), threefold:

1) To make profits
2) To lower popular expectations and tastes to a common denominator
3) To adjust the working class to the rhythms of capitalist production and consumption.

The 'mass society' argument has been widely criticised. It fails, according to some (Swingewood, 1977), to appreciate just how unstable capitalism as a system might be, that it lurches blindly from crisis to crisis, from boom to slump, thus making it difficult for the 'culture industry' to constantly distract the masses from the *reality* of their lives. It also fails to understand the different levels at which popular culture operates. Not everything that Hollywood or the music industry produces is surface novelty and escapism. Many popular movies and songs express popular hopes and aspirations of escaping from rather than simply reinforcing the habits and routines of capitalism. Siegfried Kracauer (in Hansen, 1991) saw in early popular films, such as the 'slapstick comedies' of Mack Sennett, Harold Lloyd, Laurel and Hardy and Charlie Chaplin, that:

> [O]ne has to hand this to the Americans: with slapstick film they have created a form which offers a counterweight to their reality: if in that reality they subject the world to an often unbearable discipline, the film in turn dismantles this self-imposed order quite forcefully.   (Kracauer, quoted in Hansen, 1991: 50)

In other words, not only might popular culture subvert the 'self-imposed order' of capitalism, nor are people simply passive consumers of cultural products, but actively discriminate between different styles and tastes on offer.

3) *Culture as 'a whole way of life'*

Arguments about mass society tend to be tinged by a fear of a vibrant but gaudy American consumer culture undermining 'authentic', independent British working class communities. This was shared by a new generation of literary criticism in the 1950s, such as Richard Hoggart's (1957) *The Uses of Literacy* and Raymond Williams' (1958) *Culture and Society*, as well as the more culturally attuned history of E.P. Thompson's (1963) *The Making of the English Working Class*. It is notable that such studies came from outside the discipline of sociology. Sociology had not yet established itself as an academic discipline in Britain, and was predictably resisted by the cultural traditionalists at Oxford and Cambridge (Hewison, 1981). Both Hoggart and Williams lament the 'corruption' of the 'lived culture' of the 1950s compared to the good, solid, British working class values and community of the 1930s, with Hoggart railing at the arrival of what he calls the 'shiny barbarism' from across the Atlantic inducing 'an aesthetic breakdown' and 'spiritual dry-rot'.

For the new field of cultural studies, 'culture' was no longer simply elite culture, but acquired two inter-related meanings about shared ideas and practices.

1) Culture is concerned with the common meanings and ideas that people deploy to make sense of their experiences
2) Second, 'culture' also refers to social practices and how the various elements inter-relate as 'a whole way of life'.

Culture as 'a whole way of life' seems to be what Orwell and Hoggart meant by the way that a range of activities, from the pub to the pulpit, for example, interact to produce a distinctively *English* national culture or working class culture.

Williams (1965) talks about how culture is *lived* and *experienced* through what he calls a 'structure of feeling'. This idea of a 'structure of feeling' gives a sense that the people involved may only be dimly aware of their own cultural assumptions and expectations that make up their 'whole way of life'. The term, feeling, emphasises that culture is not just about the conscious thoughts that people may have about culture, but that it is *felt* as a living, practical consciousness. Such a 'feeling' for the culture that we inhabit, such as our national identity, is never purely random or unique to any single one of us. It is also structured so that we feel it in certain ways. What we instinctively take to mean by, for example, 'Scottishness' in the earlier Rab C. Nesbitt example, we do not need to think consciously about it being intrinsically different from 'Englishness'.

In establishing a 'culturalist' perspective to the study of a 'whole way of life', Williams, though a Marxist, was also criticising the Marxist notion of 'base and superstructure' (Williams, 1980). For some Marxists, the economic 'base' of society determines its 'superstructure' (which includes politics, law, ideology and culture), on the premise that before we can do anything else the basic necessities for life need to be produced by human labour (see Chapter 2: Sociological Theory and Chapter 4: Social Class). Art and culture are, therefore, *dependent* on an economic base. Crude forms of Marxism are criticised, first for assuming that the relationship between the base and superstructure only works one-way – from the base to the superstructure; and for ignoring the many ways that art, ideology, politics and culture themselves can affect economic conditions. A second problem is that what was used by Marx as a metaphor from the principles of construction – you can only build the upper stories of a house once the foundations have been laid – gets turned into a 'social fact', as if the cultural superstructure was completely caused by the economic base.

Trigger

1. Consider the extent to which 'elite' and 'mass' culture perspectives reflect a negative view of the spread of popular culture.
2. In what ways does Williams' approach represent a challenge to these positions and offer a more positive outlook?

Hegemony and Subcultures

Raymond Williams adopts the ideas of the Italian Marxist, Antonio Gramsci (1891-1937), in an attempt to overcome what he perceived to be the 'economic determinism' of the base/superstructure formula of culture. Gramsci's (1971) central idea is that of 'hegemony' (see Chapter 2: Sociological Theory). This refers to the way that a dominant class maintains its power over the rest of society without relying on the constant use of force or coercion, or simply imposing its will without recognising the aspirations of subordinate classes. A dominant class may be said to be 'hegemonic' when it also 'leads' the rest of society intellectually, morally or culturally and subordinate classes accept its rule as legitimate (see Chapter 4: Social Class). Cultural *leadership* is exercised by the ruling class when ideas and practices acceptable to it are thoroughly interwoven throughout society. Hegemony is a social and cultural process. As such, it is always partial and never complete or finished. It can also be challenged by 'counter-hegemonic' strategies, such as the growing anti-globalisation movement, seen protesting in their hundreds of thousands in the late 1990s/early 2000s in a number of cities, including the US cities of Seattle and Washington, DC, and the ancient Italian port of Genoa. This is when subordinate classes or sections of them, like anti-capitalist protest movements, attempt to generate popular consent for an alternative set of cultural, moral and political values and practices.

Cultures as dominant, residual or emergent

Inspired by Gramsci, Williams (1977) developed a more complex idea of how hegemony is both secured and challenged. He argues that any historically concrete culture will vary thanks to changes to three inter-connected parts. These he calls:

- A *dominant* culture
- *Residual* cultures
- *Emergent* cultures.

First, an effective *dominant* culture establishes a 'selective tradition'; that is, from a whole range of possibilities only a certain version of the past is carried on as 'the tradition', since it helps to bolster dominant institutions in the present, for example, the monarchy.

Second, by *residual*, Williams means what is separate from, and perhaps in opposition to, the 'selective tradition' of the dominant culture, but is left over from the past and still continues to operate as a lived practice in the present. The dominant culture can seek to *incorporate* the residual culture. For instance, the idea of rural community might be residual where it is seen in opposition to urban industrial capitalism, but "for the most part it is incorporated, as idealisation or fantasy, or as an exotic – residential or escape – leisure function of the dominant order itself" (Williams, 1977: 122).

Finally, emergent cultures appear, consisting of substantially new meanings, new practices and new relationships alternative or oppositional to the dominant culture. New cultural formations emerge out of shifts in the social structure, like the development of new class relations, and more general shifts in the 'practical consciousness' that people have of their life situation and personal experiences, which the 'selective tradition' of the dominant classes neglect or exclude. Thus, Williams (1977: 125) argues that:

> [T]here is always, though in varying degrees, practical consciousness, in specific relationships, specific skills, specific perceptions, that is unquestionably social and that a specifically dominant social order neglects, excludes, represses, or simply fails to recognise.

Resistance through 'sub-cultural' rituals

Gramsci's ideas were further taken-up in the 1970s and 1980s by British sociologists such as Stuart Hall, whose work, was initially based around the Centre for Contemporary Cultural Studies (CCCS) at the University of Birmingham. The 'Birmingham School', as the new cultural sociology based at the CCCS became known, were initially highly critical of Hoggart and Williams for their strong bias towards literary criticism and their moralistic view of 'authentic' working class culture (Hebdige, 1988). This now seems ironic, since cultural studies soon began to use French literary theory to 'read' the symbolic 'language' of 'sub-cultural' movements like Punk (Hebdige, 1979).

Subcultures are defined in the *Penguin Dictionary of Sociology* (Abercrombie *et al*, 1984: 416-7) in the following way:

> [A] system of values, attitudes, modes of behaviour and life-styles of a social group which is distinct from but related to the dominant culture of a society. In modern society there are a great diversity of such subcultures, but the concept has been of most use in sociology in the study of youth and deviancy. For example, it has been argued that delinquent or criminal subcultures provide a solution to the problems faced by their members, who find in membership of a subculture some compensation for their 'failure' in conventional society. Youth cultures, which are often treated as deviant, develop around the adoption of styles of dress or music that differentiate them from others.

From this definition, subcultures are:

- A set of cultural meanings and practices
- Related to but distinct or deviate from the dominant culture
- Mainly, but not always, concerned with youth, style and music
- A kind of compensation for the reality of the 'failure' to 'get on' in society.

This last point emphasises that while subcultures might act as a focus for 'resistance' this is always symbolic, in the form of style, behaviour, or music, and as such fails to challenge or alter fundamentally the relationship of subordination to the dominant class and its culture. A look at a number of youth subcultures will illustrate the emphasis on style and the symbolic resistance. Bear in mind the extent to which such subcultures actually change social conditions.

Case studies of youth subcultures
Punk

Cultural movements, or sub-cultures, like punk, appropriated elements of the dominant culture and re-assembled them to form a new, alternative meaning.

> The punk subculture, like every other youth culture, was constituted in a series of spectacular transformations of a whole range of commodities, values, common-sense attitudes, etc. It was through these adapted forms that certain sections of predominantly working-class youth were able to restate their opposition to dominant values and institutions.   (Hebdige, 1979: 116)

Williams' (1980) idea of dominant, residual and emergent cultures can be seen in the punk song, 'God Save the Queen', by the Sex Pistols. This was released in 1977 at the same time as the Jubilee celebrations of Queen Elizabeth II, and its confrontational style polarised British society. Punk was an emergent culture in opposition to the dominant one, including the British monarchy. The Sex Pistols' raggedy appearance, sneering and swearing, with bent postures and contorted facial expressions seemed to pose a threat to traditional values and good taste and good order. Nothing could have been more removed from the uniform, upright British royal family than the Sex Pistols.

The song's lyrics deepened the offence to residual and dominant cultures. 'God Save the Queen' was chosen as the title precisely to maximise the level of provocation. The song's words openly flouted pop conventions by questioning the nature of the society and the role of the Crown. In the song 'the (British) state' is outrageously compared to 'a fascist regime', which has turned the Queen into its servant – informing her that "they've made you a moron" and shielded British society from the realities of its own economic and political decline, heard in the line "England's dreaming." Johnny Rotten, the singer, sneers, "We're the future – your future," implying that British society would face a serious threat, "a potential H-bomb," to its continued existence. Since the Sex Pistols made it difficult for the dominant culture to incorporate their style or music into the 'mainstream', efforts were made to suppress this emergent (sub)culture.

Reaction to the song took several forms, with workers at the record and printing plants producing the single going on strike over the songs' anti-royalist sentiment; adverts for the song were banned from TV and radio and major stores like WH Smiths refused to stock the single. This finally led to attempts to ban the group, spurred on by the creation of a 'moral panic' in the press (see Chapter 11: Crime and Deviance). When the hegemony is challenged by an emergent culture, one reaction is to try to maintain the *status quo* through suppression and playing on popular fears of a moral and cultural breakdown of the kind represented by the Sex Pistols. Punk was soon a spent force as a subculture and its shock value is now routinely incorporated into tabloid newspaper reporting of celebrity lifestyles.

Rude boys
Rebellious subcultures are not confined to the more developed capitalist countries. Take the example of the former British colony, Jamaica, out of which developed one

of the key musical styles of the late twentieth century, reggae. As an 'emergent culture', reggae grew out of Jamaica's own musical styles, bluebeat, ska and rocksteady, its violent politics and gangs, and Jamaican youth's encounter with the mystical black religion, Rastafarianism. Alongside the violent gang culture, the rude boys tended to be young unemployed or underemployed males who tended to be anti-establishment, yet lacking in any coherent ideology themselves.

Apart from their aggressive, non-conformist attitude, rude boys developed a distinctive style that would later cross to the UK. The development in Britain of a Jamaican rude boy style was initially centred on those urban areas of England in which large concentrations of Jamaican immigrants settled. The musical associations of this subculture quickly came to reflect the West Indian diaspora's experience of emigration and re-settlement. By the mid-1960s, the hopes of earlier generations of Caribbean immigrants of prosperity in Britain were being replaced by the realities of low-paid jobs and barely affordable housing. West Indian sub-cultural responses developed in ways that reflected and challenged these new conditions, emphasising especially a growing sense of personal and community dislocation from white, often racist, mainstream society. The style and attitude, though, was overwhelmingly proud and defiant. A cool black urban persona was appropriated from 'soul-brothers' in the United States and often blended with *chic* European fashions, particularly clothing from Italy. Thus:

> The rudies wore very short green serge trousers, leather or gangster-style suit jackets, and their eyes were often hidden behind moody pairs of shades. If they were 'rough, tough' and rich enough they would ride around on light, stripped down motorcycles which were covered in chrome.   (Hebdige, 1988: 72)

Disco
Within disco culture, as with other minority subcultures, fastidious attention was paid to the details of style, clothes and demeanour, and music. The much wider, mainstream 'popular' culture of disco, influenced by the dominant culture of the fashion and music industries, concealed 'emergent' sub-cultural distinctions. Even when disco music became formulaic in the late seventies, with the release of *Saturday Night Fever* (1977), there was a distinction between the predictable and the innovative fringes of the scene. Disco, as a 'fashion statement', grew out of the US gay scene and was influenced by black and Hispanic subcultures.

When it emerged in mid-seventies Britain, disco's style was altered by its male and female, predominantly working class, followers. For instance, young working class women and men in Glasgow rejected the dominant fashions of the day and wore tight 'French flares', pastel-coloured 'blouses' and adopted the 'feminine' hairstyle known as the 'Wedge'. The original Wedge cut – parted on one side, swept to the back and carved short into the nape of the neck – was created in London in 1974 and somehow made its way to Glasgow. Against the sociological idealisation of the rebel male working class subculture, the cultural journalist, Peter York (1984), sarcastically details the Wedge's adoption in southern England as a modernist revolt against both 'natural' long/lank hippie hair and the short spikes of punk:

> When they first cut it and blow it dry they keep on brushing the sides flat, pushing them back underneath the long bits at the crown so the bob part of it is resting on the pushed back horizontal part of it. The stylists trick is to let it go, so it springs out, the long bits bouncing out on top of the side, all that bouncing volume disappearing into razored flatness with nothing hippy or impromptu around the neck. Bare necks, visible ears, with bouncing subversive hair on top. What could be more irritating than this long-short combination? It makes punk spikes look obvious.
>
> (York, 1984: 72-3)

York (1984) goes into detail in order to emphasise the great lengths necessary to get the Wedge hairstyle right. This harks back to the 'cool' look of the Mods in the 1960s, which was in contrast to the convention for longish hair for men in the 1970s. Such care was an affront to the supposedly 'masculine' working class indifference to hairstyle. York takes pleasure in disturbing sociological stereotypes, 'bourgeois Bohos', of the working class rebel:

> In the original, the Wedge was for girls. Well, if the girls have it, there's no stopping the boys. And the boys wore it down the clubs where other boys, straight but loose, picked up on it and, by 1975-6, it was the uniform for the southern English, club-going, working-class soul stylist who is the hero of our story. Ah, did your ears prick up at that, middle class thinkers [sub-cultural sociologists]? Working class! Did a vision of working-class traditions, of blue-collar heroics, Neanderthal punks, or even [...] *Bruce Springsteen*, posed against *wrecked* cars or something funky and devastated, flash on? Well no [...] at this point you should be thinking of David Bowie. Bourgeois Bohos have the strangest idea of working class.
>
> (York, 1984:72-3)

Care needs to be taken that culturally generated stereotypes do not obscure the cultural meaning that different styles have for different sections of the working class. On the other hand, apart from a few good nights out critics are entitled to ask: what did disco actually change?

Rave

If disco was almost entirely ignored by sociology, then its most recent offspring, 'dance music' or 'rave', has been studied in much more depth. In its early incarnation as 'Acid House' and after the death of Leah Betts, a 15 year-old girl who died having taken 'ecstacy', raves became the target for moral outrage on the part of the media and politicians (see the reference to 'moral panics, above). Rave appeared to be a natural 'classless' phenomenon and in some senses, egalitarian, bringing together large sections of the under 40-s. Rave can be seen as part of the longer tradition we have already traced of cultural control through commercial and state action. Commercial entrepreneurs, some of them operating illegally, were central to the rave scene – like drug suppliers, fashion retailers, and event organisers. The British government used legal sanctions against rave culture, including:

- An obscure 1967 Private Places of Entertainments Act, which required commercial entertainment to acquire a license
- The Licensing Act, 1988, providing the police with greater powers to examine licensed nightclubs
- The Entertainments (Increased Penalties) Acts, 1990, which greatly increased penalties for unlicensed public entertainment
- The Criminal Justice and Public Order Act (CJA), 1994, which gave police draconian powers to arrest people they believe might be intending to attend a rave or take part in a public protest.

This last Act, the CJA, 1994, both politicised and criminalised rave culture, leading to mass demonstrations of those involved in rave culture. Despite the passing of the CJA, a deeply unequal British society seems to have so far withstood the 'inclusive egalitarianism' of rave. Class, too, does not look like it will decline as part of the social order due to rave culture. Indeed, a young group of Scottish writers, including Irvine Welsh and Kevin Williamson, came out of *rave culture* but their writing was anything but 'classless', focusing on the housing scheme environment and language of the Edinburgh dispossessed.

Subcultures as 'symbolic resistance' or 'symbolic incorporation'?
The sub-cultural case studies seem to indicate that sub-cultural fashions rise and fall over time, their symbolic resistance either incorporated or marginalized by the dominant culture. Perhaps part of the difficulty is in naming certain categories of people 'subcultures' in the first place.

Trigger

1. Can you give names to today's sub-cultures?
2. What are the main characteristics in terms of style and music for them?

As soon as you begin to order and codify subcultures, the more difficult they seem to pin down. Take the attempt in Figure 13.1 (see below) to define the main subcultures prior to the 1980s in terms of dates, names, style and music. In each case, all of the details might be argued over and other dates, names, clothes or music inserted. For instance, where would the biggest youth movement of the 1970s, disco, fit in? Because it was so widespread by the second half of the 1970s, disco is difficult to pigeonhole, which may be why it has been so readily dismissed by many sociologists of subcultures. Even more troubling is the extent to which studies of subcultures tend to focus on white, heterosexual, male groups.

\multicolumn{4}{c}{**Figure 13.1 Main British subcultures, 1950s-1990s**}
Date	**Subculture**	**Dress**	**Music**
1953-1956	Teddy Boys	Drape jacket, 'brothel creepers'	Rock 'n' Roll, Elvis Presley, Bill Haley
1958-1961	Beatniks	Duffle coat, beard	Folk/Jazz
1963	Mods	Italian-style casual wear	Soul, Tamla Motown, James Brown, The Supremes
1964	Rockers	Leathers, motor-bike	Rock 'n' Roll, Gene Vincent
1967-1972	Hippies	Long hair, kaftans, flares	'Progressive' rock, Pink Floyd
1965	Rude boys	'Baldhead' crop, Crombie coat	Ska, the Skatalites, Prince Buster
1968-1971	Skinheads	Crewcut, boots, braces, jeans, Ben Sherman shirts	Ska, rocksteady, reggae, Ansell Collins, Desmond Dekker
1971	Glam	Dyed hair, make-up, platform heels	Glam Rock, David Bowie, Roxy Music, Marc Bolan and T-Rex
1976-1977	Punk	Ripped clothes, safety-pins, spiked hair	Punk Rock, Sex Pistols, The Clash, The Damned
1981	New Romantics	'Futurist/revivalist' costumes	Club music, Spandau Ballet, Kraftwerk, Duran Duran
1983	Goths	Black clothes, black hair, make-up	Siouxsie and the Banshees, Sisters of Mercy
1985	Casuals	Designer labels	Football
1988-1992	Acid House	Baggy jeans	Techno

Postmodernism, Identity and Consumption

It seems increasingly difficult to think of culture as providing a stable sense of meaning to people's lives as it once seemed to do. Society is undergoing dramatic political, technological, economic and cultural change. The emergence of the Internet, for example, has led some sociologists, such as Manuel Castells (1998), to claim that because people are able to communicate in new ways then it will bring about far-reaching social and cultural transformations. The physical spaces between people are not so important as before. Information and communications technologies (ICTs) allow us to 'leap huge distances' in order to make instantaneous contact on 'the Net'. Castells (1998: 395-60) calls this the 'network society' and ascribes huge potential to it for improving the lot of human kind:

> The dream of the Enlightenment, that reason and science would solve the problems of humankind is within reach [...]. If people are informed, active, and communicate throughout the world; if business assumes its social responsibility; if the media becomes the messenger rather than the message; if political actors react against cynicism and restore belief in democracy; if culture is reconstructed from experience; if humankind feels the solidarity of the species throughout the globe; if we assert intergenerational solidarity by living in harmony with nature; if we depart from the exploration of our inner self, having made peace amongst ourselves. If all this is made possible by our informed, conscious, shared decision, while there is still time, maybe then, we may, at last, be able to live and let live, love and be loved.

Perhaps similar themes are evident in relation to rave culture: just like raves, ICTs have huge potential to promote global understanding and peace. However, Castells' optimistic idea of an emerging global culture seems to run counter to recent trends where large, multinational corporations like Nike and McDonalds are seen to be standardising cultural products and creating a sense of 'sameness' throughout the world (see Chapter 10: Work and its Organisation).

On the other hand, postmodernists argue that cultural identity is increasingly fragmented and the consumption of cultural goods is becoming more individualised and less standardised (see Chapter 3: Sociological Theory). For postmodern sociologists, like Mike Featherstone (1991), individuals are much more sophisticated and discriminating consumers than ever before, carefully choosing what they buy in order to create new, changing identities for themselves. Globalisation is, therefore, bringing *not* less but more cultural diversity as the consumption of cultural products continues. As indicators of taste and lifestyle, consumer goods bring people into fresh contact with each other. Culturally, globalisation "offers the prospect of a greater chance of tolerance as we enter an era in which national and cultural boundaries are more easily crossed and redrawn" (Featherstone, 1991: 147).

This more eclectic or hybrid global culture creates less fixed cultural identities. As the leading postmodern thinker, Jean-Francois Lyotard (1984: 76), put it:

> Eclecticism is the degree zero of contemporary general culture: one listens to reggae, watches a western, eats McDonald's food for lunch and local cuisine for dinner, wears Paris perfume in Tokyo and 'retro' clothes in Hong Kong; knowledge is a matter for TV games.

In the light of mass consumer choice, it no longer appears that a tiny cultural elite can impose their own narrow view of culture, such as what is good for everyone onto the rest of society. A criticism of the kind of claims made by Featherstone and Lyotard is that only certain kinds of materially well-off consumers are able to participate in the hybrid global culture. Such benign claims about cultural identity and consumption seem to ignore such issues as wars between and within states, terrorism, HIV/AIDs, starvation and repression, all of which have made the world become an increasingly unstable and dangerous place to be for much of humanity. As a recent critical review of cultural studies textbooks suggested, where once cultural studies hoped to give those on the margins a hearing, it now tended to impose its *own* meaning, seeing the marginalized in society, such as poor single mothers, minority ethnic groups and workers on unstable contracts, for example, as participants in some kind of semiotic warfare, rather than seeing them for the essentially disenfranchised groups that they invariably are (Day, 2002).

Cultural Discrimination?
We are always engaged in matters of cultural discrimination. We argue and debate about what is better and worse in our culture. Cultural populism tends to make everything as equally worthwhile as everything else. This appears to suit the elite social groups, like politicians, ministers, cultural officials, educationalists, business and media bosses, who currently define what culture is for the rest of society. Such elites deny their own existence by roundly condemning elitism in the name of the 'Ordinary People' in order to curry popular favour. Often coming from a middle class background, private school-trained and Oxbridge-educated, the cultural elites make a career out of the masses by appealing indiscriminately to 'populism'; that is, whatever a mass audience demands or is *made to want*. Elites appear as 'anti-elites' or 'inverted elites', classless, and in tune with popular tastes. To have mass appeal or popularity is seen to be a good thing in itself. An example of inverted elitism was when the New Labour government of 1997 promoted British popular culture as 'Cool Britannia' and Prime Minister Tony Blair glad-handed with the pop group, Oasis.

For the French post-Marxist sociologist, Pierre Bourdieu (1984), class is the key determinant of lifestyle and cultural consumption. 'Good' or 'vulgar' cultural tastes, such as appreciating a vintage bottle of port or a can of Irn Bru, is not something that somehow comes naturally to us. Taste *is*, arguably, a mark of distinction between the classes. Cultural distinction, though, is not something simply learned through formal education or instruction. Cultural tastes in furnishings, wallpaper or food tend to reflect your experiences of belonging to a certain social class and your distance or immediacy to material need. Working class culture tends to value 'straightforward', 'immediate', 'practical' and satisfying pleasures because of pressing material needs and the immediate pressures of work. On the other hand, middle-class people, brought up to assume that all of the daily necessities of life are guaranteed, become more generally familiar with the canons of exquisite taste – their 'cultural capital' –

because they take a more leisurely, abstract approach to education and the contemplation of works of art.

These sets of practical dispositions Bourdieu (1984) calls *habitus*, in order to emphasise their tacit, habitual character as opposed to being explicitly trained in matters of cultural taste. Such taste appears as 'naturally' cultivated, rather than how the dominant class reproduces itself by using taste as a symbol of their *objective* distance from material want and *subjective* feeling of distinction from vulgar material necessity. This makes cultural taste and its lack thereof appear natural, so much so that even mundane, everyday objects are imbued with class based cultural meanings:

> If a group's whole lifestyle can be read off from the style it adopts in furnishing or clothing, this is not because these properties are the objectifications of the economic and cultural necessity which determined their selection, but also because the social relations objectified in familiar objects, in their luxury or poverty, their 'distinction' or 'vulgarity', their 'beauty' or 'ugliness', impress themselves through bodily experiences as profoundly unconscious as the quiet caress of beige carpets or the thin clamminess of tattered, garish linoleum, the harsh smell of bleach or the perfumes as imperceptible as a negative scent.   (Bourdieu, 1984: 77)

Perhaps Bourdieu links cultural taste a bit too directly to the social distance from the daily struggle for material necessities. He also suspends his own judgement about cultural taste in order to show how the 'superior' cultural taste of the middle classes is socially produced. Yet his sense of class distinction in cultural objects and practices can be traced as modern society developed into the 'two cultures' of the 'high' and the 'low' – from amateur gentleman sports players to the vulgar proletarian professional, or the Zoot Suit and the sober dress of the monarchy. This struggle over the meaning of culture is what makes its sociological study so potentially illuminating about the kind of society we exist within.

Conclusion: The Politics of Culture

The debates about lifestyle and culture can have major political significance. Conservative thinkers like Samuel P. Huntington (1996) take the new centrality of cultural identities to argue that the fundamental divide and source of conflict in the world is that between what he calls 'the clash of civilisations'. These are the broadest 'cultural communities' imaginable, larger than villages, regions, ethnic groups, nations and religions, such as Western civilisation, Islamic civilisation and African civilisation. Civilisations, unlike nations, have no cultural community larger than themselves. While Rab C. Nesbitt may identify culturally with Govan, Glasgow, Scotland, Britain, or Europe ultimately, for thinkers like Huntington, he belongs to 'Western civilisation'.

Something like the 11 September 2001 attacks on the World Trade Centre and the Pentagon, were interpreted by US political and cultural elites, from President George W. Bush downwards, as evidence of the 'clash of civilisations'. In this account, the West is despised in parts of the Islamic world for its liberal and democratic cultural traditions. By talking about a clash of civilisations there is little need to look at issues of unequal economic, political or military power of the US and the West over the rest of the world. Instead, Huntington (1996) uses the idea of Western *civilisation* to defend the dominance of white, Christian, European-based cultural values in American national identity against 'large minority' unassimilated cultures like US Hispanics (1996: 305).

Advocates of 'multiculturalism', often used as another name for the toleration of cultural difference within a society, are seen by Huntington (1996: 305) to be the most immediate and dangerous threat to American national identity:

> In the name of multiculturalism they have attacked the identification of the United States with Western civilisation, denied the existence of a common American culture, and promoted racial, ethnic, and other subnational cultural identities and groupings. (Huntington, 1996: 305)

Huntington (1996) thus uses the broadest cultural category, 'civilisation', to support a particularly narrow and ethnically exclusive cultural category, white Euro-American nationalism.

By focusing on overcoming ignorance of the cultures of other groups, multiculturalism might in fact generate cultural diversity, though a number of critics like Sivanandan (1982: 5) have pointed out that "just to learn about other people's cultures is not to learn about the racism of one's own." Culture can, therefore, be used to support any number of political and ideological positions, from the tolerant diversity of multiculturalism to exclusive and intolerant ethnic nationalism. This is, perhaps, why sociologists tend to avoid sweeping statements about entire cultures, let alone whole 'civilisations' and focus instead on smaller-scale cultural interactions.

Chapter Summary

- The term, culture, has been variously defined both out-with and within sociology as a discipline.
- Non-sociological disciplines, such as 'sociobiology' and 'psychoanalytic psychology', assert that culture has biological roots, whereas sociologists tend to focus on culture as a social construction.

- Cultural codes of conduct and symbols, such as language, are based on 'shared assumptions'.
- The rise of popular culture can be traced back to the separation and divergence of upper and lower class culture in the late eighteenth century.
- Culture is divided both *between* classes and *within* social classes.
- A key distinction within the working class has been that of 'rough' and 'respectable' culture.
- Examples of the banning of working class blood sports and the rise of pub culture and football may show the historical emergence of state regulation and commercial control of popular culture.
- Three main theoretical definitions of culture were introduced: 1) 'Elite culture'; 2) 'Mass culture'; 3) Culture as a 'whole way of life'.
- Elite culture protects 'the best three general approaches that has been thought and said' from becoming corrupted by democracy and capitalism.
- 'Mass culture' perspectives like the Frankfurt School take popular culture seriously, but argue that the masses are being manipulated by a capitalist 'culture industry'. This is often associated with a fear of vulgar popular American culture.
- Raymond William's idea of 'culture as a whole way of life' emphasises material culture and cultural practices that help to produce a 'structure of feeling', a kind of practical, everyday consciousness.
- Williams' approach is seen to better account for cultural change than the crude Marxist idea of a cultural 'superstructure' reflecting an economic 'base'.
- Williams argues that cultures have three, inter-related dimensions: 'dominant', 'residual' and 'emergent'.
- Emergent cultures appear as distinctive subcultures, but which borrow from and oppose aspects of the dominant culture.
- Subcultures provide for working class youth a sense of symbolic resistance and compensation for failing to improve social conditions.
- Some subcultures, like punk and rave, are more studied than others. Other subcultures – rude boys and disco – have been ignored by sociologists, perhaps due to problems of ethnicity, gender, sexuality or misunderstandings about class.
- The authorities may try to either incorporate subcultures, like disco, or marginalize and criminalize them, like raves.
- Radical transformations in culture are said to be taking place in response to the presence of new forms of communication with the emergence of ICTs and altered patterns of consumption.
- Postmodern thinkers argue that cultural identities and practices have become eclectic and diverse. As a result, individuals have greater freedom to pick and choose their identities regardless of their circumstances.

- Questions are raised in opposition to this from radical thinkers like Bourdieu, who object that class position, or *habitus*, largely shapes identity and cultural consumption, and that a new elite control the flow of cultural production.
- Criticism is also made of an associated postmodern drift towards 'cultural populism' and a tendency for academics to attach cultural significance and meaning to relatively trivial practices and behaviours. This, some argue, detracts from the serious consideration of economic, political and other sociological factors.

Further Reading

Adorno, T.W. (1991) *The Culture Industry*, London: Routledge

Archer, M.S. (1996) *Culture and agency: the place of culture in social theory*, Cambridge: Cambridge University Press

Best, S. and Kellner, D. (1998) 'Beavis and Butt-head: no future for post-modern youth', in Epstein, J.S. (ed.), *Youth Culture: identity in a post-modern world*, Oxford: Blackwell

Clarke, J. *et al* (1976) 'Subcultures, Cultures and Class', in Hall, S, and Jefferson, T. (eds), *Resistance Through Rituals*, London: Hutchinson

Williams, R. (1983) *Keywords: a vocabulary of culture and society*, London: Fontana

Useful Websites

On the Zoot suit riots: http://www.pbs.org/wgbh/amex/zoot/

On youth subcultures: http://www.sociology.org.uk/ddeviate.htm

A student site: http://www.ncf.edu/culture/student.htm

On the sociology of culture: http://www2.fmg.uva.nl/sociosite/topics.html

Bibliography

Abercrombie, N., Hill, S. and Turner, B. S. (1994) *The Penguin Dictionary of Sociology*, Third Edition, London: Penguin

Adorno, T. and Horkheimer, M. (1972) *Dialectic of Enlightenment*, New York, NY: Seabury Press

Arnold, M. (1960 [1869]) *Culture and Anarchy*, Cambridge: Cambridge University Press

Bordo, S. (1993) *Unbearable Weight: Feminism, Western Culture, and the Body*, Berkeley, CA: University of California Press

Bourdieu, P. (1984) *Distinction*, London: Routledge and Keegan Paul

Brook, B. (1999) *Feminist Perspectives on the Body*, London: Longman

Carey, J. (1992) *The Intellectuals and the Masses: Pride and Prejudice in the Literary Establishment, 1880-1939*, London: Faber and Faber

Castells, M. (1998) *End of Millennium*, Oxford: Blackwell

Cosgrove, S. (1991) 'The Zoot Suit and Style Warfare', in McRobbie, A. (ed.), *Zoot Suits and Second-Hand Dresses: An Anthology of Fashion and Music*, London: Macmillan

Day, G. (2002) 'Freedom's threatened: let's go shopping', *The Times Higher Education Supplement*, 19 July

Featherstone, M. (1991) *Consumer Culture and Postmodernism*, London: Sage

Freud, S. (1961[1923]) *The Ego and the Id*, London: Hogarth

Frost, L. (2001) *Young Women and the Body: A Feminist Sociology*, Basingstoke: Palgrave

Gramsci, A. (1971) *Selections from the Prison Notebooks*, London: Lawrence and Wishart

Hall, S. (1982) 'Culture and the state', in *The State and Popular Culture (1): U203 Popular Culture, Block 7*, Milton Keynes: The Open University

Hansen, M. (1991) 'Decentric perspectives: Kracauer's early writings on film and mass culture', *New German Critique*, 54

Hebdige, D. (1979) *Subculture: the Meaning of Style*, London: Methuen

Hebdige, D. (1988) 'Towards a cartography of taste, 1935-1962', in Hebdige, D. (1988) *Hiding the Light: On Images and Things*, London: Routledge

Hewison, R. (1981) *In Anger: British Culture in the Cold War, 1945-60*, New York, NY: Oxford University Press

Hobsbawm, E. (1984) 'The formation of British working-class culture', in *Worlds of Labour: Further Studies in the History of Labour*, London: George Wiedenfield and Nicolson Limited

Hoggart, Richard (1957) *The Uses of Literacy*, London: Chatto and Windas

Huntington, S.P. (1996) *The Clash of Civilisations and the Remaking of World Order*, New York, NY: Simon Schuster

Langlands, E. (2002) 'Raves return as superclubs shunned', *Sunday Herald*, 14 July, p.7

Lupton, D. (1996) *Food, the Body and the Self*, London: Sage

Lynch, M. (ed.) (2001) *The Oxford Companion to Scottish History*, Oxford: Oxford University Press.

Lyotard, J.F. (1984) *The Postmodern Condition: A Report on Knowledge*, Manchester: Manchester University Press

Macdonald, M. (1995) *Representing Women: Myths of Femininity in the Popular Media*, London: Edward Arnold

Mass Observation (1987 [1943]) *The Pub and the People: A Worktown Study*, London: The Crest Library

McRobbie, A. (1991) *Feminism and Youth Culture*, Hampshire and London: Macmillan Press

McRobbie, A. (ed.) (1991), *Zoot Suits and Second-Hand Dresses: An Anthology of Fashion and Music*, London: Macmillan

Murray, C. (2001) *Talking Trash: When Standards are set by the Underclass*, Executive Highlights No.28, Centre for Immigration Studies (http://www.cis.org)

Orwell, G. (1981[1941]) 'The Lion and the Unicorn: Socialism and the English Genius', in *George Orwell*, London: Martin Secker and Warburg

Orwell, G. (1957) *Inside the Whale and Other Essays*, Harmondsworth: Penguin

Osgerby, B. (1998) *Youth in Britain since 1945*, Oxford: Blackwell

Pattison, I. (1992) *More Rab C. Nesbitt Scripts*, London: BBC Books

Sivanandan, A. (1982) *A Different Hunger*, London: Pluto Press

Swingewood, A. (1977) *The Myth of Mass Culture*, Basingstoke: Macmillan

Thompson, E.P. (1968) *The Making of the English Working Class*, Harmondsworth: Penguin

Tiger, L. and Fox, R. (1971) *The Imperial Animal*, New York, NY: Hoff, Reinhart and Winston

Trotsky, L. (1971[1926]) 'Culture and Socialism', in *Leon Trotsky on Literature and Art*, New York, NY: Pathfinder Press

Williams, R. (1965) *The Long Revolution*, Harmondsworth: Penguin

Williams, R. (1977) *Marxism and Literature*, Oxford: Oxford University Press

Williams, R. (1980) *Problems in Materialism and Culture*, London: Verso

York, P. (1984) *Modern Times*, London: Futura

Index

Abbott, P. 6, 169, 172
Abel-Smith, B. 182
Aberdeen 3, 6, 46, 53, 152, 195
Adonis, A. 60
agency 128, 143, 205, 239, 242, 306, 308, 309, 318,
alienation 189, 233, 241, 424, 246, 259, 261, 265, 343
anomie 233, 238, 239
assembly line production 52, 76, 249, 250, 251, 259, 242, 265, 273, 280
asylum seekers 131, 134, 136, 141, 142, 143, 144
Barker, E. 55
Barrett, M. 101, 105, 107, 165, 166, 167, 168, 169, 170, 171
Baudrillard, J. 28, 29-30
Bauman, Z. 28
Beck, U. 30
Becker, H. 269, 276, 277, 297, 313, 315
Bell, D. 73, 75, 257
Beveridge Report 180, 182
black feminism 20, 116, 104-106
Black Report 319-325, 328, 333
Blair, Tony 59, 140, 141, 151, 187, 191, 204, 227, 253, 360
Blauner, R. 259
Blom, R. 76
Blumer, H. 24
Booth, C. 179-180
Bourdieu, P. 27, 77, 215, 340, 360, 361, 364
bourgeoisie 16, 66, 67, 70, 77, 240, 241
Bowles, S. and Gintis, H. 202-206, 228
Braverman, H. 76, 233, 246-250, 264, 265
British Crime Survey (BCS) 284
Bureaucracy 244-246, 251, 252, 254, 256, 309
call centres 75, 76, 236, 259-264, 266
Callinicos, A. 77
Capitalism 18, 31, 66, 67, 71, 75, 77, 87, 100, 101-104,, 116, 127-128, 168, 169, 173, 207, 233, 234, 236, 239, 240, 240-

245, 265, 304, 311, 312, 349, 350, 352, 363
Castells, M. 358, 359
Castles, S. and Kosack 127, 131
class conflict 16, 28, 70, 71, 165, 239, 242, 245, 246
class consciousness 66, 69, 344
Cloward, R. 274, 297
Cohen, A. 274
Cohen, S. 142, 270
community 53, 62, 63, 69, 75, 105, 121, 134, 135, 136, 144, 148, 151, 188, 194, 215, 225, 273, 289, 290, 292, 293, 298, 302, 307, 323, 338, 340, 350, 352, 355, 361
Comte, Auguste 6, 67, 120, 238
conflict theory 11, 15, 16, 20, 33
consensus 12-14, 32, 33, 63, 65, 130, 131, 144, 201, 237, 238, 239, 242, 274, 277-278, 307
corporate crime 277
criminology 277, 278, 279
Croall, H. 277, 278, 280, 286
cultural capital 77, 215, 216, 227, 340, 360
cultural studies 128, 348, 350, 353, 360
culture 6, 23, 31, 32, 37, 67, 78, 79, 100, 102, 130, 131, 132, 134, 138, 143, 144, 162, 165, 177, 180, 183, 186, 188, 189, 190, 191, 196, 201, 203, 205, 207, 208, 216, 218, 221, 222, 234, 243, 245, 253, 246, 265, 269, 271, 272, 274, 275, 280, 296, 297, 337, 363
culture of poverty 78, 188, 189-190
Davis and Moore 65
democracy 30, 349, 359, 363
delinquency 172, 274, 275, 281, 290
Department of Health 319, 325, 326, 327
deskilling 76, 233, 246, 248, 249, 264, 265
deviancy amplification 276, 277, 297
deviant subculture 89

discrimination 38, 97-98, 112, 113, 115, 124-126, 129-132, 136, 138, 140, 156, 184, 185, 189, 314, 360-361
division of labour 12, 13, 16, 21, 31, 66, 70, 80, 94-95, 103, 161, 163, 166, 173, 200, 201, 237-240, 250, 255
divorce 38-40, 96, 148-149, 152, 155, 157, 236
Dobash, R. 170
domestic violence 170-171, 279, 283, 285, 286
domestic labour 93, 97, 100, 101, 166
drugs 42, 53, 270, 274, 283, 284, 293, 304, 310, 311, 329, 331
Dundee 43, 53, 135, 152, 182
Durkheim, Emile 12-18, 22, 27, 30, 33, 59, 65, 80, 188, 201, 202, 233, 237-239, 242, 245, 265, 272, 273, 296
economic determinism 69, 207, 351
Edinburgh 6, 40, 50, 51, 83, 152, 181, 194, 195, 196, 226, 287, 329-330, 357
Elites/elitism/elitist 17, 19, 73, 203, 228, 305, 337, 340, 347-348, 350, 351, 360, 362, 363
employment/unemployment 39, 56, 62, 63, 66, 74, 77, 79, 80, 83, 90, 91, 101, 102, 109-112, 115, 116, 119, 126, 127, 129, 131, 136, 137, 139, 140, 142, 143, 155, 146, 160, 166, 172, 178, 181, 182, 186, 187, 190, 193, 195-197, 207, 208, 216, 334, 225, 233, 266, 273, 280, 281, 282, 286, 293, 306, 319, 323, 324, 327, 344, 345, 366
Engels, F. 66, 67, 78, 100, 101, 165, 246
Engender 91, 114, 115
England 6, 83, 84, 86, 134, 135, 136, 137, 138, 143, 156, 158, 162, 204, 208, 217, 222, 223, 224, 225, 226, 227, 228, 285, 286, 294, 320, 321, 324, 326, 327, 329, 354, 355, 356, 366

Equal Opportunities
Commission 91, 109, 110,
112, 166
ethnicity 51, 60, 69, 80, 87,
106, 115, 119-144, 162, 177,
186, 196, 208, 219-222, 226,
228, 229, 363
ethnomethodology 23-24, 26,
33
European Union 40, 151
exploitation 18, 62, 67, 87,
91, 103, 116, 121, 127, 130,
131, 132, 167, 207, 234, 240,
246, 250
extended family 147, 148,
161, 171
Featherstone, M. 28, 359, 360
femininity 20, 93-94, 100,
108, 207, 218, 279
feminism (radical, Marxist,
black, liberal, 'dual systems',
postmodern) 20, 91, 95-109,
115, 116, 189, 216, 325
Firestone, S. 98, 103, 105,
106
flexible specialisation 252,
254
Ford, Henry/Fordism/neo-
Fordism 233, 250-254, 256,
266
Foucault, M. 209, 260, 315-
317
functionalism 11, 12-14, 17,
21, 32, 33, 65, 73, 80, 81, 82,
96, 116, 127, 130-131, 144,
160-164, 173, 200-203, 208,
313
gang culture 355
Garfinkel, H. 23
gender 20, 21, 28, 51, 60, 69,
80, 84, 86, 87, 91-116, 127,
140, 141, 143, 165, 166, 167,
168, 169, 177, 181, 183, 196,
200, 201, 208, 216-219, 222,
226, 228, 229, 235, 242, 297,
324, 343, 363
Giddens, A. 26-27, 30, 31, 80,
149
Glasgow 27, 46, 49, 50, 135,
136, 142, 143, 154, 160, 176,
195, 225, 226, 260, 262, 275,
288, 294, 328, 329-330, 339,
340, 342, 344, 350, 356, 361
Glass, D. 63, 81
globalisation 31-32, 33, 72,
86, 123, 223, 229, 254, 337,
352, 359
Goffman, E. 25, 26, 313, 314,
315

Goldthorpe, J. 60, 64, 73, 74,
75, 81, 211, 229
Gouldner, A. 77
Gramsci, A. 19, 351, 352, 353
grand narratives 107, 202
Grint, K. 234, 236, 243, 246
Hall, Stuart 128, 275, 278,
346, 247, 353
Halsey, A. 212
Hargreaves, D.H. 205
health care 304, 312, 329
Health Education Board for
Scotland (HEBS) 326
Hebdige, D. 353, 354, 355
Held, D. 31
hierarchy 62, 80, 120, 162,
203, 207, 222, 236, 244, 248
historical materialism 66, 240
Hite Report 45
Hobsbawn, E. 344, 345
hospitals 25, 51, 134, 142,
305, 332
households 40, 85, 139, 147,
148, 149, 152, 153, 154, 159,
163, 172, 194, 258, 285
housework 21, 166, 235
housing 72, 131, 138, 142,
143, 155, 159, 160, 172, 184,
185, 193, 197, 212, 214, 293,
322-324, 327, 355, 357
Huntington, S.P. 361, 362
Hutton, W. 64, 109, 258, 266
identity 18, 48, 50, 70, 71, 82,
87, 123, 127, 131, 134, 147,
165, 167, 217, 223, 234, 276,
281, 297, 314, 339, 350, 358,
359, 360, 362, 364
ideology 17, 18, 19, 38, 59,
67, 87, 102, 104, 121, 131,
165, 167, 169, 170, 171, 204,
274, 305, 312, 314, 323, 351,
355
Illich, I. 304, 308, 309, 310
immigration 119, 125, 128,
131, 133-138, 144, 163, 247
India/Indians 32, 53, 120,
136, 139, 140, 220, 236, 263-
264
inequality 59, 60, 61, 65, 68,
71, 79, 82, 83, 87, 92, 96, 99,
101-103, 109, 120, 132-133,
138-139, 143, 144, 169, 170,
171, 177-178, 183, 184, 187,
188, 192, 193, 195, 196, 197,
207, 213, 218, 224, 234, 242,
271, 274, 280, 281, 282, 287,
297, 319, 320, 322, 323, 327,
329, 330

institutional racism 119, 125-
126, 131, 141, 144
interactionism 24-26, 33, 313,
325 (see also symbolic
interactionism)
Joseph Rowntree Foundation
139
Keynesianism 251
kinship 123, 147, 148, 150,
152, 161, 167
labelling theory 229, 269,
276-277, 281, 297, 311, 313,
314, 315
Lemert, E. 276, 297, 313
Lewis, O. 189, 190
liberal feminism 20, 98-101,
116
Lombroso, Cesare 271
lone-parent households 148,
154-158
Lukes, S. 238, 239
Lyotard, J.F. 28, 359, 360
Macpherson Report 126
macro-sociology 26, 27, 33
management/scientific
management 25, 51, 53, 62,
70, 74, 84, 110, 180, 209, 225,
228, 247-253, 260-263,
265,297, 331, 333
marriage 45, 95-96, 100, 101,
149, 151, 161, 165, 167, 169,
170, 172, 173
Marx, Karl/Marxism/
Marxist/neo-Marxism 10, 11,
15-20, 22, 24, 27, 28, 30, 33,
59, 61, 65-69, 70, 71, 72, 76,
77, 78, 84, 101, 102, 104, 115,
116, 127, 128, 130, 131, 132,
140, 144, 164-165, 168, 169,
173, 177, 179, 188, 189, 192-
193, 203-205, 207, 208, 209,
233, 234, 237, 240-243, 245-
246, 249, 250, 259, 265, 275,
276, 277-278, 279, 304, 311-
313, 317, 325, 332, 340, 344,
345, 351, 363
masculinity 20, 93-94, 100,
207, 216, 217, 218, 279-280
Mead, George Herbert 24
McCrone, D. 3, 6, 7, 82, 83,
86
'McDonaldization' 254-257
McRobbie, A. 208
means of production 66, 71,
72, 127, 140, 146
mechanical solidarity 238
medicine 25, 99, 302, 303-
306, 308-313, 315-317, 318,
319, 332

meritocracy 80, 82, 203, 204, 230

Merton, R. 273, 274, 296

micro-sociology 21-27, 33

middle class 46, 59, 61, 68, 71, 73, 74-77, 84-87, 96-99, 105, 106, 154, 168, 180, 191, 192, 202, 207, 210-213, 215-218, 222, 227, 274, 275, 342-345, 346, 349, 356, 360, 361

Miliband, R. 60, 77

mode of production 240, 312

monogamy 93

mortality 177, 184, 195, 312, 320, 321, 324, 325, 328, 329, 367

multiskilling 252, 253

Murdock, George 94, 95, 161, 163, 173

Murray, C. 78-81, 132-133, 190-191, 210, 347

New Deal 80

New Labour 80, 173, 177, 185, 186-188, 190, 191, 196, 197, 204, 224-227, 228, 229, 253, 257, 260

nuclear family 147, 149, 161, 162, 163, 170, 171, 173

Oakley, Ann 21, 92, 95, 166, 318

One Parent Families Scotland 155, 157

organic solidarity 238-239

Orwell, G. 348, 349, 350

Parsons, Talcott 14, 65, 161-164, 201, 202, 205-208, 311

patriarchy 20, 27, 33, 102, 103, 106, 166, 168, 169, 318

Patrick, J. 49, 275

Popper, K. 18, 270

positivism 37

postmodernism 116, 208-210, 254, 256, 358-360, 363-364

poverty line 142, 179, 180-181, 182

prejudice 100, 104, 124, 125, 126, 134, 180

prisons 290, 293, 294

proletariat 16, 18, 66, 77, 78, 101, 132, 165, 240, 241 (see also working class)

Protestantism 135, 235, 236, 243-244, 343

punishment 25, 235, 269, 279, 280, 289-294, 298

racism 76, 104, 105, 119, 121, 124, 125-126, 127, 128, 130, 131, 132, 133, 138, 141, 144, 185, 189, 220, 221, 275, 362

refugees 131, 134, 135, 141, 142, 143

relations of production 66, 70, 73, 127, 173, 207, 240

relative deprivation 185, 282, 297

reskilling 80

Ritzer, George 251, 254-259, 266

Rowntree, B.S. 179-180

ruling class 10, 16, 17, 18, 19, 66, 72, 73, 76, 77, 82-83, 127, 240, 277, 278, 297, 351

Saunders, P. 72, 73, 81, 82, 211

Scotland 3-7, 14, 22, 31, 32, 36, 39, 40, 56, 64, 69, 78, 82-86, 91, 92, 100, 103, 109, 110, 114, 115, 119, 133-136, 137-141, 142, 145, 149, 150-154, 155-159, 160, 169, 170, 172, 173, 178, 179, 182, 193-197, 200, 203, 204, 208, 209, 212, 216, 217, 219, 222, 223, 224, 225, 226, 228, 229, 257, 260, 261, 262, 263, 264, 270, 283, 284, 285, 286, 291, 292, 293, 294, 319, 324, 326, 327, 328-332, 333, 339, 340, 342, 343, 361

Scottish Executive 143, 150, 151, 156, 171, 172, 194, 196, 197, 226, 284, 286, 292, 293, 330, 331, 332

Scottish Office 156, 289, 327, 328, 330

Scottish Parliament 4, 91, 112, 114-115, 116, 193, 225

'self-fulfilling prophecy' 205, 276, 297, 314

'sick role' 306-308

single parent 132, 153, 154, 155, 159, 279

social action 11, 26, 130, 133, 137, 243, 245

social construction 116, 265, 296, 362

social exclusion 78-80, 159, 179, 185-188, 192, 193-197, 269, 271, 282, 319, 331

social mobility 64, 75, 80-82, 85-86, 88, 99, 129, 131, 206, 222

socialism 102

socialisation (including primary and secondary) 93-94, 101, 104, 161, 167, 173, 201, 212, 215, 216, 219, 234, 242

sociological imagination 4, 32, 59

Soviet Union 15, 102

state, the 66, 101, 127, 128, 201, 202, 203, 227, 238, 239, 242, 278, 291, 298, 306, 311

stigma 79, 143, 149, 271, 276, 308, 313, 314, 315

structuration 25, 26-27

subcultures 189, 190, 221, 271, 274, 275, 297, 351-358, 363

surplus value 66, 101, 240, 241, 246, 247, 255

symbolic interactionism 24-26, 27, 33, 313-315, 325, 332 (see also interactionism)

Taylor, Frederick/Taylorism 234, 239, 247-249, 250-254, 261, 262, 264, 265, 266

Thompson, P. 246, 248, 249, 250, 252, 253, 258, 259, 260, 261, 262

Townsend, P. 182, 183-184, 185, 302, 319, 320, 321, 322, 323, 324, 328

underclass 78-80, 85, 88, 177, 129-133, 144, 177, 180, 186-189, 190-192, 210, 227, 348

United Kingdom; UK 5, 6, 7, 31, 62-64, 73, 74, 75, 76, 79, 80, 85, 91, 107, 109, 110, 111, 112, 116, 117, 129, 136-138, 139, 140, 141, 143, 147, 148, 149, 151, 152, 165, 170, 173, 178, 194, 195, 197, 226, 227, 228, 229, 233, 234, 236, 257, 260, 263, 183-184, 302, 303, 312, 319, 321, 323, 324-330, 332, 355

United States; US 80, 82, 97, 105, 124, 132, 133, 157, 166, 189, 190, 191, 202, 236, 250, 340, 349, 355, 362

upper class 61, 62, 72, 73, 82, 83, 228, 345

victim surveys 282, 284, 285, 286, 289

Wales 110, 135, 156, 158, 182, 204, 223, 225, 227, 228, 260, 285, 286, 294, 320, 329

Weber, Max 18, 22, 26, 62, 64, 65, 69-71, 72, 76, 84, 127, 128, 129-130, 131, 132, 135, 136, 140, 144, 233, 236, 237, 243-246, 251, 252, 254, 255, 256, 265, 266

Welfare/welfare state 75, 76, 79, 80, 133, 142, 171, 172,

180, 181, 182, 187, 190, 191,
193, 223, 251, 280, 290, 291,
292, 293, 298, 312
Westergaard, John 72, 181
white-collar crime 277-278,
282, 285, 286, 297
Willis, Paul 50, 54, 202-207,
217
working class 16, 17, 18, 20,
46, 54, 60, 61, 64, 66, 67, 68,
70, 71, 72, 73-74, 75, 76, 77,
78, 81, 83-85, 86, 87, 96, 99,
103, 122, 127, 128, 129, 130,
135, 140, 148, 154, 165, 179,
204, 206, 207, 208, 209, 210,
212, 213, 215-216, 218, 222,
223, 226, 229, 236, 240, 242,
246, 275, 297, 342, 343, 344,
346, 349, 350, 353, 355
youth 48, 56, 126, 142, 193,
207, 274-275, 278, 281, 282,
286, 287, 297, 337, 341, 346,
353, 254, 355, 358, 363
Zola, I. 308, 309, 310